The RISE
and FALL of
ADAM
and EVE

ALSO BY STEPHEN GREENBLATT

The Swerve: How the World Became Modern

Shakespeare's Freedom

Will in the World: How Shakespeare Became Shakespeare

Hamlet in Purgatory

Practicing New Historicism (with Catherine Gallagher)

Marvelous Possessions: The Wonder of the New World

Learning to Curse: Essays in Early Modern Culture

Shakespearean Negotiations: The Circulation of Social Energy in Renaissance England

Renaissance Self-Fashioning: From More to Shakespeare

Sir Walter Ralegh: The Renaissance Man and His Roles

Three Modern Satirists: Waugh, Orwell, and Huxley

EDITED BY STEPHEN GREENBLATT

Shakespeare's Montaigne: The Florio Translation of the Essays (with Peter G. Platt)

Religio Medici and Urne-Buriall (with Ramie Targoff)

Cultural Mobility: A Manifesto

The Norton Anthology of English Literature (general editor)

The Norton Shakespeare (general editor)

New World Encounters

Redrawing the Boundaries: The Transformation of English and American Literary Studies

Representing the English Renaissance

Allegory and Representation

The RISE and FALL of ADAM and EVE

STEPHEN GREENBLATT

THE BODLEY HEAD
LONDON

1 3 5 7 9 10 8 6 4 2

The Bodley Head, an imprint of Vintage,
20 Vauxhall Bridge Road,
London SW1V 2SA

The Bodley Head is part of the Penguin Random House group of companies
whose addresses can be found at global.penguinrandomhouse.com.

Penguin
Random House
UK

First published in the United States by W. W. Norton & Company, Inc. in 2017
First published in Great Britain by The Bodley Head in 2017

www.penguin.co.uk/vintage

A CIP catalogue record for this book is available from the British Library

ISBN 9781847922724

Printed and bound by Clays Ltd, St Ives plc

Book design by Ellen Cipriano

Penguin Random House is committed to a sustainable future
for our business, our readers and our planet. This book is made
from Forest Stewardship Council® certified paper.

To Eden and Isaiah

Contents

Prologue

In the House of Worship

When I was a child, my parents told me that, during the priestly bene-
diction that brings the Sabbath service to a close, we all had to bow
our heads and keep our eyes down until the rabbi's solemn words came
to an end. It was extremely important to do so, they said, because in
these moments God passed above our heads, and no one who saw God
face-to-face could live.

I brooded on this prohibition. To look into the face of the Lord, I
reasoned, must be the most wonderful thing any human being could
experience. Nothing that I would ever see or do in all the years that lay
ahead of me would even approach this one supreme vision. I reached
a momentous decision: I would raise my eyes and see God for myself.
It would be fatal, I understood, but the cost was surely not too high.
I did not dare to tell my parents of my determination, for I knew that
they would be distraught and try to dissuade me. I did not even tell my
older brother Marty, since I feared he would reveal my secret. I would
have to act alone.

Several Saturdays passed before I could muster the courage. But
finally one morning, standing with my head bowed, I conquered my
fear of death. Slowly, slowly while the rabbi intoned the ancient

blessings, I raised my eyes. The air above my head was completely empty. And I found I was by no means alone in looking about the sanctuary. Many of the worshipers were glancing around, staring out the windows, or even gesturing to friends and mouthing greetings. I was filled with outrage: "I have been lied to."

Many years have gone by since this moment, and I have never recovered the naïve faith that led me to prepare to sacrifice my life for a vision of God. But something lives in me on the other side of lost illusions. I have been fascinated throughout my life by the stories that we humans invent in an attempt to make sense of our existence, and I have come to understand that the term "lie" is a woefully inadequate description of either the motive or the content of these stories, even at their most fantastical.

Humans cannot live without stories. We surround ourselves with them; we make them up in our sleep; we tell them to our children; we pay to have them told to us. Some of us create them professionally. And a few of us—myself included—spend our entire adult lives trying to understand their beauty, power, and influence.

This book is a life history of one of the most extraordinary stories ever told. God created Adam and Eve, the first man and the first woman, and placed them, naked and unashamed, in a garden of delights. He told them that they could eat the fruit of any of its trees, with a single exception. They must not eat from the tree of the knowledge of good and evil; on the day that they violated this one prohibition, they would die. A serpent, the subtlest of the beasts, struck up a conversation with the woman. He told her that disobeying the divine commandment would not lead to their deaths but rather would open their eyes and make them be like gods, knowing good and evil. Believing the serpent, Eve ate the forbidden fruit; she gave it to Adam, who also ate it. Their eyes were indeed opened: realizing that they were naked, they sewed fig leaves together to cover themselves. God called them and asked them what they had done. When they confessed, He issued various punishments: serpents would henceforth be forced to crawl on the ground and eat dirt; women would bring forth children in pain and would desire the men who ruled over them; and men would be compelled to sweat and labor for their sustenance, until they returned to the ground from which they were taken. "For dust thou art, and unto dust shalt thou return." To prevent them from eating from another of the special trees—the tree of life—and living forever, the humans, by God's command, were driven forth from the garden. Armed cherubim were set to guard against any attempt to return.

Narrated at the beginning of Genesis, the story of Adam and Eve has over centuries decisively shaped conceptions of human origins and human destiny. On the face of things, it was highly unlikely ever to achieve such preeminence. It is a tale that might captivate the imagination of an impressionable child, such as I was, but grown-ups, in the past or present, could easily see that it bears the marks of the imagination at its most extravagant. A magical garden; a naked man and woman who are brought into existence in a way that no other humans have ever been born; people who know how to speak and function without the prolonged childhood that is the hallmark of our species; a mysterious warning about death that no such newly created beings could possibly understand; a talking snake; a tree that confers knowledge of good and evil; another tree that confers eternal life; supernatural guardians wielding flaming swords. This is fiction at its most fictional, a story that revels in the delights of make-believe.

Yet millions of people, including some of the subtlest and most brilliant minds that have ever existed, have accepted the Bible's narrative of Adam and Eve as the unvarnished truth. And, notwithstanding the massive evidence accumulated by geology, paleontology, anthropology, and evolutionary biology, untold numbers of our contemporaries continue to take the tale as a historically accurate account of the origins of the universe and to think of themselves as the literal descendants of the first humans in the Garden of Eden. Few stories in the history of the world have proved so durable, so widespread, and so insistently, hauntingly real.

1

Bare Bones

Why does the story of Adam and Eve—it occupies only about a page and a half out of 1078 in the modern edition of the King James Bible that sits on my desk—work so brilliantly and so effortlessly? You hear it at five or six years old, and you never forget it. The crudest schematic cartoon conjures it up at once, not perhaps in every detail but in its basic outline. Something in the structure of this narrative sticks; it is almost literally unforgettable.

In the long centuries since it was first told, it accumulated an enormous apparatus of support: teachers endlessly repeated it; institutions rewarded believers and punished skeptics; intellectuals teased out its nuances and offered competing interpretations of its puzzles; artists vividly represented it. But the narrative seems somehow independent of these complex elaborations, or rather everything that followed in its wake seems to have drawn upon an inexhaustible original energy, as if its core were radioactive. Adam and Eve epitomize the weird, enduring power of human storytelling.

For reasons that are at once tantalizing and elusive, these few verses in an ancient book have served as a mirror in which we seem to glimpse the whole, long history of our fears and desires. It has been both liberating and destructive, a hymn to human responsibility and a dark fable about human wretchedness, a celebration of daring and an incitement to violent misogyny. The range of responses it has aroused over thousands of years in innumerable individuals and communities is astonishing.

Ancient rabbis looked into the mirror and tried to understand God's intentions: What were humans that the Creator of the universe should have been mindful of them? Why were they created at all? Poring over the words of the sacred text, they concluded that the original obligation to "cultivate the ground" did not refer to agricultural labor; it referred rather to study, precisely the Torah study in which they themselves spent their days and which they regarded as their most exalted purpose in life.

Early Christians dwelt for the most part not on Adam's primordial study habits but rather on the devastating loss of Eden caused by his disobedience. The reflection that came to them from the story's depths was of sinfulness and its consequences. They followed Paul in tracing the tormenting, universal, inescapable fact of death back to the actions of the first humans, lured into evil by Satan. But they found consolation in their faith that a new Adam—Jesus Christ—had through his suffering and death undone the damage caused by the old Adam. The messiah's sublime sacrifice, they fervently hoped, would enable the faithful to recover the innocence that had been lost and to regain Paradise.

Islamic *mufassireen* (or Quranic exegetes) dwelt less on Adam's sinfulness than on his role as the original prophet of God. The Qur'an, dating from the seventh century CE, resembled early Christian texts in its identification of Satan (or Iblis) as the proud, deceitful angel who lured the first humans into disobedience. Later commentators specified that the form the malicious tempter took was not a serpent but a particularly beautiful camel: "She had a multicolored tail, red, yellow, green, white, black, a mane of pearl, hair of topaz, eyes like the planets Venus and Jupiter, and an aroma like musk blended with ambergris." As a consequence of their inconstancy, Adam and Eve were expelled from Paradise, and their descendants must always be vigilant: "O Children of Adam! Let not Satan seduce you as he caused your (first) parents to go forth from the Garden." But Islamic tradition characterized the wrongdoing that led to this expulsion as an error rather than as a heinous crime transmitted to all posterity. In the wake of his expulsion, Adam took up his role as caretaker of the earth and as religious teacher. He was a figure of prophetic illumination, the first in the line that led to the supreme Prophet, Muhammed, who would guide humanity back into the light of Allah.

Throughout Late Antiquity, the Middle Ages, and the Renaissance, a wide array of specialists teased out the implications of Adam and Eve's fate. Buried in the story, they found every urge to immerse themselves in ceaseless study; every nuance of the evil they sensed in their own hearts; every penitential impulse to mortify their flesh and crush their rebellious pride; every longing for prophetic inspiration; every dream of perfect cleansing at the end of time and a return to oceanic bliss. Ascetics, brooding on the temptations of the flesh, studied the verses for hints of alternative ways that the first humans might have been intended to reproduce. Physicians pondered the possible health benefits of a vegetarian diet of the kind our species enjoyed in the Garden. Linguists tried to determine the language that Adam and Eve spoke and to detect the traces of it that might be left. Natural scientists reflected on the ecological significance of a lost world in which relations between humans and other animals were far different from our own and in which the environment was unwavering in its gentle abundance. Among Jews and Muslims, experts in religious law probed the story's doctrinal and legal implications. In all three monotheistic communities, philosophers debated its ethical meanings. And in the Christian world, visual artists gleefully embraced the invitation to depict the human body in all of its glory and shame.

Above all, ordinary people—people who had listened to the story told from the pulpit or seen it depicted on walls or heard it from parents or friends—turned to it again and again for answers to the questions that baffled them. It helped to explain or at least to reflect back at them what was most disturbing in sexual intercourse, marital tension, the experience of physical pain and exhausting labor, the devastation of loss and mourning. They looked at Adam and Eve, and, like the rabbis, priests, and Muslim exegetes, they grasped something crucially important about themselves.

The story of Adam and Eve speaks to all of us. It addresses who we are, where we came from, why we love and why we suffer. Its vast reach seems part of its design. Though it serves as one of the foundation stones of three great world faiths, it precedes, or claims to precede, any particular religion. It captures the strange way our species treats work, sex, and death—features of existence that we share with every other animal—as objects of speculation, as if they were contingent on something we have done, as if it could all have been otherwise.

We humans, the story goes, were uniquely made in the image and likeness of the God who created us. That God gave us dominance over all other species, and He gave us something else: a prohibition. The prohibition came without explanation or justification. But at the beginning of time it was not necessary that our first ancestors understand; it was necessary only that they obey. That Adam and Eve did not obey, that they violated God's express command, caused everything that followed in the lives of our whole species, from the universal phenomenon of shame to the universal fact of mortality.

An insistence on the story's literal truth—an actual Adam and Eve in an actual garden—became one of the cornerstones of Christian orthodoxy. This insistence lies at the center of my own fascination with the story of Adam and Eve. How does something made-up become so compellingly real? How does a stone statue begin to breathe or a wooden puppet learn to stand up on its own and to dance without strings? And what happens when fictional creatures behave as if they were alive? Are they fated, for that very reason, to begin to die?

For generations pious men and women struggled to make good on a theological proposition, attempting to treat the tale of the naked man and woman and the talking snake as a strictly accurate account of the events that initiated life as we know it. Philosophers, theologians, priests, monks, and visionaries, along with poets and artists, all contributed to this massive collective effort. But it was only in the Renaissance—the age of Dürer, Michelangelo, and Milton—that brilliant new technologies of representation finally succeeded in conferring a convincing sense of reality upon the first humans and in bringing their story fully to life.

This stupendous achievement, one of the great triumphs of art and literature, turned out to have unanticipated consequences. Adam and Eve were brought together with strikingly life-like pagan statues that art-hunters unearthed from the ruins of Greece and Rome. They were examined and judged by moral standards applied not only to the distant past but also to living contemporaries. They were compared to hordes of newly encountered naked men and women in the Americas—people who appeared strangely immune to the bodily shame that all humans after the Fall were supposed to feel. Precisely because they now seemed so real, Adam and Eve raised difficult questions about language acquisition at the beginning of time, about sexual relations, about race, about mortality.

The sense of reality renewed in intensified form painful questions that had always hovered around the ancient origin story: What kind of God would forbid his creatures to know the difference between good and evil? How would it have been possible for those creatures to obey without such knowledge? And what could the threat of death mean to those who had never experienced death and could not know what it was? Authorities in the church and state reacted harshly to skeptics who insisted on asking these questions, but it proved impossible to quell a disturbance that had its roots in the very success at making the mythic first humans seem so real. With the Enlightenment, doubts multiplied and could no longer be silenced. What lay ahead was the clear-eyed skepticism of Spinoza, the penetrating gaze of Charles Darwin, and the mocking laughter of Mark Twain.

NATURAL HISTORY COLLECTIONS throughout the world proudly possess objects called holotypes. Also known as type specimens, these are the singular, officially recognized physical examples of an entire species. *This* creature in the case before you in the Museum of Vertebrate Zoology at the University of California, Berkeley, is for the entire scientific world the designated representative of the rough-skinned newt (*Triturus similans Twitty*); *that* cranium at the Centre National d'Appui à la Recherche in N'djaména, Chad, is the unique type specimen of the extinct primate *Sahelanthropus tchadensis.* The enterprise of identifying and collecting these examples began as early as the eighteenth century. The type specimen of the gray wolf, *Canus lupus,* described in 1758 by the great zoologist and botanist Carl Linnaeus, is in the Swedish Museum of Natural History in Stockholm, along with a large number of other holotypes that he and his devoted students first identified. (Since he based his description on a self-examination, the type specimen of our own species, *Homo sapiens,* is none other than Linnaeus himself.) The United States National Herbarium in Washington houses some 110,000 holotypes of plants. Berkeley's Museum of Vertebrate Zoology possesses holotypes of 364 mammals, 174 birds, and 123 reptiles and amphibians. On display in the "wet collections" in the Natural History Museum in Berlin, there are innumerable jars filled with preserved sea creatures floating in ethanol. Some of the jars are marked with red dots, indicating that they contain holotypes.

Each holotype has been designated as such by the person who has discovered a new species and then named and described it, according to certain formal criteria, in a scientific paper. In successfully publishing this paper and depositing the specimen in an appropriate collection, the discoverer is said to have "authored" the species. The holotype thereby becomes the official specimen, acknowledged by the scientific community; each is the particular, concrete touchstone from which the key features of an entire species may be derived. To date, almost 2 million species have been identified. It is estimated that there are close to 9 million species on earth.

The Genesis story imagines that God brought each beast of the field and fowl of the air one-by-one before Adam to receive its name, in something of the way that scientists assign names to their holotypes. The text did not specify the language Adam used or how long this process took or when it occurred. Bible commentaries traditionally posited that it happened on the same day that man was created, since it was only in the wake of this feat of naming that God created woman. (Most commentators were loath to believe that Adam lived alone without a mate for a very long time.) Some commentators wondered if the more noxious insects could somehow have emerged and received their names *after* the six days of creation, as a consequence of man's sin and not as part of the original plan. Others worried a bit about the fish, since the Bible only mentions creatures of the land and air. "Why were not the fishes brought to Adam?" the English clergyman and amateur scientist Alexander Ross asked in 1622, and then proceeded to answer his own question: "Because they do not so much resemble man as the beasts: secondly, because they could not be such a help to man as the beasts: thirdly, because they could not live out of the water."

There are more species in heaven and earth than were dreamed of in the Bible. But whoever created the story thousands of years ago understood, as modern science has understood, that you can only firmly grasp the whole of a species through a single representative of it. The human of the first chapter of Genesis is in effect the holotype of humanity. God authored this creature and carefully introduced him— naked, of course—on earth as the type specimen. When you contemplate Adam, you contemplate both a particular, individual figure and the entirety of humankind.

In Adam, the Bible story affirmed, you encounter not only the representative but also the very earliest instance of the species, the progenitor of all those who followed. Here too modern scientific collections have their equivalent, in this case not holotypes but rather fossils of those who are said to be our progenitors. The most famous of these is the creature known as "Lucy," an individual *Australopithecus afarensis* female who lived about 3.2 million years ago whose bones—several hundred pieces of them—were found by the American anthropologist Donald Johanson in Ethiopia in 1974. Johanson and his team jokingly nicknamed the skeleton after the Beatles' song "Lucy in the Sky with Diamonds," which they happened to be playing over and over again on a tape recorder in their remote camp.

The magic of a particular name has given this immensely distant and indirect ancestor—now preserved at the National Museum of Ethiopia in Addis Ababa—her special appeal. She was three feet seven inches tall, with a small brain like a chimpanzee, far distant from the modern humans who only emerged in Africa more than 3 million years after her species roamed the earth. But, crucially, she did not swing from the trees. Instead, she walked on two feet. No one claims that Lucy was the direct ancestor of all humanity, but there is very strong evidence that our species, *Homo sapiens,* bears a significant relation to Lucy. Hominins, the taxonomic tribe that includes modern humans and our closest extinct relatives, evolved from such bipedal primate mammals.

The implications of this evolutionary process are enormous, and they have been hotly contested. It had once seemed possible to tell a straightforward story: We *homo sapiens* are at the end of a long branch of the great tree of life. Examining our successive extinct ancestors, we could follow that branch back very slowly toward the trunk and trace the stages through which we passed in order to reach our current (and, of course, splendid) state. Now as more and more fossils are discovered—*Paranthropus boisei, Homo habilis, Homo rudolfensis, Homo ergaster, Homo erectus, Homo heidelbergensis, Homo neanderthalensis, Homo naledi,* and so forth—the overarching story becomes steadily less simple. Our ancestry, one evolutionary biologist recently wrote, resembles less a branch than "a bundle of twigs—one might even think it looks like a tangled bush."

In a room on the fifth floor of Harvard's Peabody Museum of Archaeology and Ethnology, David Pilbeam, a renowned paleoanthropologist (that is, someone who studies the kinship lines that connect our species with our near relations) kindly agreed to show me some of these "twigs." Before I arrived, he had set out bones (or plaster or plastic casts of bones), some in cardboard boxes on the formica-top tables, others assembled into skeletons and posed on little wheeled platforms. Each of the bones represents a leap back into the past, measured in millions of years before the present.

A replica of Lucy was there, in a cellophane-covered cardboard display box reminiscent of something delivered by a florist for a grand occasion—a funeral, I suppose. There is in truth not much of her to see: fragments of her skull and part of her lower jaw, a few ribs, the sacrum and part of her pelvis, pieces of her legs and arms. On a rolling dolly, a more complete model of an Australopithecus was reconstructed next to her. Nearby was the skeleton of a chimpanzee, and Pilbeam pointed out the subtle differences between its structure and that of Lucy. Subtle indeed: without his expert guidance, I would have missed almost all of them and failed to see that one is an ape and the other is my forebear.

The oldest fossil in the room was that of the Sahelanthropus from Chad. It looked to me like the skull of a small ape, but, like a detective, Pilbeam observed the telltale signs that it probably stood upright and walked on two feet. If it did so, it mastered this accomplishment very early indeed; the fossil has been dated to around 7 million years before the present, that is, not very far from the time that the Last Common Ancestor split, with one line leading to chimpanzees and the other leading to us.

As I looked around the room and jumped across millions of years, I experienced something of the queasiness that has led scientists to question metaphors of human evolution as a steady and progressive development along a clearly defined branch. In one corner, apart from the tiniest of hints, our Sahelanthropus forebear seemed to belong to a different universe from our own. In the other, the full skeleton of the Neanderthal stood there, thick of bone like a gorilla, but with a cranium very much the size of ours.

With ever greater subtlety and ingenuity, paleoanthropologists measure, scrutinize, and interpret the skeletal remains: a pelvis and spine that enable our species to walk upright, shoulder blades that help us fling lethal projectiles, the configuration of the teeth, the increasing size of the brain case. But what had once seemed a triumphal march of progress—like those cartoons that begin with an ape and end with a man sitting at a computer—now gets lost in a hundred detours and false starts, intersecting paths and dead ends. It is difficult to find the story line in a tangled bush.

Evolutionary theory is not threatened by the disappearance of the main highway. On the contrary, from the beginning Darwin insisted on the randomness of mutations, followed by the editing of natural selection, that lead to the emergence of new species. Still, it is disquieting to look around and see a wilderness of discontinuous and crisscrossing tracks. David Pilbeam once published a book called *The Ascent of Man*. It is not at all clear that he would do so today.

Nonetheless, most of us, including evolutionary biologists, continue to search for and construct stories of our ascent. For, as the Bible said long ago, we are the dominant species: "And God blessed them, and God said unto them, Be fruitful, and multiply, and replenish the earth, and subdue it: and have dominion over the fish of the sea, and over the fowl of the air, and over every living thing that moveth upon the earth" (Gen. 1:28). Our dominance is clearly linked to our intelligence, our fantastic toolmaking, our complex social and cultural life, and above all our language and symbolic consciousness. But how we developed from ancestors unable to speak, make symbols, or form abstract concepts is not at all understood. There is as yet no fully coherent, satisfying scientific story.

In the account of the creation of the human on the sixth day— "And God created the human in his image, in the image of God He created him: male and female He created them" (Gen. 1:27)—Genesis offered the equivalent of the bare bones from which scientists derive their images of our earliest forebears. And it provided (as scientists have not been able to do) a definitive starting point. But from the Bible's words it proved impossible to determine conclusively what the original human would have been like. Not that there lacked many attempts, based on the minutest examination of the text. In the second century CE, Rabbi Jeremiah ben Eleazar concluded from the phrase "male and female He created them" that the original Adam was a hermaphrodite. The third-century rabbi Samuel ben Nahman interpreted the description to mean that "When the Lord created Adam He created him double-faced, then He split him and made him of two backs, one back on this side and one back on the other side." Another argued that Adam originally filled the whole world, stretching from east to west; another that his height reached from earth to heaven; another that he could see everything in the universe; another that he had prophetic powers; another that the Lord first gave Adam a tail "but subsequently removed it from him for the sake of his dignity." Adam was "so handsome that the very sole of his foot obscured the splendor of the sun." He invented all languages and all crafts, including writing and geography. He had a kind of protective skin, a carapace, that fell off when he transgressed.

And then in the second chapter of Genesis, the creature that excited all of these speculations is gone. There are no longer bare bones or a holotype pinned to a card. Instead, there are two separate primordial human figures—the man formed out of dust and the woman fashioned from the man's rib—and these humans are involved in a story. To understand the actual nature of our kind, Genesis now insists, what is needed is not to examine a type specimen, but rather to watch the first humans in action. We have to observe their relationship, scrutinize their choices, follow their trajectory, and ponder their history. For it is not the biological nature of humans that determined their history, but their history—the choices they made and the consequences of those choices—that determined their nature.

The Bible story suggests that something happened to the species shortly after it was authored by God. Humanity did not have to turn out to be the way it is now; it could all have been different. The image of the man and the woman in the perfect garden suggests a tension between things as they are and things as they might have been. It conveys a longing to be other than what we have become.

At the center of the Genesis origin story is the human decision to take, eat, and share the forbidden fruit. The ability of narrative to depict choice and its consequence is crucial. A good story can omit details, forgo motivation, sidestep analysis, and still remain utterly compelling. The story of Adam and Eve does not use such words as "sin" or "fall" or "Satan" or "apple." The range of possible meanings is wide open: some surviving interpretations from almost two thousand years ago regard the serpent as the story's hero, for championing the acquisition of knowledge denied to humans by a jealous god. What carries the weight here, as in almost all oral tales, is the action: "And the woman saw that the tree was good for eating and that it was lust to the eyes and the tree was lovely to look at, and she took of its fruit and ate, and she also gave to her man, and he ate."

There must be a story to tell: this is the basic intuition not of Genesis alone but of virtually all ancient myths of origin, whether from Mesopotamia, Egypt, Greece, Rome, Siberia, China, the Great Plains, or Zimbabwe. Something happened at the beginning of time—some history of decision, action, and reaction—that led to the way we are, and if we want to understand the way we are, it is important to remember and retell this story.

WE KNOW, OR WE THINK WE KNOW, that chimpanzees, to whom we are so closely related, do not speculate on the origin of chimpanzee disobedience, that orangutans, though they are highly intelligent, do not brood about why orangutans are fated to die, and that pleasure-loving bonobos do not tell themselves, while grooming one another, a story about how the first bonobo male and female mated. We have ample reason to be in awe of the social complexity of ants and bees and paper wasps; we marvel at the advanced language comprehension skills of bottlenose dolphins; we have built a virtual cult around the songs of the whales. But none of them, we believe, has invented an origin story.

Humans seem to be the only animals on earth that ask themselves how they came to be and why they are the way they are. We could represent this uniqueness as an achievement, a mark of distinction, as perhaps it is. But it would be easy enough to seize upon it instead as a sign that we are lost—disoriented, uncomfortable in our own skin, in need of an explanation. Perhaps the telling of an origin story is a symptom of uneasiness—we attempt to calm ourselves by telling a story. Or perhaps our species somehow got ahead of itself, having taken, quite by accident, a developmental turn that led us along a path we cannot entirely understand and that provokes our speculative, storytelling intelligence.

We have no idea when storytelling became one of our species' characteristic accomplishments, but the adaptive usefulness of stories, as a way of transmitting knowledge as well as providing pleasure, suggests that it came early, long before the invention of writing. Five thousand years—the approximate length of humankind's written records—seems an impressively long time, given the length of any individual human life, but in fact it is next to nothing, a mere stutter, in the long history of the stories that humans have made up and recounted to one another. Would speculative accounts of human origins have been among the earliest of these stories? It is striking that small children, unprompted by adults, will ask, "Where do I come from?" The question seems to well up in us spontaneously, and the answers have obsessed priests, artists, philosophers, and scientists for as long as we can remember.

It was only fairly recently that scholars—the German brothers Jacob and Wilhelm Grimm, in the late eighteenth century, are the most famous—began systematically to collect oral tales and analyze their forms and topics. These tales had passed from generation to generation, extending back beyond any living memory. Some were stubbornly local, confined to a particular family, lineage, or community. Others had evidently leaped across geographical boundaries and languages. Virtually all cultures—from Mongolia to Oklahoma and points between—turned out to have at least one and often more than one origin story. The particular version in Genesis—the story of the naked man and woman, the talking snake, and the magical trees— has every sign of being one of these oral folktales, reaching back long before the moment that it appeared in written form in the book of Genesis, evolving out of the deep past, the past to which we have almost no access.

When I try to imagine the story's beginning, I conjure up three scenes from my life. The first and most recent was a garden in Kashan, 150 miles south of Tehran. I had been invited to Iran to address a Shakespeare congress, and I seized the opportunity to venture further afield. Kashan is a celebrated carpet city: when I was growing up, we had a Kashan rug in our dining room, and I would crawl under the table to play on a field of intricately intertwined woven flowers. But my goal was not the crowded bazaar. I wanted to see a famous late-sixteenth-century garden, the Bagh-e Fin.

The garden turned out to be a relatively small, dusty, square space with very old cedar trees lined up in rows along very straight paths walled in with brick ramparts and circular towers. The key feature was water arising from a nearby natural spring. The water was directed into straight, narrow channels and a perfectly square pool lined with turquoise tiles. At the top of the pool a two-story vaulted pavilion provided an escape from the sun.

To get there we had driven for hours from Tehran, through a miserably bleak, parched desert, a landscape of sun-baked rocks and scorched, twisted gullies stretching out all the way to the horizon. As far as the eye could see, there were no cultivated fields, no trees, not even scrub vegetation. Signs of life seemed to have been canceled as if by edict. It would have been possible in a very few minutes for the first human to name all the creatures who could be seen inhabiting this world.

Old Persian had a word for an enclosed garden like the Bagh-e Fin: they termed it a *paradaesa*. From Greek, which took over the term, we derive our word "paradise." The garden I saw in Kashan could hardly count as a setting for the creation of Adam and Eve, but I could at least imagine how in a harsh, barren land the sound of the water bubbling through its channels and the sight of the massive trees could produce wonderment and euphoria. And for the first time I fully grasped the hyperbolic extravagance of the garden in Genesis, with the headwaters of no fewer than four great rivers. The storyteller had taken what was precious in the surrounding world and fashioned from it a landscape fit for humans at their most blessed. To be driven forth from that space into the miserable salt desert that surrounded it on all sides would have been the harshest of punishments.

The second of my attempts to conjure the story's beginning occurred a few years earlier in Wadi Rum in Jordan, at a Bedouin encampment where I briefly stayed with my wife and son. It was quite cold in the desert once the sun had set, and after eating a simple meal and listening to some music played on a lute, we walked quickly to our small tent and crawled under the woolen blankets. But inevitably in the night, after having drunk so many cups of sweetened tea, I had to get up and cross to the other end of the encampment. Shivering, I lit my tiny flashlight and walked across the sand—it was a moonless night, the fire and the lanterns were out, and everyone was asleep.

When I looked up, I saw a sky implausibly, impossibly vast. It was not only full of stars, but also full of a strange feeling of depth. I turned off the flashlight and sat down on the ground and stared. I have often slept under the stars in places reasonably far from human settlements. But even distant cities throw off a tremendous amount of light. Here there was no interfering light at all; only a sense of the sheer immensity of the universe, an infinity of stars, and a need, more compelling even than the body's imperatives, to understand who we are and where we come from.

My third attempt reaches back still further in time to a memory from my earliest childhood. We are sitting, my mother and I, at a little table in our apartment in Boston's Roxbury neighborhood. It is summer, the window is open, and we can hear, from the nearby Franklin Park Zoo, the occasional roar of the lions and the screeching of the caged birds. My mother is making up a story, and it is just for me. The hero bears a name quite similar but not identical to my own. A cherished child, happy and protected, he has been strictly warned not to do only one thing: he must never, ever attempt by himself to cross Seaver Street, in order to reach the zoo whose sounds so allure him. But does he listen . . . ?

THE HUMAN FORMED FROM CLAY became a living creature, it was written in the Bible, when a breath of life was blown into his nostrils. There is a powerful truth encoded in that mythic scene. At some moment in an immensely distant past it was a breath that brought Adam to life, the breath of a storyteller.

2

By the Waters of Babylon

On the big island in Hawaii, molten lava erupts through cracks in the volcano. You can walk across the black fields of twisted, cooled lava to the cliff's edge and watch a head of burning magma force its way out, like a stupendous birth, and fly hissing into the sea. You can feel that you are present at the origin of the world, but of course the world already exists, and you know it. The whole point about stories of creation is that no one can actually claim to have been an eyewitness or to remember it or even to be part of a chain of remembrance leading back to someone who had been there.

We cannot know when someone, venturing to imagine how the universe and humankind came to exist, first told this story about what transpired in the beginning to set our species on its course. We cannot identify the person who first thought of the garden or who dreamed of nakedness without shame or who came up with the notion of the fatal fruit. There must, we know, have been a moment of inspiration, but we have no way back to it. It is lost to us forever.

There was a moment too when someone first chose to write the story down. But we have no access to this moment either, no way of knowing if the writer was a man or a woman, no clear indication of the place or the circumstances or the language, no precise or even approximate marker of the time. Some scholars think that a version could have been inscribed as early as the time of King Solomon (990 BCE to 931 BCE) and that other versions might have circulated in written form during the reigns of his successors. Since no actual manuscript traces of the story survive from these long centuries in the life of the Hebrews—all have been lost to fire, flood, and the teeth of time—the dating is speculative, sometimes wildly so. The closest we can come to an historical starting point is the moment when the story finally found its way into the book of Genesis. The precise date and circumstances are uncertain, but the fog of mystery slowly begins to lift.

Most scholars currently attribute the form in which we know the story to the sixth century BCE and think that the Pentateuch—the Greek term for the Five Books of Moses, assembled together—was probably compiled in the fifth century, roughly corresponding to the time of Ezra and Nehemiah. Even here the ground is uncertain. Every inch of the textual history has been fought over at least since the eighteenth century, and anything that I or those more learned than I am say about it will be contested, often vehemently, by someone else. Still, whatever its most distant origins, the story of Adam and Eve eventually became part of a sacred document, the Torah, whose author was said to have been Moses. At least then there was an author, someone of the utmost prestige to secure the account's truthfulness. Reasonably enough, people asked how Moses could possibly have known what transpired in the Garden of Eden, so long before his time? He could, defenders of the story's strict accuracy answered, have learned the details as they had been handed down through the generations reaching all the way to Noah and then back still further before the Flood to Adam's third son, Seth. The Bible's "begats" provided a list of these generations, extending to the beginning of time. The exceptionally long lives attributed to the early patriarchs—Methuselah was said to have reached the ripe old age of 969 years—conveniently reduced the number of links in the chain.

Since it was well known that stories had a way of changing in the course of repeated retelling, it was often added that Moses wrote at God's own dictation or at least was guided in his writing by God's spirit. That spirit could be counted on to correct any errors that might otherwise have crept in and impugned the veracity of the creation story. A work written in the second century BCE, the Book of Jubilees, went still further in an attempt to shore up the narrative's authenticity. On Mount Sinai, it declared, God instructed an angel to give Moses a faithful account of the first beginnings. The angel, along with his cohort, had been an eyewitness to the creation of the world and to the scenes in the garden. Moses simply had to reiterate the impeccably accurate report that the angel dutifully provided.

But elaborations like the Book of Jubilees—which is now regarded as canonical only by the Ethiopian Orthodox Church—were as much signs of doubt as they were reassurances. They suggest that at least some of those who read the account of the garden and the first humans and the talking snake wondered about its reliability. They wanted to know how far they could trust it, or perhaps they sensed, just outside the charmed circle of belief, its possible origin in a more familiar scene of storytelling, the realm of fantasy.

The Torah could have begun, after all, at what would have seemed a far more obvious and secure historical juncture: the origin not of the first humans but of the first Jews. "And the Lord said to Abram, 'Go forth from your land and your birthplace and your father's house to the land I will show you. And I will make you a great nation and I will bless you and make your name great, and you shall be a blessing" (Gen. 12:1–2). Instead, it began with events that clearly precede any possible historical record: the creation of the cosmos and of humankind. To understand why it seemed critically important to the Jews to launch their sacred book with an account of the beginning of time, before they themselves existed, it is important to understand the disaster that had befallen them.

• • •

IN THE ANCIENT WORLD, the fall of kingdoms was often followed by wholesale massacre of the vanquished, but Nebuchadnezzar II, the ruler of the great Babylonian Empire, thought that deportations made more sense. After the small kingdom of Judah, ruled by a venerable dynasty that called itself "the house of David," surrendered to his armies in 597 BCE, he set up a puppet government in Jerusalem and deported a significant number of Hebrews, including the toppled king and his court, to Babylon. Across a vast gulf of time, Psalm 137 manages to convey their misery, homesickness, and rage: "By the waters of Babylon, there we sat down,/yea, we wept, when we remembered Zion."

The Hebrew exiles, living testimony to Nebuchadnezzar's latest triumph, swelled the labor pool that his enormous ambitions required. After a long period of decline, Babylon was once again in the ascendant. There were irrigation ditches to dig, fields to tend, vines to dress, innumerable bricks to bake, fortifications, ziggurats, and palaces to build. The Hebrews were not the only exiles who sweated in the work gangs and dreamed of their lost home. They labored alongside Assyrians, Medes, Scythians, and Egyptians, and in the company of native-born Babylonians who had fallen hopelessly into debt. Defeat and enslavement produced in Babylon a kind of servile cosmopolitanism.

The bustling, culturally diverse city on the Euphrates was wealthy, sophisticated, and famously beautiful. Two of its legendary building projects—the immense city walls and the hanging gardens—were counted among the Seven Wonders of the World. In its glazed-brick grandeur, the famous Ishtar Gate, reconstructed today in the Pergamon Museum in Berlin, bears witness to the city's majesty. If the Hebrew exiles could hardly be expected to feel at home in Babylon, they were not complete aliens, for they thought of themselves as having come in the distant past from this part of Mesopotamia. Abraham, the founding figure of the Jewish faith, began his life in nearby Ur, and a return to these roots was evidently not unbearable to everyone. When the opportunity finally came to go back to Judah, a significant number of Hebrews opted to remain where they were. From the period of exile flowered a Jewish community in Mesopotamia that lasted well into the Iraq of the twentieth century.

For the pious among the Hebrew exiles by the banks of the Euphrates, the great challenge was not to give up on Yahweh. Yahweh had long been their chief god and protector. Occasionally they had been drawn to the worship of other gods as well; that was the point of Yahweh's repeated injunction "Thou shalt have no other gods before me." But for the most part, even in difficult times, they had been able to keep Yahweh foremost in their hearts and to worship him through the ritual observances and animal sacrifices they conducted in the great Temple in Jerusalem.

Those rituals continued intact for a decade after Judah's surrender to Nebuchadnezzar. But then another disaster: Zedekiah, the Hebrew quisling whom the conqueror had put in place, was foolhardy enough to lead an uprising against his masters. The Babylonian army besieged Jerusalem, and the Egyptian allies, on whose aid the Hebrews had been counting, failed to materialize. The siege dragged on, with famine, disease, and desertion taking their terrible toll. Finally the wall was breached, and the Babylonian troops swarmed in. At the king's command, vengeance was then meted out on the city which had, up to this point, been spared. The great Temple, the palace, and other civic buildings were burned to the ground. The chief priest, his principal assistant, and many other leading figures were put to death. Zedekiah's sons were executed before his eyes; he was then blinded and carried off in chains. And once again a large number of people were deported, joining those who had already been in exile in Babylon for a decade. A few years later, in the wake of the assassination of the Babylonian governor, still more of the population from the unruly province was deported. The lives of the Hebrews had been shattered.

Now that the Temple had been destroyed, its desolation seemed to bear mute witness to the overwhelming fact that Yahweh had been unwilling or perhaps unable to protect his chosen people. His abject failure in 597 and again in 587 must have confirmed every subversive thought that less pious Hebrews had ever had about their tribal deity: Yahweh was a priestly fraud, a figment of the collective imagination, or perhaps simply a weakling, the god of losers. The mocking voices have been suppressed—the Bible is written, for the most part, from the perspective of the pious—but they left behind traces of themselves. "The fool hath said in his heart, There is no God," begins Psalm 14. Fool perhaps, but the psalmist is certain that there are enough such fools in his midst to warrant quoting and attacking them.

How could it have been otherwise? The national disaster tapped the wellsprings not only of sadness but also of doubt and irony. Yahweh did not exist; or Yahweh did not care; or Yahweh had been bested decisively by the Babylonian god Marduk. In the wake of the fall of Jerusalem and the mass deportations, the skeptics must have found it maddening to listen to the prayers of the pious, imploring aid from a god who was missing in action. Conversely, for the pious, the mockery of the skeptics must have been unendurable. "All they that see me laugh me to scorn," says the speaker of the 22nd psalm; "they shoot out the lip, they shake the head, saying,/He trusted on the Lord that he would deliver him: let him deliver him, seeing he delighted in him" (22:7–8). And if there is no deliverance in sight, if there is only continuing humiliation and mockery and the cruel dashing of hopes, what then? For the faithful, in exile in Babylon, the central psychic experience was anguish. Where was Yahweh? Centuries later this terrible sense of abandonment surged up in another forlorn Jew who at the moment of his execution quoted the opening words of this very psalm: "My God, my God, why hast thou forsaken me?"

As an antidote to despair, the Hebrews could tell themselves that the disaster was all Yahweh's doing, punishment for his people's refusal to obey his divine ordinances, but the doubters in their midst could easily shake their heads and dismiss the fantasy as pathetic. To make matters worse, faithful and skeptics alike were surrounded by the jubilation of the conquerors and by their hymns in praise of their triumphant god. The exiles would have looked up every day at the glorious Babylonian temple complex called the Esagila—"the house of the raised head"— and at the enormous seven-story ziggurat Etemenanki, "the temple of the foundation of heaven and earth." Years later the Hebrews' memory of that astonishing sight, suitably reinterpreted to signify overweening pride and arrogance, became the Tower of Babel.

Nebuchadnezzar had rebuilt both temple and ziggurat in honor of the Storm God, Marduk. Long the city's patron deity, the god had grown so powerful that his worshipers feared to pronounce his holy name and simply called him Bel, "the lord." Marduk was exalted as the master of the universe. Having managed to assume for himself the attributes of the surrounding deities, having drawn into his powerful gravitational field the whole rich body of Mesopotamian mythology, he was now in a position to absorb the powers of all rival gods, including Yahweh. From his holy of holies within the Esagila and from the golden shrine at the dizzying summit of Etemenanki, Marduk's image looked down at peoples whose destiny he seemed to control.

Every year the Babylonians observed a grand New Year's festival in Marduk's honor. Statues of other gods, paying homage to the city's divine protector, were taken down from their niches and carried in a grand public procession to the main sanctuary. On the festival's fourth day, led by the king himself, there was a solemn recitation of a sacred text that had been first inscribed on clay tablets in the remote past. The venerable text, bearing the prestige of its immense antiquity, was the *Enuma Elish*, the Mesopotamian origin story. In the beginning, it related, there was sex: a stream of fresh water—the god Apsu—rushed into the sea, the goddess Tiamat. From this primordial intercourse, all the other gods in the Babylonian pantheon were formed, like silt deposited at the mouth of a river.

But the story did not celebrate reproduction as an unambiguous blessing. On the contrary, it focused on the murderous rage that may surge up in a parent, when its quiet is disturbed. The newly created gods proved to be intolerably noisy, and Apsu, unable to rest, eventually decided that he would destroy his offspring. Though her repose had also been disturbed, Tiamat counseled forbearance: "What? Shall we put an end to what we formed?" Apsu persisted. He wanted his rest, and if that meant killing the children, then so be it. The intended victims got wind of the plan to destroy them. Most of them wandered about in despair or sat silent, uncertain what to do. But the cleverest of them, Ea (or Enki, as he is called in the Sumerian versions), managed to avert destruction. He contrived to lull his father Apsu to sleep and then killed him.

In the beginning then, there was murder as well as sex. In the *Enuma Elish,* this original murder was not tinged with horror or condemned; it was celebrated. Life, with its energy and noise, had triumphed over sleep and silence. But, while celebrating this triumph, the Babylonians did not simply repudiate the value of repose. Ea built his palace on the body of the father he had slain, and then, after uttering a cry of triumph, he withdrew: "In his chamber, in profound quiet, he rested./He called it 'Apsu.'" Apsu, the vanquished creator, lived on in the name that the victorious murderer, his own son, gave to the shrine of his deepest rest.

Perfect tranquility, however, did not reign. Now it was the first mother, Tiamat, who rose up in menace. The other gods were terrified—once again their parent was set on destroying them—but Ea's son Marduk came forward and offered to save them, if the gods swore eternal fealty to him. The gods eagerly agreed. As Ea had killed the primordial father Apsu, so Marduk dealt with the primordial mother Tiamat:

He split her in two, like a fish for drying,
Half of her he set up and made as a cover (like) heaven.
He stretched out the hide and assigned watchmen,
And ordered them not to let the waters escape.

Once again the murder was not condemned but celebrated, and once again the victim's corpse was put to good use: the universe was made from the divided female body, an upper sphere of water that formed the sky and a lower sphere of water out of which the earth emerged.

In the wake of his great victory, Marduk's heart prompted him "to make artful things" on behalf of those whom he had saved. The junior gods were sick of doing chores for themselves; they too wanted to rest. "I shall compact blood, I shall cause bones to be,/. . . I shall create humankind," Marduk declared. Humans—*lullu,* as the *Enuma Elish* calls them, "the black-headed people"—were brought forth for lives of unceasing labor. By building shrines, digging irrigation canals, planting and harvesting crops, preparing food offerings, and singing praises, they enabled the gods to relax and enjoy their existence, and thereby fulfilled the design of their savior, the supreme god Marduk.

In the sixth century BCE, when generations of captive Hebrews were forced to encounter it year after year, the *Enuma Elish* was already shrouded in great antiquity. Its age conferred upon it a special prestige that it shared with several other ancient Mesopotamian stories of human beginnings. One, called the *Atrahasis,* told the story of a primordial flood that almost destroyed all of humanity; another, *Gilgamesh,* recounted the love of a semidivine hero for a human fashioned from clay. These works feature gods—a whole pantheon of them—but Yahweh is nowhere among them, let alone their lord and master. So too they recount the creation of the first humans, but these are not called Adam and Eve and their maker is not the supreme Creator-God of the Hebrews. It would have made perfect sense for the Hebrew captives to embrace the beliefs of the Babylonian victors and to abandon a provincial, local, and, above all, failed god. But they—or at least a pious remnant among them—clung fiercely to his memory.

"By the waters of Babylon, there we sat down, yea, we wept, when we remembered Zion." The misery that Psalm 137 conjures up is not linked to any obvious oppression: there is no image of laboring in the broiling sun under the lash of harsh taskmasters. Instead, we are given a strange scene in which all that the victor asks of the vanquished is a song: "For there they that carried us away captive required of us a song; and they that wasted us required of us mirth, saying, Sing us one of the songs of Zion." To the psalmist, the commandment to sing in the shadow of the ziggurat—to perform one's culture for the conquerors' amusement—was unendurable. It seemed like a violation of memory, a primal loss of selfhood:

> How shall we sing the Lord's song in a strange land?
> If I forget thee, O Jerusalem, let my right hand forget her cunning.
> If I do not remember thee, let my tongue cleave to the roof of my
>   mouth; if I prefer not Jerusalem above my chief joy.

The conquerors may even have thought that singing one of the songs of Zion would for the conquered be an agreeable form of nostalgic remembrance. But the psalmist bitterly refuses, implying that such remembrance would be tantamount to forgetting. Why? Because it would have acceded to the victor's wishes; because it would have threatened to trivialize deeply held belief; because it would have acknowledged the possibility of detaching that belief from the place held sacred by the Hebrews, the place that the conqueror had destroyed. Perhaps too because the allure of the dominant Babylonian culture—its landscape and its buildings, its rich fund of songs and stories and its great Storm God Marduk—was intense and because the Hebrews were uncomfortably aware of how much and in how many ways they were being shaped by it.

Such an awareness—a queasy sense of unwelcome but inescapable influence—may lie behind the weird eruption of violence in the psalm's closing lines:

> Remember, O Lord, the children of Edom in the day of Jerusalem;
> who said, Rase it, rase it: even to the foundation thereof.
> O daughter of Babylon, who are to be destroyed: happy shall he
> be that rewardeth thee as thou hast served us.
> Happy shall he be, that taketh and dasheth thy little ones against
> the stones.

The sudden whiplash of rage still has the power to shock. One moment the exiles are sitting and weeping and clinging to memories of home; the next moment they are dreaming of throwing babies against the stones. The pivot point that turns melancholy into thoughts of murder is recollection of the destruction of Jerusalem. The Hebrews must have known perfectly well that the order to raze the temple came not from the daughter of Babylon but from Nebuchadnezzar and his general Nebuzaradan. But their anger is directed at a whole culture and its people.

The triumphant Babylonians want to hear a little music from their slaves. The psalm's closing words express hatred in its purest form, hatred that wells up from the seething resentment of a defeated and demoralized people. The psalm begins with a gesture of refusal—the captives have hung their harps on the willows—and then, after shifting to a lament, it gives the Babylonians a song all right, but not a song calculated to heighten their mirth. The dream of killing Babylonian babies takes the remembrance of disaster and the feeling of being vulnerable and turns them into imagined violence against those who are still more vulnerable.

The Babylonian Captivity, as it is traditionally called, lasted for decades. It must have seemed as if it would never come to an end. The

elders died; those who had been children at the time of the deportations of 597 grew old; their children and grandchildren knew nothing
but the shadow of the baked-brick ziggurat and old, half-crazed stories of a beautiful stone city with a grand temple that had once been
theirs. The exiles from Judah kept Hebrew as their national language,
but they ordinarily spoke its linguistic cousin, Aramaic, which was,
along with Neo-Babylonian, the language of everyday life in Babylon. There was no language barrier then between themselves and their
captors, and for the well-born Hebrews at least there was only a modest social barrier. The Babylonians allowed the upper classes of those
whom they deported to live in the royal court. Some of the more
learned exiles may also have acquired knowledge of Old Akkadian,
Old Babylonian, or even Sumerian, the ancient languages in which
the ritual life of Nebuchadnezzar's kingdom was conducted and in
which the Babylonian scribes continued to keep the sacred stories of
their people. Whether the Hebrews were fascinated or repelled by
what was going on around them—the songs, the festivities and observances, the folklore, and the elaborate myths—they could not possibly
block it out.

Then, with startling suddenness, the Babylonian Empire began to
fall apart. In the wake of Nebuchadnezzar's death, there was a succession crisis that weakened the state just at the time that a new and
dangerous threat was gathering, under the leadership of Cyrus, in
neighboring Persia. When in 547 the formidable Cyrus conquered
the immensely wealthy Lydian king Croesus (from whom we get the
phrase "rich as Croesus"), he consolidated a powerful empire that then
moved relentlessly southward into Mesopotamia. On October 12, 539
BCE, Babylon surrendered to the Persians. A canny politician, Cyrus
paid homage to Marduk, but he also liberated the enslaved Hebrews
and allowed them to go back to Judah.

To pious Hebrews, permitted after so many years of exile to return
to their homeland, Cyrus could only have been the chosen agent of

their god. "He is my shepherd," Yahweh says of Cyrus in the book of Isaiah, "and shall perform all my pleasure: even saying to Jerusalem, Thou shalt be built; and to the temple, Thy foundation shall be laid" (Isa. 44:28). The Persian conqueror might have been surprised to discover that he was the tool of a deity of whom he had probably never heard. But Yahweh, as Isaiah imagines him, spells out the situation directly to the conqueror: "I am the Lord, and there is none else, there is no God beside me: I girded thee, though thou hast not known me" (Isa. 45:5).

The Hebrew exiles who returned to Jerusalem undertook the immense labor of rebuilding the Temple, enabling them to resume the ancient sacrifices to Yahweh. (Visitors to Jerusalem today who stand by the side of the Western Wall and gaze at the enormous stone blocks flung down in 70 CE by the Romans can get some sense of the scope of the enterprise.) But this building project was not enough for them: they embarked upon the comparably immense intellectual labor of forging out of all of their diverse records and repeated stories a sacred book.

For a thousand years or more, the Hebrews had done without a single, collective sacred text. But in Babylon they had heard over and over again the *Enuma Elish* with its praise of Marduk, who created the first humans. The trauma of exile, along with the threatened loss of cultural memory, may well have triggered the key determination to bring together the stories and the laws with which the Hebrews defined who they were. For it is in this strange soil—a defeated and embittered people, repatriated at the whim of a foreign prince—that the Bible as we know it seems to have taken root.

Behind the decision to compile the sacred book lay the fear expressed by Ezra the scribe—the leader of a large body of the exiles back to Jerusalem—that the Hebrews had "not separated themselves from the people of the lands" (Ezra 9:1). Already before the exile, this fear of contamination had been a major theme. The prophets raged that the cult of Yahweh had become twisted together with observances they regarded as abominations. Seventy years of exile had only made things much worse. The Hebrews had adopted the customs, beliefs, and dress of others. They had intertwined the cult of Yahweh with cults devoted to rival gods. And most threatening of all, they had begun to intermarry.

According to Ezra, the homeland to which the Jews returned was "an unclean land with the filthiness of the people of the lands, with their abominations, which have filled it from one end to another with their uncleanness" (Ezra 9:11). Ezra wept, tore his hair, rent his garments, and launched a campaign against intermarriage. And when the ethnic cleansing was complete and the foreign wives and children were all sent away, he gathered the people before him, stood up upon a pulpit of wood, opened a book, and began to read it out loud.

What do you do when warnings and denunciations are not enough? How do you eradicate old legends to which people had been long devoted or stop new cults that were constantly entering the land along the trade routes? It is one thing to pull down an altar you regard as an abomination. The act is relatively easy, particularly when the forces of monotheistic piety are in the ascendant. But the suppressed cults tend to spring up again like weeds. You can, in a frenzy of xenophobia, send away foreign wives and children, but the emotional cost must have been very high. And after a few years, there would always be more foreign wives and children, along with more alluring alien cults. How do you uproot deeply held beliefs?

You change the story.

The dream of the master text, the truth stripped of all uncleanness, was part of a concerted effort to resist the powerful culture of the surrounding peoples, to refuse their reigning divinities, abjure their forms of worship, and reject their accounts of the world. It is likely that this dream originated even before the return to Jerusalem, when the Hebrews were still weeping by the waters of Babylon. Significant portions of the book, such as the story of Adam and Eve or of Abraham and Isaac, may have already been available, written independently in separate parts over many centuries. Bringing these parts together would have served as an alternative to the ruined Temple, a substitute for what had been lost. In the long history of the Jews, in any case, this role is precisely what the sacred text, the Torah, played.

The Torah helped to turn Hebrews—a tribal people occupying a particular, highly vulnerable territory—into Jews. Already the prophets had begun to envisage a new covenant, not between Yahweh and the nation, but between Yahweh and the individual. Marduk might seem for the moment quite overwhelming, but he was a god inseparably linked to the city he protected and to the king whose power he upheld. When the walls crumbled, the king was toppled, and Babylon became the haunt of foxes and jackals, then Marduk would fall. There was no doubt in the minds of the prophets that this time was coming. And when it did, they, the Jews, would remain. They would be in possession of a sacred book—not an esoteric tract bound up with the fate of a particular city and its priests and king, but a collective treasure that recorded for all humankind the deeds of Yahweh, the all-powerful Creator. They would become what in Hebrew is called *Am HaSefer,* the People of the Book.

The Torah as a whole, most scholars agree, was first redacted in the fifth century BCE, but what exactly does "redacted" mean? It means that one or more editors took multiple strands that had reached them from the past, compared them, corrected them, cut pieces from them, added pieces to them, adjusted them, reconciled them to the best of their abilities, and wove them together. No one knows who these editors were, how many there were, or who chose them. No one knows if there were competing factions, or if there was a dominant figure, someone who adjudicated disagreements and made the final decisions. And no one knows for certain how many strands—full-scale narratives, mythic fragments, genealogical tables, chronicle histories, law codes, letters, tribal records, and the like—these editors, whoever they were, consulted and assembled.

In 1883 a thirty-nine-year-old German professor, Julius Wellhausen, published his *Prolegomena to the History of Israel* (*Prolegomena zur Geschichte Israels*). Notwithstanding the less-than-thrilling title, the book caused an immediate sensation. The son of a Lutheran pastor, the author deftly summarized a growing consensus among Bible scholars that, whatever might have been revealed to Moses at Mount Sinai (an event variously assigned by rabbis to 1312 or 1280 BCE), the written Torah as we know it was not the work of a single author. Advancing what he called "the documentary hypothesis," Wellhausen identified and chronologically ordered four distinct strands or strata that were woven together when the Torah took the form in which we know it. Each represented a distinctive set of features, preoccupations, and ways of referring to God; each emerged at a different moment in the historical development of ancient Israel; each responded to different pressures and represented different institutional interests and theological ideas. What a falling-off there was from the myth of origin: in place of Moses, Wellhausen referred to what he called J, E, D, and P.

Wellhausen hypothesized that J (for Jahwist, after the German spelling of YHWH or Yahweh as *Jahweh*) was the earliest of the sources, dating from around 950 BCE. It was followed by E (for Eloist, after *Elohim*, a plural noun used to refer to the deity), dating from around 850 BCE. J and E, he thought, were woven together relatively quickly. He estimated that D (for Deuteronomist) was composed around 600 and P (for Priestly) around 500 BCE. In Genesis, he thought, J (or, more probably, a conflation of J and E) were conjoined with P.

Very few scholars would at this point deny the basic premise that there is more than one strand in the story of the first humans and, more generally, in Genesis. The multiple strands are immediately apparent in the fact that the God of chapter 1 is called "Elohim," while in chapters 2 and 3 he is called "Yahweh Elohim." But from here on we enter exceedingly difficult terrain, every hillock and pothole of which is fiercely contested, often on dauntingly technical but nonetheless murky grounds. And even if all the battles were fought and won, and sweet concord reigned in the world of biblical scholarship, we would still bump up against the fact that for thousands of years, the story of Adam and Eve was received not as an intertwining of distinct strands but as a single story, a story by which men and women were fascinated, disturbed, and moved.

Outside the charmed circle of faith, the belief that Moses himself wrote down the creation story told in the first chapters of Genesis is no longer credible. But that pious belief had one great advantage: it is difficult to credit a committee of redactors with the fashioning of a work of art so powerful and so enduring. True, at least two distinct strands may be detected in those opening chapters, but why should the perception of such elements frighten us away from the idea of authorship? When Shakespeare sat down to write *King Lear,* he had before him Geoffrey of Monmouth's *History of the Kings of Britain,* Holinshed's *Chronicles,* Harrison's *Historical Description of the Island of Britain,* Higgins's *Mirror for Magistrates,* Spenser's *Faerie Queene,* Sidney's *Arcadia,* and the anonymous *True Chronicle History of King Leir and His Three Daughters.* Close attention reveals fault lines and tension among these sources. Do we think for a moment that Shakespeare was not the author of his great tragedy? Would we ever refer to Shakespeare as "the redactor" of *King Lear?*

The writer—or the compiler or the transmitter of tradition—who set out to construct a Hebrew counternarrative to the Babylonian creation story may have had more than one old manuscript in front of him; he may have had other old stories stored away in his memory; he may have turned to colleagues for suggestions and support and criticism. None of this is surprising, for nothing comes from nothing. But at the end of the day, someone—let us, for convenience, call him the Genesis storyteller—had to pull the multiple pieces together and to write the Hebrew creation story that has come down to us over the centuries. In that story Adam and Eve, whenever they were first conceived and whatever their status had been in the earlier centuries, came into their own. They were a proof of Yahweh's supreme power.

Yahweh was not, or not merely, a territorial deity; he was, the Genesis storyteller affirmed, the Creator of the universe; he was everywhere and all-powerful. This meant that he must have created the first humans, just as he must have willed the destruction of Jerusalem and the exile of his chosen people as a punishment for their disobedience. It followed that Nebuchadnezzar was merely a tool in his divine hands. The fact that the Babylonians took Jerusalem and razed Yahweh's temple was decisive proof of Yahweh's power, since the greatest empire in the world only served the disciplinary purposes of the Hebrews' god.

To skeptics this claim might have seemed pathetic and almost laughable—a Monty Python–like absurdity in which the most obvious evidence of defeat is trumpeted as proof of omnipotence. But oddly enough it seems to have been the position that triumphed historically, not only among Jews who have for millennia affirmed Yahweh's power in the face of overwhelming evidence of his failure to protect and defend them, but also, and even more successfully, among Christians who took this argument to a new level. Their omnipotent savior was beaten, spat upon, and executed in the manner reserved for criminals and slaves, but that miserable fate was precisely proof of his fulfillment of the designs of the omnipotent father.

A god who wielded such absolute power—who could treat the likes of Nebuchadnezzar as his vassal—was not only the master of the universe but its creator, not only the chief among the gods but the one true god, not only the maker of the Jews but the maker of all humankind. The Hebrew Bible that was stitched together so brilliantly after the return from exile could therefore not begin with Abraham and the origins of the Hebrews. It had to begin with Adam and Eve.

3

Clay Tablets

Whether we believe in the story of Adam and Eve or regard it as an absurd fiction, we have been made in its image. Over many centuries, the story has shaped the way we think about crime and punishment, moral responsibility, death, pain, work, leisure, companionship, marriage, gender, curiosity, sexuality, and our shared humanness. Had history developed in a different direction, the *Enuma Elish*, the *Atrahasis,* and the epic of *Gilgamesh* might have served as our own bundle of origin stories and would undoubtedly have shaped us other than as we are. That it did not work out this way had consequences.

Like the Bible, the Mesopotamian works that we now read almost certainly had behind them, as the wind in their sails, centuries of oral storytelling to which we can have no access. But even the written records of these great narratives stretch back into deep time, far deeper than any surviving traces of the Hebrew Bible. When and why someone in Mesopotamia first had the idea of writing down creation myths is not clear, but fragments of them survive from almost four thousand years ago.

Most of the speculative genius of early humanity is lost to us forever. But it is as if in these remarkable works a fragile breath—the breath of those in the remote past who wondered who we are and how we became that way—miraculously left its traces. The survival of the traces has everything to do with their place of origin—the sloping alluvial plains along the Tigris and Euphrates, whose carefully tended fields sustained the inhabitants of large, well-organized walled cities—and with the medium in which they were recorded: wet clay tablets inscribed with legible marks and subsequently dried in the sun or baked in a kiln.

The writing on these tablets, a mix of phonetic signs and visual symbols, was done with a sharpened reed that, when pressed into the moist clay, left wedge-like marks. Since the word "wedge" is *cuneus* in Latin, the script became known as *cuneiform*, that is, "wedge-shaped." Once widely used by the Sumerians, Akkadians, Babylonians, Assyrians, Hittites, and other peoples of Mesopotamia, cuneiform was gradually displaced by the simpler, easier writing in alphabetic characters, and by the time the Romans took control of the region, it had fallen into disuse. The last-known cuneiform inscription, an astronomical text, was made in 75 CE. Before long the wedge-shaped marks became completely indecipherable.

When the tablets could no longer be read—when they had become like the old floppy disks to which I no longer have access—the *Enuma Elish*, the *Atrahasis*, and *Gilgamesh* sank into a dreamless sleep. It did not happen suddenly: their existence must have lingered in the memories of those who recalled distant times when the account of creation was read aloud from the ziggurat. But as vanquished Babylon and the other Mesopotamian cities fell into ruin, the ancient stories gradually ceased to be told. With their vanishing any grasp of the influence the stories had once had upon the imagination of everyone in their orbit, from mighty kings to Hebrew slaves, vanished as well.

In the scriptures that they compiled after their return from exile, the adherents of Yahweh had no interest in acknowledging a debt to Babylonian myths. On the contrary, they were determined to eradicate anything that looked like a trace of an "abomination." This eradication—a massive, collective act of forgetting—was largely successful. With the passing of the centuries, less and less was known about Babylon and its neighboring cities, apart from what was written in the Bible. Marduk shrunk into a generic idol, one of those stocks and stones that only a fool could believe in. Nebuchadnezzar became a grotesque tyrant who was reduced to madness—"he was driven from men, and did eat grass as oxen, and his body was wet with the dew of heaven, till his hairs were grown like eagles' feathers, and his nails like birds' claws" (Daniel 4:33)—and then, recovering his wits, he humbly acknowledged the sovereignty of Yahweh.

More reliable, if quite modest, information about Babylonian religion remained just barely accessible, thanks to a priest of Marduk named Berossus who was active in the early third century BCE. A gifted astronomer, he is credited with the invention of the semicircular sundial hollowed into a cubical block, Berossus also wrote in Greek a *History of Babylonia*. That history was lost, but before its disappearance it was excerpted in the work of two later historians. That work in turn was lost, but before vanishing it was used by two still-later historians. Their work too was lost, but not before it was used in the third century CE by Eusebius, bishop of Caesarea. Eusebius's original Greek text was also lost, but an Armenian translation of it somehow survived. The early Christians who encountered Eusebius might have noticed that the ancient Babylonians had a creation myth with certain odd echoes of Genesis. Of course, given the extreme unreliability of the transmission—a translation of a lost copy of a lost copy of a lost copy of a lost original—it was perfectly reasonable to think that any echoes were simply garbled versions of the Hebrew account, which was assumed to be far more ancient and, in any case, was taken on faith to be true.

In the fullness of time then, the psalmist's fondest dream had come true. No one any longer worshiped Marduk (or Baal or El, the comparable West-Semitic storm gods). He became extinct, like Ishtar, Shamash, Ashur, and innumerable other vanquished deities. (Marduk today is principally known as the name of a Swedish heavy metal band.) In the wake of violent conquest, ruthless pillaging, and long, slow neglect, all that remained of Babylon and the neighboring cities were enormous mounds of dirt, with scarcely a broken pillar or a headless statue above the ground to indicate what had once been there.

But by a strange twist of fate, the historical disasters that destroyed so many records of past civilizations helped to preserve these, for when in wars and invasions the great Mesopotamian cities were burned down, the sun-dried tablets in the libraries and royal archives were in effect baked into durable form. In their death-agonies, the palaces and the temples had become kilns. Even the violent floods that on rare occasion swept through the ruins could not wash away what these kilns had hardened. Moreover, there was no incentive to recycle or destroy the indecipherable texts on which permanence had been so unwittingly conferred. Parchments could be scraped clean of whatever had been written on them and then reused; papyri were convenient for lighting fires and keeping the stove warm. But fire-hardened clay tablets were worthless: if you smashed them, all you got was a handful of dust.

In the Middle Ages and the Renaissance, foreign travelers to the Near East occasionally came across the cuneiform tablets and brought some home as souvenirs or as objects to puzzle over. But it was not until the nineteenth century that the extent of what had survived was grasped. From the 1830s on, Western archaeologists began systematic explorations of the buried cities along the Tigris and Euphrates, discovering what were evidently the archives of rulers whose scribes kept careful records. It turned out that the ancient Mesopotamians had systematically gathered and saved tablets; they had in effect invented the idea of the library. In his capital Nineveh, on the eastern bank of the Tigris, the Assyrian king Ashurbanipal in the seventh century BCE assembled the largest, most comprehensive, and best-organized library ever created. Ashurbanipal—whom the Greeks called Sardanapalus— had a personal interest in these collections: unlike most of the region's kings, he had received scribal training and was proud of his ability to read not only the simplified cuneiform of his contemporaries but also the ancient Sumerian and Akkadian scripts. Centuries before the Ptolemaic kings of Egypt established their famous library at Alexandria, this learned ruler in what is now northern Iraq brought together under his lordly gaze the wisdom of the whole world.

And then it was all gone. In 612 BCE, shortly after Ashurbanipal's death, Nineveh was besieged by a coalition of enemies. The walls were breached, and after fierce house-to-house fighting, the city was sacked, its houses and temples set on fire, its citizens massacred. In the murderous conflagration that destroyed the city, the library's shelves, on which cuneiform tablets in their thousands had been carefully arrayed, collapsed; the floors buckled with them; and the whole mass was buried under tons of rubble.

Nineveh was abandoned and forgotten until the 1840s, when archaeologists burrowing through the rubble began to make their finds. Along with the more obviously valuable and impressive statues, reliefs, and ornamental gateways, huge numbers of tablets or fragments of tablets—at the time completely unreadable—were shipped back to European imperial capitals and particularly to London. The archaeologist Hormuzd Rassam, a Chaldean Christian who converted to Anglicanism and eventually became a British subject, is alone credited with adding some 134,000 tablets to the holdings of the British Museum.

As with the deciphering of hieroglyphics by means of the Rosetta Stone, the key to cracking the cuneiform code was the discovery of a trilingual inscription. "I am Darius the king," it began, in parallel Old Persian, Elamite, and Akkadian scripts, "the son of Hystaspes, the Achaemenid, the King of Kings, the Persian, the king of Persia. . . ." Two of the scripts were in legible script; the third was in cuneiform. Slowly, painstakingly, the mystery of the tablets began to be unraveled. The central figure in grasping their significance was a young working-class banknote engraver, George Smith, who had become captivated by the objects on display in the sculpture galleries of the British Museum. With little formal education and no social credentials but driven by a deep fascination, Smith read everything that he could get his hands on in the nascent field of Assyriology. He soon began to show an extraordinary aptitude for deciphering the wedge-shaped signs.

Laboring feverishly over newly found tablets as well as tablets that had been languishing on the shelves for years, Smith identified and succeeded in translating the *Enuma Elish*. After two thousand years of forgetting, both deliberate and accidental, it became clear that the Hebrew origin story had not stood alone, in solitary splendor. The opening of Genesis was evidently a response to what the captives heard over and over again when they sat and wept by the waters of Babylon. Those captives determined not to swell the number of the *lullu,* the black-headed people who sang hymns to Marduk. They would make clear that it was Yahweh, not Marduk, who fashioned the universe and who created the first humans.

The sublime simplicity of the opening of Genesis was polemical. Creation for the Hebrews was not a tangle of incest, conspiracy, and intergenerational bloodletting; it was the act of Yahweh and Yahweh alone. He did not grapple with a rival or impregnate a goddess. Indeed there was no one else in all the vastness at the beginning of things, no consort, no assistance, and no resistance. The humans were created in God's image and likeness, animated not with the blood of a murdered rival but with his own breath. He did not produce these creatures in order to serve him and make his divine existence easier. God did not need servants. The building of cities, the digging of canals, the tending of the flocks, and the exhausting work in the fields were of no interest to him. Rest—the repose of the seventh day—was important to Yahweh, as it was to Apsu, but it could not be impertinently threatened or disturbed. When Yahweh decided to take his rest, he simply took it.

The Hebrews were determined to distinguish themselves—from the very beginning of time—from their former captors. The Genesis storyteller was in effect burying a hated past. At the same time, in the wake of Smith's deciphering, it was possible to catch distant echoes, like sounds coming to us from under mounds of rubble, of what had been buried. A god, hovering over the restless deep, engenders everything that will come to exist; he divides the waters in two, shaping one into the sky and the other into the sea; he forms a primordial human from clay and assigns him agricultural work. Are we in Jerusalem or Babylon?

The echoes were striking enough in themselves, but they were amplified to a spectacular degree in a further shattered tablet, partly caked with deposits of lime still covering some of the cuneiform signs, that Smith came across in November 1872. The young Assyriologist found himself reading what seemed to be an account of a devastating flood and a boat that enabled a tiny remnant of humanity to survive. Once the tablet was thoroughly cleaned, he grasped that his initial surmise was correct. When he began to read over the lines and saw that "they contained the portion of the legend he had hoped to find there," a colleague later recalled,

> he said, "I am the first man to read that after more than two thousand years of oblivion." Setting the tablet on the table, he jumped up and rushed about the room in a great state of excitement, and, to the astonishment of those present, began to undress himself.

The undressing that so shocked Smith's colleague may, as the literary historian David Damrosch has observed, have been only a loosened collar: this was, after all, Victorian England. But almost any level of excitement could have been justified by the discovery.

Here at last, resurrected from a distant past, was overwhelmingly powerful evidence of the deep currents that linked ancient Mesopotamian mythology and the Hebrew scriptures. Smith had found a flood story considerably older than the date on which Moses was traditionally said to have received the Torah on Mt. Sinai. It is not simply that the clay tablets, which reach back astoundingly to 1800 BCE, gave an account of an immense, destructive deluge; they included many of the key elements that feature in the Noah story: the enraged god's determination to eradicate all human life; lifesaving advice to one particular human who finds divine favor; the careful building and provisioning of the ark; the terrifying storm and rising waters; the ark coming to rest on a mountaintop; the release of birds to see if the waters had receded; the offering of a sweet-smelling sacrifice in gratitude for the recovery of dry land.

The flood story that Smith initially happened upon—out of the vast number of tablets in the storeroom of the British Museum—was from the great epic *Gilgamesh,* but it was told there in abbreviated form. Continuing his search, the indefatigable scholar managed to find an even older and more complete version. This version, the *Atrahasis*, linked the flood, in a manner reminiscent of the *Enuma Elish*, to the problem of noise, but now it was not the noise of the junior gods but human noise. Humans had been created in order to help out with the most disagreeable chores, but they had an irrepressible penchant to reproduce:

> The land had grown wide, the peoples had increased,
> The land was bellowing like a bull.
> The god was disturbed with their uproar.

This restless god repeatedly tried to reduce the human population through a succession of catastrophes—plague, drought, and crop failure—but his efforts were thwarted each time by a fellow god, Enki. Enki had established a pleasant relationship with a particularly intelligent human—*Atrahasis* in Akkadian means "Extra Wise"—to whom he gave advice on ways to avert through sacrifice the worst consequences of the divine attacks. After every disaster, the human population, and with it the unbearable human noise, rebounded.

At last, losing patience, the angry, sleep-deprived god decided to do away with humans once and for all by unleashing a terrible flood. Enki advised Atrahasis to abandon his house and build a boat—"Forsake possessions, and save life"—in order to survive. The flood was suitably catastrophic: at the spectacle of destruction, the corpses clogging the river like dragonflies, Atrahasis's "heart was broken, and he was retching gall." But thanks to the boat, a remnant of humanity was saved.

In the wake of this survival, a brilliant solution—a kind of sinister bargain—was finally devised. From henceforth the great god would not try to eliminate humanity altogether. He would simply reduce the human population on a regular basis by making some women infertile and by causing large-scale infant mortality. Misery for humans, but happiness for a god who wanted his rest.

The Genesis storyteller embraced this ancient text, taking over for his tale of Noah both the general outline and many specific details. But something happened in the retelling, something that marked off a decisive difference between the Hebrews and the Babylonians. The Babylonian god was angry because his rest was disturbed, but not so the Hebrew god. Yahweh did not need to sleep, and he was indifferent to human noise. He did not want to reduce human numbers; indeed he commanded the first humans to be fruitful and multiply.

Fine. But why then did he unleash the flood? What was his motive? In the Babylonian source, it all makes sense, from the creation of the first humans to their noisy multiplication to the attempt to exterminate them and finally to the compromise that would keep the burgeoning population down through infertility and infant mortality. Noise is a characteristic of humans, as everyone who has lived in a crowded city knows particularly well. The myth of Atrahasis seems perfectly suited to an urban culture such as that of Babylon.

But the Hebrews did not think of themselves primarily as urban dwellers; they clung, if only in fantasy, to their rural or nomadic roots. Imagining an all-powerful God who is indifferent to noise, they gave him an entirely different motivation for murderous anger: "And God saw that the wickedness of man was great in the earth, and that every imagination of the thoughts of his heart was only evil continually" (Gen. 6:5). To the Hebrews' way of thinking, there had to be a *moral* reason that accounted for the disasters that humans encounter, something in their actions and their inner lives ("every imagination of the thoughts of his heart"). The flood was a response to human evil.

This radical rewriting of the ancient Mesopotamian story was in its way a tremendous achievement. Humans—the black-headed people who reproduce and swarm noisily across the land—must not be conceived of as thoughtless nuisances. They bear moral responsibility for their actions. Even those things that seem to link them to the fate of all living creatures, such as their shared vulnerability to a disaster like the flood, are in the case of humans the consequence of their own choices, their willed decisions. Besides, the Genesis storyteller seemed to ask with a hard look back at Babylon, what kind of God is it that needs slaves in order to eat, or that cannot sleep because of the racket, or that would visit destruction on his own creatures because his nap has been disturbed?

Yet any rewriting of myth comes at a cost, and this particular rewriting, for all its sublimity, cost dearly. There is, after all, much to be said for explaining infertility and infant mortality and a terrible vulnerability to drought or plague or flood not as punishments for moral failings but as divinely mandated devices to keep down the human population. The devices are cruel, but at least they do not attribute guilt, either to the individual victims or to humanity as a whole. Human reproduction is not limitless; there will be constraints, painful, structural, and largely indifferent to good and evil. Recognition of this indifference did not need to be a call for mere fatalism: wisdom and piety, of the kind embodied in Atrahasis, were rewarded. But it is not as if humans had done something wrong, as if they should have tried to reproduce less or be quieter. Atrahasis was not encouraged to regard those who were swept away in the flood as somehow deserving of their fate. On the contrary, he was literally sickened when he saw the destruction.

There is a lot to be said as well for a religion that regards certain gods as beneficent protectors of mankind and others as malevolent threats. One god might argue openly against the destructive design of another god or work secretly to circumvent a planned outcome. A worshiper could imagine playing one god off against another and could express ambivalent feelings toward the acknowledged rulers of the universe. It is difficult to find a place for such feelings in Genesis. The Hebrew Bible has many moments of subtle negotiation with Yahweh and of veiled protest against his divine decrees, but these all occur within an overarching understanding that Yahweh, at once just, compassionate, and wise, is the ultimate locus and arbiter of all moral value. This understanding promises a greater coherence: the Babylonian pantheon (like that of the Greeks and the Romans) seems by contrast a confused jumble of competing powers. But it opens up queasy questions of responsibility that haunt the biblical story of Noah and reach back still further to haunt the biblical story of Adam and Eve.

In the Genesis storyteller's account of the Flood, the divine smiter and the divine protector are one and the same. This reduction to one supreme divinity from multiple gods, one cleverly thwarting the destructive design of the others, preserves the omnipotence of the Creator who has made all things and now, at his own will and discretion, can destroy them. But doing away with multiple gods introduces certain problems, starting with the very notion of an all-powerful, all-knowing god who nonetheless repents what he has himself created. Did the wise maker not anticipate what his creatures would do? How is it possible for an omniscient divinity to regret what he has done?

And how is it possible to justify or even comprehend the arbitrariness and cruelty of the destruction that he unleashes, destruction that sweeps away not only adult malefactors but also small children, newborn lambs, virgin forests?

In the Mesopotamian origin story, neither the murderous gods nor the irrepressibly noisy humans are morally judged for what they do. But in Genesis, humans bear responsibility for their actions and for what befalls them. God is neither arbitrary nor capricious. It was the fatal wickedness of Noah's contemporaries that led God to regret his creation of humans. And lurking somewhere behind that wickedness are the first humans and the behavior that led God to expel Adam and Eve from their perfect garden. But how could such wickedness have arisen from creatures made in God's image?

These questions had been there from the beginning, troubling the minds of the pious as well as the doubters. Notwithstanding all the efforts of prophets and preachers, inquisitors and artists, moral philosophers and systematic theologians, they continued over the centuries to linger in the shadows of cozy parish churches and to slumber just below the surface of familiar, well-thumbed pages. George Smith understood that what he had stumbled upon, after more than two thousand years, would reanimate the half-buried disturbances and unsettle even his most complacent Victorian contemporaries. It was as if you had grown up with an inheritance you thought you perfectly understood and in which you took great pride, but now that inheritance had been made to seem less comfortable, coherent, and sustaining. Your stories were no longer entirely your own. You had strange ancestors you never dreamed that you had.

Smith lost his life in search of these ancestors. In October 1875, at the urging of the British Museum, he set out for Nineveh, in present-day Iraq, hoping to find more tablets. There were bureaucratic delays in Istanbul, an outbreak of plague, disquieting reports of political unrest in the area where he intended to dig, increasingly unbearable heat. He fell ill with dysentery and died at the age of thirty-six in a small village north of Aleppo. His claim to immortality, of the kind scholars hope to attain, rests on the moment he jumped up and began to tear off his clothes, the moment he discovered *Gilgamesh*.

There may have been a real ruler named Gilgamesh who reigned in the city of Uruk (now Warka, in southern Iraq) and ordered the construction of its walls and ramparts some five thousand years ago, but the Gilgamesh in the tablets Smith deciphered is a mythical figure, two-thirds god and only one-third human. The tablets bear the name of the person who compiled them, the scholar-priest Sin-lequi-unninni. About Sin-lequi-unninni nothing is known, except that, like Homer or the Genesis storyteller, he was a brilliant artist who was working with already existing materials, texts and oral legends that reached far, far back into the past. The Torah was probably assembled in the fifth century BCE; the *Iliad* somewhat earlier, perhaps between 760 and 710 BCE. But Sin-lequi-unninni wrote his text sometime between 1300 and 1000 BCE, and the earliest surviving written tales of Gilgamesh date from around 2100 BCE. Older by more than a thousand years than either Homer or the Bible, *Gilgamesh* is quite possibly the oldest story ever found.

Already by the time of the Babylonian captivity, Uruk had lost much of the political influence it once exercised in the region. Still, it retained a peculiar prestige, for it was there in the far distant past that something amazing had been invented. Over an area covering some 5.5 square kilometers small settlements had come together to form an unprecedented economic and administrative whole. Even at the time, people understood that they were participating in a phenomenon of singular importance. What was emerging was the first city in the ancient Near East and perhaps the first city in human history.

The setting of *Gilgamesh* is not a garden at the beginning of time but a crowded city. The work does not attempt to reconstruct a world before humans existed; it seems to imagine rather that we have always lived in communities and always shared stories. And yet though it does not give us a moment before which nothing existed, it includes a remarkable scene of creation, one that resembles the primal moment depicted in the *Enuma Elish*. As the work begins, the people of Uruk are suffering under the uncontrolled and uncontrollable desires of their ruler. One-third human, two-thirds god, Gilgamesh is a mighty warrior and a great builder, but his sexual appetites are destroying the city's morale. Heeding the people's complaints, the gods launch a complex, roundabout scheme. The first step is taken when the mother goddess Aruru washes her hands, pinches off a piece of clay, and forms a creature out of it. The creature—"Shaggy with hair was his whole body" (1:105)—is named Enkidu.

Eating grass and drinking from water holes, Enkidu roams naked in the wilderness with gazelles. When he sees traps set for his animal companions, he breaks them, and he fills in the pits that the hunters have dug. One day a frustrated hunter catches sight of the wild man. Understanding now why his attempts to capture game have been failing, the hunter travels to Uruk, a three-days' journey, to ask Gilgamesh for advice. Gilgamesh counsels the hunter to go to the Temple of Ishtar, the sex goddess, and request help from a priestess named Shamhat. The priestess is a temple prostitute skilled in all pleasures.

Shamhat accompanies the hunter back to the waterhole and waits for Enkidu. "Toss aside your clothing," the hunter urges her, "Let him lie upon you,/Treat him, a human, to woman's work!" (1:184–85). It comes to pass just as the hunter had hoped. Shamhat and Enkidu spend six days and seven nights in fervent lovemaking. Then at the end of this time, when Enkidu attempts to rejoin the gazelles and other wild creatures, they all run off. He is bewildered at no longer being able to keep up with them, but his disorientation and loss are the preludes to a new state of being: "You are become like a god," Shamhat exclaims. "Why roam the steppe with wild beasts?" (1:207-8). It is not only his body that has changed but also his mind. He is no longer a beast among beasts.

When the benevolent Shamhat tells Enkidu about Gilgamesh, her words seem to awaken some longing in him. But they cannot instantly go to the city. Civilized life requires initiation, accommodation, and an extended learning process. The harlot begins by dressing her naked charge: "She took off her clothing, with one piece she dressed him,/ The second she herself put on" (2:20–21). The clothing is not a response to a feeling of shame, nor even an adaptation to the environment. It is a mark of the movement from nature to culture.

That movement continues when Shamhat takes Enkidu to dine in a hut with shepherds. The rustic meal is simple, but to someone accustomed to browsing on grass and suckling the milk of gazelles, it is as strange as the first morsel of solid food on the tongue of an infant. Shamhat teaches him to eat bread and to drink beer. Having drunk seven goblets, Enkidu, who has become carefree and cheerful, "treated his hairy body with water,/He anointed himself with oil, turned into a man" (2:42–43). The lines may simply mean that he washed his hair, but they may also suggest that he rubbed the fur off of his body. We are watching the ascent of man.

This ascent sets the stage for the friendship between Gilgamesh and Enkidu, a friendship carefully prepared long before they set eyes on one another. "Let me show you Gilgamesh," Shamhat exclaims, giving her charge a vision:

> He is radiant with virility, manly vigor is his,
> The whole of his body is seductively gorgeous. (1:236–37)

So too in Uruk, she tells Enkidu, Gilgamesh will dream of a star that has fallen from the heavens. "I fell in love with it," Gilgamesh tells his mother, to whom he has related his dream. Interpreting the dream, his mother explains to him that the star to which he was drawn is the friend he is fated to meet: "You will fall in love with him and caress him like a woman" (1:273).

The powerful erotic charge leads into their first encounter, but in a surprising way. Arriving in Uruk, Enkidu takes it upon himself to block Gilgamesh's access to a bride whom he intends, as is his custom, to rape on her wedding day. The desperate prayers of the people have been answered: the wild man barring Gilgamesh's way is the fulfillment, by an extremely circuitous route, of the gods' plan to save the city.

Gilgamesh is enraged that anyone should oppose his wishes. He and Enkidu lock bodies in a mighty struggle that shakes the doorframes and the walls of Uruk. When Gilgamesh is finally victorious, the victory is sealed with an embrace: "They kissed each other and made friends" (2:115). The bride is forgotten. Inseparable friends from this moment forth, Gilgamesh and Enkidu embark together on a succession of reckless, heroic adventures.

But at a certain moment, the gods decree that Enkidu must sicken and die. The terrified human blames Shamhat, who has taken him from the life of the gazelles ranging the hills to the anguish of a mortal man: "May you never make a home that you can enjoy," he bitterly curses her; "May you never caress a child of your own" (7:71–72). The issue here cannot be mortality itself—after all, as Enkidu knows, the gazelles had been hunted and killed—but rather the peculiar human awareness of mortality. That awareness, the special anguish that is our lot, is the terrible cost of the initiation into civility so lovingly conducted by the temple prostitute. The beneficent sun god Shamash, the god of fairness and moderation, directly intervenes to remind Enkidu of all he owes to that initiation: food and drink that have sustained and delighted him, beautiful clothing he wears, honors of which he is proud, and above all his deep friendship with Gilgamesh. Before he dies, Enkidu, though still frightened, repents his curses and blesses the prostitute who has made him fully human.

Gilgamesh, who has lovingly attended his friend through the long death agonies, goes into deep mourning. The pain of loss is bound up with fear for himself:

Enkidu, my friend whom I loved, is turned into clay!
Shall I too not lie down like him,
And never get up forever and ever? (10:69–71)

The inconsolable hero leaves Uruk and embarks on a search for a way
to avoid death. He is determined somehow to find the survivor of the
ancient flood, Utnapishtim, reputed to be the only human who has
ever achieved immortality.

The search leads the wanderer to the shores of the sea, where he
encounters an alewife, Siduri, who keeps a tavern. When he explains
to Siduri that he is set on crossing the sea to find Utnapishtim, she
urges him to accept the way things are. It makes no sense for Gilgamesh or anyone else to torment himself with longings for immortality. He should embrace whatever joys life has to offer:

As for you, Gilgamesh, let your stomach be full,
Always be happy, night and day,
Make every day a delight,
Night and day, play and dance.
Your clothes should be clean,
Your head should be washed,
You should bathe in water.
Look proudly on the little one holding your hand,
Let your mate be always blissful in your loins. (10:82–90)

The alewife's words epitomize the wisdom of the everyday, the advice
summoned up by the spectacle of too much heroic striving: know your
limits, accept the human condition, savor the ordinary sweet pleasures
that life offers. "This, then," she concludes, "is the work of mankind."

Gilgamesh cannot accept this counsel, even after he finds Utnapishtim and learns that the immortality conferred by the gods upon
him and his wife after the great flood was a unique event. Taking pity

on the tormented hero, the ancient man and his wife give him one final hope: they reveal that a secret tree of life, a thorny plant, grows beneath the sea and magically confers rejuvenation. Tying heavy stones to his feet, the daring hero dives down and seizes the plant.

But the dream of rejuvenation is shattered. When in the course of his return to Uruk Gilgamesh stops to bathe in a pool of fresh water, a serpent steals the plant away. The plant clearly was effective— before vanishing into the reeds, the rejuvenated serpent sheds its scaly skin—but it is now irrevocably lost. Gilgamesh sits down to weep, knowing that his quest for immortality has failed. He will not be able to escape death. But he consoles himself with the recognition that he will leave behind something splendid: the vast foundation platform and staircases and brick walls, the temples and orchards and ponds, of his city.

This is the great epic that circulated in the Near East for many centuries before the Hebrews decided to write their account of humankind's earliest days: a tale of joyous sexual initiation; a gradual ascent from wildness to civility; a celebration of the city as the great good place; a difficult, reluctant acceptance of mortality; above all, a life that has at its center the experience not of marriage and family but of deep same-sex friendship. Then, with the collapse of the cities of Mesopotamia, it vanished. Until its chance recovery in the nineteenth century, the love story of Gilgamesh and Enkidu had been forgotten for millennia, written in a script no one could any longer read and buried under the mounds of rubble. It did not become part of our collective inheritance. Instead, we inherited Genesis.

Though the epic of *Gilgamesh* meant nothing to Augustine, Dante, or Milton, it was almost certainly known to the Genesis storyteller. In addition to its account of the deluge and the ark, it provided a narrative of a god who makes a human from clay and an account of the first experience of sexuality, love, suffering, and death. Even in the broken fragments that survive, it is a beautiful and compelling story. If the Hebrews had to answer the *Enuma Elish*, so too they may have felt compelled to respond to *Gilgamesh*.

There was no room for such a response in the terse, impersonal style of the opening, with its successive days of creation culminating in the making of the human in God's image and likeness: "Male and female created He them." This cosmology, in its sublime abstraction, could not even hint at the experience of human life that *Gilgamesh* so brilliantly represented. For that, whoever put Genesis together had to begin again, to launch a new story.

The narrative that unfolds in the second and third chapters of Genesis begins where the opening left off. Yet it is not a simple continuation. In chapter 1, God had "created the human in his image," but there was no mention of any material with which God worked, any more than there was for the sun and the moon. They all came forth through the power of His word. At the risk of a contradiction, in chapter 2 the writer provided a different account, one that responded more directly to the challenge posed by Enkidu where the goddess Aruru forms a man from clay. Yahweh too now forms a man from clay, as the punning name of the species insists: clay in Hebrew is *'adama,* and the word for human is *'adam*. Instead of adding some substance from his body to this clay figure, the Hebrew god blows into its nostrils "the breath of life." Not a substance but a breath. The image brilliantly captures the miracle of animation: the matter is the same as the inert dust of the ground, but it is not inert. The clay breathes; it lives. God has fashioned it and awakened it to life, but He is not in it. Therein lies the possibility of freedom and of alienation.

In *Gilgamesh* the human formed from clay is a wild man, with flowing hair (possibly all over his body) and the strength and manner of life of the animals. In Genesis the clay human is created "in the image of God" and has from the beginning the status of one who is not a companion to the other animals but of one who dominates them. There is no slow evolution toward full humanness; in Genesis the clay creature animated by God's breath is already fully human. That he does not need to learn anything or experience anything to realize his identity cuts away at a stroke the whole basis for Enkidu's initiation story.

Adam's goal is not the city—or rather, if for his descendants urban life lies ahead, it represents only a further disaster in the wake of the expulsion from the Garden of Eden. In chapter 11 of Genesis, some men decide to build a city on the plain of Shinar. As if in acknowledgment of Mesopotamia's primacy in this invention, the text makes clear that the people are set on building a city not made of stone, like the cities of Canaan, but of bricks.

> And they said to each other, "Come, let us bake bricks and burn them hard." And the brick served them as stone, and bitumen served them as mortar. And they said, "Come, let us build us a city and a tower with its top in the heavens, that we may make us a name, lest we be scattered over all the earth." (Gen. 11:3–4, Alter trans.)

"Go up," Gilgamesh proudly tells his boatman, "pace out the walls of Uruk./Study the foundation terrace and examine the brickwork. Is not its masonry of kiln-fired brick?" (11:95). The Genesis storyteller almost certainly knew this passage, and he also seems to have had in his mind the passage from the *Enuma Elish* in which Marduk approves the making of a great city: "Create Babylon, whose construction you requested!/Let its mud bricks be moulded, and build high the shrine!" In Genesis this brick-built metropolis is a disaster:

> And the Lord came down to the see the city and the tower that the human creatures had built. And the Lord said, "As one people with one language for all, if this is what they have begun to do, now nothing they plot to do will elude them. Come, let us go down and baffle their language there so that they will not under-

stand each other's language." And the Lord scattered them from there over all the earth and they left off building the city. Therefore it is called Babel, for there the Lord made the language of all the earth babble. (Gen. 11:5–9, Alter trans.)

Pious Hebrews who had always feared and hated cosmopolitan Babylon must have loved this story. They must have laughed at the punning reference to the babel of languages and at the inability of the ambitious builders to finish their proud tower. And they must have relished the transformation of the city as fulfillment of human destiny into the city as emblem of human arrogance and futility.

For the author of Genesis 2 and 3 the garden, not the city, was the great good place, the place that Yahweh designed for the human he created, endowing it with "every tree lovely to look at and good for food." There is no need to venture forth, as Enkidu and Gilgamesh do, to cut down trees in order to build grand gates. In the Genesis story, there is no trace of any structure in the garden in which the human lives, no sign of a hut, let alone an altar, shrine, or palace. The trees are valued for fruit and beauty, not for architecture. The human's role is not to build anything in the garden but only "to till it and to watch it."

These tasks imply labor as an essential part of human existence from the very beginning. The term "paradise" was not used in the Hebrew Bible but was given by the Greek translators who may have dreamed of a realm of perfect leisure not imagined by the Hebrews. The dream in Genesis is not leisure but rather purposive work—tilling and watching—that is experienced as pleasure. Labor yes, but not the hard labor that was an essential part of the Sumerian origin myth. Indeed the fact that Yahweh's design includes a river that "went out of Eden to water the garden" (2:10) seems to lift the heavy burden of digging irrigation ditches that figured so prominently for the Babylonians. God has created the conditions that enable man through his efforts to feed himself and his offspring. We learn later that this provision of vegetarian sustenance was easy, for there were no weeds, and the labor evidently did not cause the man to sweat.

In *Gilgamesh*, the gods create from clay a wild man who becomes the hero's friend or life partner. In Genesis, God, seeing that it is not good for the earth man to be alone, forms the woman out of a piece of the man's own body. This second, separate creation is an astonishingly creative response to the Mesopotamian story. It captures the same deep longing for companionship, the acute need for "help," the ecstatic pleasure in the existence of another person with whom one's own life is bound up, but at the same time it completely transforms them.

What is the nature of the transformation? What difference does it make, in representing the central human bond, to shift, as Genesis does, from a man and his male friend to a man and a woman? Both accounts feature the importance of human company: the individual, no matter how powerful and independent, cannot function alone. Both convey the pleasure and excitement, as well as the utility, of human company. Both capture the sense that, in its heroic achievements and its tragic losses, human destiny derives from shared decisions and collective actions. To this extent there is little difference.

The Genesis storyteller does not, as one might have expected, depict the relationship between the first man and the first woman as fundamentally hierarchical. Nothing suggests that the woman God fashions is unequal to the man in either strength or rank. And though in chapter 1 of Genesis humans are commanded to be fruitful and multiply, in chapter 2, when the woman is formed from the man's rib, that commandment to reproduce is not reiterated. Neither hierarchy nor reproduction seem to have seized the storyteller's imagination.

What Genesis emphasizes instead is the experience of "cleaving" together. Its account is much briefer. It does not, as *Gilgamesh* does, represent the couple in conversation with each other, or depict their disagreements, or show how they reached a joint decision or endured loss. But within his tiny scope the Genesis storyteller finds the time to repeat and repeat the strange, ecstatic feeling that the man and the woman are what he calls "one flesh."

When God brings the woman to the man, the man utters a jubilant welcome, an ecstatic poem that expresses his sense that the creature he sees before him is at the same time a piece of his own body:

> This one at last, bone of my bones,
> and flesh of my flesh. (Gen. 2:23, Alter trans.)

The woman is part of the man's actual substance and at the same time different, so that the man, awaking from his deep sleep, sings an ecstatic song about what he sees before him—"This one"—that is at the same time an ecstatic song about himself.

There is nothing like this in *Gilgamesh*. However intimate the relationship between Gilgamesh and Enkidu—and the poem depicts the emotional current between them as very deep indeed—they do not possess this peculiar feeling, at once metaphor and literal description, of shared being. It is a feeling that the Hebrew writer captured in a play on words, as if the letters themselves could convey the eerie sense that the man and woman are interlaced:

> This one shall be called Woman (*ishah*),
> for from man (*ish*) was this one taken. (Gen. 2:23, Alter trans.)

Gilgamesh and Enkidu kiss, embrace, and hold hands; sworn brothers in arms, they share dangerous adventures; they are sufficiently close that the death of one of them devastates the other. Their relationship is much more developed, intense, nuanced, than the relationship between Adam and Eve. But they are not "one flesh."

Perhaps the eerie sense that the man and the woman are fused—*ish* and *ishah*—is linked to procreation. After all, offspring are the living embodiments of the intertwining of flesh and bone. But as anyone who has been deeply in love can attest, the feeling of union is independent of offspring and very often precedes the production of offspring. Certainly it precedes it here: part of the brilliance of Genesis is precisely to separate the commandment to reproduce—and the fact of reproduction—from this intense feeling of being one flesh.

The Genesis writer underscores this key difference from *Gilgamesh*: "Therefore does a man leave his father and his mother and cling to his wife and they become one flesh" (2:24, Alter trans.). Becoming one flesh is linked, in this verse, to a momentous idea not found in *Gilgamesh*: the idea of leaving one's parents (absurd in the immediate context of Genesis, where there are no parents to leave) and forming a new unit. The Bible declares that the man leaves his mother and father—where in *Gilgamesh* it is precisely Gilgamesh's mother who facilitates and remains central to the relationship between Gilgamesh and his friend. Deep friendship does not necessarily entail the creation of a new family unit, but the bringing together of the man and the woman as one flesh does.

The description in Genesis ends with the vision of the couple in the garden—not in fact a single hermaphrodite, as the metaphoric "one flesh" repeatedly implies, but two people: "And the two of them were naked, the human and his woman, and they were not ashamed" (Gen. 2:25, Alter trans.). A trace of the mythical oneness remains, not in their nakedness but in the fact that they were not ashamed of this nakedness. This simple vision is the sum total of their life in the garden together, but it is enough.

For the Genesis storyteller, there is no initiation, no passage to civility, in order to make the primordial relationship possible. Life was somehow unfinished and unsatisfying before the creation of the woman, but now it is complete. There are implied glimpses forward—to clothing, to shame, to the way things are now—but they are marks of suffering or vulnerability after the violation of the divine prohibition. Genesis rewrites initiation as transgression.

"You have become like a god," the temple prostitute tells Enkidu after his sexual initiation. The Genesis storyteller remembered these words and used them to depict not the rise but the ruin of the man and the woman. The serpent who robs Gilgamesh of the branch that would have enabled him to escape death is transformed into the serpent who robs the man and the woman of their hope of eternal life. And the promise with which the serpent persuades the woman to eat the forbidden fruit is the very vision that Shamhat offered to Enkidu: "You will become as gods." Enkidu did not actually become a god. Clothed and instructed in proper ways to eat, he became fully human, capable of civility, deep friendship, and heroism. There is a price—he was now conscious of his mortality—but mortality itself was always his lot. Like the gazelles with which he used to run, he simply did not know it.

The man and the woman in Genesis could also be said to become fully human only after they eat the fruit. But, while for Enkidu the transformation is ultimately a blessing, for Adam and Eve it is a disaster: their clothing is a response to shame and privation, and their food must be extracted from a recalcitrant, thorny earth. Above all, their lives will be cut short by a death they might otherwise have avoided. They too have achieved greater understanding—the knowledge of good and evil—but it is an understanding purchased at an almost insupportable price.

If the Hebrew storyteller intended to unsettle deeply held Mesopotamian beliefs, he succeeded brilliantly. He turned the ancient origin story upside down. What was a triumph in *Gilgamesh* is a tragedy in Genesis.

4

The Life of Adam and Eve

In late 1945 an Egyptian peasant, Mohammed 'Ali al-Samman, went off with one of his six younger brothers to the mountains near his village north of Luxor in search of *sabakh*, a fertilizer formed from decaying matter in old cemeteries and abandoned settlements. Digging with his mattock, he accidentally unearthed a sealed red earthenware jar, about three feet high. At first he was afraid to open it, for fear that it was under a spell and would release an evil spirit, but, curiosity and avarice winning out, he broke the seal and reached inside. To his disappointment, he discovered not a cache of gold coins but only thirteen books, bound in leather, along with a few other loose scraps of paper. He took what he had found back to his village, where he tried largely unsuccessfully to trade the books for cigarettes or a few piasters. He off-loaded a few of them and threw the others on a pile of straw used in his home to heat the large clay bread oven. His mother tore some sheets off to keep the fire going, but the discoverer must have had some inkling that his find might be worth more than fuel, since he rescued the rest and set it aside.

News of Mohammed 'Ali's discovery began to trickle out beyond the confines of the village. By various serpentine routes, and with some further pages lost along the way, the trove eventually reached Cairo, where the antiquities dealers quickly grasped its potential value. Before the books found buyers, however, the Egyptian government got wind of their existence and, managing to seize all save one, placed them in Cairo's Coptic Museum. There they sat on a shelf for a decade before a project to transcribe and translate them was launched.

The books that came out of the jar date from around 350–400 CE and are copies of earlier texts. The whole cache has come to be known as the Nag Hammadi Library, after the town nearest the site where they were found. They were made out of sheets of papyrus, not glued together into scrolls (an ancient format familiar from the Torah scrolls still used today in synagogues) but stitched together as codices, the more convenient design we continue to use in our printed books. Christians were among the first to embrace codices for their sacred texts, and here, almost miraculously, was a whole collection of them.

Their survival depended on climate and sheer chance, but also on deliberate concealment. Written in Coptic, the language that flourished in Egypt before the Arab conquest, the books had been hidden away. Not surprisingly, those who carefully sealed them in the jar and buried them in so remote a place did not identify themselves, but they were probably monks from a nearby monastery who had been alarmed by the increasingly stringent policing of books deemed heretical by Christian authorities. The church in this period regarded it as important to settle the boundaries of the canon and to distinguish sharply between acceptable beliefs and those, such as the ones at Nag Hammadi, that were deemed dangerous. Whoever hid the books evidently did not want to destroy precious possessions, many of which reached back for centuries. Perhaps they hoped that the persecution would come to an end and that they could then return to the texts over which their community had long pored. But as it happened, the hunt for heterodoxy only intensified, and the manuscripts they had buried remained untouched and then forgotten for fifteen hundred years.

When the hidden library finally returned to the light, interest worldwide was aroused by the unique copy of the so-called Gospel of Thomas, with its claim—still hotly debated—to disclose unknown sayings of Jesus. But in many ways the most startling finds were texts about Adam and Eve. One of these, the Apocalypse of Adam, professes to be in the voice of the first human speaking to his beloved son Seth. "When God had created me out of the earth, along with Eve, your mother," the father recalls, "I went about with her in a glory." The glory in question, Adam makes clear, was not solely his possession. On the contrary, he owed it to his wife: "She taught me a word of knowledge of the eternal God." And the knowledge that they then shared made them both immensely powerful: "We resembled the great eternal angels, for we were higher than the god who had created us and the powers with him, whom we did not know."

"We were higher than the god who had created us": in this version of the Genesis story the creatures become stronger than God, God grows increasingly jealous and fearful, and man depends upon the courage and wisdom of woman. Eve is the real hero, for it was she who boldly grasped for herself and for all humanity the knowledge that the envious Creator had been withholding.

Another of the Nag Hammadi treatises, The Testimony of Truth, is written not from the perspective of God or Adam and Eve but from that of the serpent. God's limitations, according to The Testimony of Truth, are dismayingly clear. What kind of deity would refuse to permit humans to eat from the tree of knowledge? A truly loving Creator would surely have fostered knowledge, not forbidden it to his creatures. The God of Genesis is not our friend. It is the serpent who, in this version of the story, was the humans' great benefactor.

Evidently, to some members of this community, the story of Adam and Eve meant something radically different from anything we have come to expect. They were gripped by the suspicion that Yahweh was envious and mean-spirited. They attributed to the first humans words that we do not read in the sparse verses of the Bible. They celebrated the serpent who urged the humans to eat and the woman who in the pursuit of knowledge dared to violate Yahweh's prohibition. To be sure, their interpretation lost out: that is why they had to bury their books in a sealed jar that was forgotten. Perhaps that is why they themselves were forgotten.

But monks in the desert were not the only ones at the time who were asking questions about the origin story and straining to hear words that the Bible did not provide. Here are the opening words of The Life of Adam and Eve, a text that began to circulate in Greek in the first century CE:

> When Adam and Eve were expelled from paradise they made for themselves a tent and spent seven days mourning and lamenting in great sadness. But after seven days they began to be hungry and sought food to eat and did not find any. . . . Walking about, they searched for many days but did not find anything like they had in paradise. They only found what animals eat. Adam said to Eve: "The Lord gave these things to animals and beasts to eat. Ours, however, was the angelic food."

Probably originating in a Jewish milieu and composed in a Semitic language, this account of the first humans quickly migrated to early Christian communities and appeared in an array of other languages, from Latin to Coptic, Armenian, Georgian, and Slavonic. It continued to be read for centuries.

Together with a massive body of commentary, both rabbinic and patristic, the international popularity of The Life of Adam and Eve indicates that by late antiquity the verses of the book of Genesis had come to seem at once tantalizing and parsimonious, a blend of ethical conundrums and baffling silences. Readers demanded to know more. How did the first humans react to their expulsion from Paradise? Did they beat at the gate and beg for permission to return? Did they even understand what had happened to them? Where did they go, and how did they manage to survive? What did they say to each other in the months and then years that followed? Did their love endure? What did they tell their children about what they had done? Did the Creator watch the spectacle of their suffering with indifference or pleasure or possibly a twinge of regret? And how did they experience mortality— first their son Abel's murder and then their own dying?

The questions were not without risk. These imagined scenes, unrecorded in the Bible, had a bearing on contested topics: the sources of sin; the nature of marriage; the moral difference, if any, between women and men; the justice of God's anger; the hidden identity of Satan, humankind's mortal enemy; the possibility of redemption. Both Jews and Christians were struggling to sort out which would be the central, approved sacred texts of the faith—the canon—and which texts would lie outside the boundaries, in the zone designated "apoc-rypha," from the Greek word for "hidden." The process was long and fraught, full of bitter arguments, some of which have not been entirely resolved to this day.

Notwithstanding its wide circulation, The Life of Adam and Eve was never, in any of its many versions, accepted into the canon, nor did it make it into the apocryphal books that often appeared as an appendix in manuscript Bibles and later in printed editions. Instead, it lingered always on the outside, impossible fully to embrace and impossible to suppress. Venturing into the territory of fiction, the anonymous author or authors responded to the almost irresistible impulse to imagine the newly expelled Adam and Eve as people facing a terrible predicament. Hence the opening scene at which we have already glanced. In Para-dise the humans' diet had been identical to that of the angels. When the fallen pair first felt desperate hunger, they realized, to their dismay, that their appetite could only be assuaged with the same food that animals eat. For the first time, then, the humans were forced to grasp that they were themselves animals.

The ancient biography went on to imagine that Adam proposed a desperate ritual of penitence. He told his wife that he would stand up to his neck in the waters of the Jordan for forty days; as the weaker of the two, Eve could limit herself to thirty-seven days immersed in the Tigris. But before the period had ended, an angel appeared to Eve and told her that merciful God had heard her groaning and accepted her repentance. He had been sent, the angel declared, to take her to the food she had been craving and that God had lovingly prepared for her. Eve came shivering out of the river—"Her flesh was like grass from the water's coldness"—and hurried happily to her husband. But when Adam saw her, he cried out in anguish that she had once again been deceived. The angel of light was their enemy Satan in disguise.

Eve flung herself to the ground and asked Satan why he so hated them. The Life of Adam and Eve then rehearses what became one of the major motifs in the elaboration of the origin story. The devil explained to Eve that it was because of Adam that he and his fellow rebel angels had been driven out of heaven. When called upon to worship the newly created man, they refused, since they regarded themselves as older and superior. For this refusal, they had been cast down into hell. They would take their revenge now in any way that they could.

Adam, still standing in the water and determined to complete the full term of his ritual of penitence, was bitterly angry at his wife. Eve wandered off in despair to the west, determined to live out her life in solitude until death came for her. Theirs was not only the first marriage, then: it was also the first separation. But it turned out that Eve was three months pregnant, and when the time of childbirth was upon her, she cried out in pain. Hearing her cries, Adam rejoined her, and they resumed a life together with their newborn. "At once the infant stood up and ran out and brought some grass with his own hands and gave it to his mother. His name was called Cain."

There is not a hint of any of this in Genesis. But the anonymous author of The Life and those who eagerly read it were trying to think through the aftermath of the disaster, to conjure up the existence of original ancestors, and to find a comprehensible motive—and a plausible identity—for the serpent. They wanted what in the theater is called a backstory, a hidden history that would make sense of behavior that in the Bible's terse narrative seemed to come from nowhere: "And the serpent said to the woman, 'You shall not be doomed to die. For God knows that on the day you eat of it your eyes will be opened and you will become as gods, knowing good and evil'" (Gen. 3:4–5). Even setting aside the problems of a serpent that somehow talks—with what vocal cords? in what language? with what degree of consciousness?—there was the problem of a rationale.

Rabbinical sages long pondered God's words in chapter 1 of Genesis, "Let us make a human in our image." Who was the "us" here? (Ancient Hebrew apparently does not have a "royal we.") In the religion of Babylon or Rome, the plural would suggest that Yahweh was speaking to his fellow gods, as Marduk or Zeus often did. But if that had ever been a possible idea for the Hebrews in some distant past, anyone who proposed it in rabbinical times would have been labeled a heretic, particularly after the early Christians began to claim that the plural referred to the Trinity.

In the late third century CE, Rabbi Samuel ben Nahman imagined what must have happened when Moses, taking down the Torah from divine dictation, reached that word "us." "Why dost Thou furnish an excuse to heretics?" Moses asked. "Write," God replied. "Whoever wishes to err may err."

The correct explanation, most rabbis thought, was that God was consulting with the angels. But they went on to speculate that some of the angels were quite upset and broke up into competing parties.

The angelic party of Love supported the proposed creation; the angelic party of Truth opposed it. So too Righteousness was in favor; Peace against. Rabbi Hanina suggested that to undermine the opposition to his plan, God told the angels about all the piety that would spring from mankind and concealed from them all the wickedness. And while the parties squabbled with one another, God went ahead and did what He proposed to do anyway.

Some rabbinical commentators began to develop an account that attributed opposition to the creation of man not to parties upholding one or another heavenly principle but rather to angels motivated by envy or malice—the feelings confessed by Satan in The Life of Adam and Eve. Early Christians, starting with this speculation, gradually elaborated a grand narrative focused on the Prince of Darkness and his legions. Moslems later developed a comparable account focused on the refusal of the devil, Iblis, to obey Allah's command and bow to Adam. Allah asked, "What prevented thee from prostrating when I commanded thee?" And Iblis replied, "I am better than he: Thou didst create me from fire, and him from clay." For this pride and arrogance, Allah cursed Iblis and consigned him to Jahannam, the Islamic hell.

Christians proposed a further resolution to the problem of the mysterious "us" in "Let us make a human in our image." In the opening words of his gospel, the evangelist John seemed to allude to the opening words of Genesis: "In the beginning was the Word, and the Word was with God, and the Word was God." The "us," they concluded, must refer to the divine Logos, the Word that became incarnate in Jesus Christ. It was Christ then who carried out, against the malicious hostility of the demons, God's plan of creation. And it was Christ who through his sublime sacrifice would redeem humankind led astray by the lies that Satan, in the form of the serpent, had told.

But none of these interpretive schemes ever satisfied everyone or silenced the arguments or quieted the need for further exploration. In

Genesis, vast stretches of Adam's life history are summed up in a very few words: "He lived nine hundred and thirty years, and then he died" (Gen. 5:3–5). "And then he died" is a phrase that called out for elaboration, for this was the first natural death in the history of humankind. In The Life of Adam and Eve, Adam summoned his children and told them that he was ill—"I am in great pain"—but they could not even understand what he meant by the words "illness" and "pain." How could they have done so? In anguish, Adam sent Eve and his favorite son Seth to the doors of Paradise to plead for the healing oil of mercy, but the angel Michael sternly refused.

When they returned and reported the refusal, Adam, grasping that death was imminent, took the occasion, as he had repeatedly done throughout this account, to blame his wife: "Adam said to Eve: 'What have you done? You have brought on us a great affliction, fault and sin unto all our generations.'" He knew that the fate he was now suffering would be visited on his descendants, and he was eager that the source of their misery be made clear to his entire lineage. He instructed his wife therefore to tell their offspring what she did.

Eve's turn to die came six days after Adam's death. As if in fulfillment of Adam's injunction, she called Seth and her other children together, but she subtly modified the message. There was no reason why her children and her children's children should believe that the blame was entirely hers. They and their entire lineage are condemned to die, she told them, because of what both she *and* Adam did.

She then made a crucial provision, the provision of a cultural transmission that depends not only on speech but also on a more durable inscription. The Life of Adam and Eve attributes to the first woman the idea of writing.

Make tablets of stone, and other tablets of earth, and write on them my whole life, and that of your father, which you have heard from us and seen.

If he judges our race by water, the tablets of earth will dissolve, but the tablets of stone will endure. If, however, he judges our race by fire, the tablets of stone will be destroyed, but the tablets of earth will be fired.

Determined that the story survive whatever catastrophes lie ahead, Eve carefully prepared for the possibility of either flood or fire.

The Life of Adam and Eve provided the elaboration of the sparse Genesis account that many people craved. But for some Jews and early Christians, the expansion of the story only intensified the old, disturbing ethical questions. What was the point of it all? "Why didst thou weary thine undefiled hands and create man," asks the visionary Sedrach in a dialogue written in the second or third century CE, "since thou didst not intend to have mercy on him?" God replies that Adam violated his explicit commandment, and "being beguiled by the devil ate of the tree." But invoking the devil does not settle the matter. "If thou lovedst man, why didst Thou not slay the devil?" The argument continues back and forth, ending only when God shuts it down with the kind of question that silenced Job: "Tell me, Sedrach, since I made the sea, how many waves arose and how many fell"?

Demanding to know the number of waves in the ocean may serve to close this particular conversation, but it obviously did not quiet the larger doubts that the story of Adam and Eve continued to provoke. The most extreme solution was offered by a very early Christian bishop named Marcion, born in the Black Sea city of Sinope around the year 85. Marcion proposed that the church simply abandon the Hebrew Bible altogether as the basis for faith in Christ. The God whose acts and intentions are recorded in the history of the Jews, he argued, is manifestly tainted by evil. A divinity who forbids humans access to knowledge in the Garden of Eden and then punishes them horribly for an act that only the possession of such knowledge could have prevented is not the pure, spiritual, holy, and good God whose spark redeemed Christians find within their own bosoms. Marcion conceded that Yahweh was indeed the Creator, as Genesis affirms, but he was an evil creator. He was the father of the implacable law given to the Jews but not the father of Jesus Christ. Marcion drew the sharpest possible line between the old god and the new. The worship of Yahweh should go the way of the cult of Marduk, Ammon Ra, or innumerable other gods swept away by the new revelation.

But, though his views drew a large following, Marcion was eventually denounced as a heretic. The church committed itself to the Hebrew scriptures whose God was the ruler of the universe and whose ancient prophecies Jesus had fulfilled. Jesus made sense precisely as a response to Adam. St. Paul had established the crucial connection: "For since by man came death," he wrote to the Corinthians, "by man came also the resurrection of the dead." It was, the apostle's words suggested, impossible to understand Christ without understanding the sin of the first humans and the consequence of that sin. Christianity could not do without the story of the Garden of Eden.

In the imagination of Christian theologians, each moment in the cosmic scheme began to fall into place: the day on which Christ was incarnated was mystically linked to the day on which God formed man out of the ground; so too the day the holy infant was put to the breast and the day on which God formed the stars; the day the Savior suffered on the cross and the day Adam fell; the day Christ rose from the dead and the day God created light. The links between the Hebrew scriptures and the New Testament, integral to the whole vision of Jesus's life and mission as recounted in the gospels, were forged with tireless zeal and ingenuity. The method, known as typology, exerted a huge, enduring influence on the Christian faith.

Typology insisted on the historical reality of the events described in Genesis. If those events only found their ultimate meaning in the New Testament, that meaning did not make them less real in themselves. The dust from which Adam was formed and the animating breath in his nostrils, the wound made in his side in order to extract the rib to fashion Eve, the garden with its ominous tree, the sweat on his brow when he was set to labor, all were perfectly real and at the same time were "fulfilled" in the life of Christ—in his incarnation, in the bitter "tree" to which he was nailed, in the wound that the soldier's lance made in his side, and so forth. To call into question these elaborate connections, as Marcion and his followers had done, was to incur charges of heresy. Already by 180 CE, in St. Irenaeus's book *Against Heresies*, it was spelled out clearly: Christians were not permitted to repudiate Yahweh or to claim that the Savior was a previously unknown and hidden god or to forswear the story of the first humans. No Adam, no Jesus.

But the tale of the naked couple and the snake and the forbidden fruit remained troubling. It was, or so it was claimed, an essential foundation stone for the Christian faith, but to some the stone felt unstable or even embarrassing. How was it any different from the most ridiculous pagan origin stories? The sophisticated fourth-century CE Roman emperor Julian treated all such myths with equal contempt. The ancient Greeks, he wrote in *Against the Galileans,* invented "incredible and monstrous stories." But the Hebrew story about Adam and Eve, which Christians profess to believe, is no better. What sort of language, the emperor asked derisively, are we to say the serpent used when he talked with Eve? And is it not strange that the Hebrew God would deny to the humans he made the power to distinguish between good and evil? Surely that power is one of the key attributes of wisdom, "so that the serpent was a benefactor rather than a destroyer of the human race."

When Julian died of wounds he received in an ill-fated campaign against the Persians, imperial skepticism died with him, and Christianity resumed its place as the official religion of the empire. But the uneasiness with the Hebrew creation story did not disappear. A technique for quieting the uneasiness, at least among some intellectually sophisticated Jews and Christians, had already emerged around the time that Jesus was active in the Holy Land. It was principally the work of Philo, a Greek-speaking Jewish philosopher from Alexandria who understood perfectly well why people who had read Plato and Aristotle might find certain Bible stories primitive and ethically incoherent.

Philo's solution, radical and brilliant, can be summed up in a single word: allegory (Greek, "speaking otherwise"). The whole effort to take these stories literally has to be scrapped. Each detail instead has to be treated as a philosophical riddle, a hint toward a concealed and more abstract meaning. The Bible says that in six days the world was created, he wrote, "not because the maker was in need of a length of time—for God surely did everything at the same time." Days are mentioned because "things coming into existence required order." The first human—the human created in chapter one of Genesis—was not a creation of flesh and blood, according to Philo, but rather a kind of Platonic idea of a human. The Garden of Eden bore no resemblance to gardens we might encounter. As for the Tree of Life in its midst, "No trees of life or understanding have ever appeared on earth in the past or are ever likely to appear in the future."

The key for Philo was not to focus on the literal details of the narrative. Instead, they must be understood as symbols, "which invite allegorical interpretation through the explanation of hidden meanings." In picturing Adam in the garden, Moses was not asking his readers to conjure up the image of a naked peasant who has been set to work in some rural wilderness. The original ancestor, the cosmopolitan Philo wrote, was "the only real citizen of the cosmos," and the actual garden in which he was meant to labor was his soul. The Tree of Life was a symbol for the highest virtue, reverence for God. The serpent was not a garden-variety snake; it was "a symbol for pleasure, firstly because it is a legless creature which lies face-forward on its stomach, secondly because it takes clumps of earth as food, and thirdly because it carries poison in its teeth, by which it is able to kill those whom it bites."

Philo's strategy enabled Hellenized Jews, steeped in Greek philosophy, to approach the fabulous elements of the story not with embarrassment but with the subtlety and sophistication called forth by myths like the cave in Plato's *Republic*. His intellectual stance set the course of Jewish exegesis for centuries, extending even to the present. But it was not for Jews alone that Philo's allegorical method served as an inspiration and a powerful model. He influenced key figures in early Christianity, most importantly the Alexandrian scholar known as Origen Adamantius (the "Unbreakable").

Born in 184 CE, some two hundred years after the birth of Philo, Origen was the son of a Christian who was martyred during one of the cycles of imperial Roman persecution. An intensely pious young man, he thought that his own destiny would also lead him to the glory of dying for his faith. Instead, perhaps to his disappointment, he merely became a hugely influential teacher and a theologian. Aided by a team of scribes who took his dictation in relays, he is said to have written some six thousand works. "Works" here meant what would fit on a single papyrus roll, something like a chapter. Even so, this is a staggering achievement, and, though much has been lost, Origen's surviving output—celebrated volumes of biblical scholarship, richly detailed commentaries, collections of homilies, polemics, theological meditations—confirms its magnitude.

There was always something alarming about Origen, something that aroused the anxiety of church authorities and provoked the conflicts that forced him to lead a deeply unsettled, peripatetic life. Immensely learned, unsleeping, devout, and self-punishing, he possessed many of the qualities that often led to beatification and canonization. But Origen was never made a saint. Some of his theological positions—and, of course, in six thousand works there were a startling number of them—violated what eventually became church doctrine.

He suggested that God the Son was subordinated to God the Father, and he hinted at times that all creatures, including Satan himself, would in the end be saved and reconciled to God. Both ideas were ultimately deemed to be heretical.

But it was not a matter of doctrine alone. A radical ascetic, he brooded on the answer that Jesus gave to his disciples, when they asked him if he was implying that it would be better never to marry. "All men cannot receive this saying, save they to whom it is given," Jesus replied, adding,

> For there are some eunuchs, which were so born from their mother's womb; and there are some eunuchs, which were made eunuchs of men: and there be eunuchs, which have made themselves eunuchs for the kingdom of heaven's sake. (Matt. 19:12)

Longing to be one of those who made themselves eunuchs for the kingdom of heaven's sake, Origen took a knife and castrated himself.

Though it was not formally condemned as a practice until the fourth century CE, the church took a dim view of self-mutilation. They ruled that Jesus's words here, like many others that he spoke—"Let the dead bury their dead"; "If thy right hand offend thee, cut it off"; "Call no man your father on earth"—had to be understood metaphorically. You were not permitted, let alone encouraged, to treat any of this literally.

The irony of Origen's cruelly literal understanding of heavenly eunuchs is that he became the greatest early Christian advocate for the allegorical interpretation of the Scriptures. He made his position clear in response to a pagan attack written by a Greek philosopher named Celsus. (Celsus's book, *The True Word*, has not survived, but substantial parts of it are known through Origen's reply.) "The Jews then, leading a groveling life in some corner of Palestine, and being a wholly uneducated people," Celsus had written, wove together some "incredible and insipid" stories such as the creation of Adam and Eve, upon which Christians stake their faith. In the face of this challenge, Origen ran away as fast as he could from the literal sense. The words of scripture should be treated, he wrote, precisely in the way that pagan intellectuals like Celsus treated their own classics. Why interpret Moses's profound fables with dull literalism, while the comparable fables in Hesiod and Plato are accorded subtle readings? Plato too would sound like a joke if you read his myths flat-footedly and failed to admire the way in which he concealed great philosophic mysteries under the cloak of storytelling.

Thus in Genesis, Origen insisted, Adam must not be conceived as an individual; the Hebrew term signifies the nature of man in general. Paradise refers not to a particular place but to the condition of the soul. And the expulsion of the man and woman from Paradise, and their being clothed by God with tunics of skins, is not some crude folktale; it contains "a certain secret and mystical doctrine (far transcending that of Plato) of the soul's losing its wings, and being borne downwards to earth, until it can lay hold of some stable resting-place." Origen's many followers continued and further refined his interpretive work: "Eden" was Jesus Christ, "Paradise" was the church, the "woman" was sense perception, and the "man" reason. Slowly, as in a painstaking archaeological dig, philosophical treasures were excavated from beneath the stony surface of the Genesis story.

If Origen's approach had triumphed, Adam and Eve would gradually have faded into arcane symbols, interesting perhaps for the ways in which they pointed to subtle philosophical problems but not otherwise compelling. They would have ceased to lay claim to reality and would have begun the slow march to oblivion. But though allegory seemed to some like the perfect solution to the discomfort and risk of literal readings, soon after Origen's death treating the story of Adam and Eve as an allegory came under sustained and devastating attack. Contemporary surveys indicate that many millions of people even now, in the wake of so much scientific evidence, still profess to believe in the story of Adam and Eve not allegorically but literally. The reason for this literal belief has little or nothing to do with ignorance. It has everything to do with the history of Christianity, a Christianity stamped by a still more durable philosopher than Origen the Unbreakable: Augustine of Hippo.

5

In the Bathhouse

One day in the year 370 CE, a father and his sixteen-year-old son went to the public baths together in the provincial city of Thagaste, in what is now Algeria. On the face of things, the visit could not have been more routine: Thagaste, resembling hundreds of other Roman cities in the ancient world, had certain predictable municipal features, including some combination of markets, temples, gardens, law courts, schools, housing blocks, theaters, forums, workshops, animal pens, amphitheaters, gymnasia, brothels, barracks, and, of course, bathhouses.

The baths varied widely in size and luxury, from the famously sumptuous Baths of Diocletian in the great capital of the empire to modest provincial facilities of the kind the father and son would have entered, but the basic experience—the soaking, the sweating, the massages, the final cooling down and resting—was everywhere the same and has continued virtually unchanged to the present.

So what could possibly have transpired there more than sixteen hundred years ago that left a trace that has reached our own world? At some point in their visit the father may have glimpsed that the boy had an involuntary erection, or simply remarked on his son's recently sprouted pubic hair. Hardly a world-historical event, but the boy was named Augustine, and decades later he still remembered what happened. He recalled the moment in his famous autobiography, the *Confessions*, written around 397, a few years after he had become a bishop in North Africa. That day at the public baths, he wrote, his father "saw the signs of active virility coming to life in me, and this was enough to make him relish the thought of having grandchildren."

It is easy, even across a vast distance in time and culture, to conjure up a teenager's exquisite embarrassment. But embarrassment—the intense longing to make his father stop looking or to sink through the floor of the bathhouse—was not what fixed itself in Augustine's memory. What stayed with him instead is what happened when they got home. His father, he recalled, "was happy to tell my mother about it." Even here it is not embarrassment that he wanted to share with the God whom the *Confessions* addresses:

> He was happy to tell my mother about it, for his happiness was due to the intoxication which causes the world to forget you, its Creator, and to love the things you have created instead of love you, because the world is drunk with the invisible wine of its own perverted, earthbound will. But in my mother's heart you had already begun to build your temple and laid the foundations of your holy dwelling. . . . So, in her piety, she became alarmed and apprehensive. (2:3)

The evidence of the adolescent's sexual maturity had become the occasion—not the first and certainly not the last—for a serious difference between his parents, Patricius and Monica.

Of the two, though Augustine wrote very little about him, the father seems easier for us to understand. A man of modest means, Patricius had high hopes for his eldest son, whose promise he and the whole family clearly recognized. The young Augustine had already been sent to study for several years in the pleasant town of Madauros. He had done well enough there to merit being sent on to the university at Carthage, from whence he would be launched on a brilliant, potentially lucrative career. The gifts he had already shown—a way with words, a facility in interpretation and declamation—suggested something in teaching, law, or public service. The Roman Empire needed bright young administrators, all the more so in the rich African provinces where so much of its food was grown, packed up, and shipped to Rome and the other great cities on the Italian peninsula. At the bathhouse Patricius allowed himself to leap ahead in his fantasies and to imagine himself surrounded by his grandchildren, the offspring of his successful son.

The fantasies must have been all the sweeter because this was a difficult time for Patricius. The adolescent Augustine was back in Thagaste for a reason: his father did not have the money to send him to Carthage and was scrambling to raise it. He was not poor—he owned some property and slaves—but a university education was extremely costly. Other fathers, even ones far richer, Augustine recognized, would not have gone to the trouble and expense. The effort was no secret in the town. "No one had anything but praise for my father who, despite his slender resources, was ready to provide his son with all that was needed to enable him to travel so far for the purpose of study." But the beneficiary of all this paternal care did not look back as an adult and join in the chorus of praise. "This same father of mine," he told God, "took no trouble at all to see how I was growing in your sight or whether I was chaste or not."

We are back then to the scene in the bathhouse and to the abyss that opened up at home between his father and his mother. Under intense, if quiet, pressure from his ardently Christian wife to become baptized, Patricius resisted. Though he had allowed his child at birth to be signed with the Cross and though he himself had recently agreed to listen to Christian instruction (as a so-called "catechumen"), he did not concern himself with his son's spiritual development in the sight of Jesus, nor did he regard the evidence of his son's virility with anything but delight. If he had been asked to justify this delight, he might have invoked the goddess Venus whose erotic power knit together the whole universe, or he might simply have said, with Shakespeare's Benedick, "The world must be peopled."

Chastity, in any case, was not high among Patricius's concerns. Though he admired his wife's virtues, he was, Augustine wrote, unfaithful to her. The *Confessions* does not say how or when the rumors reached him, but it is clear that the son had talked about his father's infidelity with his mother, who knew all about it and chose not to make it a cause of quarreling. His father, though kind, had a temper, which his mother was careful not to provoke. Augustine remembered that many of his mother's friends appeared with bruised and battered faces, complaining of their husbands' violence, but that his mother would reproach them: by the laws of matrimony, they were, she would remind them, their husbands' *ancillae*, slave-girls.

It is all the more telling then that on her son's behalf, rather than her own, Monica was willing to make a scene. Patricius's sexual behavior was one thing; her son's quite another. When her husband beamed at what he had seen at the bath, she began to dread, Augustine wrote, "that I might follow in the crooked path of those who do not keep their eyes on you but turn their backs instead." It is not difficult to see just whose path Monica feared her son might be following. She set about deliberately and systematically to drive a wedge between son and father. "She did all that she could," Augustine recalled admiringly, "to see that you, my God, should be a Father to me rather than he" (1:11).

About one thing the father and mother completely agreed: their brilliant son should obtain the education his remarkable gifts deserved. (Augustine was the chosen one. He had at least one brother and sister whose education does not seem to have figured in his parents' schemes.) It took a year of paternal scrimping and networking to come up with the needed funds, and then he was off to Carthage. When he left Thagaste for the big city, Augustine must have seen his father for the last time, for in the *Confessions* he casually mentioned that when he was seventeen Patricius died. The mention is a conspicuously cool one.

If, mingled with her mourning, the widowed Monica felt some relief at the disappearance of her husband, so dangerous an influence on her beloved son Augustine, any hopes she might have had that he would embark at once on the straight path of chastity were quickly dashed. "I went to Carthage," he wrote, "where I found myself in a midst of a hissing cauldron of lust" (3:1). What was brewing in the cauldron? The phrase "I muddied the stream of friendship with the filth of lewdness" sounds like an overheated account of masturbation or homosexuality, while other equally cryptic phrases suggest a succession of unhappy affairs with women. The feverish promiscuity, if that is what it was, resolved itself fairly quickly into something quite stable. Within a year or two of arriving in Carthage, Augustine had settled down into a relationship with a woman with whom he lived and to whom, in his account, he was faithful for more than thirteen years.

Though it would not have made her happy, this concubinage—a conventional arrangement by the standards of the time—would probably have been the best that Monica could envisage at this stage for her son, given his restless sexual energies. It was a hasty marriage that she most feared, a marriage that might hinder his advancement. Merely living with a lower-caste woman posed much less of a threat, even when the woman gave birth to a son, Adeodatus. At least from Augustine's perspective—and that is the only perspective we have—there was no thought of marrying the woman, whose name the *Confessions* does not even bother to provide. He understood, and he expected his readers to understand, "the difference between the restraint of the marriage alliance, contracted for the purpose of having children, and a bargain struck for lust, in which the birth of children is begrudged, though, if they come, we cannot help but love them" (4:2).

"A bargain struck for lust": in Augustine's memory of these years, his whole life was such a bargain. Sex was only one part of it. Priding himself on his cunning and unscrupulousness, he studied law; he honed his rhetorical skills; he entered dramatic competitions for reciting verse; he consulted astrologers; he spent his time with friends whose moral and intellectual failings he complacently observed.

Already as a boy he had developed a love for literature. At school, he recalled, he had "learned to lament the death of Dido, who killed herself for love, while all the time, in the midst of these things, I was dying, separated from you, my God and my Life, and I shed no tears for my own plight" (1:13). Now in Carthage, he found himself attracted to the theater, where he joined audiences who love feeling sad at spectacles of imaginary misery by which they would be horrified in their own lives. The fictional nature of the distress makes it pleasurable, Augustine thought, because it only grazes the skin.

Fables and fictions, in his view, were the perfect fare for someone who was determined to keep his existence as superficial as possible. Warding off dangerous introspection, avoiding real intimacy, refusing to own up to his own choices, he tried to live life on the surface: a relationship that did not count; a child whose birth he begrudged; the ambitious pursuit of meaningless prizes; a restless search for trivial stimulation.

Still, something in him was not satisfied. He was a profoundly serious young man trying to play at being lighthearted. Once, remembering his mother's faith and the precepts in which he had been instructed, he picked up the Scriptures to "see what kind of books they were" (3:5). But he was disappointed. Their language—he would have been reading them in the *Vetus Latina*, the earliest Latin translation—was no match for the stateliness of Cicero's. To someone whose literary tastes were shaped by Virgil and Ovid, these texts were crude in style, while their content seemed disappointingly humble compared with the sophisticated philosophical treatises to which Augustine and his friends were drawn.

Even in his most determined effort to stay on the surface of things, Augustine's tastes, as the *Confessions* makes clear, did not run to comedy and light entertainment. He was drawn to spectacles of suffering, as earlier he had been drawn in his reading to the tragic fate of the abandoned Dido. Why, he repeatedly asked himself, is there so much misery in the world? Why do humans again and again make destructive choices? What is the cause of the cruelty, degradation, and violence that everywhere characterizes the human condition? He found the answers to these difficult questions in a cult that, though illegal, had made significant inroads across the Roman world of the fourth century. He became an adherent of the Manichees, a religious system that had originated in Persia in the previous century.

Though the system's visionary founder, the prophet Mani, called himself an "apostle of Jesus Christ," Augustine's adherence was not the conversion to the Catholic faith for which the pious Monica had been praying. Quite the contrary. For the Manichees, the universe was not ruled by a single omnipotent God who sent His beloved son to save mankind. Rather it was divided between the powers of light and darkness, two warring and irreconcilable worlds. Jesus was one of the avatars of light. In the long history of Manichaeism, which spread along the trade routes through Central Asia and as far as China, Jesus took his place alongside other figures of luminous purity, including the Buddha, Zoroaster, and Krishna.

The divine forces on the good side of the universe tried to help pure souls, lodged in human bodies, to rise up toward the light. But set against this effort was an evil side, a formidable world of greed, violence, injustice, and fathomless sexual appetite. Like Marcion, the Manichees had little patience with the Hebrew scriptures. They ridiculed as a naïve and ethically incoherent folktale the opening chapters of Genesis. They identified the Hebrews' Yahweh not as the father of Jesus but as the demonic power that created the dark, fallen world. The struggle between light and darkness was recapitulated at every level of the universe, from the vast reaches of interstellar space to the inner-most recesses of the isolated individual.

The true believers at the center of this cult—those who not only mastered its complex, sinuous system of thought but also translated its principles into a way of life—were strict ascetics known as the Elect. This was an exclusive circle to which Augustine would not, or at least not yet, have aspired to join. Comfortably settled into a relationship with his mistress and small son, and just starting to make his way as a teacher, the young man was hardly a prime candidate for Manichaean asceticism. He was rather in the outer circle of believers, one of those who were known as "Hearers."

As we might expect of someone articulate and philosophically agile, Augustine was an extremely good "Hearer." A restless intel-lectual who had escaped from a pious, anxious, overbearing mother in a provincial town, his membership in a sophisticated countercultural secret society must have been thrilling. Perhaps too he was drawn to the esoteric, syncretic nature of the cult, its claim to know the hidden truth that lay behind everything in the universe. But above all, Man-ichaeism answered a question on which Augustine had been anxiously brooding for some time. It solved the tormenting riddle of where evil—in the world and in himself—came from.

If, as the Jews and Christians claimed, a single, all-powerful, all-knowing God created everything, why should He have made a world with so much wickedness? And why should Augustine, who wished to be pure and good, feel such inner conflicts? Could God will both good and evil? Or, worse, could God, as some people claimed, be indifferent to good and evil? Better to believe that the God of perfect, unblem-ished goodness was not all-powerful, but that He had to contend with an evil counterpart, a satanic enemy just as clever and resourceful. And better too to believe that the purity, goodness, and light that Augustine found lodged in himself, in the hidden recesses of his innermost being, were set about by the hostile, alien powers of darkness.

Such were the convictions that Augustine carried with him, along with his mistress and his son, from Carthage to Thagaste, when he decided to return there to take up a post as a teacher of literature. They still remained his convictions when he went back to Carthage, where he began to give courses on public speaking, and then when he moved on to Rome and Milan. These were years of impressive, even spectacular, professional advancement, of the kind his father had dreamed for him. Augustine won a poetry prize; he dazzled everyone with an interpretation of Aristotle; he published his first book, a treatise on aesthetics; he surrounded himself with impressive friends; he obtained the support of an influential patron. Carthage was a significant step up from Thagaste; Rome, the glittering object of everyone's fantasies, a huge leap, both in prestige and salary. And, though compared with Rome, Milan might seem less alluring, it was in fact the city where the imperial court resided, and Augustine had been named there to a hugely prestigious professorship of rhetoric.

In this decade-long ascent from one rung in the career ladder to the next, there was only one major problem, and her name was Monica. When he went from Carthage to Thagaste for his first teaching position, Augustine's mother initially refused to share the same house with him, not because of his mistress and child—Monica, still focused on making a socially advantageous marriage for her son, regarded the mistress as an irrelevance—but rather because of his Manichaean beliefs. Those beliefs were loathsome to her, and she made a conspicuous show of weeping bitterly, as if her son had died. Augustine recalled that it was only when an angel assured her in a dream that "if she looked carefully, she would see that where she was, there also was I" that his mother consented to inhabit the same house and share meals. Even then, he added, "she gave no rest to her sighs and her tears" (3:11).

As anyone who has survived the overbearing love of an anxious mother can testify, the emotional satisfactions of being the object of so much concentrated attention and concern must be weighed against its considerable costs. At some point in his young life Augustine may have wished to supersede his father and his siblings in his mother's love. If so, he had clearly got his wish and then some. But there is every sign that he now wanted to escape.

Since Augustine had refused to abandon his Manichaeism, we may be certain that his mother's sighs and tears, along with her emotional claims upon him, continued unabated. And they were redoubled when he prepared to leave Carthage for Rome: "She wept bitterly to see me go and followed me to the water's edge, clinging to me with all her strength in the hope that I would either come home or take her with me" (5:8). Unable to tell her directly that he was leaving, he lied and, saying that he was only seeing off a friend, persuaded her to spend the night at a shrine near the harbor. "During the night, secretly, I sailed away."

Augustine must have been aware that he was reenacting in his own life the scene in Virgil's *Aeneid* that had once so moved him: the scene in which Aeneas, treacherously abandoning his lover Dido, secretly sails off from Carthage to become the founder of Rome. That literary moment had implanted itself deep within him. He clearly used it to make sense of what he had done, to represent himself as an epic hero, acting under divine mandate, while at the same time acknowledging the intensity of the suffering that his departure caused, as if he had witnessed it for himself: "The next morning she was wild with grief, pouring her signs and sorrows in your ear," he told God, "because she thought you had not listened to her prayer."

He must have felt some guilt. And yet, in remembering this moment, he allowed himself for once to express some of the anger toward his mother that must have long been building up within him: "You used her too jealous love [*carnale desiderium*] for her son as a scourge of sorrow for her just punishment." The phrase Augustine uses for her love—"carnal desire"—would seem more appropriate for a lover than a mother. Monica had taken whatever was blocked or unsatisfied in her relationship with her husband and transferred it to her son. Her son, suffocating, had to flee. And the suffering that his escape had visited upon her was her due, Augustine reflected, as a woman: "the torments which she suffered were proof that she had inherited the legacy of Eve, seeking in sorrow what with sorrow she had brought into the world."

In Genesis, Eve's legacy is twofold: women are condemned to bring forth children in pain and to yearn for the husbands who dominate them. As Augustine looked back at his relation to his mother, he cast himself in his imagination as both her child and her husband: she brought him with sorrow into the world and she sought him with sorrow through the world. For his grieving mother's search for her son did not end at the harbor in Carthage. A few years later, when Augustine had taken up his post in Milan, Monica sailed from North Africa to join him.

This time he did not continue to flee. He told her that he had become increasingly disenchanted with Manichaeism. Though he was not ready to embrace Catholicism and be baptized in the faith, he had been impressed by the Catholic bishop of Milan, Ambrose. Ambrose's approach to the Scriptures was in the tradition of Philo and Origen. Discovering allegories hidden in seemingly naïve stories, his intellectually compelling sermons helped to undermine Augustine's erstwhile contempt for the Hebrew Bible. What had struck him as mere absurdities, when taken in a literal sense, began to seem like profound mysteries. As a Manichee, he had been drawn to an esoteric system that only a small number of adepts could fully grasp. Now he found himself drawn in the opposite direction: in its apparent simplicity, the Bible was accessible to everyone, but it addressed the deepest questions anyone could ask.

All the while, his career continued on its course. He met his students in the morning; he spent his afternoons with his close friends discussing philosophy. His mother, settled in his household along with his longtime mistress and their son, busied herself with arranging the advantageous marriage that had long been her goal and had likely become his as well. He was thirty years old. A suitable Catholic heiress was found whose parents consented to the match. But the girl, probably only ten or eleven years old, was some two years shy of marriageable age, so the wedding, though agreed upon, had to be delayed.

In the meantime, Monica was able to engineer a second related change in her son's life. "The woman with whom I had been living was torn from my side as an obstacle to my marriage," Augustine wrote, "and this was a blow which crushed my heart to bleeding, because I loved her dearly" (6:15). There is no reason to doubt the reality of this pain: the couple had been living with each other for thirteen years and had raised a child together. But though he sensitively represented his own acute suffering—"At first the pain was sharp and searing, but then the wound began to fester, and though the pain was duller there was all the less hope of a cure"—Augustine left us barely a glimpse of his nameless mistress's feelings. He wrote only, "She went back to Africa, vowing never to give herself to any other man, and left me with the son whom she had borne me." And then she is gone from his account, expunged as if she no longer mattered, as if her fate meant nothing to him. All that was left was the gnawing sexual appetite that she had served to appease. With almost two years to wait, he related, he quickly took another mistress.

Augustine had long compared himself with his intimate friend, Alypius. Though in his early adolescence, Alypius admitted, he had some experience of sexual intercourse, "it had not become habitual" with him (6:12). Now, he said, he found the act degrading, and he lived a life of utmost chastity. For Augustine, by contrast, sexual desire was a constant presence, and intercourse had indeed become habitual. He could not imagine life without this intense bodily pleasure. Ambrose's sermons, with their ardent praise of virginity, their urging of sexual continence, and their dream of an escape from the body, only seemed to mark out the abyss separating Augustine from the highest aspirations of Christian piety. Spiritually ambitious, he longed to fulfill these aspirations himself, but he knew that it was impossible.

Yet, as he would soon come to testify, God's grace works in strange ways. In little more than a year's time, Augustine had converted to the Catholic faith. Shortly thereafter, now baptized, he had broken off his engagement to marry, resigned his professorship, vowed himself to perpetual chastity, and determined to return to Africa and found a monastic community. By running away from his mother, he had without realizing it embarked on a course that would fulfill and surpass her utmost dreams.

Augustine described the process of his conversion, the most important event in his life, in loving detail. Two moments stand out. The first took place in a garden attached to the house in Milan in which he, his mother, and his friend Alypius were living. Augustine was still struggling with whether or not to accept baptism, for he knew that this decision would mark a decisive, irrevocable transformation of his whole existence. He felt torn in opposite directions, as if there were within him two distinct wills, bitterly at war with one another and yet both aspects of his own single self. He wanted desperately to convert, once and for all. He envisaged the chaste beauty of Continence—the renunciation forever of sexual relations—beckoning to him, urging him to close his ears to the unclean whispers of his body. But those whispers, his old desires, refused to be silent. His inner conflict growing more and more unbearable, he flung himself down beneath a fig tree and began to weep, crying out "How long shall I go on saying 'tomorrow, tomorrow'? Why not now?" (8:12).

As he was obsessively asking himself these questions, he heard a child in a neighboring house, repeating again and again in a singsong voice the words *tolle lege, tolle lege,* "Take it and read, take it and read." Understanding this as a divine command, Augustine rushed to his copy of the Holy Scriptures, opened it, and read the first passage that met his eyes. They were words from St. Paul's Epistle to the Romans: "Not in reveling and drunkenness, not in lust and wantonness, not in quarrels and rivalries. Rather, arm yourselves with the Lord Jesus Christ; spend no more thought on nature and nature's appetites." The conflict was over. Augustine had converted.

He went inside to tell his mother. At his announcement—"I no longer desired a wife or placed any hope in this world but stood firmly upon the rule of faith"—Monica was jubilant, having received more than she had dared even to pray for. The joy she felt, Augustine wrote, was "far sweeter and more chaste than any she had hoped to find in children begotten of my flesh."

Monica had triumphed in the conflict that had arisen so many years earlier when Patricius, reporting what he had seen at the bathhouse, chuckled in anticipation of grandchildren. True, a grandson had been born, the outcome of the relationship Augustine had renounced, but there would be no legitimate offspring and no further sexual relations. Though all Christians were not under an obligation to renounce intercourse—"Better to marry than to burn," Paul had written—Augustine's own conversion in the garden in Milan was marked precisely by such a renunciation, one that deeply shaped his interpretation of the Garden of Eden.

"Therefore," Genesis tells us, when Adam and Eve are brought together, "does a man leave his father and his mother and cling to his wife and they become one flesh." In his own life Augustine managed to undo this trajectory. For many years, to be sure, he left his parents and clung to his mistress. To his father at least he never returned. But, though he had once slipped away from her at Carthage, his mother was the love of his life on this earth, as he was of hers, and shortly after his vow of perpetual continence they shared together a remarkable mystical experience.

Together with the family and friends who had decided to return with him to Africa to found a monastic community, Augustine was in the Roman port of Ostia, from whence the small company planned shortly to set sail. Looking out from a window at the garden of the

house where they were staying, Augustine and his mother were standing alone and talking. Their conversation, serene and joyful, led them
to the conclusion that no bodily pleasure, however great, could ever
match or even remotely approach the happiness of the saints. And then,
"as the flame of love burned stronger in us," something happened: they
felt themselves climbing higher and higher, through all the degrees
of matter and through the heavenly spheres and, higher still, to the
region of their own souls and up toward the eternity that lies beyond
time itself. "And while we spoke of the eternal Wisdom, longing for it
and straining for it with all the strength of our hearts, for one fleeting
instant we reached out and touched it" (9:10). It is difficult to convey in translation the breathless power of this account and of what it
meant for the two of them, the thirty-two-year-old son and the fifty-
five-year-old mother, to reach this instant together. And then it was
over: *suspiravimus.* "We sighed," Augustine recalled, and returned to
the sound of our speech.

The two of them looked back and tried to understand what had
just happened to them. What they had experienced could only be captured, Augustine thought, in perfect silence, which he then attempted
to conjure up in an astonishing, unbroken sentence of 184 words, a sentence of which any English translation is a pale, disjointed reflection:

> Suppose, we said, that the tumult of a man's flesh were to cease
> and all his thoughts can conceive, of earth, of water, and of air,
> should no longer speak to him; suppose that the heavens and even
> his own soul were silent, no longer thinking of itself but passing
> beyond; suppose that his dreams and the visions of his imagination
> spoke no more and that every tongue and every sign and all that is
> transient grew silent—for all these things have the same message
> to tell, if only we can hear it, and their message is this: We did
> not make ourselves, but he who abides for ever made us. Suppose,
> we said, that after giving us this message and bidding us listen to

him who made them, they fell silent and he alone should speak to us, not through them but in his own voice, so that we should hear him speaking, not by any tongue of the flesh or by an angel's voice, not in the sound of thunder or in some veiled parable, but in his own voice, the voice of the one whom we love in all these created things; suppose that we heard him himself, with none of these things between ourselves and him, just as in that brief moment my mother and I had reached out in thought and touched the eternal Wisdom which abides over all things; suppose that this state were to continue and all other visions of things inferior were to be removed, so that this single vision entranced and absorbed the one who beheld it and enveloped him in inward joys in such a way that for him life was eternally the same as that instant of understanding for which we had longed so much—would not this be what we are to understand by the words *Come and share the joy of your Lord?*

The spiritual climax that Augustine and his mother shared was the most intense experience in his life, perhaps even, as Rebecca West remarked, "the most intense experience ever commemorated." A few days later Monica fell ill and on the ninth day she died. The *Confessions* does not take the story of Augustine's life any further. It turns instead to a philosophical meditation on time and the beginning of an interpretation of the book of Genesis.

In the more than forty years that succeeded his moment of ecstasy—years of endless controversy and the wielding of power and feverish writing—Augustine, priest, leader of a community of monks, and bishop of the North African city of Hippo, spent an extraordinary amount of his time trying to understand the story of Adam and Eve. He thought about it when he sat, book in hand, on his bishop's chair (his *cathedra*), when he addressed his clergy and congregation in solemn assembly, when he grappled with complex theological issues, and when he tirelessly dictated letter after letter to his network of friends and allies. He brooded on it all through his bitter polemics against heretics. He continued to ponder its mysteries when he heard the terrible reports in 410 of the three-day sack of Rome by a Visigothic army led by Alaric. Over the decades, he had persuaded himself that it was not a story at all, at least not a story in the sense of a fable or myth. It was the literal truth, and, as such, it was the scientific key to the understanding of everything that happened.

Through intellectual mastery, institutional cunning, and overpowering spiritual charisma, this one man managed slowly, slowly to steer the whole, vast enterprise of Western Christendom in the same direction. It is to him preeminently that our world owes the peculiarly central role that Adam and Eve came to occupy. There were many dissenters, for then as now the Bible's account of the first humans in the magical garden seemed at first glance more like fiction than history. But Augustine did not yield. He insisted that the divine plan, and hence the fate of individuals and nations alike, was bound up with the reality of what had occurred in that garden. Nothing shook his faith, and at the end of his long life, with some eighty thousand Vandal warriors besieging Hippo as Roman rule in Africa collapsed, Augustine still looked for the underlying meaning of the disaster befalling his world in what Adam and Eve had done in the beginning of time.

6

Original Freedom, Original Sin

In the company of pagan and Manichaean intellectuals, the young Augustine had once looked down with contempt on the apparent simplicity of the ancient biblical narrative. Then in Milan, listening with rapt attention to Ambrose's sermons, the ground shifted. "I fell in Adam, in Adam was I expelled from Paradise, in Adam I died," he heard Ambrose proclaim; and Christ "does not recall me unless He has found me in Adam." But the sermon's stirring words posed an urgent question: just what did it mean to be "in" Adam?

Augustine knew that he was throwing himself into a problem whose final resolution had eluded the great theological minds of the Christian faith. What could he bring to the attempt that his remarkable predecessors had not already brought? He had grown up with a confident sense of his brilliance, but it would not be enough to invent another sophisticated allegorical interpretation. He was convinced that the only way he could truly understand his relation to Adam was to look into himself. There was no other way back to the beginning of time. All recorded traces of those first crucial moments, apart from the enigmatic words of Scripture, were gone. But he could find a key in the hidden places of his own inner life.

Reflecting on his agony of irresolution in the garden in Milan, before he was able to bring himself to accept baptism, Augustine struggled to analyze his tormented inner state. "I was at odds with myself," he wrote:

> When I was trying to reach a decision about serving the Lord my God, as I had long intended to do, it was I who willed to take this course and again it was I who willed not to take it. . . . It was part of the punishment of a sin freely committed by Adam, my first father. (8:10)

His self-analysis led him back to the sinfulness of his father, not Patricius but rather his "first father." Adam's sin was still alive in Augustine, as was the punishment that an angry God justly visited upon it, and conversely Augustine was still "in Adam."

Looking back into his childhood, Augustine thought he could even identify a particular moment in his life that replicated Adam's original crime. The moment occurred during his unhappy return to Thagaste, while his father scrambled for money. The sixteen-year-old boy, out after dark with some of his friends, went to a neighbor's pear tree and shook down the fruit. The tree was not theirs, and they were not hungry. They threw the pears—which were good neither to look at nor to eat—at the pigs. Why did they do something that they knew was wrong? "Our real pleasure," Augustine wrote, "consisted in doing something that was forbidden" (2:4).

The fact that the act had no point—that it was inexplicable and gratuitous—was precisely the point: if there had been a grand motive, a terrible compulsion, it might have seemed that there really was an independent force of evil in the world, as the Manichees said. But Augustine had renounced Manichaeism. An orthodox Catholic Christian, he now believed that in all the universe there was a single God, all-knowing, all-powerful, perfectly good. Evil, in such a scheme, could only be empty and derivative, a mere parody of the good.

Though it was not always easy to work out exactly which of God's powers a particular sinful action was parodying, this notion of evil as mere imitation helped solve the Manichaean challenge with which Augustine had long been grappling. But the solution did not diminish the magnitude of human viciousness and human suffering, and in fact much of the time Augustine wrote as if evil were anything but a pale imitation of something good. In the case of rowdy teenaged boys taking some fruit that did not belong to them, the transgression might seem negligible, but if understood rightly, it contained all you needed to know about human sinfulness. A few years after he wrote the *Confessions*, Augustine managed to find in Adam's eating of the forbidden fruit a whole litany of sins: pride, blasphemy, fornication, theft, avarice, even murder ("for he brought death upon himself"). What seemed like nothing turned out to be everything.

Then as now, the world was full of unspeakable crimes. Adults abused defenseless children; gangs conspired to attack and mutilate their enemies; rapists preyed on unprotected women. How could Augustine, so subtle and intelligent, actually claim to see fornication and murder in the eating of a piece of fruit and to attribute all subsequent criminality and misery to that single distant act? He had, of course, inherited the Genesis story, and with it St. Paul's claim that Jesus had come to undo the catastrophic consequences of Adam's disobedience. But how could that primal disobedience in Eden possibly explain human wickedness and the sheer weight of human suffering? These were easy enough to account for if the body was part of the dark side of a universe divided between an evil god and a good one. But if there was only one God—the Creator who made everything and saw that it was very good—why was life so appallingly difficult? Why did so many infants die, often along with the mothers who bore them? Why were there starving or abused children? Why did some people go blind or deaf or mad?

Some of those who suffered were clearly guilty of evil actions, but with the great bulk of human wretchedness, it was not so obvious. Augustine was determined to save the divine creation from any imputation of injustice. Yet, if God was not either unjust or impotent, then they, the humans, must bear the responsibility. Condemned to exhausting labor, pain, and death, the human race got what it deserved. God is good, but He is also just, and justice demanded the punishment of crime.

As Augustine knew perfectly well, the Manichaean belief that there was an evil as well as a good god was not the only alternative to the ethical monotheism that orthodox Christianity espoused. The followers of the Greek philosopher Epicurus believed that the moral order was not, as it were, hard-wired in the universe. Morality was what human themselves managed to create and maintain. Humans might wish to claim that their codes of behavior were issued by a divine lawgiver, but such claims were superstitious fantasies. Laws were an entirely secular, contingent work-in-progress. Moral judgments have meaning in this life only, for there is no afterlife. The soul, Epicureans held, is made up of atoms, just like the body, and when the body dies, so too does the soul. Hence no postmortem punishments, and no rewards.

Augustine understood the allure of this account, which he talked over with his friends when they were struggling to understand the nature of good and evil. "In my judgement," he recalled in the *Confessions*, "Epicurus would have won all the honours, were it not that I believed that the soul lived on after death and received the reward or punishment which it deserved" (6:16). Augustine did not want to live in a universe in which the moral reckoning would be left unpaid, in which human suffering meant nothing but the vulnerability of matter, in which wickedness would not be punished or exceptional piety receive an eternal reward. It was better to believe that accounts were being kept to the last scruple by an all-seeing God, even one who was murderously angry at humanity, rather than to believe that God was indifferent or absent.

Given the magnitude of human wretchedness, what this meant, Augustine reasoned, is that appalling criminality must lie hidden in seemingly innocuous actions. Otherwise the goodness of God—His patience and forbearance and loving-kindness—would be called into question. The world as God made it was good, perfectly so, and it would have remained good, had it not been for the original, terrible act of human perversity. All the miseries that have followed—the endless succession of ghastly crimes, the horrors of tyranny and war, the seemingly natural disasters of earthquake, fire, and flood, and what Hamlet calls the thousand natural shocks that flesh is heir to—are just punishments meted out by a just God. Such is the meaning of being "in" Adam.

On the face of things, this seems insane. Was it really possible to insist that all suffering was the consequence of a crime committed by a distant ancestor, a crime one could not possibly remember and whose reported nature seemed too minor to justify any serious penalty? Could anyone actually claim that a sweet child dying of wasting illness was only getting what she deserved?

Augustine saw quite clearly what was difficult and indeed repellent in such claims. But the alternative seemed to him far worse. He refused to believe with the Epicureans that human behavior, good and ill, was a matter of divine indifference. There was, he insisted, a single, omniscient, omnipotent, and benevolent creator-god. And yet how to account for the sufferings of those who seemed innocent?

Augustine started characteristically at home, that is, with memories of his own childhood sufferings. As a schoolboy, he hated being beaten, which was then, as for centuries afterward, the principal pedagogical technique for encouraging diligent learning. He earnestly prayed to God that he might be spared the whip. But his prayers were to no avail: if he were idle, he was flogged. It seemed grotesquely unfair, since the adults who did the flogging were themselves guilty of idleness and worse, and the *Confessions* registers, with subdued passion, the outrage that still lingered in his breast. Yet this outrage did not lead him to condemn the beating of schoolboys. Quite the contrary. For though the beatings were unfair, Augustine reflected, they did the child good, by driving him to learn against his inclination to play. I deserved to be punished, Augustine wrote, "for I was a great sinner for so small a boy" (1:12).

"A great sinner." Young children deserve to be beaten, even though those who beat them are doing so for the wrong reason and are still worse than those they beat. The deeper Augustine ventured back into his own infancy—and he did so with a sympathetic intelligence unrivaled in the entire ancient world—the more disturbing were the things he perceived:

> I began to smile as well, first in my sleep, and then when I was awake. Others told me this about myself, and I believe what they said, because we see other babies do the same. But I cannot remember it myself. Little by little I began to realize where I was and to want to make my wishes known to others, who might satisfy them. But this I could not do, because my wishes were inside me, while other people were outside, and they had no faculty which could penetrate my mind. So I would toss my arms and legs about and make noises, hoping that such few signs as I could make would show my meaning, though they were quite unlike what they were meant to mime. And if my wishes were not carried out, either because they had not been understood or because what I wanted would have harmed me, I would get cross with my elders, who were not at my beck and call, and with people who were not my servants, simply because they did not attend to my wishes; and I would take my revenge by bursting into tears. (1:6)

Anyone who has ever watched a small baby, and still more anyone who has ever tried in vain to satisfy a wailing baby's needs, will grasp the acuteness of Augustine's observations, observations that probably take us into a room where he sat with his mistress and intently watched their infant Adeodatus.

It is here, when we seem to be approaching familiar and reassuring territory, that we encounter Augustine's theological purposes. For it turns out that what he observed—wishes, indignation, revenge— marked for him the full presence in the infant of the moral catastrophe of adult life. It is all there already in the nursery: the violence, the will to enslave others, the urgency of capricious desires. The fact that the infant is impotent—that he can merely fling his arms about and cry— does not alter what for Augustine is the hard truth: there is something morally wrong with us from birth.

The baby who cries for the breast and makes his imperious demands for attention, Augustine wrote, deserves to be rebuked, even though custom and common sense do not permit us to do so. Custom and common sense are good enough in their way; they keep us from being laughed at or regarded as strange by our neighbors. But they prevent us from seeing the truth of things. In God's sight, "no man is free from sin, not even a child who has lived only one day on earth" (1:7).

What might seem cruel in human suffering then was only fair. And though He had every reason to hate sinners, God was merciful: He gave His only son to satisfy the strict claims of justice and to redeem errant humanity. Those who embraced this revealed truth— and who embraced it in the way that the church authorized—would ultimately be saved. All others would be damned. It was no excuse if you happened to be born before the coming of Christ or if you lived in some corner of the world where the news could not have reached you. And if you were unbaptized it made no difference whether or not you lived a life of moral rectitude. You would spend eternity in hell, and justly so, because of the taint you had inherited from the sin of Adam and Eve.

This position became one of the cornerstones of Christian orthodoxy. But, from its inception, it did not reign undisputed. Chief among those of Augustine's contemporaries who found it both absurd and repulsive was a British-born monk, Pelagius. Arriving in Rome around 390 CE, Pelagius impressed everyone with the breadth of his learning, the eloquence of his speech, and the ascetic simplicity of his life. Almost exactly Augustine's age, he was in a certain sense his secret sharer: an upstart from the margins of the Roman world who by force of intellect, charisma, and ambition made his way to the great capital and had a significant impact upon the empire's spiritual life.

Pelagius and his followers were moral optimists. They believed that all human beings were born innocent. Infants do not enter the world with a special endowment of virtue, but neither do they carry the innate stain of vice. We possess in ourselves the possibility of choosing good over evil. True, we are all descendants of Adam and Eve, and we live in a world rife with the consequences of their primordial act of disobedience. But that act in the distant past does not condemn us inescapably to sinfulness. How could it? What would be the mechanism of infection? Why would a benevolent God permit something so monstrous? No: we are at liberty to shape our own lives, whether to serve God or to serve Satan.

Why is it then that the great mass of men and women are so sinful? The answer, Pelagius thought, was essentially social: we become whoever we are largely through imitation, and we develop in the course of a lifetime habits that are extremely difficult to break. "The long custom of sins" that begins in childhood gradually brings us more and more under its power "until it seems to have in some degree the force of nature (*vim naturae*)." But it is important to grasp that it is not in fact our nature that compels us to sin.

We have not inherited a disposition to sin from our first parents; we have inherited a cumulative history. But history is a nightmare from which we can awaken. "We say," Pelagius affirmed, "that man is always able both to sin and not to sin." Why? "We have free will."

It is in defense of this freedom that Pelagians rejected the belief in innate sinfulness and insisted on the innocence of newborns. Adam's sin has no determining effect on his posterity, and it is possible at least in principle for all individuals to be perfectly good. As for death— which Augustine and others viewed as the direct consequence of that sin, not only for Adam and Eve themselves but for all mankind— Pelagius argued that it was simply a condition of the physical nature of humans. Adam would have died anyway, whether he had sinned or remained sinless. To die is not a punishment; it is part of what it means to be alive.

When these views reached North Africa, Augustine was horrified. His whole conception of the human condition, corrupted from birth and doomed to death by the fall of Adam and Eve, seemed under attack. Pelagius had found favor among several aristocratic Roman families, but Augustine too had powerful friends in Rome to whom he now wrote, urging them to launch a counterattack. Pelagius was accused of heresy and brought to trial. Augustine and his allies penned long, bitter theological treatises and sent them off to Rome as witnesses for the prosecution. (The writings of the defense—the losing side—were all destroyed, but the positions may be reconstructed from the quotations included in the attacks.) Fearing that treatises alone might not secure the condemnation of his doctrinal enemy, Augustine was careful to send, through an ally, a magnificent gift of eighty Numidian stallions to the papal court. Pelagius was condemned, excommunicated, and exiled to Egypt.

By around 420, Pelagius was dead, but the fight was by no means over. Julian of Eclanum, an Italian aristocrat extremely well connected both in the church and at court, quickly emerged to raise the Pelagian standard. Augustine's hardline position on divine punishment, Julian argued, was at once sinister and grotesque, an attempt to impose upon the community of Christians an unnatural and singularly cruel doctrine. The church was at risk, he thought, of being poisoned by a set of weird, uncivilized beliefs concocted by a domineering, psychologically twisted African demagogue. Should Christians, Julian asked, really think that a merciful, loving God would torture infants just because they were not baptized? If a Gentile— that is, a non-Christian—clothes a naked man, "is it a sin because it is not by faith"? Is the chastity of a pagan woman not chastity? And what of the non-Christian who delivers someone from danger, binds up an injured man's wounds, or refuses to bear false witness even when tortured? Could such a person be hated by an angry God simply because he is not a Christian? Are all the virtuous heroes of the world before Christ doomed for eternity? Augustine answered implacably that yes, they are all sinners, all damned.

Julian tried ridicule: "If it be maintained that the chastity of unbelievers is not chastity, then for the same reason it must be said that the body of pagans is not a true body, and the eyes of pagans have not the sense of sight, and the crops growing in pagans' fields are not true crops, and many other consequences so absurd they could move an intelligent man to laughter." But Augustine was not to be budged. It was, he insisted, the Pelagian's position that was absurd: "Your laughter will move intelligent men, not to laughter, but to tears, as the laughter of the insane moves their sane friends to weeping." There was no room for compromise.

The core of the problem, Julian argued, was Augustine's view of sex, and for once Augustine completely agreed. Julian believed that the human experience of sexual intercourse was natural and healthy, an essential part of God's design reaching back to the moment when He commanded the first humans to be fruitful and multiply. It was here, Augustine contended, that Pelagians made their crucial mistake. For sex as we know it is not natural and not healthy. The problem is not merely with sex outside of marriage, with practices and positions not focused on procreation, and with homosexuality—though Augustine, along with many others, assailed these all as abominations. The problem is that even the most legitimate form of sexual intercourse—between a husband and wife mutually bent on engendering a child—is also corrupt. The current of sinfulness that courses through it is precisely the mechanism that carries the stain of evil from one generation to the next and infects the dreams of those most determined to keep themselves pure and chaste. Human sinfulness is a sexually transmitted disease.

Augustine knew that he would have a difficult time making this case, if not perhaps within the church then at least among the laity. Then, as now, most people regarded their sexual pleasure as legitimate and good. Julian argued that by Augustine's mad logic, all parents were murderers, since the very act that brought forth their children also doomed them to destruction. What the gloomy bishop of Hippo condemned as a sin is simply the "vital fire" that is, by God's own design, our natural way of reproducing.

Augustine countered that our way of reproducing was corrupted by Adam and Eve and has remained corrupted ever since. It is impossible, even for the most pious married couple determined to restrain their sexual intercourse within the narrowest approved boundaries, to get anywhere at all "without the ardor of lust" (*On Marriage*). And this ardor, to which Augustine gives the technical name "concupiscence," was not simply a natural endowment or a divine blessing; it was a curse, a mark of punishment, a touch of evil. The action of a married man and woman who intend to beget a child is not evil, Augustine insisted; it is good. "But the action is not performed without evil" (*Against Julian*). How much better it would be if there were no need for sexual desire, if it were possible to bring children into the world in some other way than through the pleasurable stirring of the genitals by lust.

In the world as we know it, this pious wish is not possible. Augustine's obsessive and tormented recognition of the fact—of the inescapable presence of arousal not only in conjugal love-making but also in what he calls the "very movements which it causes, to our sorrow, even in sleep, and even in the bodies of chaste men"—shaped his most influential idea, one that weighed down the centuries that followed and from which we his heirs have only partially freed ourselves: *originale peccatum,* Original Sin.

We are all marked from the beginning with evil. It is not a matter of particular acts of cruelty or violence, specific forms of social pathology, or this or that person who has made a disastrous choice. It is hopelessly shallow and naïve to think, as the Pelagians do, that we start with a blank slate or that most of us are reasonably decent or that we have it in our power to choose good. Look around. There is something deeply, structurally, essentially wrong with us. Our whole species is what Augustine called a *massa peccati,* a lump of sin.

No trace of this idea is found in the reported words of Jesus, nor does it exist as a significant theme in the vast body of rabbinical writing that flowed into the Midrash Rabbah and the Talmud or in the comparably vast Islamic tradition. Some anticipations of it can be found—in the strange Hebrew Book of Jubilees from the late second century BCE, for example, and in the writings of the bishop of Lyons Irenaeus (c. 130–c. 202 CE), among others—but no one had given it the power and the doctrinal importance it assumed in the works of Augustine. And no one before Augustine had ventured to offer such proof, the proof that makes itself felt in the stirrings of sexual arousal and in our knowledge that all of us come into the world only through this arousal. We originate in sin, and sin never ceases to manifest its hold over us.

Julian and the other Pelagians cried foul: Augustine, they said, was simply reverting to the old Manichaean belief that the flesh was the creation and the possession of a wicked god. Surely this was a betrayal of Christianity, with its faith in a messiah who became flesh. Not so, Augustine responded. God chose to become man, but he did this "of a virgin, whose conception, not flesh but spirit, not lust but faith, preceded." Jesus's existence did not depend upon the minutest touch of that ardor through which all other human beings are generated. And we could all have been like Jesus; that is, we could have entered the world and survived in the world and reproduced in the world untouched by lust. That we are not untouched by lust is our fault, the consequence of something that we have done.

It is here, when Augustine had to produce evidence of our individual and collective perfidy, that he called in witness Adam and Eve. For the Original Sin that stains every one of us is not only a sin that inheres in our individual origins—that is, in the sexual arousal that enabled our parents to conceive us—but also a sin that may be traced back to the couple in whom our whole race originates. It is the moral equivalent of a disease, a genetic flaw, that we have inherited from our most distant ancestors. And though it is our inescapable inheritance, we bear the guilt for it, a guilt that attaches to our species.

In order to protect God from the charge that He was responsible for the innate defects in His creation, Augustine had to show that in Paradise it could all have been otherwise, that our progenitors Adam and Eve were not originally designed to reproduce as we now reproduce, that they perversely made the wrong choice, and that we inescapably reiterate their crime. For proof he burrowed into the enigmatic words of Genesis more deeply than anyone had done before. He was determined to reconstruct the lost lives of our remote ancestors, to find his way back to the Garden of Eden and watch our first parents making love.

Long before his encounter with the Pelagians, before he had even been ordained as a priest, Augustine had attempted to crack the ancient code. At the end of August in the year 388, in one of the first works he wrote after his conversion, his *On Genesis: A Refutation of the Manichees* treated the opening chapters of Genesis as a subtle allegory. It was not in reference to the physical body that man was made in God's image; indeed, Adam was originally endowed with a spiritual body, if not yet pure soul then at least "soulish." Eden is less a place than a spiritual experience. Eve is a figure for the soul that each human should love. The commandment to be fruitful and multiply did not originally refer to the flesh but to "a spiritual brood of intellectual and immortal joys filling the earth." The trees likewise were symbols of spiritual joys. And as for the disturbing verse, "lest he put forth his hand, and take also of the tree of life, and eat, and live forever: therefore the Lord God sent him forth from the Garden of Eden" (Gen. 3:22–23), the words properly understood mean the very opposite of what they seem to say on the surface: "The reason the man was sent away to the wearisome labors of this life was *in order that* at some time or other he might indeed stretch out his hand to the tree of life and live for ever. The stretching out of the hand surely is an excellent symbol of the cross, through which eternal life is regained."

Augustine came to feel that this clever early exercise in allegorical interpretation, in the manner of Origen, was a mistake. It barely concealed a certain embarrassment about the verses it pretended to embrace. It conceded, in its aversion to the body, a great deal to the very Manichaeism it hoped to refute. By treating Adam and Eve not as recognizable humans but as symbolic figures, it risked opening the way to treating Jesus too as a mythic symbol rather than as the living Savior. And it completely failed to find in its emblematic reading of the story any basis for Original Sin.

By the year 400, in the wake of the completion of the *Confessions,* Augustine's approach had begun to change. The way forward, he became convinced, was first and foremost to take the words of Genesis as literally true: as literally true as his own life and that of his parents, his former lovers, and his friends. The story of the naked man and woman, talking snake, and magical trees might seem like a folktale of the sort he had looked down upon when he was a young man. But the task of the true believer was not to try to save it by treating it as the naïve covering of a sophisticated philosophical mystery. The task rather was to take it as the unvarnished representation of historical reality and to convince others to take it that way as well.

Plunging into the project, Augustine studied hard and wrote feverishly. He embarked on a work entitled *The Literal Meaning of Genesis,* whose goal was to talk "about the scriptures according to their proper meaning of what actually happened, not according to their riddling, enigmatic reference to future events." For about fifteen years he continued to labor on this work, resisting the urgings of his friends to complete it and make it public. Of all of his many books it was probably the one to which he devoted the most prolonged and sustained attention.

In the end it defeated him, and he knew it. He struggled to take literally the Hebrew account of the creation of the cosmos, but he could not bring himself to think that the days in which God formed the universe were anything like our days, or that the light brought forth on the first day (before the creation of the sun) bore any resemblance to our light, or that God actually rested on the seventh day, in the way that tired humans rest after labor. He knew that the Bible said that God formed man from the dust of the ground, but "that God molded the man from mud with actual material hands," he admitted, "is an excessively childish notion." God spoke to Adam, but it was foolish to think that God had divine vocal cords. Everywhere he turned, there were comparable problems. Toward the close of his life, looking back on what he had written in *The Literal Meaning of Genesis*, he acknowledged that "it is a work in which more questions were asked than answers found; and of those that were found only a few were assured, while the rest were so stated as still to require further investigation."

And yet . . . he returned again and again to the insistence that the story—if not every element then at least its core elements—must be taken literally. Overcoming his resistance, he affirmed that Adam was an actual person formed from mud as an adult male. There was a real tree whose real fruit he was commanded not to eat, lest he die. God spoke to Adam not mystically but "with such vocal signs as he would be able to understand." All of the animals were actually brought before Adam, not rounded up by God Himself "in the way hunters and fowlers track down and drive into the nets whatever animals they catch," but impelled by angels to appear in the right place at the right time. Why should we doubt that God literally fashioned the woman from the man's rib—"we who could not know about a tree being made from the shoot of a tree in the trunk of another one, if we were likewise ignorant of how farmers serve God in his act of creating these things?"

Woe to the person who does not hold on, whenever possible, to the literal sense of the Bible's words. Eve disobeyed the divine warning—"if you take a bite of it, you shall die the death"—because she assumed disastrously that God's words were not to be taken literally. She preferred to believe that God, being merciful, could easily forgive any transgression. "That is why she took some of its fruit and had a bite, and also gave it to her husband." Far better had she clung to the harshest, most literal-minded understanding of God's injunction.

The problem is that, however much one tries, not every word can be taken literally, and Augustine could find no simple, reliable rule for the appropriate degree of literal-mindedness. The Bible tells us that after Adam and Eve ate the forbidden fruit, "the eyes of both of them were opened" (Gen. 3.7). Does this mean that they had been made with eyes sealed shut "and left to wander about blind in the paradise of delights, feeling their way, and so to reach and touch all unawares the forbidden tree too, and on feeling the prohibited fruits to pick some without knowing it?" No, it cannot possibly mean this, for we have already learned that the animals were brought to Adam, who must have seen them before he named them; and we have been told that Eve saw that the fatal tree was good for eating "and pleasing to the eye." All the same, because one word or phrase is used metaphorically did not mean that the entire passage should be taken as an allegory. It was imperative to discover the literal core.

Small wonder that Augustine struggled for fifteen years to write *The Literal Meaning of Genesis*. It is not as if the stakes were low: it was a matter of life or death, not only for the first parents but also for all of their descendants. Whenever he could put his hands on it, Augustine clung for dear life to the literal sense. Adam and Eve were not literally blind, he granted, before they ate the fruit. But there had to be some way to understand the words "Your eyes shall be opened" other than as a figure of speech. There had to have been something, he insisted, that the couple actually saw for the first time after their transgression, something not merely metaphorical. But what could that possibly have been? The answer came to him: "They turned their eyes on their own genitals, and lusted after them with that stirring movement they had not previously known."

The key to this understanding had been hidden in Augustine's experience at the age of sixteen in the bathhouse, that is, in the signs of *inquieta adulescentia* that his father had observed. The stirring movement that delighted the adolescent's father and horrified his mother could now be traced all the way back to the original moment in which Adam and Eve felt both lust and shame. They saw for the first time what they had never seen before, and if the sight aroused them, it also filled them with shame and impelled them to reach for the fig leaves to cover as with a veil "that which was put into motion without the will of those who wished it." Until this moment, they had possessed—for the only time, Augustine thought, in the whole history of the human race— perfect freedom. Now, because they had spontaneously, inexplicably, and proudly chosen to live not for God but for themselves, they had lost their freedom. And with them we lost our freedom as well.

Augustine came to believe that the sign of this loss, both his own and that of the first humans, was not arousal but rather its involuntary character. More than fifty years later, he was still brooding on its underlying significance. If we are healthy, he wrote, we are free to move other parts of the body—eyes, lips and tongue, hands and feet—as we wish. "But when it must come to man's great function of the procreation of children, the members which were expressly created for this purpose will not obey the direction of the will, but lust has to be waited for to set these members in motion, as if it had legal right over them."

How weird it is, Augustine thought, that we cannot simply command this crucial part of the body. We become aroused, and the arousal is within us—it is in this sense fully ours—and yet it is not within the executive power of our will. The stiffening of the penis or its refusal to stiffen depends on the vagaries of a libido that seems to be a law unto itself. It was characteristic of Augustine and indeed of his whole age to think about sex in male terms, but he was certain that women must have some equivalent experience to male sexual arousal. That is why in Genesis, in the wake of the first transgression, the woman as well as the man felt shame and covered herself. "It was not a visible movement the woman covered, when, in the same members, she sensed something hidden but comparable to what the man sensed, and they blushed at the mutual attraction."

Augustine's experience of sexual arousal, so intense and insistent and deeply mysterious, returned him again and again to the same set of questions: Whose body is this, anyway? Where does desire come from? Why am I not in command of my flesh? "Sometimes it refuses to act when the mind wills, while often it acts against its will!" The teenaged boy confronted a weird split between his will and his body. So too, Augustine acknowledged, did the aged monk, tormented in his cell by the irruption of "voluptuous thought," "disquieting memories associated with base pleasures," "a certain uproar of sordid interruptions." There are other bodily appetites as well, of course, which even the most pious and disciplined person inevitably experiences. But with eating and drinking, Augustine wrote, it is possible to retain some control and, in the midst of satisfying appetite, to continue to think about things of the mind and the spirit. Sexual desire is different: "Does it not engage the whole soul and body?"

But what was the alternative that Adam and Eve—and we—lost forever? How, specifically, were they meant to reproduce, if it was not in the way that all humans do and have done for as long as anyone can remember? The Pelagians had argued that human sexuality was a natural, happy part of God's design. The first man and the first woman were human, in exactly the way that we are human, and they would have reproduced just as we do. Did Augustine think, Julian asked, that Adam and Eve were not of our species?

Augustine could not evade the question, as he had once tried to do, by arguing that Adam and Eve were "soulish" spirits rather than bodily beings. Having committed himself to a literal understanding, he had come to believe that the first humans had material bodies, just as we do. They were not giants, as some had speculated, nor were they endowed with superpowers. They were no doubt perfect versions of what we so inadequately and partially embody, but they were still our kind.

But there was—or there would have been, had they continued to dwell in Paradise—a crucially important difference. Adam and Eve were meant to reproduce, Augustine insisted, without involuntary arousal. "They would not have had the activity of turbulent lust in their flesh, . . . but only the movement of peaceful will by which we command the other members of the body." Untroubled self-command— arousal only when you will yourself to be aroused; no arousal when you do not—was for Augustine the heart of what it meant to be free.

To those of us accustomed to think of freedom in political or social terms, this conception of freedom as unruffled inward tranquility and bodily control seems very strange. But to someone deeply troubled by the problem of involuntary arousal, it made sense. And Augustine was certain that he was not alone. He drew upon a long tradition of moral philosophy, pagan as well as Christian, that centered on the achievement of a control over the self that nothing, not even excruciating pain or exquisite pleasure, could disturb. In Paradise, he wrote in *The City of God*, Adam and Eve—with no pain, no fear of death, no inner disturbance—would have known perfect serenity, a serenity that was meant to extend to sexual intercourse. The coming together of male and female in the reproductive process was designed to be utterly calm. Without feeling any passion—without sensing that strange goad, as if something were driving you forward—"the husband would have relaxed on his wife's bosom in tranquility of mind."

How would this have been possible, the Pelagians asked, if the bodies of Adam and Eve were substantially the same as our bodies? Just consider, Augustine replied, that even now, in our current condition, some people can do things with their bodies that others find impossible. "Some people can even move their ears, either one at a time or both together. Others without moving the head can bring the whole scalp—all the part covered with hair, down towards the forehead and bring it back again at will." Still others—as he personally had witnessed—could sweat whenever they chose, and there were even people who could "produce at will such musical sounds from their behind (without any stink) that they seem to be singing from that region." Why should we not imagine then that Adam, in his uncorrupted state, could have quietly willed his penis to stiffen, just enough to enter Eve? It all would have been so calm that the seed could have been "dispatched into the womb, with no loss of the wife's integrity, just as the menstrual flux can now be produced from the womb of a virgin without loss of maidenhead." And for the man too there would have been "no impairment of his body's integrity."

It was awkward to think about Adam and Eve making love. Augustine knew that it would make his readers uncomfortable or, still worse, make them laugh. He was doing his best to imagine a time when sexual intercourse was not shameful, but precisely because we are fallen, we cannot recover that time. Even though he was deliberately restraining his eloquence in the service of modesty, he understood that any attempt to describe the sexual intercourse of our first parents would trigger a sense of embarrassment. There was a further awkwardness: to discuss sexual activity in a sermon or a conversation inevitably leads to the conjuring up of mental pictures. Those pictures carry over into dreams where it is impossible to distinguish between fantasy and reality. "The flesh is at once stirred into movement," Augustine reflected at the end of *The Literal Meaning of Genesis*, "and the result is what usually follows upon this movement."

But involuntary wet dreams, his own (which he seems to be acknowledging here) or those of his readers, are a risk worth taking. For it was crucial, in order to understand who Adam and Eve were and what the human condition was meant to be, to grasp precisely how they were meant to reproduce. The embarrassment we feel when we try to envisage them having sex is part of the problem. "Everyone knows," Augustine observed in the *City of God*, what act a married couple perform for the procreation of children. The whole marriage ceremony is all about the consecration of that act. "And yet when this act is being performed, with a view to the birth of children, not even the children who have already been born as a result of such an act are permitted to witness it." "Not even the children": did Augustine imagine then that in Paradise children would have been permitted to watch their parents in the act of copulation? Yes, that is precisely what he imagined, since the event would have been unnoticeable, unremarkable, and without a trace of involuntary arousal.

This was how it was all meant to be for Adam and Eve. But, Augustine concluded, it never happened, not even once. Their sin happened first, "and they incurred the penalty of exile from paradise before they could unite in the task of propagation as a deliberate act undisturbed by passion." So what was the point of the whole elaborate exercise of imagining their sex life? Augustine might never make all the world's Christians believe that their sexual feelings were unnatural or evil, but he could try to win an important doctrinal debate with the Manichees and the Pelagians and shore up a doctrinal vision of Jesus as the miraculous child of a virgin who became pregnant without the experience of ardor. And in matters of doctrine, whenever there was an encounter between a moderate, commonsensical position and a hard, intransigently radical position, the latter stood a very strong chance of success.

Along with these doctrinal purposes, Augustine's obsessive engagement with the story of Adam and Eve spoke to something in his life. What he discovered—or, more truthfully, invented—about sex in Paradise proved to him that humans were not originally meant to feel whatever it was that he experienced as an adolescent in Thagaste. It proved to him that he was not meant to feel the impulses that drew him to the fleshpots of Carthage. Above all it proved to him that he, at least in the redeemed state for which he longed, was not meant to feel what he had felt again and again with his mistress, the mother of his only child; the woman he loved for thirteen years (a period almost as long as the one during which he struggled to write the book on the *Literal Interpretation of Genesis*); the one he sent away at his mother's behest; the one who declared that she would never be with another man, as he would never be with another woman; the one whose separation felt to him, he wrote, like something ripped from his side (*avulsa a latere meo*).

Adam had fallen, Augustine wrote in the *City of God*, not because the serpent had deceived him. He chose to sin because of pride—a "craving for undue exaltation"—and because he "could not bear to be severed from his only companion." Augustine had, as best he could within the limits of his fallen condition, undone Adam's choice. He had tried, with the help of his sainted mother, to move away from ardor, to flee from arousal. True, he still had those involuntary dreams, those unwelcome stirrings, but what he knew about Adam and Eve in their state of innocence reassured him that someday, with Jesus's help, he would have perfect control over his own body. He would be free.

7

Eve's Murder

Augustine's account of his mother's tearful longing to save her husband and son from sin was so powerful that over the centuries it resulted in a cult. When eventually her remains were brought to Rome from Ostia, where she had died, miracles were said to have occurred all along the route. In a basilica built near the Piazza Navona and dedicated to her son, her sacred relics were deposited for veneration in a special chapel to the left of the high altar. The basilica's handsome façade, as can still be admired today, was clad with travertine torn off the Colosseum; the symbolism would not have escaped either the son or his mother. Prayers invoking her aid entered the Roman Breviary, and the feast day of Santa Monica—patron saint of patient wives, long-suffering mothers, and abuse victims—is kept on August 27. A small Spanish encampment in California became a flourishing city (and freeway) that still bears her name. She served for her wayward son—and through her son's eloquent words for many others—as a path back toward paradisal innocence.

As for the other woman Augustine loved, his sexual partner and the mother of his son, she simply disappeared from his voluminous writings, as she had disappeared from his life. He was not interested in using her as an emblem of carnal temptation or holding her responsible for his own sexual desires. After all, his underlying model for the disruptive presence of those desires was solitary arousal: a young man's stirring manhood in a bathhouse and an old man's erotic dreams.

But if Augustine did not choose to focus on woman as the primal source of temptation and the loss of innocence, others did. By making the story of Adam and Eve the central episode in the drama of human existence, Augustine opened the floodgates to a current of misogyny that swirled for centuries around the figure of the first woman. It did not matter that the rabbinical tradition had very little interest in focusing the blame upon Eve or that the Qur'an depicted Adam and Eve as equally culpable. It did not matter that Christianity in its formative years had welcomed women, along with slaves and criminals and others oppressed by the Roman social order, and had offered them a place at the table of the blessed. It did not matter that Augustine and numerous theologians in his wake held Adam principally responsible for the catastrophe that befell humankind. Many other authorities, both inside the church and out, were happy to assign responsibility almost entirely to Eve.

In doing so, they could draw at least indirectly upon an ancient pagan tradition that blamed women for the woes of the world. Virtually everyone, Christians as well as pagans, would have known the story of Pandora, most famously related by Hesiod, a venerated Greek poet of the eighth century BCE. The god Zeus, the story went, had been tricked by the titan Prometheus and was enraged at him. Since the titan had shown special favor to men, it was on them that Zeus determined to get his revenge. He commanded the blacksmith god Hephaestus to fashion a beautiful figure, the first woman, out of clay, and he directed each of the gods in turn to give her a gift. Athena taught her to weave; Aphrodite gave her seductive charm; the Graces gave her golden necklaces; the Seasons wove spring flowers into a crown; and sly Hermes gave her "the morals of a bitch."

The irresistible Pandora—the name means "all-gifted"—was then sent to Prometheus's brother Epimetheus, who had been warned not to accept any presents from Zeus. But Epimetheus, of course, was smitten and forgot the warning. Once in his house, Pandora opened the lid of a jar (mistranslated in the sixteenth century as a box) and, before she closed it again, out flew all of the ills that have afflicted humankind ever since. Only one item remained in the jar, just under the lid: hope.

Mankind, in this account, had been caught in the middle of a struggle between a god and a titan. As there was no human transgression in the first place, so too no human ritual of penitence could possibly appease the angry divinity. Men had once lived free from illness and heavy toil, but, thanks to Pandora, that life is gone forever. There is no great moral lesson to be learned. All that can be salvaged from the disaster, apart from the knowledge that Zeus always wins, is an awareness of the source of life's miseries: "the deadly female race and tribe of wives."

Early Christians did not embrace the myth of Pandora, any more than they embraced the rest of the Greek and Roman pantheon. But the faithful could not help looking over their shoulders at the culture they were rejecting. Pandora may never have existed, wrote the second-century theologian Tertullian, but the seductive temptation she symbolized continued to cause terrible harm. In his book on women's apparel, he grimly rehearsed the punishments God meted out on Eve and her descendants. Then he continued with mounting outrage:

And do you not know that you are (each) an Eve? The sentence of God on this sex of yours lives in this age: the guilt must of necessity live too. *You* are the devil's gateway: *you* are the unsealer of that (forbidden) tree: *you* are the first deserter of the divine law: *you* are she who persuaded him whom the devil was not valiant enough to attack. *You* destroyed so easily God's image, man. On account of your desert—that is, death—even the Son of God had to die. And do you think about adorning yourself over and above your tunics of skins?

Though widely read, Tertullian seems to have been regarded with wariness by orthodox Christians. Nonetheless, his emphasis on woman's incorrigible vanity and moral failings found many echoes.

More in the mainstream of early Christianity was Augustine's contemporary Jerome, whose translation of the Bible into Latin (known as the Vulgate, after the Latin word for "popular") became its principal conduit in the West. Hugely influential and admired—he is the patron saint of translators, librarians, and the writers of encyclopedias—Jerome returned again and again in his works to those feminine adornments and enhancements that so outraged Tertullian. He fulminated against women "who paint their cheeks with rouge and their eyes with belladonna, whose faces are covered with powder . . . ; whom no amount of years can convince that they are old; who heap their head with borrowed tresses; who polish up past youthfulness in spite of the wrinkles of age."

But the unmarried Jerome went much further than the married Tertullian. It was no longer enough to issue warnings against cosmetics or to insist that women cover their hair or keep themselves indoors. Surrounded by a circle of ardently pious women who were his generous patrons and with whom he maintained an extensive correspondence, Jerome actively disparaged marriage. He could not retroactively undo such marriages as they might already have made, but he sternly counseled widows against remarrying.

"A widow who is freed from the marital bond," he wrote in 384 CE to a woman named Marcella, "has but one duty laid upon her, and that is to continue as a widow." Neither the widow's age nor the circumstances of her life mattered. The Christian widow must resolve to avoid falling for a second time into marriage: "If the scorpion, jealous of her resolute purpose, with soft words urges her to eat again of the forbidden tree, let a curse crush him instead of a boot, and let her say, as he lies dying in the dust that is his due; 'Get thee behind me, Satan.' " "To eat again of the forbidden tree": for Jerome marriage itself was the Fall.

•   •   •

SOMETHING HAD CHANGED. The Hebrew creation story seemed to include an ecstatic celebration of marriage—"This one at last, bone of my bones and flesh of my flesh"—and of procreation. The rabbis had interpreted the divine blessing to be fruitful and multiply as a solemn commandment. If you were married and capable of having children and you failed to do so, you had, according to the Talmud, committed the equivalent of murder.

Augustine and Jerome were at the center of a radical rethinking of spiritual life and with it a rethinking of the lives that truly pious Christians should aspire to live. Most of the faithful, they recognized, would inevitably continue to marry and to produce children; such was the way of the world. But if the highest calling were a life of chastity, ascetic renunciation, and contemplation in the company of other celibate monks or nuns, then the whole account of Adam and Eve's ideal existence in the Garden of Eden would have to be recast.

In a fierce polemic against a Christian writer named Jovinian who had written in praise of marriage, Jerome maintained that, in Paradise, Adam and Eve were virgins, living a blessed life of bodily abstinence. So long as Adam fasted, he wrote, "he remained in paradise; he ate, and was cast out; he was no sooner cast out than he married a wife." So too, he reminded one of his young female followers, in Paradise, Eve was a virgin. "Paradise is your home," he told her. "Keep therefore as you were born." The young woman duly took a vow of perpetual virginity and followed Jerome to Palestine, where she lived a radically austere life.

These ascetic views were not uncontested in Christian communities of the fourth century, but Jerome and his allies prevailed. Jovinian's writings in praise of marriage were condemned and burned. Convicted of heresy and labeled by his enemies "the Epicurus of Christianity," he was flogged and then exiled to a small island in the Adriatic. Others who argued that marriage was as holy as virginity were similarly deemed heretics and punished, often brutally. Many Christians, both men and women, may have secretly thought that marriage was nothing inferior to monastic abstinence, that sexual relations between husband and wife were wholly good, and that women were the moral and intellectual equals of men and should feel free to speak out in church, but they were well advised to keep their opinions to themselves.

The women who followed Jerome renounced lives of wealth and privilege. Helping to found nunneries in a harsh and dangerous environment, they were bold, determined, and impressively learned. Against all odds, they set out to recover at least the traces of the purity of the first woman, before she fatally reached out and tasted the forbidden fruit. But this spiritual achievement and the power that came with it did not free them altogether from their inherited taint. For there was no denying that Eve had sinned, and the consequences of that sin reached even the most pious of her descendants. One of her punishments, imposed directly by God, was that woman would be dominated by man: "and he shall rule over thee." Everyone had to understand that whatever authority women wielded was strictly constrained by limits that were traced back to the sin of the first woman.

Like many others who shared his perspective, Jerome drew support from a foundational document of the Christian faith. He cited a passage in the First Epistle to Timothy, one of three pastoral letters attributed to the apostle Paul:

Let a woman learn in silence with full submission. I permit no woman to teach or to have authority over a man; she is to keep silent. For Adam was formed first, then Eve; and Adam was not deceived, but the woman was deceived and became a transgressor. (1 Tim. 2:11–14, New Revised Standard Version)

Though in Galatians St. Paul had affirmed that "there is no longer male and female: for ye are all one in Christ Jesus" (3:28), in his letter to Timothy, gender difference reappeared with a vengeance. And its underlying justification was not merely the local customs in Ephesus, where Timothy served, but rather an ineradicable difference reaching back to the beginning of time.

"Adam was not deceived, but the woman was deceived and became a transgressor": those words were repeated again and again over the centuries. They were drilled into small children, invoked whenever the balance of power between husband and wife was threatened, thrown up at intelligent, articulate women who did not seem to know their place. "A woman was the effective cause of damnation," wrote a canon lawyer almost a thousand years after Jerome, "since she was the origin of lying." She certainly should not be allowed to teach. "A woman taught one time," a thirteenth-century Spanish friar put it, "and the whole world was overthrown."

This endless harping on Eve's sin and the defects of all of her daughters obviously suited the mental world of monks and friars who had taken vows of chastity and abjured—at least officially—the companionship of the other sex. And it suited as well those husbands who were locked in a struggle to dominate their wives and daughters. The miseries brought by Eve became a standard talking point in the battle of the sexes, a predictable and highly useful charge because it seemed to carry the authority of the Bible itself.

The obstreperous Wife of Bath, in Chaucer's fourteenth-century classic *Canterbury Tales*, provides a comical glimpse of a typical skirmish. Her husband Jankin, she declares, was inordinately fond of reading her lessons night and day from an endless array of misogynistic authors, including inevitably a cardinal named Saint Jerome "that made a book against Jovinian." One night, she recalls, her husband

Read on his book as he sat by the fire
Of Eva first, that for her wickedness

Was all mankind brought to wretchedness,
For which the Jesus Christ himself was slain.

Jankin underscored the conclusion: "Woman was the loss"—that is,
the ruin—"of all mankind."

The Wife of Bath had had enough. Reaching down, she tore
three pages out of the "cursed book" and struck her husband in the
face, making him fall backward. He rose up and hit her on the head
hard enough to knock her out. But, she says, it all worked out splen-
didly: fearing that he had killed her and repenting his violence, Jankin
pledged to abandon his claim to domination: "He gave me all the
bridle in mine hand,/To have the governance of house and land." As
the perfect sign of his pledge, he burned the book—Jerome's *Against
Jovinian*—that chronicled Eve's wickedness.

Chaucer's comical outcome may have had its real-life equivalents,
but the moral emblem of Eve's transgression was endlessly reiterated in
images and sermons, lighthearted jests and bitter denunciations. It had
the force of scientific proof.

It was not only men who invoked it and drew out its misogynistic implications. Many pious women, such as those who funded and
accompanied Jerome, accepted and embraced the judgment against
women's nature. There were occasional exceptions: daring, saintly
women who challenged the routine denigration. But for the most part
the dominant account held sway, even among those Christians who
had displayed their indifference to the reigning social assumptions of
the times. Mere social rules were one thing—they were made to be
challenged or broken. Eve's transgression was presented as something
else: historical fact, anthropological truth, biological nature, religious
doctrine. The miseries of human existence could all be traced back to
Eve, and Eve's daughters bore the stain.

The fierce condemnation of Eve was often linked to the ardent
celebration of Mary, who was represented as undoing the first

woman's sin. Early on, the antithesis was worked out in detail. Eve was pulled from the flesh of the old Adam; the New Adam was born from the flesh of Mary. Encountering the virgin Eve, the serpent's word crept into her ear; encountering the Virgin Mary, the Word of God had crept into her ear. Through Eve, the serpent's word built the edifice of death; through Mary, the Word of God built the fabric of life. The knot of disobedience that Eve had tied by her unbelief Mary opened by her belief and her obedience. Eve gave birth to sin; Mary gave birth to grace. *Eva* became *Ave.*

This elaborate counterpoint helped launch over the centuries an astonishing array of images: drawings, book illuminations, sculptures, frescoes, and paintings. On the left side of the great eleventh-century bronze doors at Hildesheim, Eve nurses Cain, while on the right Mary nurses Jesus. In a painting in Boston by the Netherlandish master Rogier van der Weyden, St. Luke draws a picture of the Virgin while she nurses her baby. Carved on the arm of the wooden throne on which she sits are the tiny figures of Adam and Eve. If you look very closely, you can see that Eve is reaching to take an apple: Original Sin and the redemption are thus brought together. So too a splendid altarpiece in Cortona by Fra Angelico shows the annunciation in the foreground, while in the distance the angel Michael is expelling Adam and Eve from Paradise. And a fifteenth-century Italian illumination of Dante's *Paradiso* plays an even more radical game with time and space. On the right, in front of a small chapel, the angel Gabriel kneels down to Mary. Just behind him to the left the naked Adam and Eve, covering their genitals, look at the scene in rapt wonder.

Since Marian devotion in the Middle Ages was often linked to anti-Jewish polemics—the Jews, after all, were said to have been responsible for the Virgin's sorrows—depictions of Eve and Mary often extend the contrast to that between Jews and Christians. In a German Bible illumination from 1420, Eve stands on one side of the fatal tree, and Mary on the other. The naked Eve reaches up with one hand to seize an apple; with her other hand, she touches a death's head held by one of a group of bearded Jews wearing conical hats. The gowned Mary reaches up to hold a crucifix and looks benignly back at a group of priests and monks. The opposition is between synagogue and church—and thus between law and grace, death and life.

In an unforgettable painting of 1605–6, now in the Borghese Gallery in Rome, Caravaggio depicted the Virgin bending down to put her bare foot on the head of a writhing snake. She holds her naked son, who places his foot on top of hers; their weight together will crush the snake. In the shadows the child's grandmother, Saint Anne, her face wrinkled and weary, looks on. Though she is nowhere to be seen, Eve is also implicitly present, for the event had been foretold at the beginning of time. "And I will put enmity between thee and the woman, and between thy seed and her seed" (Gen. 3:15), God told the serpent who had lured Eve into transgression. Now the New Testament savior and his virgin mother are fulfilling the Old Testament prophecy. This is the triumph of Christianity, and accordingly the child Jesus is conspicuously uncircumcised.

The whole symbolic contrast could be used to suggest that Eve's sin was a blessing in disguise. It was, after all, her action that ultimately led to Mary and, through Mary, to the birth of the Savior. And yet, since Mary was everything that Eve was not, setting them side-by-side often served to intensify the condemnation of the rashness, vanity, and pride that first woman had bequeathed to her offspring. Theologians seemed to compete with one another in berating women for their inherited defectiveness. Even that supremely intelligent and morally sensitive philosopher Thomas Aquinas concluded that man is more the image of God than woman. The woman, he wrote, is a *vir occasionatus,* a defective or mutilated man. The notion was an ancient, pagan one; Thomas took it from Aristotle. But it found a ready home in medieval thought, where it seemed to account for the belatedness of woman's creation, for her origin in what was called a crooked rib, and for her fatal succumbing to the serpent's blandishments.

Why then, Thomas asked, had God created her in the first place? She was meant to be a helpmeet, but, as Augustine had observed centuries earlier, another man would have been better for help with agricultural labor. So too, Thomas wrote, "for living together and keeping each other company, it is better for two [male] friends to be together than a man and a woman." Her creation only made complete sense, he concluded, for the purposes of procreation.

Women's procreative power was acknowledged and honored, above all in the innumerable tender, reverential images of Virgin and Child. But though the cult of the Virgin Mary steadily grew in importance, it did not diminish the denigration of Eve. In at least some medieval Christians, particularly those living in monastic communities, misogyny reached levels that now seem to us clearly pathological. That the misogynistic rants did not seem so at the time was due to the fact that they found a relatively comfortable place within a larger structure of belief and within institutions that rendered them acceptable. St. Peter Damian, an eleventh-century Benedictine, was particularly devoted to Mary—he penned a celebrated *Officium Beatae Virginis*—but that devotion did not soften his frenzied attack on "the cause of our ruin:"

> You bitches, sows, screech-owls, night owls, she-wolves, blood suckers, [who] cry "Give, give! without ceasing" (Prov. 30:15–16). Come now, hear me, harlots, prostitutes, with your lascivious kisses, you wallowing places for fat pigs, couches for unclean spirits, demi-goddesses, sirens, witches, devotees of Diana, if any portents, if any omens are found thus far, they should be judged sufficient to your name. For you are the victims of demons, destined to be cut off by eternal death. From you the devil is fattened by the abundance of your lust, is fed by your alluring feasts.

In this crazed language of loathing, the human pair in Genesis—
"So God created man in his own image, in the image of God created he him, male and female created he them"—has morphed into
something sinister. More particularly, the woman, far from being the
partner of man, has become his mortal enemy. Though she too is ultimately Satan's victim, she is also the ally of the Evil One and the principal agent of humanity's downfall. Somewhere lurking in the saint's
mind as he sits brooding in his cell are suspicions older than Christianity, older too than the religion of the Jews. The woman is not merely
Satan's ally; she is his lover, joining her body to his in filthy rites.

The serpent in these obscene fantasies is sometimes the form in
which Satan couples with the woman. Alternatively, it is the woman
who is the real serpent. Learned commentators remarked that the
Hebrew name Eve was related to the Aramaic word for snake, but the
misogynists did not need philology to lead them in this direction. The
woman used her sexual allure to tempt and ultimately to destroy the
man. The actual victimization of women was conveniently forgotten,
or rather it was seen as the fault of the women themselves, who have
learned, as the daughters of Eve, to arouse male desire.

In the most extreme forms taken by this argument—less an argument than a mental disturbance or compulsion—the woman ceased to
be fully human. "A woman is a menstrual animal," wrote an early commentator on the Church's canon law, "by contact with whose blood
fruits do not produce, wine turns sour, plants die, trees lack fruit, rust
corrupts iron, the air darkens." The dehumanization of women, like
the comparable dehumanization of Jews, was an invitation to violence.

In 1486, two Dominican friars, Heinrich Kramer and Jacob
Sprenger, published a celebrated book, *The Hammer of Witches,* in which
they described the inquisition that the pope had authorized them to
conduct in an extensive area of Germany and Switzerland. Their inves-
tigations, drawing on confessions extracted by torture, had led to the
identification of a significant number of alleged witches, among them

a few men but for the most part women accused of trafficking with the devil. The accused were condemned and executed. The inquisitors were eager to justify what they had done and to encourage others to take up their important mission.

Citing church fathers and many others, Kramer and Sprenger explained why so many more women than men are drawn to the practice of witchcraft. It is, they wrote, because of a natural proclivity in all females to do evil. Of course, there have been heroic, pious, and even holy women: like Peter Damian, Sprenger was particularly devoted to the cult of the Virgin Mary. But truly good women are rare exceptions: as a whole they are a very bad lot. "Since they are defective in all the powers of both soul and body," the inquisitors wrote, "it is not surprising that they cause more acts of sorcery to happen against those for whom they feel jealousy."

Acts of sorcery, the inquisitors insisted, are not mere fantasies; the witches enter into actual binding contracts with the devil, whom they worship and serve in exchange for evil powers. "Demons can, in assumed bodies," they explained, "speak with sorceresses, see them, hear them, eat with them and beget with them." The demonic powers conferred upon the witches are often quite local—to kill a neighbor's cow or cripple a child or render a man impotent—but they can also reach far beyond the village: "we find that virtually all the kingdoms of the world have been overturned because of women."

It all goes back to Eve. The fatal defects, they wrote, "can be noticed in the original shaping of woman, since she was formed from a curved rib, that is, from the rib of the chest that is twisted and contrary, so to speak, to man." True, the devil misled her, but it was the woman, and not the devil, who misled Adam and brought about man's ruin. That she did so only confirms the theory that women are imperfect animals: "in terms of the intellect or the understanding of spiritual matters they seem to belong to a different variety than men."

Only the small shred of verbal caution—"they *seem* to belong to a different variety than men"—kept Kramer and Sprenger from stating directly what their book so often implied: that women were not fully human. Though it was prefaced by an elaborate official approval of its orthodoxy, the theologians at the University of Cologne identified heretical errors in it, and three years after its initial publication *The Hammer of Witches* was condemned by the Inquisition as false. Despite this condemnation, it managed to circulate widely in multiple editions, and Heinrich Kramer, the more enthusiastic of the inquisitors, was repeatedly licensed by church authorities to go about his sinister work. Innocent women continued to die for what was imagined to be an innate propensity to evil that was traced all the way back to mother Eve.

But though the misogynistic strain built deep into the origin narrative was drawn upon to justify the cruel mistreatment of women, though Eve's transgression licensed anything from casual insults to judicial murder, the Genesis story was not always and inevitably used to prove the innate defectiveness of all women. All major Christian theologians, from Augustine and Aquinas to Luther and Calvin, held that the first woman, like the first man, was created in the image of God. That conviction placed a certain brake on the most extreme denigrations of Eve. And on occasion even her alleged defects could be used to defend women or at least to deflect their guilt. In the mid-fifteenth century the impressively learned humanist Isotta Nogarola argued with wry eloquence that women's imperfections—their ignorance and inconstancy—were part of their God-given nature and therefore a mitigation of their sinfulness. Properly understood, Eve was "like a boy who sins less than an old man or a peasant less than a noble." Adam, being made perfect and endowed with free will, had no such excuse.

Many Christians, men as well as women, shared the view that Adam was the more culpable of the pair. The woman had been deceived by Satan; the man had transgressed freely. And even when the first woman was said to bear the principal burden of guilt for the ruin of all humanity, there was still a way to mitigate her crime by recalling, as the early church fathers had done, the salvation her act had helped to bring about.

Early in the fifteenth century, a remarkably learned woman, the French humanist Christine de Pizan, imagined herself in conversation with the "Lady Reason." "If anyone would say that man was banished because of Lady Eve," Reason assures her, "I tell you that he gained more through Mary than he lost through Eve." Rightly understood, Eve was humanity's benefactor: "Man and woman should be glad for this sin."

A few bold interpreters went further. Perhaps the most remarkable was a very articulate, very unhappy nun in an enclosed Benedictine convent in Venice. The nun, Arcangela Tarabotti, was one of eleven children. Born in 1604 with a congenital disability—like her father, she was lame—she had been consigned to the nunnery as a very young girl, a strategy frequently adopted by parents who either wanted to save on a dowry or thought that their daughter would not find a suitable husband. By her seventeenth birthday she had taken the irrevocable vows that shut her up in the convent for the rest of her days. But she did not quietly resign herself to her fate, and in the course of her life she repeatedly found ways to communicate with the world beyond her cell.

Her most famous book, published in 1654 two years after her death at the age of forty-eight, is *Paternal Tyranny,* a scathing indictment of the cruelty that led to the misery that she and others like her suffered and an indictment too of the lies men used to justify this cruelty. Understood properly, the Bible makes clear that the first woman was not merely the equal to the first man but rather his superior. Adam was formed of mere clay, Eve of the nobler substance of the human body; he was born outside of Eden, she in Paradise itself. She was the compendium of all perfections, God's final and supreme masterpiece.

Notwithstanding their evident inferiority, men have contrived through violence and deceit to subjugate women, and they have cloaked their wickedness by blaming everything on Eve. She is unjustly held responsible for all the ills that have befallen humankind. And the vicious slander against her has been used for centuries to justify and reinforce the virtual enslavement of all women. What a lie, Tarabotti wrote; God "did not tell Adam 'You will rule over woman.' Both male and female were born free, bearing with them, like a precious gift from God, the priceless bounty of free choice." But men will not allow the opposite sex the freedom that they themselves cherish. They imprison women in oppressive marriages or still worse in gloomy convents where, apart from the few who have true vocations, the inmates are condemned to a miserable existence: "Their lives have no beginnings and no ends, gnaw but do not consume, kill but do not put to death."

A seventeenth-century nun could hardly call into doubt the whole story of the first humans in the Garden. But if the author of *Paternal Tyranny* could not deny the truth of Holy Writ, she could at least wrest its interpretation in a more humane direction. Eve was induced to eat of the forbidden fruit not because of pride but because of her thirst for knowledge: "hardly a blameworthy desire." Her beauty may have contributed to Adam's fall, but that was hardly the fault of the woman: "You vain men hate women's beauty because your impure hearts prevent you from enjoying her presence without lust."

Immured for life in her convent cell, Tarabotti struggled mightily to unmask the sinister uses to which the story of Adam and Eve had been put. "I do not find literally or symbolically a hint of a shadow that God wished there to be women enclosed in convents against their wills," she wrote. "The blessed Creator, in whose mind the numerous future procreation of the human race was present, could have entrusted to our first father Adam the task of founding religious orders of women dedicated to His service. But He did not do so. . . ." In the Bible story the woman succumbed to the blandishments of the devil in the shape of the serpent, but as Tarabotti retold it, God made clear how unfairly Eve and all women since had been treated: "Truly," God tells Eve, "the devil stands for the male, who from now on will cast on to you the blame for his failings and will have no other purpose than deceiving you, betraying you, and removing all your rights of dominion granted by my omnipotence."

It is possible that other women, both inside the convent and beyond its walls, agreed with Tarabotti, and it is possible that she had male allies as well. But, assuming they existed, few or none of them were in a position to say so openly. *Paternal Tyranny* was immediately attacked, and in 1660 the Inquisition condemned it in its entirety, banned any future publication, and placed it on the index of prohibited books.

Despite the heroic efforts of Arcangela Tarabotti, Isotta Nogarola, and others, it was almost impossible completely to erase the curse of Eve's culpability from within the faith. No matter how much one assigned the greater blame to Adam or how fervently one celebrated the redemptive power of Mary, the taint of misogyny remained, like the bitter residue in a cask one can never completely scrub clean. It was only from a position firmly outside the story that the feminist Mary Wollstonecraft could look back in anger: "Probably the prevailing opinion, that woman was created for man, may have taken its rise from Moses's poetical story," she wrote in 1792 in *A Vindication of the Rights of Women,*

yet, as very few, it is presumed, who have bestowed any serious thought on the subject, ever supposed that Eve was, literally speaking, one of Adam's ribs, the deduction must be allowed to fall to the ground; or, only be so far admitted as it proves that man, from the remotest antiquity, found it convenient to exert his strength to subjugate his companion, and his invention to shew that she ought to have her neck bent under the yoke, because the whole creation was only created for his convenience or pleasure.

Near the end of the eighteenth century, in the wake of the Enlightenment and the American and French revolutions, Wollstonecraft presumed that "very few" thoughtful people ever took the story of Adam
and Eve in a literal sense. It was possible then for her to argue openly
that it served—and that it had always served—as a device to justify the
subjugation of women.

People were no more credulous in the 1480s than they were in
the 1780s or, for that matter, than they are now. In the case of witchcraft accusations, there is widespread evidence of skepticism, including
within the church. The stories of flying through the air and mysterious trysts with the devil and occult power to maim and kill were frequently denounced as delusions, the fantasies of the mentally ill or of
those with hidden agendas. But Augustine had succeeded in establish-
ing as a key principle the literal reality of the events in the Garden. The
insistence on the reality of Eve's conversation with the serpent gave
witch-hunters like Kramer and Sprenger the opening they needed, and
their claims were reinforced by the mass-produced and increasingly
powerful images of the fateful scene in the Garden of Eden.

Among the greatest of these images were paintings, woodcuts,
and etchings by the early sixteenth-century German artist Hans Baldung Grien, who also produced the most brilliant, intensely disturbing
images of witches. Their long hair flying out like flames around their
plump naked bodies, the witches cavort with one another in obscene
satanic rituals. Those rituals are never far from the way Baldung
Grien imagined Eve. In one of his most famous paintings, now in the
National Gallery of Canada in Ottawa, a fleshy Eve with flowing hair
stands, holding an apple in one hand behind her back, next to the fatal
tree. No stray branch discreetly covers her nakedness; on the contrary,
her body is turned fully toward the viewer. But she is not looking out
at us; with a sly expression on her face, her eyes are directed down at
the snake that has wrapped itself around the tree. In a gesture whose
erotic implications are clear, she reaches out and fingers the snake.

The artist made the consequences of this little sex game unmistakably clear. Behind the tree, smiling at Eve and holding her arm as he reaches up with his other hand to pick one of the fruits, stands Adam. But it is not the Adam we expect to see in Paradise. Already a corpse, his flesh is falling in tatters off his bones. The snake completes the circle by biting the rotting arm that the husband has extended to touch his wife. Better never to have had a wife, better never to have been sexually aroused, better never to have seen a woman's body. But the painting itself centers caressingly on the body of Eve, and it is very obviously—indeed pornographically—meant to arouse.

8

Embodiments

Beneath the streets of modern Rome, there is a vast network of catacombs, a city of the dead, much of it unexcavated. Paths tunneled in
the tufa extend for many kilometers, twisting and turning in a baffling,
unlit labyrinth. In the third and fourth centuries CE, pagans tended to
cremate their dead; they placed the ashes in funerary urns deposited
in what were called *columbaria,* from their resemblance to dovecotes
(a dove in Latin was a *columba*). But, in the belief that the end of the
world was near, Christians in this period opted for burial rather than
cremation: why make resurrection more difficult, they thought, by
reducing the body to ashes? Therefore, along the twisting paths of the
catacombs, they laid their dead—by the thousands—in slot-like niches,
known as *loculi.*

The corpses of the wealthy were sometimes placed in niches topped
by arches, or, as a still more costly option, in small rooms called *cubiculae.* These rooms, where whole families were interred, possess the most
interest today, since they were decorated on the walls and ceilings with
frescoes. Over the centuries, between the humid air and the smoke
from the lamps of mourners and pilgrims, the frescoes were coated
with a black layer that turned out to protect them. When the black

layer is removed, the images glow in brilliant colors, as if they had been painted yesterday and not more than sixteen hundred years ago.

In the Catacombs of Saints Marcellino and Pietro—an extraordinary site in a rather dreary, out-of-the-way neighborhood in Rome—certain figures recur again and again: the raising of Lazarus, Noah opening the ark and seeing a dove with a branch in its beak, Daniel in the lion's den, and a narrative sequence that shows Jonah thrown overboard, swallowed by the great fish, spit out on land, and then happily relaxing in the shade of a vine. These are scenes of mortal peril overcome, designed to reassure the dead or rather to comfort the living, not only the bereaved but also the pilgrims who came to the catacombs to pray near the relics of saints and martyrs. Scattered in the *cubiculae* arrayed along the maze of narrow, underground tunnels are other signs of reassurance as well: images of Christ as the Good Shepherd carrying His sheep, Christ enthroned with the Apostles, the blessed sitting at a banquet, the woman with the issue of blood touching the hem of Jesus's robe, Jesus talking with the Samaritan woman at the well, and even, somewhat anomalously, Orpheus, who in pagan myth descended into the underworld and then returned to the light.

The artists who painted these scenes paid a surprising homage to the people responsible for the creation of the catacombs: mourners and pilgrims were treated to several large and unusually realistic depictions of the diggers, wearing work clothes and carrying their tools. Their backs turned to the viewers, these stalwart workmen were depicted excavating the tufa to make more graves. Still more surprising, in the torch-lit darkness, visitors could look up at wall paintings of the naked Adam and Eve standing on either side of a tree.

Whoever created these images of the first humans had few or no models to draw upon from the Hebrew world that had given birth to the story. To be sure, Adam and Eve had always been imagined to have bodies of some kind or other—for some rabbis, as we have seen, the bodies of enormous giants; for others, bodies covered, while they were still in Paradise, by a protective carapace; for still others, bodies tethered to the Edenic ground by a kind of magical umbilical cord. But the Jewish prohibition of graven images meant that there were almost no graphic depictions of these bodies, no guides to picturing them, as it were, in the flesh.

Early Christians had no comparable anxiety about graven images. And since the Romans who embraced Christianity were heirs to centuries of Greek and Roman art, we might have expected them to depict the first man and the first woman, who were said to be the most beautiful of all humans, as unabashedly naked. Instead, Adam and Eve in the Catacombs of Saints Marcellino and Pietro have bodies bent over and humbled, already in the grip of shame. Their heads lowered and their arms hunched forward, they are anxiously covering their genitals. All around them are emblems of hope. On the wall to the left, the corpse of Lazarus, still completely shrouded, emerges from his tomb; to the right, Moses strikes the rock to release the life-giving waters. Above their heads Noah arises like a jack-in-the-box out of a tiny ark. But the Adam and Eve figures here have no touch of redemption. They have every reason to be ashamed: they are the pair responsible for the death that made the catacombs necessary in the first place.

By the third century, Romans of all persuasions had distanced themselves from the public nudity permissible in ancient Greece— the Greek word *gymnasium* means a place to exercise naked. But, even when modesty became the order of the day, statuary in Rome continued to copy Greek models and therefore to celebrate gods and heroes comfortable in their well-toned, beautifully proportioned nude bodies. Christians would have seen such figures everywhere. Nothing could signal a greater distance from Apollo or Venus than these emblematic paintings in the gloom of the catacombs of Adam and Eve, crushed by shame.

With the conversion of the emperor Constantine the Great, Christianity definitively came out into the sunlight of the Roman world, but the faithful remained committed to the imagery of shame they had embraced in the underground burial chambers. Around 359 CE the powerful Roman senator Junius Bassus died and was buried in a magnificent marble sarcophagus. As befitted a recent convert—"newly baptised," as the inscription declares, he "went to God on the 8th day of the Calends of September"—his sarcophagus was elaborately carved with images from the Old and New Testament. The naked Adam and Eve were there, but not to represent the paradisal bliss to which the senator hoped to ascend. Rather they represent, in the words of St. Paul, "the body of this death," from which the deceased was delivered. By the fatal tree, around which the serpent is coiled, they look down and away from one another. Disgraced, ashamed, and now painfully alone even in each other's company, they press fig leaves to their genitals.

Other Christian sarcophagi from the same period and in the centuries that followed repeat the same vision. Even when Adam and Eve are depicted at the moment before the transgression, they are already ashamed of their bodies. Reaching for the fruit with one hand, they awkwardly cover themselves with the other. The fruit may be still untasted, but the Fall has happened before it actually happens, or rather for anyone who sees the figures, it has already happened, decisively and irreversibly. After all, the viewer has fallen as a result of what took place in the Garden, and there is no escape from shame.

In early medieval depictions of Adam and Eve, the only significant exceptions to the rule of shame are of the story's early moments, before it lurches toward its tragic denouement. A beautiful carving in ivory from around 400 CE, now in the Bargello Museum in Florence, shows Adam with the animals that were brought to him to name. He is not, as we might expect, standing before them, like a general reviewing his troops. Instead, along with bears and lions and other beasts, he seems to be floating, as if in a Maurice Sendak drawing, in a kind of dream space—entirely unashamed of his nakedness. More common are scenes of the creation, and especially of the creation of Eve. Adam lies asleep while God pulls the form of Eve from his side. Both are naked, and they do not reach to cover themselves, so here at least we are at a moment in which the body does not display the awareness of its disgrace.

But even these bodies imagined to be in a state of perfect innocence seem somehow to have shrunk back into themselves, as if they were already ashamed. The figures have lost most of the exuberance of the flesh that had characterized pagan representations; instead, they are on the way to becoming gaunt and wasted. The illuminated Grandvier-Montval Bible from around 840 and the sumptuous First Bible of Charles the Bald, from the same period, each depict the unfallen and naked Adam and Eve almost as if they were bodies risen like Lazarus from the grave.

This way of representing the first humans as stripped-down, ascetic figures, little more than skin and bones, continued for centuries. My personal favorite is a fifteenth-century illuminated manuscript, of Bohemian origin, in the Vatican Library. The text is by the twelfth-century French theological writer known as Peter Comestor—his last name is a Latin nickname, "the Eater," not because he distinguished himself at the dinner table but because he was an insatiable devourer of books. Many readers in the Middle Ages encountered Genesis not in the Bible, which was only infrequently read, but in Peter Comestor's popular and often illuminated paraphrase. In the version in the Vatican Library, naked Adam lies fast asleep on a kind of rock couch, while robed God stands behind him, delicately holding in his left hand a rib on whose top sits Eve's head. He has not yet formed the rest of her body, so that she looks exactly like a stick puppet, but with his right hand God is already giving the bare rib his blessing. As Augustine had urged, the artist adheres to his understanding of the literal sense: "And the rib, which the Lord God had taken from man, made he a woman" (Gen. 2:22).

Such figures in creation scenes are in effect a gesture toward the nakedness of Adam and Eve in Paradise, but for the most part in

Christian art of late antiquity and the early Middle Ages, the bodies of the first man and woman are only notionally there. The artists who crafted such images were not ignorant of the pagan past; they could still have seen around them many remnants of classical nudes in shameless beauty. They could, if they wished, have taken these nudes as models for the original humans in their perfection and their unfallen innocence. But they chose to fashion something else, something that marked the threshold of faith that had been crossed.

That threshold did not, of course, also mark the abandonment of artistic ambition. Quite the contrary, as attested by innumerable Romanesque and Gothic churches adorned with magnificent paintings and sculptures. In the decorative schemes of these churches, Adam and Eve appear quite frequently in the form of small sculpted naked figures carved on the portals, or depicted in paintings as an aged patriarch and matriarch freed by Christ from Limbo, or simply, in the case of Adam, as a skull at the foot of the Cross in Golgotha, "the place of the skull," where Jesus was crucified.

There are tens of thousands of these painted skulls to be glimpsed on church walls or in medieval prayer books or now in the world's museums. Very few modern viewers any longer realize what a medieval viewer would have known at once: that the skull is that of Adam, who brought death into the world. In the village of San Candido, situated in an obscure valley in the part of the Dolomites known as the Alta Pusteria, there is an ancient church that has above its high altar a painted wooden crucifix. A bearded Jesus looks out impassively from the cross on which he has been nailed, his bleeding feet resting directly on a head. The head, in this case, is not quite a skull, for it still has flesh and features: the worshiper is in effect looking into the face of Adam. He has fallen, as a result of his transgression in the Garden, but through Christ's sacrifice, he will be redeemed.

One of the most remarkable medieval representations of this vision of fall and redemption was created about a thousand years ago in an ancient city in northern Germany near Hanover. A rich and impressively well-educated nobleman who had served as tutor to the Holy Roman Emperor Otto III was, as a reward for his service, made bishop of Hildesheim in 993. Having visited Italy and seen the wonders of the ancient world, this nobleman, Bernward, was determined to turn his bishopric into a new Rome. He had walls built around the cathedral hill and set to work on an elaborate decorative scheme, which he personally supervised. The results are only somewhat visible today, in part because of subsequent rebuilding and in greater part because on March 22, 1945—two months before the end of the war—Allied planes heavily bombed the medieval center of Hildesheim. Fortunately, the cathedral's artistic treasures, having been removed for protection, survived and were restored to their place in the postwar reconstruction. The greatest of these, two enormous bronze doors with figures in three-quarters relief, prominently feature Adam and Eve.

Bernward's doors, each cast in one piece, were a fantastic technical achievement: nothing at that scale had been made in bronze since the fall of the Roman Empire. The sixteen scenes depicted upon them form an elaborate storytelling program, ranging from the creation of Adam and Eve, at the top left, down through the Fall of Man to the murder of Abel at the bottom, and then upward on the right-hand door from the Annunciation to the Virgin through the Crucifixion to the risen Christ's appearance in the garden to Mary Magdalene. The whole scheme is elaborately choreographed, with the Old Testament events on one side carefully coordinated with the New Testament events on the other.

Adam and Eve are the central figures on the left-hand door, their entire history conjured up on successive panels. Even in the scenes before the Fall, there is nothing confident, independent, or beautiful about these first humans: in their postures and their forms, they are more like awkward children, not fully at home in the world or in their own bodies. The figures are particularly eloquent in conveying the medieval vision of the body in disgrace: after the Fall, the crouching Eve holds a fig leaf over her genitals with one hand, while with the other she points down at the serpent, depicted in a dragon-like form with its tail between her legs. Cowering Adam, also crouching and covering himself, tries to shift the blame toward Eve, while God (fully dressed, of course) points an accusing finger directly at him. Who would not shrink before such a finger?

The creation scene in the first of those panels has posed a riddle that has not been solved to anyone's satisfaction. At the panel's center God is bending over and sculpting with his divine fingers a human who lies on the ground. Presumably, the human is Adam being formed at this instant from clay. But to the right, on the other side of a tree whose form strikingly resembles a heart, there is another figure, evidently also Adam, staring in amazement. The creature being made at the center then might be Eve, but there is no sign of a rib, and the amazed onlooker is wide awake. Perhaps, as some scholars have suggested, God has removed the rib from Adam's side and is now finishing the task by adding some clay? Or perhaps the scene depicts Adam looking back in wonder at his own creation? Or perhaps the artist was thinking not of chapter 2 of Genesis, with the creation of the male from clay and later the female from the rib, but rather of chapter 1, where both humans are created at once: "male and female created he them"? That would at least help to explain the apparent absence of any sexual differentiation. The figures are androgynous, and they remain androgynous on the panels until the scene of the Fall, where Eve, luring Adam, holds the fruit directly in front of her apple-like breasts. Sexual difference is clearly part of the disgrace that is about to befall them. And that disgrace makes it impossible for medieval artists to give them naked bodies proud and unashamed.

The rule of shame, so prominent in the eleventh-century Hildesheim doors, continued into the later Middle Ages. Yet some artists began to explore new and surprising ways of representing nakedness, even under the sign of its disgrace. The most spectacular of these explorations is found in the town of Autun, in eastern France. There around 1130, on a lintel above a portal of the church of Saint-Lazare, a stonemason named Gislebertus carved a life-sized image of Eve. The image is only a fragment of a larger decoration, the rest of which is lost. The Eve too would have been lost, had it not been incorporated into the masonry of a house, where it was discovered when the house was being demolished in 1856.

Gislebertus's Eve bears the traditional marks of shame: her genitals are discreetly hidden by the sculpted trunk and leaves of a small tree, and though stretched out on the ground, she is kneeling as if in penance. She rests her head on her right hand, in a gesture that might represent sadness or remorse. And yet here the conventional imagery of the abject body strangely vanishes. This Eve has a powerful erotic allure. Her long hair falls loosely over her shoulders, and her upper torso is turned outward toward us, showing her beautiful breasts. Her slender left arm reaches back along her body, while her hand grasps a fruit from a tree behind her, a tree in which a snake's body appears to be twisted. Her hand seems to be operating on its own, without her conscious will.

The more one looks, the more this medieval Eve at once tantalizes and resists clear resolution. She is evidently in the act of plucking the fruit, but she has not yet carried it to her mouth, and indeed, as she leans her head on her hand and looks out musingly, she seems far away from that fatal moment. Perhaps she is still innocent, and, since in that case she would not yet feel shame, the leaves that shield her private parts from our gaze are only in the right place by happy accident. The allure of her body would not therefore be a sign of *her* awakened sexuality; insofar as we are aroused, it is rather a sign of *our* fallenness. At the same time, her kneeling and her melancholy gaze suggest inescapably that she has already fallen. She must have lost her innocence after all, and the twisting of her beautiful body toward us is a deliberate provocation. She is then a siren, a mermaid, a serpent.

Which is it, innocent or guilty? a temptress or a penitent? an emblem of everything we are meant to leave behind when we enter the church, or a model of deportment appropriate for the sacred space? Impossible to say, and the conundrum centers on whatever it is that is hidden behind the serpentine vegetation blocking our view of her waist. For it is there, out of sight, that her body pivots in a way that is impossible for the actual human body to do. Gislebertus was able to use the nonnaturalistic conventions of medieval art and the intellectual subtlety of medieval philosophy to create an Eve who is at once aware and unaware of sin. The sacrifice that the sculptor made was of an entirely believable human body, as the Greeks and Romans had so magnificently represented it, but that classical heritage was in the distant past, and Gislebertus, if he recognized it at all, would have regarded it as a small price to pay for the effect he so brilliantly achieved.

Medieval artists did not need the resources of ancient painting and sculpture in order to explore with extraordinary subtlety the intricate meanings of the Genesis origin story. In a vast number of sculpted lintels, carved choir stalls, panel paintings, and manuscript illuminations, they depicted Adam's mysterious sleep when the rib was removed from his side; God's artisanal fashioning of the first woman; the wily serpent twisting itself around the tree; the fatal act of reaching out for the fruit; the primal experience of shame; and the moment of expulsion through the gates of Paradise. That moment was particularly dramatic, for it represented the key transition from life in the purpose-built garden, with all human needs met by divine design, to life in a harsh, recalcitrant, death-driven world. Thus in the St. Albans Psalter, created in England in the first half of the twelfth century (and now in Hildesheim, Germany), God himself pushes Adam and Eve out past the slender columns that signify the gates of Paradise. Dressed in skins, they are carrying implements, the man a sickle, the woman a distaff. Adam looks back at God and at the cherub who is poised to guard the gates; Eve looks forward and points a finger out toward whatever lies ahead. The expressions on the cartoon-like faces are difficult to make out, but Eve seems to have a slight smile, as if she at least is not entirely devastated. In the beautiful Crusader Bible, made about a century later in France (and now in New York's Morgan Library), Adam and Eve, driven by a sword-wielding angel through the gate of a narrow tower, are less prepared for the world. They have no clothes and no tools. Still naked and ashamed, they are covering their genitals with fig leaves. Both bend their heads decorously in a sign of their sadness.

But nothing in the innumerable depictions of this scene could have anticipated the emotional intensity of the fresco of the expulsion painted around 1425 for the church of the Carmelite nuns in Florence. This fresco, by a young Tuscan artist, Tomasso di Ser Giovanni di Simone, or, as he is better known, Masaccio, has come to stand for the vast and momentous shift that took place under the pressure of the intellectual and artistic movement known as the Renaissance.

When I first saw this fresco, in the 1960s, the figures of Adam and Eve were modestly, if scantily, dressed in fig leaves. But a thorough cleaning in the 1980s removed the fig leaves—they turned out to have been a later addition—and disclosed that Masaccio's original Adam and Eve were stark naked. Under the impulsion of the sword-wielding angel, along with certain mysterious rays that seem to be spewing from the gate behind their backs, the figures are stepping forward, Eve's weight on her right leg, Adam's on his left.

They are both utterly bereft and miserable. Her head tilted back, her eyes closed, and her mouth open in a soundless wail, Eve attempts to cover her genitals with one hand, her breasts with the other. Excruciatingly aware that she is exposed, she responds, like the naked women in those infinitely cruel photographs taken by the Nazis, to a sense of shame that bears no relation to the scene in which she finds herself. That is, it is not a social emotion, not a preservation of dignity, which drives her to try to conceal her sex; it is a primordial sense of what she must do in the face of an unendurable exposure. Adam's response is different: his head bent down, he covers his face with both hands in a paroxysm of misery.

The art historian Michael Baxandall has suggested that there is a moral distinction drawn in the fresco between the woman and the man: Eve's gestures reveal that she is experiencing shame, while Adam's disclose his sense of guilt. Perhaps. Masaccio's unforgettable figures depend, in any case, on their overwhelming sense of embodiment, an illusion of actuality conjured up by perspective and heightened by the shadows that they cast and by the effect of movement. Adam's right foot still touches the threshold of Paradise, but not for long. They are in the world now, and unlike the angel who possesses wings, a beautiful garment, a sword, and a kind of magic carpet, the humans are utterly unprepared. The prime source of their misery no doubt is the shame and guilt they feel as a result of their transgression, but the glimpse of the barren soil on which their feet now tread might suggest another, more material source as well. They are entering a very harsh environment, and they have nothing whatsoever to shield or protect them. From this perspective Adam's penis, strikingly central in the fresco's composition once the overpainted fig leaves were removed, is less a sign of his virility than of his being what Shakespeare calls "unaccommodated man."

Masaccio died in 1428, at the age of twenty-six, but in his brief lifetime he almost single-handedly transformed Italian art. Young painters came to study what he had done and to emulate the revolutionary new techniques that gave to his images so much dramatic power. His Adam and Eve were no longer abstract, decorative emblems of human guilt; they were particular suffering people who had bodies with volume, weight, and, above all, movement.

At almost the same moment, in the north of Europe, another great artist, the Flemish master Jan van Eyck, found a comparably radical way to give Adam and Eve a startlingly new bodily reality. The figures on the outer panels of his celebrated Ghent Altarpiece from 1432 are not dramatic in the way that Masaccio's are. They do not howl in grief or shudder in guilt, nor are they being violently driven out of the Garden. They stand in painted niches at the far ends of a vast vision of redemption through the mystic Lamb of God.

Redeemed at the end of time will be all of those whom God has elected to save, an immense multitude of the descendants of the first humans. Van Eyck depicts them in the central panel, gathered around the fountain of living waters. Adam and Eve themselves, it was thought, will be included in this multitude, so the figures are there in their niches not only as the pair who initiated sin but also as among the saved.

There was nothing new in this theological expectation. What was new in these panels was the truly startling life-likeness of the naked man and woman. They are almost life-sized, and, since the painter's miraculous brushwork is concealed, they seem somehow present in every pore beneath the perfectly finished surface. In today's Ghent the viewer is no longer allowed to approach the great altarpiece; it has had, after all, a melancholy tradition of violation, including Nazi theft and, in the nineteenth century, the painting of clothing on Adam and Eve. But with digital imaging, it is now possible to get eerily close, and still the figures seem to be there in the flesh. They cover their genitals with fig leaves, but the gestures of modesty seem only to intensify their exposure and to invite an almost compulsive, amazed inspection of their nakedness. Adam's expression is sober; his hands are reddened, probably from labor. Eve holds an odd-looking fruit in one hand, probably some kind of citrus; her belly—the womb from which we all descended—is strikingly prominent. Everything, in the minutest detail, seems to be open to view; Adam's clipped toenails and his random hairs are particularly disturbing.

No artist, including Michelangelo, who painted his famous fresco of the creation of Adam on the Sistine ceiling some eighty years later, has ever matched, let alone exceeded, the astonishing realism of Van Eyck's Adam and Eve. That Van Eyck was fully aware of what he had done is implicit in his entire conception of the work, but a small, invisible detail provides a special insight into this conception. An infrared reflec-togram—a modern technique for looking beneath the layers of paint in order to see the artist's original intentions and the alterations made as the work developed—revealed a startling change in the orientation of Adam's right foot. Van Ecyk had at first depicted Adam as standing fully within his niche, with both of his feet parallel to the picture frame. But at a certain point, presumably as the figure increasingly acquired the effect of bodily reality, he changed his mind. He turned the foot outward, so that the toes seem to be projecting out of the niche and toward the viewer. It is as if Adam had come alive and were stepping into our world.

In the fifteenth century, when the altarpiece was painted, Adam could only have this magical effect on viewers who happened to be in Ghent and went to St. Bavo's Cathedral and saw the altarpiece in its open state. The same need to be present in a particular place was true, of course, of Masaccio's Adam and Eve in the Carmine in Florence or the hundreds of other Renaissance paintings that participated in the project of conferring bodies on the first humans. All of these works were site-specific. In some cases, their reputation may have spread; sketches may have been produced and circulated. But their actual effects could only be experienced by those who ventured in person to the place to which they were firmly attached.

All of this changed in 1504, when the thirty-three-year-old Ger-man artist Albrecht Dürer produced his engraving of the *Fall of Man*. The engraving quickly became famous, and since the copperplate tech-nology meant that it could be handsomely reproduced again and again, it was successfully marketed and circulated. Thousands of people across Europe saw the same compelling image and were convinced that they now knew what the first humans in the Garden of Eden had looked like before the Fall. Almost nothing in the long history of Adam and Eve has had such satisfying specificity.

Dürer's engraving represents Adam and Eve, their glorious bodies fully facing us, on either side of the Tree of the Knowledge of Good

1. From the catacombs in Rome, one of the earliest surviving images of the Bible's first humans. *Adam and Eve,* third century CE, fresco.

Photo PCSA Archives.

2. The fallen Adam and Eve on the sarcophagus of a Roman Christian. *Sarcophagus of Junius Bassus* (detail), *c.* 359 CE.

3. Adam with some of the animals which he names. *Adam in the Garden of Eden,* fifth century.

4. The scenes on these bronze doors form an elaborate storytelling program, with scenes from Genesis on the left panel carefully paired with scenes from the gospels on the right. Bernward Doors, *c.* 1015.

5. A famous problem: who is the person looking on?
The Creation of Eve (detail from the Bernward Doors).

6. Adam blames Eve, Eve the serpent, and God all three. *The Judgment of Adam and Eve by God* (detail from the Bernward Doors).

7. God himself pushes Adam and Eve, carrying the implements they need for labor, out of paradise, twelfth century.

8. The twelfth-century figure of Eve, from the portal of the Cathedral of Saint-Lazare, seems suspended between penitence and provocation. Gislebertus, *The Temptation of Eve, c.* 1130.

9. As in this thirteenth-century crucifix, the head beneath the bleeding feet of Jesus is traditionally thought to be Adam, *c.* 1200.

10. Here God has only begun to turn the rib, taken from the sleeping Adam's side, into the woman.

11. Eve, in the company of Jews, brings death into the world, while Mary, holding the crucifix, offers redemption to the Christian faithful. *Mors per Evam, vita per Mariam, c.* 1420.

12. In Paradise, Dante and Beatrice see all of salvation history, from the Fall to the Annunciation to the Crucifixion. Giovanni di Paolo, *The Mystery of Redemption* from *Paradiso Canto VII, c.* 1450.

13. In the seventeenth century, long after they were painted, Masaccio's Adam and Eve were given fig leaves that were only removed in the 1980s. Masaccio, *The Expulsion* (from a photograph taken *c.* 1980, before its restoration), 1424–1428.

14. Masaccio emphasizes the nakedness and abject misery of Adam and Eve. Masaccio, *The Expulsion,* 1424–1428.

15. Adam and Eve seem to stand in their niches as if they were fully, eerily alive. The scene above Adam depicts the offerings of Cain and Abel; that above Eve depicts the murder of Abel by Cain. Jan and Hubert van Eyck, interior of left and right wings of the Ghent Altarpiece, 1432, oil on panel, Saint Bavo Cathedral, Ghent.

and Evil. Gone is the imagery of the enclosed, carefully manicured garden or the decorative gothic towers and archways. They are standing in a deep forest; a rabbit, an elk, and an ox are visible in the shadows behind them. The only glimpse of the sky is in the far distance, above a crag on which a mountain goat, barely visible, seems poised to jump. The fatal tree is not strikingly different in form from any other tree around them, but it is bearing fruit that hangs on the branches just above Eve's head. Eve holds one of these fruits in her left hand; in plucking it, she has taken some of the tree along with the fruit, for a twig extends from its stem across half of her body. There is no trace of shame in her posture, but the leaves on the twig just happen to cover her genitals. In her other hand, she is also holding a fruit in her fingertips. She is presumably receiving it from the serpent that is coiled around the tree, but her gesture is delicate and ambiguous enough to suggest that she could be feeding the animal instead of being fed by it. She has turned her head, her long hair flowing out behind her, and is looking intently at the serpent and the fruit.

Adam has also turned his head, but he is directing his gaze at Eve. Reaching back with his right hand, he holds onto the branch of a tree, presumably the Tree of Life; a smaller branch from lower in the trunk of that tree happens to cover his genitals. His left arm reaches out toward Eve, and his hand is open, as if ready to receive the fruit that she is taking from the serpent's mouth. They are still perfectly innocent and unashamed, but this is the last moment. Adam is about to let go of his hold on the Tree of Life. Human nature will change forever, and in the same instant, all of nature will change.

The Bible said nothing about whether the animals in the Garden of Eden were fated to die natural deaths. The verses in Genesis only suggested that the first creatures were all vegetarians: "And to every beast of the earth, and to every fowl of the air, and to every thing that creepeth upon the earth, wherein there is life," God declares, "I have given every green herb for meat" (Gen. 1:30). This diet will soon be altered forever. Adam nearly steps on the tail of a small mouse, while a cat dozes by his other foot. We know that as soon as the fatal fruit is eaten, the cat will pounce and the poor mouse too will be eaten. But like the suspended leap of the mountain goat in the distance, it is all in the realm of the not-quite-yet.

The depiction of this final moment of innocence, captured as if by a camera with a very fast shutter speed, is brilliant enough to account for the work's almost instant celebrity. Connoisseurs marveled at the artist's astonishing technical skill, a skill that, as a great Dürer scholar remarks, "does equal justice to the warm glow of human skin, to the chilly slipperiness of a snake, to the metallic undulations of locks and tresses, to the smooth, shaggy, downy, or bristly quality of animals' coats, and to the twilight of a primeval forest." But what most seized Dürer's contemporaries was the sheer unconstrained beauty of the two naked figures, our first parents, and particularly the beauty of Adam. It was as if almost no one had seen such bodily perfection before, certainly not in Masaccio's despairing Adam, or Van Eyck's bulb-shaped Eve, let alone Hildesheim's bronze icons of shame.

To be sure, many equally splendid nudes were created precisely at this time or shortly thereafter. Seized by the desire to resuscitate ancient art, with its plethora of idealized nudes, Renaissance painters and sculptors turned to Adam and Eve, who could be represented unclothed in all their unfallen majesty. The whole of the sixteenth century is rich in such representations, with particularly celebrated paintings by Titian, Tintoretto, and Veronese in Italy, and by the elder and younger Cranach, Lucas van Leyden, Hans Baldung Grien, and Jan Gossaert in the north. And, of course, literally looming over all of these paintings is the giant Adam awakened to life on Michelangelo's Sistine ceiling.

But even in this vast field of genius, the influence of Dürer's Adam and Eve is preeminent. It is as if the copperplate engraving was an enormous stone thrown into a pond where it continued to produce endless

ripples. Even when the artist pushed back aggressively against Dürer—
as when Baldung Grien turned Adam into a decaying corpse—the
master's fingerprints are detectable. The 1504 image, so public and so
perfect, was the almost inescapable model.

This perfection did not come easily; it was the consequence of a
decades-long search, and, as with other great advances in the Adam
and Eve story, it drew upon everything in the artist's whole career and
life. Prodigiously gifted from childhood, trained first in the shop of his
goldsmith father and then as an apprentice to a painter, Dürer mastered
the art of representing virtually everything that attracted his keen
gaze: a pond in the woods, the shimmering colors in a bird's wing,
a clump of grass, a beetle. The humbleness of many of the objects
on which he expended his stupendous gifts did not embarrass him:
"I believe that no man liveth," he wrote, "who can grasp the whole
beauty of the meanest living creature." He was astonished and thrilled
by the inexhaustible variety of things: "If to live many hundred years
were granted" to a skilled artist, he wrote, he would have more than
enough "daily to mold and make many new figures of men and other
creatures, which none had before seen nor imagined." It is precisely
artistic skill—a combination of God-given talent and immensely hard
work—that enables the observer to perceive this marvelous variety,
as well as to capture at least a few of its innumerable manifestations.
Where the untrained eye sees only a small repertoire of forms tediously
reduplicated, Dürer saw a vast panorama of diverse objects. His particular training as a maker of woodcuts and engravings heightened his
sensitivity to this diversity, for he knew, as he wrote, that it was impossible for the most skilled artist to produce the exact same picture twice
or even to print identical images from the same copperplate.

At thirteen years old, Dürer turned his formidable powers of attention on himself. He stared into a mirror (an uncommon household
object at the time) and drew what he saw. Some forty years later, after
he had become so renowned that even his casual scraps were treasured,

he came upon this drawing among his papers and wrote a signed note upon the top of the sheet: "This I fashioned after myself out of a mirror in the year 1484 when I was still a child." An impressive display of skill, the drawing initiated a lifelong practice of self-portraiture, a practice analyzed in a superb study by the art historian Joseph Koerner. One of the most unusual of these self-portraits was made in 1503, the year before the engraving of Adam and Eve: with a pen and brush, Dürer drew himself nude. Silhouetted against a dark background, he leans slightly forward, weight on one leg, his long hair pulled back in a net, his face sober and alert, his muscles taut. His nakedness is without a touch of shame. To call this self-portrait unusual is an understatement: there is, as Koerner notes, nothing like it in all of Western art until Egon Schiele in the early twentieth century.

Whatever Dürer thought he was doing, whether he was motivated by self-love or by self-concern, whether he was celebrating himself or grimly diagnosing the effects of an illness, the drawing must bear some relation to the naked bodies in the nearly contemporaneous Adam and Eve engraving. Dürer had already been thinking about that engraving for some time, imagining possible poses, drawing life studies and abstract geometrical models, sketching hands holding or reaching for fruit, brooding about the ideal shape of the human body. He had studied and drawn many nudes; when the Renaissance reawakened an interest in the statuary of Greece and Rome, this became a central element in any artist's training and an important part of studio practice. But the 1503 nude self-portrait is something different; it bears witness to the search for the original, the essential body.

Dürer was a descendant of Adam—of that he was sure—and this descent must mean that his own naked body had, at least to a small extent, to resemble Adam's. Of course, in Paradise Adam's body was perfect, and all bodies since that time had fallen away from the original perfection. Nonetheless, to grasp Adam's body—so far back in the past, so inaccessible—Dürer evidently felt that he had to grasp himself.

It did not matter that no artist before him had gone this far: he was compelled to look at, to assess, and to represent with characteristic intensity his own unmasked, unprotected flesh. Far from concealing his genitals, his nude self-portrait makes them strikingly central, as if to disclose what is ordinarily hidden behind the fig leaf of clothing. But whether his family resemblance to the first human confirmed the artist's narcissism or undermined it by calling attention to how far his body was from perfection is not clear.

What is clear is that Dürer felt he could not use any body he had ever observed—his own or that of anyone else—as the life model for his Adam. He had to make Adam perfectly beautiful. Though there was beauty to be glimpsed everywhere in the world, including in the image he stared at in a mirror, that beauty was not the same as what was embodied in the first man and the first woman—the only two humans created directly by God. "Originally," Dürer wrote, "the Creator made humans the way they ought to be." To conceive that beauty in the imagination, let alone to capture it in an image, was almost impossible; after all, there was, he believed, no one alive who could grasp the whole beauty even of a blade of grass.

All the same, as he made clear in his *Four Books on Human Proportion* and other theoretical treatises, he set himself the task of seeing—and accurately representing—the whole beauty of the most beautiful of all living creatures: the naked human body as God first intended it to look. Though the challenge was all but impossibly great, Dürer told himself that it befitted him to rise to it: "Let us not," he wrote, "take unto ourselves thoughts fit for cattle." And, though he knew he might fail, he was confident that his training, his study, and his particular genius had prepared him better than anyone living for this undertaking.

Dürer had a sharp eye for endless differences, even among the superficially similar creatures of the same species. He had ventured out in the world and knew that there were more things in heaven and earth than were dreamed of in and around Nuremberg. By 1500 he had almost certainly heard of the discoveries made by Columbus, discoveries that unsettled the geographical and ethnographical map of the world. (Years later he would see for himself some of the objects sent back by Cortés from Mexico and would write that this treasure "was much more beautiful to me than miracles.") As a Christian, he believed in a single truth for all humankind, but that truth did not erase all distinctions. Beauty celebrated in one place was not necessarily celebrated in another. "There are many different kinds of men in various lands," he noted; "whoso travels far will find this to be so and see it before his eyes."

But in the search for the true form of Adam and Eve, Dürer was committed to finding "the most beautiful human figure conceivable," that is, the one perfect model for all humanity, in all times and in all places. "I will not advise anyone to follow me," he wrote, "for I only do what I can, and that is not enough even to satisfy myself." He decided that the best, possibly the only, way forward was to imitate the ancient Greek painter Zeuxis. No work by Zeuxis, who lived in the fifth century BCE, had survived, but among the many stories that were still in circulation about him was one that told how he successfully managed to depict Helen of Troy, the most beautiful woman in the world. Unable to find a suitable model, he gathered instead five beautiful women to serve as his models and selected from each of them their finest feature, which he then blended together into a triumphant portrait. Dürer thus set about observing and collecting particular features.

A sheet of drawings survives in which Dürer, with his exquisite attention, observed the way that hands reach for or grasp a piece of fruit, and especially the wrinkles in the wrist caused by such an action. Whose wrist this was remains unknown, but the key point is that it belonged to a particular person at whom the artist, pen in hand, stared. You could not, as Dürer wrote, simply make up from within yourself what you longed to represent. Even the greatest artist had to look and sketch and store up in his mind what he had actually seen. "Thence the gathered, secret treasure of the heart is openly manifested in the work, and the new creature, which a man createth in his heart, appeareth."

In the secret treasure of Dürer's heart were stored many particular bodies and parts of bodies—this wrist, that shoulder, these thighs, and the like—along with such crucial details as the precise way the toe touches the ground when the weight is being carried on the other foot, or the way the hip rises and the side creases when the arm is extended. It seems to be Dürer's own side—as he had observed it in a mirror and sketched it in the nude self-portrait—that served as the model for what Adam looked like when he reached out his hand for the fatal fruit. But at this distance it is impossible to identify with any certainty the sources of most of Adam and Eve's features.

Perhaps there is a hint. In one of his notebooks, Dürer jotted down observations about Africans he had seen. (Several powerful drawings attest to his interest.) He remarked that their shinbones were too prominent and their knees and feet too bony. But then, having listed these problems, he went on to write, "I have seen some amongst them whose whole bodies have been so well-built and handsome that I never beheld finer figures, nor can I conceive how they might be bettered, so excellent were their arms and all their limbs." No evidence survives that Dürer used black models for his first humans. But, as he was obsessively in search of figures that could not be bettered and as he wrote that he had seen such figures among the Africans he observed, it is tempting to think that he had such excellent arms and limbs in mind when he engraved Adam and Eve.

The problem remained that even when he gathered and conjoined the best features that he could find, he knew that a sufficiently gifted artist could always claim to find a more beautiful figure. He felt he himself had seen and sketched instances of such superior beauty in the classical nudes that the Renaissance had once again put into circulation. The source of superiority, he concluded, must reside not so much in the particular features as in the proportions, but since there were so many differences among individuals, calculating the exact proportions of perfect beauty eluded him: "It seemeth to me impossible for a man to say that he can point out the best proportions for the human figure; for the lie is in our perception and darkness abideth so heavily about us that even our gropings fail."

In 1500, Dürer encountered an artist, the Venetian painter Jacopo de' Barbari, who claimed to have come up with the answer: "He showed me the features of a man and a woman that he made according to a canon of proportions." This canon of proportions was what Dürer was looking for: not or not only nude bodies, including his own, with all of their peculiar differences, but rather a set of objective geometrical measurements that would enable the artist to draw the ideal human body. Unfortunately, Jacopo evidently regarded the crucial details as trade secrets, and he refused to share them with the talented young German painter. "I would now rather see what his method was," Dürer later wrote, "than behold a new kingdom."

By the time he met Jacopo, Dürer may have had trade secrets of his own. Around 1490, near Anzio, south of Rome, an ancient marble statue had been unearthed. Nearly intact, it was a second-century Roman copy of a Greek depiction of the sun god Apollo. Even before Pope Julius II installed it in the Vatican cortile, where it became known as the *Apollo Belevedere,* the statue had begun to arouse the interest of artists. When he traveled to Italy in 1494–95, Dürer did not see it for himself, since he did not get all the way to Rome, but he must have seen careful drawings of it or copies in wax or bronze. It was, he began to think, the solution to the riddle he had been desperate to solve. He measured and calculated. Here were the exact proportions he was seeking: head one-eighth of body length, face one-tenth; square of chest one-sixth, with its base at one-third from the crown of the head.

Starting as early as 1495, Dürer drew the figure again and again, trying to capture not only its proportions but also its precise form, the way the weight was carried on one leg, the way the knees were bent, the way one arm reached back and the other up, the way the head was turned. Sometime around 1503 he took his ruler and compass and once again with pen and brown ink measured out the proportions of the figure. The arms and hands are unfinished—they could be intended to hold a goblet and snake, as in a drawing he made in 1501, or a scepter and sun disk, as in a drawing he made in 1502. But this time he turned over the sheet on which he had made his preliminary sketch and, using it as his guide, drew a man holding onto the branch of a tree with one hand and holding an apple with the other. He had turned Apollo into Adam.

This then was how Dürer exquisitely created his Adam: a figure made up out of beautiful pieces of bodies stitched together according to an idealizing geometrical scheme drawn from a pagan idol. For his Eve—though, to my eyes, slightly less successfully—he did the same. Then, smoothing the copperplate and coating it with wax, he drew the figures in mirror image. Next he took the burin—the sharp, tempered-steel tool of which he was the absolute master—and carefully incised the dense network of lines on the plate. When the plate was heated and inked, he made the first print and saw what he had made. He had every reason to be immensely pleased. Reproduced again and again, sold throughout Europe and, eventually, around the world, the engraving became the definitive image of Adam and Eve, or as close to definitive as any single representation of figures so widely and frequently depicted could possibly be. Of course, along with everyone else who picked up a pen, Dürer continued to draw and paint images of Adam and Eve. But all subsequent images, his own and those of others, have an odd way of seeming to allude, deliberately or inadvertently, in homage or in opposition, to the 1504 pair.

The Fall of Man engraving secured his name and fame, as Dürer seems to have been confident that it would. Just behind the branch onto which Adam holds, there is another branch, so close that it almost looks like an extension, on which there sits a parrot, one of those creatures whose beauty the artist longed to capture. Next to the parrot, just over Adam's shoulder, there hangs—at once naturalistically and with the utmost implausibility—a tablet on which, along with his monogram, is inscribed "ALBERT DVRER NORICUS FACIEBAT 1504" (Albrecht Dürer from Nuremberg made this, 1504). The Latin verb actually has the sense of extended time—not "made" but "was making." The sign suggests that there in the Garden at the decisive moment in the history of the world the artist was present, and not merely present but at work. It is because of Albrecht Dürer's "making"—the work that he did in engraving the copper plate and the work that continues every time the image on the plate is reproduced—that we, in our fallen condition, have a vision of those perfect bodies that existed before time and labor and mortality began.

9

Chastity and Its Discontents

If the most influential contribution to the image of Adam and Eve was made by Albrecht Dürer in 1504, the most influential contribution to their story was made almost two centuries later by the English writer John Milton. *Paradise Lost* is—or so I and many others believe—the greatest poem in the English language. But it is something more: an unprecedented, even shocking fulfillment of Augustine's injunction to interpret Genesis literally. Milton took this injunction as a challenge to make Adam and Eve real. And like Dürer, he brought to the challenge both every resource the Renaissance had crafted and every facet of his own turbulent life and times. His poem forever transformed the ancient narrative.

The decisive event of Milton's life—the experience to which his imagination ever afterward obsessively returned—was not his meeting with Galileo in Florence, not the outbreak of the English Civil War, not the beheading of the anointed king, not even his own descent into blindness. Rather it was the scant month or five weeks that he spent as a newlywed in the summer of 1642 with his young bride, Mary Powell. About the actual day-to-day experience of that brief period we know next to nothing; a curtain has been drawn that is impossible to pull back. Yet something happened in July of 1642, when he was thirty-three years old, that realigned everything in Milton's life and decisively shaped the great poem he would eventually write about Adam and Eve.

The eldest son of a wealthy moneylender and notary who had a passion for music, Milton was a brilliant, insatiable student. Everything in his education at London's elite St. Paul's School and then at Christ's College, Cambridge—his study of Greek, Hebrew, and Aramaic, his intense Bible reading, his immersion in theology—pointed in the direction of a conventional career as a learned Anglican churchman. Yet Milton, anything but conventional, never took orders and instead became a thorn in the side of the church establishment.

Already at Cambridge there were signs of trouble ahead. In the fall of 1626, the seventeen-year-old student had a serious altercation with his principal academic supervisor, his tutor William Chappell. The precise details are unknown, but Milton was whipped and then rusticated—sent home to London—for a term. The irate tutor maintained that Milton deserved to be turned away "both out of the University and out of the society of men." For his part, in a Latin poem he wrote to his best friend, Milton declared that he did not miss Cambridge in the slightest; he was having a far better time reading poetry, going to the theater, and ogling pretty girls.

All of this might suggest that Milton was a rowdy undergraduate—an enemy later wrote that he had been "vomited out" of the university after "an inordinate and riotous youth"—but something like the opposite was the case. An intellectually intense, long-haired aesthete, he despised both the university's academic curriculum, which he thought hopelessly antiquated, and its student culture, which he found fixated on heavy drinking and sexual exploits. His fellow students nicknamed him "The Lady of Christ's."

It is easy to imagine the cruel teasing that the fastidious poet must have received, but Milton was not unarmed: he possessed an unshakable self-confidence conjoined with verbal skills finely sharpened to draw blood. He did not need to establish his manhood by drinking and whoring, he told his classmates, any more than by farm labor. He would demonstrate his virility not in the brothel but in his writing. His prose was aggressive and cutting, while his poetry was full of erotic fantasies, thinly disguised in classical robes.

Milton shared his poems with his companions, above all with his friend Charles Diodati. It was to this intimate friend that he revealed his deepest literary ambition. "Listen, Diodati," he wrote in a letter of 1637, "but in secret, lest I blush; and let me talk to you grandiloquently for a while. You ask what I am thinking of? So help me God, an immortality of fame." Milton knew that there was something embarrassing about a young, largely untested writer having fantasies of soaring like Pegasus. Five years after he had graduated from Cambridge, Milton was living at home in the country—his father had recently moved from London to a small village near Windsor—and still endlessly reading. Many of his contemporaries had already married and had launched themselves into careers. Diodati, following in his father's footsteps, had become a physician. The twenty-nine-year-old Milton remained single, a perpetual student. But he was dreaming, as he confessed to his friend, of being celebrated as a great poet.

He was hardly making steady progress toward this goal. Long periods would pass without his producing anything of value. But, though he was living, as he put it, in "obscurity and cramped quarters," and though he granted that he should be blushing, he nonetheless felt stirring within him a sense of possible greatness. And in the fall of 1637 he was not, after all, without a reason to hope. He had already penned several works of extraordinary beauty: "L'Allegro" and "Il Penseroso," companion poems about joy and melancholy; "Lycidas," a poignant elegy on a college friend who had drowned; and, most ambitiously, a dramatic poem known as *Comus,* commissioned for the wealthy and powerful Earl of Bridgewater and performed at Ludlow Castle on September 29, 1634.

Comus was what was called a masque, a theatrical entertainment created for a single formal occasion. The occasion was a gala celebration of the earl's appointment as the chief administrator of Wales, and the performers included the earl's own children, his fifteen-year-old daughter Alice and her two younger brothers. The Bridgewaters were near the top of the English social hierarchy, but they had a skeleton rattling noisily in their closet: a few years earlier the earl's brother-in-law had been executed on charges of sodomy and rape. The details were the stuff of film noir: greed, sexual perversity, incest, and murder all tangled together. At the sensational trial that led to his conviction, the principal witness against him was his wife.

The scandal was recent enough to make the Bridgewaters highly sensitive to the potential stain on their public image, and they may therefore have directed the young poet to write something in praise of sexual propriety. Milton, who was in his mid-twenties at the time, clearly found the theme congenial and could well have come up with the idea on his own: a masque that celebrates the special power of chastity. His plot centers on a girl—called simply "Lady"—who, together with her two brothers, becomes lost in the woods on the way to meet their parents. When the brothers go off to search for food and water and fail to return, she falls into the hands of the evil sorcerer Comus. Comus leads the unsuspecting virgin to his pleasure palace where, once seated on an enchanted chair, she finds herself unable to move, fixed to the spot with "gums of glutinous heat." The wily sorcerer, praising the pleasures of sensual indulgence, offers her a drink from his magical cup, but she spurns his "brewed enchantments" and invokes the aid of temperance and chastity. Protected by her steadfast virtue, she is eventually rescued, reunited with her brothers, and led to her loving parents.

Milton turned this fairy-tale story of a young girl's triumphant virginity into a magnificent display of learning and poetic skill: he presented the Bridgewater family over a thousand lines of gorgeous verse, rich in classical allusions and musical effects. *Comus* was a grand public spectacle in honor of the elite recipients, and not the author's private statement. Yet Milton's one venture in the masque form was charged with a peculiar and deeply personal intensity. When the "lewd and lavish act of sin," the Lady's brother warns, "Lets in defilement to the inward parts,/The soul grows clotted by contagion." The "lewd and lavish act of sin" must at all costs be avoided. *Comus* was a display of the poet's commitment to preserving his own virginity and keeping his soul from becoming clotted.

The mockery he encountered from the fellow undergraduates who called him "Lady" makes it clear that Milton's view was not typical of the young men of his day. Then, as throughout most of history, concern with virginity focused on unmarried girls. Milton believed that this focus was a reversal of what should rightly be the case. He had, he later wrote, thought it all through. If unchastity in a woman is a scandal, then it must be even more dishonorable in a man, who is "both the image and glory of God."

Augustine and his friend Alypius would have entirely approved: in taking monastic vows, they committed themselves to lives of sexual continence. Yet, though he had kept his virginity intact throughout his twenties, Milton was not arguing for the Catholic ideal of the monastery and nunnery. As a good Protestant, he embraced instead the ideal of "married chastity." The purity he longed to protect and preserve in himself was, he believed, fully compatible with sexual intercourse, provided that this intercourse was sanctified by marriage. He must preserve his virginity until his wedding night.

The fervid evangelical religious climate of the early seventeenth century aroused similar anxieties and similar convictions in other earnest young men, though they remained a distinct minority. What was altogether unusual was any link to poetry. Milton's fear that the "lavish act of sin"—premarital sexual intercourse—would threaten his poetic inspiration and compromise his dream of immortality was distinctly peculiar. Then, as for many centuries before (and after), poetry was inseparably bound up with erotic longing and fulfillment. Creative power was ordinarily thought to be heightened by sexual desire, not extinguished by it. Steeped in Ovid and Catullus, Shakespeare and Donne, Milton grasped this perfectly: his sorcerer Comus speaks the seductive language of *carpe diem*. But the Lady—the Lady in the masque and the Lady of Christ's—would firmly resist the seduction.

Milton's effort to preserve his virginity for marriage may have been a difficult one, first at Cambridge, then London, and then in the country. The brothels were open for business on the outskirts of Cambridge, prostitutes plied their trade at the London theaters that Milton frequented, and the bookish young man must at least on occasion have gazed longingly at the pliant milkmaids. But he resisted. In one of his later works, he remarked, presumably glancing back at himself, that it is possible to control sexual desire through diet—avoiding certain foods believed to provoke lust—and exercise. And, of course, he cultivated his intense male friendships, buried himself in books, and surfaced to write at least some of the poetry that this sexual restraint was meant to protect and enhance.

The real test must have come in 1638 when the thirty-year-old Milton, accompanied by a servant, embarked for the Continent. After a brief stop in Paris (which he seems not to have liked), he traveled on to Italy, where he remained for more than a year, visiting many cities and staying for extended periods in Florence, Rome, Naples, and Venice. Fluent in Italian, the cultivated Milton was welcomed by an impressive array of intellectuals, poets, artists, and scientists, along with their aristocratic patrons. In Florence he called upon the seventy-five-year-old Galileo, under house arrest for life, "a prisoner," as Milton put it, "to the Inquisition, for thinking in astronomy otherwise than the Franciscan and Dominican licensers thought." Everywhere he went in Italy, he toured rich libraries, attended concerts, and exchanged Latin poems with newfound friends. In the letters he sent home to his nephew and others, he praised the natural beauty of the landscape, the splendid climate, the refinement of the language, "the nobleness of the structures, the exact humanity and civility of the inhabitants."

In the many surviving traces of this extended trip, there is absolutely no hint of sexual adventures. This may not seem so surprising: why would any such hints survive? But, by Milton's own account, he returned to England from this extended sojourn abroad with his virginity, as well as his Protestantism, safely intact. If true (and there is no reason to doubt it), then Milton may have been among the very few young Englishmen of his day who came back from such travels in a state of sexual innocence. For English gentlemen on the Grand Tour, Italy was the world of Marcantonio Raimondi's *Modi* (celebrated engravings of sexual positions, accompanied by Aretino's lubricious sonnets); of paintings by Giulio Romano, Annibale Carracci, Correggio, and many other masters of erotic arousal; of sculptures that captured in stone the touch of fingers on warm flesh. And the pleasures were not only virtual: contemporary English travelers to Italy routinely bore witness to the beauty of its women and, more to the point, to the sophisticated delights of its courtesans.

Though he moved easily in Italian high society, from literary and scientific academies to aristocratic salons to the courts of cardinals and bishops, Milton seems to have gone out of his way to signal what he took to be his moral superiority. In Counter-Reformation Italy of all places, he should hardly have been outspoken about his religious convictions—he was, after all, a guest, received with extraordinary graciousness by his Catholic hosts—but he evidently refused to be discreet. In a letter to a friend, the Dutch poet Nicolas Heinsius reported that "the Englishman"—Milton—"was hated by the Italians, among whom he lived a long time, on account of his over-strict morals." The ardently Protestant thirty-year-old virgin made it clear that he would not be seduced.

Milton was in Naples, contemplating extending his travels to Sicily and Greece, when he heard disquieting reports from England: the political situation, already tense when he departed, had deteriorated, and the country seemed to be drifting into increasingly dangerous waters. He decided that, rather than voyaging out still further, he would return home. All the same, he did not hurry. He had not resolved the vocational problem that had been weighing on him. He clearly loved being in Italy, "the lodging place," as he put it, "of *humanitas* and of all the arts of civilization." And he may not have felt ready to face directly a grievous personal loss: at some point after August 1638 he had received word that his beloved friend, his soul mate Charles Diodati, had died.

Shortly after he returned to England, in the summer of 1639, Milton sat down and commemorated his friend's death in a long pastoral elegy in Latin. The conventions of the genre—a lamenting shepherd and his flocks in an idyllic, classical Greek landscape—create a kind of formal distance from the real world, but the poem is nonetheless intense, intimate, and revealing. When the terrible news reached him in Italy, he wrote, he did not fully allow himself to register its reality. It was only at home that he experienced the full immensity of his grief. Was it so important, he now asked himself, to travel far away in order to see "Rome in its grave" and to stay away so long, when he could have remained in the company of his dearest friend? Had he not put such a distance between them, he would at least have been able to touch the hand of his dying companion and say farewell. Now he was left with a sense of unutterable loneliness. The consoling thought to which Milton clung at the end of his poem is that Charles—"a youth without stain"—must have ascended in glory to the heavens. "Because the joy of the marriage bed was never tasted," Milton addressed his dead friend, "virginal honors are reserved for you."

How much consolation the thirty-two-year-old Milton's own "virginal honors" seemed to him at this point is not clear. He was no longer a promising youth at the threshold of a brilliant career, but what exactly was he? Money was not really the issue: his moneylending father had assigned some loans to his son's name, so that Milton, who set himself up in London, now had a small independent income. He supplemented that income by undertaking to educate a few private pupils, starting with his two nephews. But all of that obsessive study and the massive learning and immense intellectual ambition—would it wind up in a schoolmaster whipping a handful of young charges for failing correctly to conjugate Latin verbs?

The dream of literary immortality had not died in him. Milton filled pages of notes—they survive in the library of Trinity College Cambridge—with the titles and brief outlines of possible literary projects, most of them for tragedies on biblical themes. There are multiple sketches of a five-act play on the fall of man, one of them titled "Adam unparadiz'd" and another, "Paradise Lost." Milton carefully listed the characters: they would have included Adam and Eve, of course, along with a range of figures from Lucifer to Moses, and from Mercy to Discontent. Then he crossed the whole list out. He would no doubt have found it a difficult play to write, given his scant experience of women. In any case, Milton did not get far with any of his projects. History intervened.

The country was falling apart, bitterly divided between Charles I, who dreamt of absolute rule, and a hostile, increasingly intransigent Parliament. As in the chaotic months leading up to the French or Russian revolutions, there were innumerable factions, jostling opinions, failed attempts at compromise, unlikely allies, shifting enmities. But to Milton in the early 1640s, there was a single great struggle: the godly against the ungodly. At the center of the ungodly, in his view, were the bishops of the Church of England: wealthy, worldly, cynical, swollen with conceit, and hopelessly mired in error. At the center of the godly were the enlightened visionaries of radical religious reform, men and women sometimes called by their enemies Puritans. These brave reformers had allies in Parliament who were willing to stand up to the armed legions controlled by the bishops and the king.

In the early 1640s matters began to come to a head. In the City of London, not far from Milton's house, Puritan-inspired mobs rioted, demanding "Root and Branch" reforms to save England from popery by abolishing the episcopacy. Accounts of arrests, demonstrations, Parliamentary grievances, troop movements, and massacres filled the broadsheets that clandestine printing presses ground out in enormous numbers.

Immersed in his books and occasionally surfacing to drill his pupils in Greek, Latin, and Hebrew, Milton had thus far been observing the growing turmoil from the sidelines. But beginning in 1641 he could no longer hold himself back in watchful waiting. In five long treatises, written and published in a remarkably short time, he unleashed upon the bishops and their apologists all of the contempt and rage, along with the massive learning, that had been bottled up within him. The long apprenticeship spent honing his sarcasm in response to the teasing of his boozing, wenching classmates and the intellectual aridity of his overbearing teachers suddenly made sense: the two enemies, in his imagination, fused into one. The bishops, he wrote, typically were men who "spend their youth in loitering, bezzling [i.e., boozing], and harlotting, their studies in unprofitable questions and barbarous sophistry, their middle age in ambition and idleness, their old age in avarice, dotage, and diseases."

But what justification did Milton offer for setting himself up as the judge of those so high above his station and venting upon them what he called a "sanctified bitterness"? Who was he—a perpetual student who had written a masque on chastity and taken a Grand Tour to Italy—to weigh in on the fate of the nation? His answer, in a work he published in April 1642, lay in the same deep reading and moral discipline on which he hoped to found his career as a great poet. His authority and inspiration, he asserted, came not solely from his intellectual rigor but from his purity. He had never been defiled by sex out of wedlock with any woman. He was a thirty-three-year-old virgin. *That* was his moral authority.

Little more than a month after he published this account of himself, Milton rode to a manor house called Forest Hill, near Oxford, concerning an outstanding loan, one of those investments that his prudent father had made on his behalf. The borrower, Richard Powell, had received £300 and had agreed to pay 8 percent interest in two yearly installments. The nation remained tense with the possibility of civil war—Milton himself had been training with a militia—but the roads between London and Oxfordshire were open, and the interest on the loan was due. Milton arrived at Forest Hill in June and returned to London in July. Whether he had obtained the £12 owed to him is not known. What is known is that he brought home with him a wife, the eldest daughter of the man who owed him money, seventeen-year-old Mary Powell.

Marriages between people of means in the seventeenth century were often more like protracted business negotiations than romantic courtships, but the suddenness of this one suggests, at least on Milton's part, something other than calculation. True, Milton had been long thinking about the nature of love, the moral qualities he hoped to find in a bride, the chastity compatible with the joys of the marriage bed, and so forth. But this was hardly the calculation typical of the marriage market. Rather, on the June afternoon when he first encountered the young girl, Milton seems to have felt the tantalizing possibility of bliss. And true, when the whirlwind courtship was concluded, Milton had a pledge from the girl's father for a dowry of £1,000, a very handsome sum indeed. But there had been no time for due diligence; the ardent suitor knew nothing about his father-in-law's solvency. In fact, Richard Powell was a shady land speculator who had no prospect of repaying the original £300 loan, let alone honoring the marriage settlement he expansively promised.

What the bride knew about her husband may have been equally negligible. Her family was staunchly Royalist in sympathies, and Milton had quickly established himself as one of the most fiercely outspoken enemies of the bishops. At a moment when the whole country was about to explode, could they really have avoided the subject altogether at the dinner table at Forest Hill? Perhaps Richard Powell, eager for the match, told his daughter and everyone else in his family to keep a wide berth of politics; and perhaps Milton, dazed and happy, gave his rage a rest.

However much or little they actually knew each other, John and Mary arrived, a married couple, at the small house on Aldersgate Street. The teenaged bride was accompanied to London by some of her relations—probably her parents and a few of her many siblings—who came to celebrate the nuptials. After several days the visitors left, and the newlyweds had time to begin to think about what they had done.

Milton had not, he fervently believed, compromised the chastity on which, for so many years, he had founded his sense of himself, his moral authority, and his poetic vocation. "Marriage," he wrote, "must not be call'd a defilement." God Himself had instituted it before the Fall, in the Garden of Eden, when Adam and Eve were still perfectly chaste and pure. A wedded couple could enjoy the state of innocence granted to Adam and Eve. When he married Mary Powell of Forest Hill, Milton could have said to himself, in Adam's words, "This is now bone of my bones, and flesh of my flesh." And if on the threshold of the bedroom he experienced a twinge of anxiety, he could have recalled the words that followed in Genesis: "And they were both naked, the man and his wife, and were not ashamed."

He was, he thought, about to enter Paradise.

•   •   •

MARY POWELL LASTED IN her new life as Mrs. Milton for little more than a month before she moved back to Forest Hill. The official excuse was an "earnest suit" by her mother for her daughter's company, with a promise that she would return to London in about four weeks' time, that is, toward the end of September. Neither she nor her husband left a direct account of the domestic misery that must have sent her packing so soon after the wedding and with so flimsy an excuse. Milton's nephew put the blame on the "philosophical life" at Aldersgate Street, irksome to a young woman who was accustomed to a lively country house. The seventeenth-century gossip John Aubrey, ferreting around for further details, heard that Mary had been raised "where there was a great deal of company and merriment, dancing etc." She found herself in a somber house that no one came to visit, its quiet broken only by the weeping of the young schoolboys whom her husband was beating in the adjoining room. So much for joys of the philosophical life. Aubrey jotted down in his notebook a further cause of dissension: Mistress Powell was a Royalist, and "different religions do not well on the same bolster."

Mary did not return at the appointed time, nor did she send word to clarify the situation. It was the abandoned husband who wrote to her, but he received no answer. He wrote again and then again, but still there was no response from Forest Hill. In the meantime, the national crisis worsened. Accounts of the past tend to keep the personal and the political in separate spheres, but of course they always bleed into one another.

In August 1642 a very young, unhappy woman fled from a marriage in which she felt trapped, and in the same month King Charles I took the fateful step in Nottingham of gathering his troops around him, raising his standard—a banner on which was written the motto "Give Caesar His Due"—and launching a civil war. Two events could not be more unlike, and yet they did not occur in separate universes.

Milton and his bride may not have argued in bed over points of difference between Anglicanism and Puritanism, but the outbreak of hostilities would certainly have exacerbated and hardened whatever tensions had already been simmering. At the most practical level, travel between London—the heart of the Parliamentary party—and Royalist Oxfordshire became at first difficult, then risky, then extremely dangerous. Milton did not go to Forest Hill himself to fetch his wife, but when his letters went unanswered, he dispatched a servant. The servant returned, Milton's nephew Edward Phillips recalled, not only without a satisfactory answer but also with the news that he had been "dismissed with some sort of contempt."

The bride's family had no doubt been enthusiastic at first about the match to the wealthy Londoner to whom they owed a great deal of money. At a different time, they might have urged, even compelled, their unhappy daughter to return to her lawful husband. But in the fall of 1642, from the perspective of Forest Hill, it appeared that the king, who had established his headquarters at nearby Oxford, would soon make mincemeat of his enemies. Once the court party gained the upper hand and restored order to the land, there would be a reckoning with the troublemakers. And among those who had disturbed the peace was the intemperate and arrogant man who had written those incendiary tracts against the bishops. Mary stayed put at Forest Hill.

And Milton? Milton remained in his house in London. It was not a pleasant time. He had made a catastrophic mistake, and he did not have the excuse of green youth. He had long prided himself on his profound learning, his moral rectitude, and his eloquence. He harbored—not as a well-kept secret but as an open promise to himself and the world—a sense that he was destined for greatness. Now he had shown himself to be a fool, the object at once of pity and of ridicule.

By late October the king's army was moving steadily down the Thames valley toward London. The end of the insurrection was tantalizingly in sight. The royal forces reached Turnham Green—close enough to be the site now of a London Underground station on the District Line—only to encounter fortifications hastily erected by the trained militias, citizen bands of shopkeepers and artisans and apprentices, with a modest intermingling of old veterans. The king hesitated, assessed the situation (including the ominously approaching Parliamentary troops, led by the Earl of Essex), and pulled back. London was never again within his grasp.

Though Milton had been in training—a fastidious, long-haired poet shouldering a pike and marching up and down a parade ground—when the king's army approached, he did not emerge from Aldersgate Street and rush to Turnham Green to erect barricades. Instead, he wrote a sonnet that he tacked to his door (or perhaps he only imagined doing so). The poem begged whoever happened to approach his defenseless house to protect the person within from harm. Why? Because this was the house of a poet, and a poet possesses the ability to "spread thy name o'er lands and seas." This is not, it is fair to say, Milton at his most heroic. But it conveys, half-playfully and half-seriously, his faith in the power of poetry and in his own vocation. And the truth is that he was in his own way extraordinarily brave, though it was not a form of bravery that would catch the attention of a military historian.

At this moment of national crisis, Milton could have been expected either to lie low or, if he were determined to act rashly, to renew his polemic against the bishops. Instead, he did something else, something that took unbelievable courage or, alternatively, unbelievable self-absorption. He threw himself into writing a succession of impassioned tracts demanding that no-fault divorce with the right to remarry be made legally available to all English men and women. It was justified, he argued, by a proper understanding of the story of Adam and Eve.

Milton's contemporaries found these tracts shocking, and for good reason. In seventeenth-century England, marriages were considered binding for life; they came to an end only with the death of a spouse.

Back in the early sixteenth century, Henry VIII had broken with the Roman Catholic Church over what is often said to have been his demand for a divorce from Catherine of Aragon, his wife of eighteen years. In fact he was not seeking a divorce, nor did he receive one from the Protestant archbishop of Canterbury. Rather he was granted an annulment. The Church of England did not significantly change the Catholic understanding of marriage. It would take more than three hundred years before the changes for which Milton called were finally made legal in the Divorce Reform Act of 1969–73.

If a man and woman were legally wed—if there was no bigamy, incest, insanity, or other circumstance that should have prohibited betrothal in the first place and if the marriage was consummated—then the knot could not be untied. A wife whose husband repeatedly beat her or violently sodomized her might arouse sympathy. If the abuse was sufficiently cruel, she might even be granted a formal separation "from bed and board," though these were by no means easy to obtain. But, short of a case of adultery or heresy, there would be no grant of divorce and no right to remarry. So too in cases of desertion: if a wife deserted her husband (or vice versa), the abandoned spouse might well be pitied, but neither he nor she could find another mate and start over again. As for incompatibility—the recognition that a relationship had broken down and could not be repaired—that was a traditional subject for comedy and not a matter for the courts.

As it stood then, Milton was stuck in a marriage that he regarded as a catastrophic mistake—and so, for that matter, was Mary. Everything in Milton's nature rebelled against passively accepting the situation in which he now found himself. For years he had been saving himself for marriage. He was destined, he was absolutely convinced, for something better than the fate of quiet, melancholy compromise, seething resentment, or sly cheating that he saw all around him. Besides, the more he thought about it, the more the whole existing law seemed a nightmare, not just for him alone but for everyone.

The overwhelming problem was not that this law rested, as it did, on time-honored custom, hardened into the regulations of canon law. The free soul of a brave and learned person, Milton wrote, can easily sweep away "the rubbish of canonical ignorance." The truly serious issue was that the Messiah himself, citing the story of Adam and Eve, seemed explicitly to prohibit divorce, except on grounds of adultery.

In the gospel of Matthew, the Pharisees ask Jesus about the lawfulness of divorce. In reply, Jesus reminds them that in the book of Genesis the first man cleaves to his wife, and they become one flesh. "What therefore God hath joined together," the Savior declares, "let not man put asunder" (Matt. 19:4–6). No Christian who hoped to change the divorce laws could ignore or easily evade this passage.

Facing the difficulty squarely, Milton reinterpreted Jesus's words by invoking what was traditionally called "the law of charity." The New Testament was good news; it could not possibly intend to make the Mosaic law more inflexible and burdensome. Therefore, he wrote, Jesus's harsh pronouncements on divorce must not have meant what they seemed to mean. The Savior gave the Pharisees the answer that those "arrogant inquisitors" deserved. But the answer that he intended for men and women of good faith is entirely different, and the clue is his reference to Adam and Eve.

Jesus is instructing us to go back to the beginning of human life, to picture Adam alone in the Garden, and to grasp the end for which the Creator fashioned Eve. That end, Milton argued, was not first and foremost about sex. To believe that the bond of wedlock was principally instituted to satisfy and regulate the desires of the flesh was a fundamental error, one that collapsed humans into the category of mere beasts. The church, both Catholic and Anglican, had reduced what it meant for a man and a woman to be "one flesh" to the crude fact of ejaculation, what Milton called in one of his wilder phrases "the quintessence of an excrement."

Still less, he thought, was the principal purpose of marriage the generation of children. Even the church court was not foolish enough to believe that a marriage was invalid because it failed to bring forth offspring. God commanded the first humans to be fruitful and multiply, along with the cattle of the fields and the birds of the air. But the first marriage—the marriage of Adam and Eve—was instituted for a different reason, perfectly encapsulated in God's own words: "It is not good that man should be alone." There is nothing complicated or obscure here; everyone should be able to grasp its meaning. "Loneliness is the first thing which God's eye nam'd not good." The principal end of marriage is neither sex nor children; it is companionship. A solitary Adam, though he dwelt in Paradise, would have been condemned to unhappiness. It was, as Milton put it, for the "prevention of loneliness to the mind and spirit" that God created woman and brought her as a helpmeet to the man.

Confident that he grasped the purpose of the original, paradisal marriage, Milton tapped into his personal anguish. He articulated clearly and forcefully, perhaps for the first time ever, an experience to which anyone who has been in an unhappy marriage can attest. If you are married to the wrong person, your loneliness—"God-forbidden loneliness"—is not diminished but heightened. It should not be possible, for your spouse is there in the room with you, but you feel more alone than when you were solitary. The silences are charged with pain, and words, even ones meant to end the isolation, only intensify it. That is what those weeks in the summer of 1642 had taught him. He found the lesson unbearable.

And what about Mary? It was she, after all, who had left behind her parents and eleven brothers and sisters and the familiar servants in lively, bustling Forest Hill, she who came at the age of seventeen to the somber house on Aldersgate Street, she who might well have found her much older, bookish, fiercely argumentative husband strange and off-putting. Mary was the one who in her new life must have felt excruciatingly lonely. It would be agreeable to think that Milton recognized her suffering, as well as his own, and in principle at least he was poised to do so. The incendiary pamphlet that he published anonymously in August 1643, a year after Mary had abandoned him, was entitled *The Doctrine and Discipline of Divorce, Restored to the Good of Both Sexes*. Both sexes, not just the male.

Yet everything in the way that Milton described the dilemma he took it upon himself to solve suggests that he was only truly alert to his own misery. He deemed his own performance as a husband to be perfectly just and proper; he thought that the words he spoke to his bride were met with maddening resistance. He was, he felt, the victim of a mute and spiritless mate who had deprived him of the "cheerful conversation" that was the whole point of marriage and that was only possible "when the minds are fitly disposed."

How then could he have made so disastrous a mistake? He looked around at the marriages of his friends and acquaintances, including those whom he deemed far inferior to himself in both intelligence and morals, and he recognized that many of these marriages, perhaps all of them, were happier and wiser than his own. In the divorce tracts, though never directly acknowledging that he is reflecting on himself, Milton struggles to explain how it could have happened. The "bashful muteness of a virgin," he now understood, may hide her sloth and dullness. Or the suitor may not have been granted sufficient "freedom of access" until it is too late. Or, if he has any lingering doubts, there are inevitably friends who try to persuade him "that acquaintance, as it increases, will amend all."

But none of this quite accounts for why outright scoundrels often make good marriages, while those who "have spent their youth chastely" can so easily blunder into terrible ones. The answer, Milton thought, is that those who have flitted wildly from one lover to another have accumulated funds of valuable experience. But the chaste and inexperienced youth, if he makes a single fatal mistake, is told that there is nothing to be done: he must endure it for his whole life.

Milton refused to do so, at least not without a fight. Deprived of the cheerful conversation of wedlock and certain that he would never find it with the woman he had married, he felt arising in himself a different emotion he did not hesitate to name: "Then enters Hate," he wrote about failed marriages, "not that Hate that sins, but that which only is natural dissatisfaction and the turning aside from a mistaken object." Love had turned to loathing.

Milton was sickened by the thought of entrapment for life in a loveless marriage. He knew that he would never turn for solace to the brothel or to adultery. But to have sex with a partner you hate—"to grind in the mill," as he put it, "of an undelighted and servile copulation"—was a form of "forced work." Instead of one flesh, he wrote bitterly, there were "two carcasses chained unnaturally together," or rather "a living soul bound to a dead corpse." Could God be such a tyrant?

If God intended to inflict this misery upon him, then Milton would have to believe that rather than being one of the elect, he was what Calvinists called a reprobate, a sinner rejected by God. And if he refused to believe that he was one of the damned? There was for Milton a still worse fear, more terrible and perhaps more tempting than the feeling of reprobation. A sensitive person trapped forever in an unhappy marriage could begin to doubt that God had anything to do with it at all. The last and worst of a series of miserable alternatives that began with the whorehouse and the neighbor's bed was atheism.

But none of it, Milton reasoned, was truly necessary. For the God who ordained marriage in the Garden of Eden could not possibly want to condemn all those who made an innocent mistake to a lifetime of unhappiness. If love, mutual help, and intimacy were to be an integral part of marriage, as God intended, then there had to be the possibility of divorce. Led astray by a corrupt church, men and women had been penned up in a prison of their own making, from which they desperately needed someone to lead them. A person who could provide the thread "that winds out this labyrinth of servitude," Milton argued, "deserves to be reckoned among the public benefactors of civil and humane life, above the inventors of wine and oil."

He understood that by 1644 his personal situation would be well known to many of his readers. It was a small world, one in which he had already made himself highly visible by his vehement published attacks on the bishops. Now that his young wife had left him, he knew that his arguments for divorce would seem to some a mere personal brief. But what of that? He would transform a private crisis into the largest possible public claim, and in doing so he would be the savior of marriage itself, someone worthy of more grateful admiration than the inventors of wine and oil.

When in 1643 he first brought out *The Doctrine and Discipline of Divorce* (the title means in effect "the theory and practice" of divorce), he did so anonymously. But in the next year, after two printings sold out almost immediately, he issued a revised and expanded version, this time boldly affixing his name to the title page: John Milton.

Instead of admiration, there was a rush of ridicule and outrage. *The Doctrine and Discipline of Divorce* deserved "to be burnt by the Hangman"; its arguments were "little less than blasphemy against Christ himself." As for Milton's account of the intolerable loneliness felt by someone married to the wrong person, one of his opponents sneered, "You count no woman to due conversation accessible . . . except she can speak Hebrew, Greek, Latin, and French, and dispute against the canon law as well as you."

Milton had argued that children of an unhappy marriage—"the children of wrath and anguish," as he termed them—are worse off than those whose parents agree to a "peaceful divorce." So too, he thought, unhappy wives have as much reason to welcome divorce and the possibility of remarriage as unhappy husbands. Why should women, any more than men, be forced to remain yoked to a spouse they have come to hate? But to almost all of Milton's seventeenth-century contemporaries, these arguments seemed either wicked or appallingly naïve. They would license men, it was thought, to abandon their responsibility and undermine the institution that God himself had established in Eden. The poet who had once prided himself on his virginity and written a masque in celebration of chastity was clearing a broad path for libertines.

Milton struck back. Had his critics, he asked, actually bothered to read *The Doctrine and Discipline of Divorce* and take in its arguments? God could have created a male companion for Adam—a thousand of them, if He had chosen to do so—"yet for all this, till Eve was given him, God reckoned him to be alone." That was not only or even primarily because of sexual intercourse; it was because "there is a peculiar comfort in the married state beside the genial bed which no other society affords."

Normally so effortlessly eloquent, Milton struggled to describe what this comfort—which he had not himself yet experienced—must be like. It had to be deeply satisfying, since God intended Adam, as Milton put it, "to spend so many secret years in an empty world with one woman." But if it was not sex—if it was something "beside the genial bed"—then what exactly was it? It was, he wrote somewhat awkwardly, "a kind of ravishment and erring fondness in the entertainment of wedded leisures." That was the closest he could come.

Milton had no comparable difficulty finding words to describe his critics: "idiot," "brain-worm," "arrant pettifogger," "odious fool," "gourmand," "barbarian," "cockbrained solicitor," "presumptuous lozel," "mongrel," "brazen ass." But the enemies did not slink away under this torrent of abuse. A complaint against *The Doctrine and Discipline of Divorce* was lodged with a Parliamentary committee empaneled to investigate the unlicensed publication of immoral and irreligious works. Milton felt himself in the maddening position of a liberator who is spurned by the very people he is attempting to free.

Milton characteristically refused to accept defeat. Ferreting through theological tomes to find supporting arguments, he continued to write and publish tracts, ranging in tone from the scholarly to the furious, that advocated divorce. The feverish effort came at a cost, or so it seemed to Milton. For it was at this time that he began to experience digestive problems that plagued him through the rest of his life and to notice a still more serious problem: "Even in the morning, if I began as usual to read, I noticed that my eyes felt immediate pain deep within and turned from reading, though later refreshed after moderate bodily exercise; as often as I looked at a lamp, a sort of rainbow seemed to obscure it." He did not know then, of course, that the deterioration of his vision, whatever its actual cause, would lead in a few years to total blindness, but he must have felt that he was paying a very high price for his labors.

In 1644 he published *Areopagitica,* one of the most eloquent and influential defenses of a free press ever written. Milton had long been against censorship. Now in responses to demands that his book be burned by the common hangman, he wrote: "As good almost kill a man as kill a good book," for "who kills a man kills a reasonable creature, God's image, but he who destroys a good book kills reason itself, kills the image of God, as it were, in the eye." How did his opponents imagine that the truth would ever emerge, if not through the public clash of competing ideas? Did they think that humans were mere puppets, designed—as in the shows that the seventeenth century called "motions"—only to mouth lines ventriloquized for them by the authorities? "Many there be that complain of divine providence for suffering Adam to transgress. Foolish tongues!" Milton declared; "When God gave him reason, he gave him freedom to choose, for reason is but choosing; he had been else a mere artificial Adam, such an Adam as he is in the motions." Whatever else he was or might become, Milton was not going to be an artificial Adam, a puppet spouting someone else's words and accepting laws that he was convinced were unjust. Were we not created by God to be free?

Three years had passed since the disastrous honeymoon in the summer of 1642, and Milton had not, so far as we know, heard a word from Mary. But history—the same history that had turned London and Oxford into enemy camps—now intervened in the marital stalemate. The tides of war turned. The Royalist victory that had seemed almost in reach at the time when Mary returned to her family at Forest Hill shimmered and vanished, like a mirage. By the spring of 1645, Parliament was in the ascendant. Under siege, Royalist Oxford began to run out of provisions, and King Charles decided to lead his troops in person against the massed enemy forces in the north. The Royalist soldiers felt buoyed by the king's presence; many of the wealthier officers' wives and mistresses rode out in their carriages to witness the expected triumph. But on a foggy mid-June morning in 1645, at the Battle of Naseby, the Parliament's New Model Army, under the command of Thomas Fairfax and Oliver Cromwell, crushed the king's forces in what proved to be the decisive battle of the Civil War.

When the news of the disaster reached Oxfordshire, the Powells, facing ruin, knew that they had to act quickly, but how? Their eldest daughter was married, at least in name, to an important figure on the Parliamentary side, but she had deserted him. And Milton, who had made no secret of his miserable loneliness in the company of a wife he had come to hate—"a living soul bound to a dead corpse"—could hardly be expected now to welcome her back. The strategy the Powells hit upon depended on the cooperation of Milton's cousins, William and Hester Blackborough, who lived near him in London and must have been eager to effect a reconciliation. One summer day, very shortly after the Royalist defeat, Milton stopped by, as he apparently did regularly, to visit his relatives. A door opened, as Milton's nephew relates, "and on a sudden he was surprised to see one whom he thought to have never seen more." The scene was carefully, even brilliantly stage-managed. Mary fell to her knees in submission before the husband she had abandoned and begged for his pardon.

Milton, who believed fiercely in the "freedom to choose," could have freely chosen to turn away. But he did not. He took up his repentant bride and led her home. This time the marriage endured. The children whom Milton tutored still no doubt wept under his rod, and the house must still have seemed gloomy to the twenty-year-old Mary. But she could no longer even think about running off to her family's lively manor house in the country. Forest Hill, occupied by Parliamentary troops, was finished, and with it the expansive social world in which she had been raised.

The £1,000 dowry, always a will-o-the-wisp, was now out of the question. Mary's family, rendered homeless by the Parliamentary victory, obtained permission to come to London. Where were they going to live? Where indeed? The whole crowd of them—Richard Powell and his wife Anne, along with young George, Archdale, William, the two Elizabeths, and perhaps even others of their innumerable brood—moved in with their daughter and with the son-in-law they had hated.

By autumn Mary was pregnant, and on July 29, 1646, the Miltons' first child, a daughter, was born. In a Latin letter written on April 20, 1647, to his Italian friend Carlo Dati, Milton reveals at least something of what he must have felt about his new living arrangements. "Those who are closely bound to me by the mere fact of proximity," he writes, "although they have nothing else to commend themselves to me are with me daily, they deafen me with their noise and, I swear, torment me as often as they please."

And Mary? Had she actually come to regret the separation and blame herself or her interfering mother for it? Of her feelings after she returned to the marriage, we know nothing. In October 1648, she gave birth to a second daughter (christened Mary); in March 1651 she gave birth to a son (christened John); by the summer's end she was pregnant again—four pregnancies in six and a half years.

The end of the marriage came about not through divorce but through the means that the marriage ceremony itself imagined: "till death us depart." On May 2, 1652, Mary Milton brought her fourth child into the world, but a few days later, at age twenty-seven, she was dead. "My daughter Deborah was born the 2nd of May being Sunday somewhat before 3 of the clock in the morning, 1652," Milton wrote in his Bible, and then continued, with startling vagueness, "my wife her mother died about 3 days after."

Though Mary left no record of her inner life—no diary or letters of hers have survived—there is an astonishing attempt to imagine what she might have thought and felt. This imagining is, in its way, moving, but also entirely indirect and unreliable, for it is Milton's own. In his divorce tracts Milton, hurt and angry, could not allow himself to reflect at all on what his unhappy bride must have been experiencing, and, as far as we can tell, he did not seem to interest himself in the precise state of her feelings after her return. But years later he tried to record what her voice might have sounded like, had he been able to hear it. Even then, he did not, from our perspective, give it full and robust presence, and he may, for all we know, have been hopelessly wrong. Yet it was remarkable for Milton to hear anything at all, other than the echo chamber of his own unhappiness. Imagining himself as Adam, he called the woman whose voice he conjured up Eve.

10

The Politics of Paradise

In 1381, preaching to impoverished English peasants, the priest John
Ball pointed out that when humans began life in the fallen world there
were no pampered nobles lording over oppressed serfs. To grow his
crops the first man had to dig in the earth himself; to make clothing
the first woman had to spin her own wool. Ball used a revolutionary slogan that quickly became famous: "When Adam delved and Eve
span, who was then the gentleman?" In case his listeners didn't get it,
he spelled out the meaning of his incendiary little rhyme: "From the
beginning all men were created equal by nature." Rebels torched court
records, opened jails, and killed officials of the crown.

When the insurgency was crushed, the instigator was treated to the
grisly end specially reserved for traitors: his head was stuck on a pike on
London Bridge, and his body was hacked into four pieces which were
sent as a warning to four different towns. Though Ball's fate marked
the end of the fourteenth-century Peasants' Revolt, his slogan was not
forgotten, and his death did not kill off radical readings of Adam and
Eve. Those readings always lurked in the story—both in the untram-
meled freedom of Paradise and in the manual labor of Adam and Eve

after the Fall—and were available to anyone in search of ways to justify and legitimate social protest.

In periods of political and social unrest, time has a strange way of buckling, with the present seeming to collapse into the past or the past bursting its containment and inhabiting the present. It was not only biblical figures who suddenly became contemporaries. In the wake of the Renaissance in Italy, it was often the classical, pagan past that surged up. In fourteenth-century Rome a tavern-keeper's illegitimate son, Cola di Rienzo, had himself crowned tribune and called for the unification of Italy and a new Roman empire. Leaders of the American and French revolutions at the end of the eighteenth century were depicted wearing togas. German followers of the Russian Revolution imagined themselves as the direct heirs of the Roman slave rebellion led by Spartacus. But in the overheated religious climate of seventeenth-century England, a culture of ardent Bible readers, it was above all the story of Adam and Eve that seemed eerily close.

It was so close to some, or so at least it was rumored, that they met in secret, men and women together, took their clothes off, and worshiped God as Adam and Eve would have worshiped him in Paradise. Whether these people—known as Adamites—actually existed is not clear, but even as a fantasy in the minds of alarmed defenders of orthodoxy, the rumor reveals the perceived potency of the Genesis story. Conservative authorities, nervous about excessive religious enthusiasm, made efforts to fix the events in the Garden securely in the remotest antiquity. The scholarly James Ussher, a politically moderate Anglican bishop, pored over the historical records, carefully counted the generations inferred by all the biblical "begats," and calculated that the world was created on the night preceding October 23, 4004 BCE. He added that Adam and Eve were driven from Paradise on Monday, November 10. Those dates put the primordial events in their place.

But many of Ussher's contemporaries agreed rather with the physician and natural scientist Sir Thomas Browne when he declared that "the man without a navel still lives in me." Historical distance was meaningless; Adam, in his proneness to temptation, stirred and breathed within Browne himself. Even those who adhered to the notion that the Fall occurred as a specific event long, long ago often insisted, with the preacher John Everard, that "We must bring these histories home to ourselves: otherwise what does it mean to me that there was Sinai and Zion, Hagar and Sarah?"

Bringing the histories home was not only a matter of taking personal responsibility for sinfulness; it could also mean recovering a sense of lost innocence. Near the end of the seventeenth century, the founder of the Quakers, George Fox—repeatedly jailed for religious dissent— testified that through his faith he was lifted back in spirit into Paradise: "All things were new, and all the Creation gave another Smell unto me than before." "I came up into the state of Adam," explained Fox, "which he was in before he fell." For some of Fox's contemporaries this perfect innocence had never been lost; it was the possession of all humans in the simple experience of childhood. Augustine's gloomy insistence that all children, even newborn infants, were already corrupt and sinful by nature was a lie. "I was an Adam there," wrote the poet Thomas Traherne, recalling his earliest years; "A little Adam in a sphere/Of Joys."

The deep truth, all of these seventeenth-century searchers believed, could be found in Genesis. Milton never ceased to search there. Sketching in his notebook the idea of a tragic drama on the fall of Adam and Eve, he briefly hoped that this would be the great work of art that had been secretly gestating within him. But the play refused to get written. He continued to believe that God had given him the talent to make something that would endure in human memory, as the works of Homer and Virgil had endured, and yet that talent in him seemed to lie buried. He worried that he was belated, that the crucial moment of opportunity had eluded his grasp, that his time was running out and still the creative achievement was not happening.

As he reached his fortieth birthday in December 1648, it must have been clear even to him, propped up though he was by an enormously robust ego, that he was nowhere close to writing the masterpiece of which he dreamed. He could tell himself, with utmost justification, that there were other things to think about. The country, which settled into an uneasy truce in 1646, had less than two years later lurched once again into civil war. This time, after a second round of sieges, destruction, and bloodletting, the triumphant New Model Army was not inclined to negotiate a compromise settlement. In an unprecedented move, the king was tried on charges of high treason and convicted, with fifty-nine judges signing the death warrant.

On January 30, 1649, Charles I mounted a scaffold erected in front of the Banqueting House of Whitehall Palace. After making a speech that only those standing near him could hear, he said a prayer, put his head down on the block, and signaled his readiness. The hooded executioner—his identity, carefully concealed, remains unknown—severed the head from the trunk in a single stroke. One eyewitness, a Puritan minister and hence no friend to the king, reported that at the instant when the blow was given, there was "a dismal universal groan among the thousands of people that were in sight of it," a sound such "as I never heard before and desire I may never hear again." England had embarked on a radically new course toward an unknown destination.

A prudent person would have elected at this moment to lie low, but John Milton was anything but prudent. He had already made himself notorious for the vehemence of his attacks on the bishops and, still more, for his championing of divorce. Now he went much further. On February 13, 1649, only two weeks after the execution of Charles I, he published *The Tenure of Kings and Magistrates*. With this long polemical pamphlet, Milton, who had had no responsibility for the regicide, was in effect stepping forward and publicly signing the death warrant. Kings always pretend that they are God's elect, he wrote, but in fact the "divine right of kings" is a lie, just as it is a lie to claim that the king's subjects are born to obey his commands. In terms that recall John Ball and strikingly anticipate the American Declaration of Independence, Milton formulated what he took to be the essential principle: *"All men naturally were born free."*

Like Ball, Milton reached his radical position by thinking hard about Adam and Eve in Paradise:

> No man who knows aught can be so stupid to deny that *all men naturally were born free*, being the image and resemblance of God Himself, and were by privilege above all the creatures born to command and not to obey.

God's words in Genesis to the first humans—"Have dominion over the fish of the sea, and over the fowl of the air, and over every living thing that moveth upon the earth"—were for Milton a political statement, a declaration of innate, unfettered freedom. Humans lived in this freedom until "from the root of Adam's transgression, falling among themselves to do wrong and violence, and foreseeing that such courses must needs tend to the destruction of them all, they agreed by common league to bind each other from mutual injury and jointly to defend themselves." Political arrangements then are social contracts, nothing more. If the ruler violates his part of the contract, the subjects are under no further obligation to obey.

As John Adams and Thomas Jefferson, a century later, fully understood, these claims were revolutionary. For Milton they followed naturally from his reading of Genesis, a reading that led to the stance he had taken in attacking the bishops: "We have the same human privilege that all men have ever had since Adam, being born free." In the wake of his unhappy marriage, he drew out the implications of this stance. Marriage, as the creation of Eve proved, was about the pursuit of happiness, not about unbreakable bonds. "He who marries," he wrote in *The Doctrine and Discipline of Divorce*, "intends as little to conspire his own ruin, as he that swears allegiance." He made the political analogy explicit: "As a whole people is in proportion to an ill government, so is one man to an ill marriage." The unfolding events of the Civil War gave the words Milton penned in 1643 a weird prophetic force: in 1649 the people of England demanded a divorce, and when the king refused to grant one, they did what needed to be done in order to recover the freedom and happiness that was their birthright from the first humans.

To many revolutionaries at this decisive moment, Adam and Eve seemed like key allies. Shortly after the king's execution, a man named Gerrard Winstanley called his followers together. A tailor from the north of England who had gone bankrupt in the economic turmoil brought on by the war, Winstanley had hit close to rock bottom: to stay alive, he had become a cowherd. But he had not despaired. He reflected obsessively on the original man and woman in Eden, on why society had taken such a disastrous turn after the Fall, and on how it would be possible to reverse the damage.

On April 1, 1649, Winstanley led a small group of like-minded men and women to dig and plant crops on St. George's Hill in Surrey, about twenty miles from London. They were Adam and Eve, their leader said, and together they would re-create the Garden of Eden. They were careful not to appropriate anyone else's property; the land they cultivated was common, the time-honored possession of the entire community. But local landowners immediately understood the radicalism of their symbolic action. The "Diggers"—as members of the commune were called—were mounting a challenge to private ownership and to a whole class structure that concentrated wealth, land, status, and power in the hands of a tiny elite group, while consigning the rest of the population to powerlessness and penury. The warped system, enforced by violence, allowed the privileged few to fence off as their own possession what God intended for everyone.

The Fall was not, Winstanley told his followers, an event that occurred in the archaic past; it is something that is constantly happening here and now, whenever a person, drunk with self-love, becomes greedy and begins to tyrannize over others for the sake of accumulating wealth. "When a man falls, let him not blame a man that died 6000 years ago, but blame himself." Private property is the fatal fruit.

Paradise, Winstanley wrote, is not something that only our distant progenitors knew briefly and then lost forever. It is the life that each of us has already experienced when we were young:

> Look upon a child that is new born, or till he grows up to some
> few years: he is innocent, harmless, humble, patient, gentle, easy
> to be entreated, not envious. And this is *Adam*.

The preachers who tell us that in this life we can never regain innocence are lying. We not only possess it as children but we can also recover it as adults, provided we do away with our possessiveness and our possessions: "There shall be no more buying or selling, no fairs nor markets, but the whole earth shall be a common treasury for every man, for the earth is the Lord's." The whole social hierarchy that has grown up alongside our acquisitiveness and greed must be dismantled. There will be no more masters and servants, no gentlefolk and commoners. Men will no longer lord it over women. All will be equal. On St. George's Hill, the Diggers set out to prove that this vision was not an idle dream; it was a life that could be realized here and now.

The local landlords complained, but the authorities sent by the New Model Army at first saw nothing threatening in a group of nonviolent visionaries who merely wanted to plant crops on common lands. When the army refused to act, the property-owners took matters into their own hands. They were not going to allow a radical commune to attempt to establish a class-free paradise in their neighborhood. Surrey was no place for a new Adam and Eve. In 1650 armed thugs were hired to beat up the settlers, destroy their crops, and burn down their huts. Though Winstanley's impassioned tracts—*The New Law of Righteousness*, *The Fire in the Bush*, *The Law of Freedom*—continued to circulate, his social experiment was over.

Politically radical though he was and steadfastly opposed to censorship, Milton was never sympathetic to the likes of Winstanley. The sects that sprung up all over England in the 1640s and '50s—Diggers, Familists, Muggletonians, Quakers, Ranters—were, he wrote, "but winds and flaws to try the floating vessel of our faith." The great project at hand was the redemption not of this or that small group of visionary purists but of the nation as a whole. Milton had no intention of shivering in a hut after planting cabbages all day or of taking communion in the nude with a gaggle of wild-eyed would-be Adams and Eves.

At the very time that the landlords' enforcers were driving the Diggers off St. George's Hill, Milton had accepted the position of Secretary of Foreign Languages for the newly formed Republican Council of State. He had been offered the position, which paid a handsome £288 per year, only a month after he published his pamphlet defending the execution of the king. He had moved then from the margins, as the notorious advocate of no-fault divorce, to a place near the center of power. He was the principal champion in Europe of the English Commonwealth, the learned, indefatigable defender of king-killing and Parliamentary rule.

Milton's charge was to respond at length to the many attacks, from the shocked defenders of monarchy across the Continent, on what the English revolutionaries had dared to do. The arguments were no more polite in Latin—the language in which the debates were conducted—than they were in English, but Milton had always been able to give as much as he got. The problem was that his dream of literary immortality seemed further away than ever and, more ominously, his eyesight was steadily deteriorating. The rainbow that had plagued his vision when he was writing the divorce tracts gave way to worse symptoms: a mist seemed to hover in his forehead and temples; objects on which he tried to focus floated and refused to stay still; intense lights flashed before his closed eyes. He tried every medical therapy he could find, but nothing helped except rest, and there was no time for rest.

By 1652, at age forty-four, he was completely blind. His enemies said that the affliction was divine punishment for his collaboration in the regicide, but he observed wryly that by the same logic you would have to conclude that God had brought about the regicide in order to punish the king's crimes. It was more reasonable to think that his blindness came from natural causes exacerbated by his tireless labors. For all that, Milton did not abandon his post as Secretary of Foreign Languages. The Council still needed him and, renewing his appointment, provided assistants to read the documents to him, fetch books, and take dictation. Endowed with a formidable memory, he trained himself to follow complex arguments, to compose, revise, and translate in his head, and to dictate the results. The training turned out to be crucially important in the future, when he finally came to write the great poem he believed was within him.

At the same time that he was serving the state, Milton was busy in his domestic life. He needed to adjust in innumerable ways to his loss of vision. There were investments to attend to, legal squabbles, friends to visit or to receive at his house. Managing his household must have been an exceedingly complex task, even with ample resources. The death of Mary in 1652 left him a blind widower with three small daughters, the eldest of whom was only six. He somehow got through the next four years with the help of servants and perhaps with help (despite the animosity between them) from Mary's mother. Then, in his forty-eighth year, he married Katherine Woodcock, twenty years his junior. A year later she gave birth to a daughter, Milton's fourth, but the family had almost no time to settle into its new configuration.

Only four months later, Katherine was dead—"of a consumption," according to the notation in Milton's Bible—and her baby lived for only another month.

In 1658, following a urinary tract infection, the fifty-nine-year-old Oliver Cromwell suddenly died of septicemia. He was succeeded by his son Richard, but the conflicting forces that his tough, wily father had managed to hold together began to turn viciously on one another. The Republic collapsed into irreconcilable factions, and there was a surge of popular support for a return to the way things had once been. The dead king's son was invited to reclaim the kingdom that was rightfully his—that had been his all along, it was said—and on May 29, 1660, his thirtieth birthday, Charles II entered London, to the ringing of bells and the ecstatic cheering of his loving subjects.

Milton should not have been caught unawares by this turn of events, but he evidently was, at least to the extent that he failed to conceal or secure for himself and for his daughters all of the money he had saved—the very large sum of almost £2,000—from his salary as Secretary. That and other wealth tainted by his service to the Commonwealth would be confiscated, he realized too late, just as the Republicans had earlier confiscated the property of prominent Royalists.

But that was perhaps the least of Milton's problems. The Restoration, he knew, would be christened with blood. As the royal authorities named those whom it held principally responsible for the regicide and its aftermath, Milton's enemies were calling loudly for the arrest and execution of the blind traitor. The traditional sentence for those convicted of treason was to be "hanged by the neck, and being alive cut down, and your privy members to be cut off, and your bowels to be taken out of your belly and there burned, you being alive." To avoid this fate, some of his Republican associates escaped to Holland or other places where they might receive protection, but the blind Milton, who would easily have been spotted by watchers stationed at all the ports, did not attempt to flee the country. Instead, he went into hiding at a friend's house in London. The identity of the friend has never been discovered, but whoever it was took a serious risk.

The immediate and most obvious targets for Royalist justice were the fifty-nine judges who had presided over the trial of Charles I and others closely associated with his execution in 1649. Some of these had already died; others fled. (Among those who managed to elude capture were three signatories to the death warrant who made it all the way to New Haven, Connecticut, and are now commemorated in street names: Dixwell, Whalley, and Goffe.) Ten, less agile or fortunate, were duly arrested, tried, and executed. But these hideous deaths were not enough to settle accounts either for the ax blow that had killed the king or for the eleven subsequent years of Republican rule.

The newly crowned son of the royal martyr was affable, tolerant, and more interested in sexual conquest than in revenge. But the reckoning was not over. Eager to demonstrate their loyalty, the Commons and the Privy Council assembled a further shortlist of those it deemed worthy of punishment, whether execution or life imprisonment. Milton was a prime candidate for inclusion. He had, after all, found in the story of Adam and Eve the principal justification for the killing of the king: "All men naturally were born free." But though his name was mentioned, it was left off the final list, almost certainly because of the effective intervention of influential friends both in Parliament and at court. When the king subsequently signed an Act of Indemnity and Oblivion to pardon all others who had served the toppled regime, Milton was safe.

Though he emerged from hiding and returned home, he remained in seclusion. According to one of his earliest biographers, Milton "was in perpetual terror of being assassinated." Many people wished him dead, but whether he had grounds for his fear is not clear. His public life, in any case, was over. A royal proclamation was issued calling for anyone who possessed copies of his "wicked and traitorous works" to deliver them to the authorities, who would see to it that they were burned by the public hangman.

Milton was reunited with his three daughters, aged fourteen, twelve, and eight. The blind father needed help. Though he had lost much of his wealth, he was still a man of means, and servants continued to do many of the basic household tasks. But the able assistants that he once had, in his office as Secretary, who fetched him books and read to him, were gone. His life's blood was reading, and now, thrown back on himself, he craved more than ever access to his precious books. When some loyal friends paid him visits, he could recruit them to read, and he hired a young Quaker who had some Latin to come daily to his house. But the young man was periodically arrested—it was illegal to be a Quaker—and his help, in any case, was not enough. Milton began to demand that the girls read to him, often in languages that they did not know. He taught them how to recognize and sound out the Greek, Hebrew, and other characters, but he who had so deeply concerned himself with the education of children did not bother to teach his own daughters how to understand what they were reading. When visitors to his house remarked on the strangeness of his daughters' reading so many languages without comprehension, their father would remark jokingly that "one tongue is enough for a woman." It was evidently regarded as a witty reply.

In 1663, five years after the death of his second wife, Milton married again, this time to Elizabeth Minshull—Betty, he called her—a yeoman's daughter thirty years younger than he. At this point relations with his teenaged daughters, in particular with his eldest daughter Mary, had almost completely broken down. When Mary was told of her father's approaching marriage, she replied that it "was no news to hear of his wedding; but if she could hear of his death, *that* was something." The family all continued to live together under one roof for six years, but there is no sign that relations ever improved.

His political hopes lay in ruins; his grinding labor and eloquent writing over more than twenty years were for nothing; his exultant enemies laughingly burned his books; most of his wealth was gone; many of his friends were dead or in hiding; his daughters, whom he had alternately neglected and bullied, hated him; he was unable to wield a pen, let alone read a book; blindness and fear of assassins kept him cooped up. All was lost—and yet: his inner world had vastly, incalculably expanded. Each night or in the early hours of the morning, if we can believe him, he had in this inner world of his a female visitor.

Milton called his nightly visitor Urania. The name was pagan, the ancient Muse of astronomy, but in Latin its literal meaning is "heavenly one," and she was for Milton the mysterious force within him that was enabling him at long last to write the great epic poem that he had dreamed all his life that he was destined to write. His prior attempts to write such a work had gone nowhere. He was able to show friends some scattered verses, but nothing more. Shakespeare had died at fifty-two, having already retired to Stratford and given up his active career as a professional writer. What could the ruined Milton, who turned fifty-two in the year that Charles II returned to England, expect to accomplish at this late stage of his life? Yet suddenly here it was, through the virtually miraculous assistance of a being he called his "celestial patroness."

I think we must take Milton's claim of celestial visitation, however strange it sounds, seriously. The Muse would come to him, as he put it, "unimplored." With her protection he would descend into the underworld; he would soar into "the Heaven of Heavens"; above all, as if he still could see, he would wander by shady grove or sunny hill or along the sacred brook that bubbled up by the holy sites of Jerusalem. And he would emerge from these reveries filled with a peculiar music that he had never been able to sound, that had never before been sounded by anyone.

He settled upon a routine. He would awaken at four in the morning (at five in the winter) and lie in bed for half an hour, listening to someone read to him, preferably from the Hebrew Bible. Then for an hour or two he would sit quietly in contemplation. By seven he was ready. An amanuensis would arrive, and Milton would begin to dictate the verses that he had composed in his head—that had come to him from on high or welled up inside him. If the amanuensis was late, the blind poet would begin to complain, as if he were in pain from what he was forced to hold back: "I want to be milked."

It would emerge from him in a rush: he could dictate as many as forty lines of verbally dense, syntactically complex, unrhymed iambic pentameter verse. He would have the lines read back to him, and then, sitting in an easy chair with his leg swung over one of the arms, he would begin to adjust and cut and tighten, often reducing the forty lines to twenty. The whole morning was spent this way.

And then it was over for the day. Fearing his belatedness and anxious to bring to fruition what he had finally begun—"long choosing and beginning late" (9:26), as he put it—Milton felt keenly the pressure of time and must have been eager to press on. But he knew that he could not force more lines to come. He had to wait for another night, another unbidden visitation. After lunch he paced in his small garden for three to four hours at a time, or if the weather would not permit him to be outdoors, he would sit on a swing he had devised, pulling himself back and forth. In the evening, he played music, received a few visitors, listened to poetry. By nine o'clock he was in bed, courting sleep and the return of the Muse.

For long months, extending into years, these returns continued, as if by miracle. The mornings would bring forth more verses, more occasions to be "milked." The task was to keep going, to dodge the assassin's knife that he feared was hanging over him, and, more realistically, to avoid infection from the bubonic plague that periodically ravaged London's population.

By the summer of 1665 he had a draft—over 10,000 lines—of a stupendous poem to show his young Quaker assistant. What had seemed impossible had actually happened. Published in 1667 and then again, in revised form, in 1674, *Paradise Lost* was the bid for poetic immortality that Milton had confessed dreaming about in his youthful letter to his best friend. He had actually succeeded in rivaling Homer and Virgil. He had ascended the peak that Shakespeare had climbed. He had written one of the world's greatest poems.

11

Becoming Real

A creative achievement of this magnitude, as Milton's own talk of nightly visitations from the Muse suggests, is almost impossible to account for rationally. But the one piece of it that makes perfect sense is that the poem had to be about Adam and Eve. Those figures had haunted every facet of Milton's experience, from his expectation of marital bliss to his plea for divorce, from his educational schemes to his understanding of Jesus, from his political radicalism to his understanding of why the revolution had failed. The story in Genesis was for him the key to unlocking the meaning of virtually everything: anthropology, psychology, ethics, politics, faith. And like Augustine, who shared this obsession, Milton brought to the story his whole life.

Bringing to the story his whole life did not mean that he turned the characters into personifications of his contemporaries—Mary Powell as Eve, Cromwell as Satan, himself as Adam, and so forth. But it did mean that everything that mattered most to him—his travels as a young man, his intense reading of the classics and of Shakespeare, his sexual longings, the disastrous honeymoon with Mary, the loneliness expressed in the divorce tracts, his theological broodings, the Civil

War, the council meetings he attended as Cromwell's Secretary, the bitter experience of defeat, all of it—found its way into the poem.

Everything mattered for the most fundamental of reasons. Every one of us, he believed, is the literal heir to the central figures, Adam and Eve. They were as real as we are, and their destiny directly affected our own.

Milton was sure of that, for he shared Augustine's conviction that the literal truth of Jesus Christ was bound up with the literal truth of Adam and Eve. The Savior's actual blood canceled the debt incurred for all of us by the actual transgression of the actual first humans. Milton was well versed in the spiritual levels of scriptural interpretation that, alongside the literal sense, medieval theologians like Hugh of St. Victor (c. 1096–1141), St. Bonaventure (1221–74), and St. Thomas Aquinas (c. 1225–74) had painstakingly elaborated. He knew that the historical figures and events described in the Bible formed only one part of a much larger set of meanings posited by what was called the "four-fold method" of reading. He was steeped in scriptural typology, teasing out the *allegorical* links between the events in the Old Testament and the life of the Savior. He was gifted at deriving *moral* guidance for the present from the traces of the sacred past. And he brooded constantly on the beatific vision to which a reader skilled in *anagogical* interpretation could climb. (The term "anagogy" is related to the Greek for "upward ascent.")

Milton knew then that it was possible to extract from the Old Testament's story of Adam and Eve and the New Testament's story of Jesus and Mary a rich and elaborate set of symbolic associations, ethical lessons, and spiritual intimations. But he was convinced that everything had to spring from and return to the literal truth of the Bible's words. In the absence of that truth, Milton's Christian faith and all the positions he had taken on the basis of that faith would be robbed of their meaning. If the Garden and its first inhabitants were merely allegorical fables, then the whole interlocking structure of sacred stories would slide into myths no more reliable than the pagan fables of Prometheus and Pandora.

Fortunately, his faith assured him, Moses had in Genesis provided infallible written testimony that Adam and Eve were real people. Milton undertook to make good on this reality. But how to do it? And why should he be able to do it more successfully than Augustine, who had left his book *The Literal Meaning of Genesis* unfinished after fifteen years of struggling to complete it? The answer, Milton understood, lay not only in himself—in those talents that he was confident God had bestowed upon him—but also in the great good fortune of his timing. On the face of it, that timing would appear to have been a disaster: his dreams for his nation had been shattered, and his career lay in ruins. But, properly understood, it was providential.

He had arrived as a poet in the wake of the greatest revolution in artistic representation since the ancient world. The Renaissance had altered all the rules. Painters like Masaccio, Paolo Uccello, and Piero della Francesca had developed linear perspective: the figures in their paintings were situated in a geometrical, mathematically calculated space. Their depicted size and their relation to one another no longer depended on their spiritual or social importance, as they had in medieval art, but on exactly where in that space they were standing. Using devices like foreshortening and a shared vanishing point in a single, unified scene, artists were able to achieve an unprecedented illusion of life.

But it was not only technical innovation that had changed everything; it was also the release of titanic creative energies. Milton was now blind, but he had spent more than a year in Italy, and what he had seen and felt then remained etched in his consciousness. He left no record of these encounters, but he must have encountered some works by Mantegna, Titian, Tintoretto, Botticelli, Leonardo da Vinci, and Raphael. Above all, as anyone who has ever read Milton inevitably wonders, would there not have been a day in which someone—perhaps his friend Lucas Holstein, the Vatican librarian—took the poet into the heart of the Vatican and showed him Michelangelo's Sistine Chapel? Perhaps Milton's staunchly Protestant sensibility would initially have been shocked by the sight; the dazzling, kaleidoscopic colors might at first have struck him, as the interior of St. Peter's struck George Eliot's heroine in *Middlemarch*, like "a disease of the retina." But it is impossible not to imagine the future author of *Paradise Lost* raising his eyes, still unclouded by the disease that eventually blinded him, and gazing up in wonder at the stupendous vision on the ceiling. Surrounded by angelic *putti*, the majestic white-haired God with the flowing beard, his left arm around a beautiful naked woman (presumably Eve, yet unborn) reaches out with his powerful right arm and extends his index finger to touch the slack finger of Adam. That touch, we instantly grasp, will animate the first human, still lying prone on the ground, and will bring his magnificent body to its feet. We are viewing the origin of our species, the moment that all human life—and hence the very possibility of our own existence—began.

Michelangelo's unforgettable scene is part of a still more capacious vision, a tremendous sequence of scenes from Genesis that chronicles both the creation of the universe and the eventual tragic alienation of humans from their Creator. The whole scheme then ties together, in the way sanctified by Christian tradition, the Old Testament and the New, leading up to the grand spectacle of the Last Judgment frescoed on the altar wall. Michelangelo's contemporaries were in awe of what they called his *terribilità*. A single artist of immense skill, visionary intensity, and almost infinite ambition had managed to capture everything in one vast work. It was as if he had not merely represented or imitated God's own creative power but had actually appropriated that power for himself.

Milton had his own literary version of Michelangelo's *terribilità*. Steeped in the culture of Renaissance humanism, with its dream of recovering the glory of the ancient past, he was determined to give

Adam and Eve the compelling presence that Homer had given Hector and that Virgil had given Aeneas. The opening chapters of Genesis, he recognized, lacked the thrilling struggle of the Trojan War or the historical specificity of the founding of Rome. But he was certain that the origin story narrated in such brief form was far more important and, rightly understood, at once more heroic and more poignant than either the Greek or Latin masterpieces. The question was how to expand the sublime but terse biblical narrative in order to give it the sustained grandeur of the pagan epics.

The Christian tradition had long engaged in this process of expansion. Developing the ancient midrashic speculations that some of the angels had objected to the creation of the first humans and envied the qualities that God conferred upon them, Ambrose, Augustine, and their contemporaries began to posit behind the serpent's temptation of Eve a backstory: the rebellion of Satan and his legions. By the Middle Ages these speculations had been elaborated into an account of a full-scale war in heaven, with Satan leading a third of the angels in a reckless, mad, doomed uprising against God and then, in defeat, plotting to harm God's creatures, the first man and woman.

Milton seized upon this legend as an opportunity to emulate and even outdo the great battle scenes in the classical epics. *Paradise Lost* includes extravagant accounts of heavenly warfare, complete with flashing swords, the flinging of whole mountains, and even the diabolic invention of gunpowder. But the poet who once posted a sonnet on his door pleading for mild treatment from any passing soldier could not conjure up the grim, unforgiving urgency of Homer and Virgil's warriors. And there was an insurmountable problem: angels, good and bad, may have the wind knocked out of them by the impact of a mountain, but being made of immortal substance, they soon recover. Still worse, since God's power is infinite and absolute, the outcome is in no doubt at all. Milton himself recognized that he could not expect his readers to take entirely seriously his attempt to confer on the biblical narrative the martial power and the tension of epic. When God urges his son to help him prepare a defense against the approaching enemy army, the son instantly recognizes that his father is making a joke. God has no need for help.

What Milton could bring effectively to the depiction of the rebellion in heaven derived from his years as Cromwell's Latin Secretary, listening intently to the deliberations of the Council of State. Probably no great epic poet—certainly not Dante and not even Virgil—has ever had such sustained, daily, and intimate access to the halls where powerful, ambitious men attempt to assert their political will. In *Paradise Lost* this privileged access probably helps to account for the astonishing air of conviction carried by the council scenes in hell in which Moloch, Belial, Mammon, and Beelzebub debate the best policy for the devils to pursue.

Milton undertook to turn the literal into the real not as the great visual artists had done, through line and color and form, but rather through incantatory rhythm, rhetoric, metaphor, and the rich sounds of his native tongue. There were very few Renaissance precedents for bringing the story of Adam and Eve to life in a work of vernacular literature. Artists felt free to depict the Garden of Eden in any way that they chose, but writers had to tread more carefully. It was difficult and possibly dangerous to take too many liberties with the words of sacred Scripture. But in his poetry as in his politics, Milton was exceptionally bold. And he knew exactly where he could turn for literary inspiration. In addition to the Greek and Latin poets that the Renaissance had cultivated anew, he had native resources near at hand upon which to draw.

He could find in his own world, close enough almost to touch, an astonishing embodiment of the literary power for which he longed. Shakespeare's First Folio, which celebrated the great playwright, in Ben Jonson's words, as "not of an age but for all time," was published when Milton was fifteen years old. The second edition in 1632 included a

new poem in praise of Shakespeare: "Thou in our wonder and aston-
ishment," it proclaims, "Hast built thyself a lasting monument." The
anonymous author of those words was the young John Milton: it was
his first published poem in English.

In order to invent a compelling Satan, Milton carefully studied
how Shakespeare had done it. The depiction of Macbeth's murderous ambition and despair provided a psychological and rhetorical tem-
plate for the Prince of Darkness, and Milton added notes he took from
Richard III and from Iago. He was almost too brilliant a student, for
the result was a character so vivid that he threatened to take over the
poem, particularly in its early books. In the later books Milton chose
deliberately to diminish Satan in order to make room for the characters
who were at the center of his lifelong obsession, Adam and Eve.

But Adam and Eve posed a challenge much greater than any that
bedeviled his depiction of heaven or hell. There were almost no precedents, literary or otherwise, for the sustained depiction of a marriage.
Shakespeare had almost nothing to offer Milton, nor did Homer or
Virgil, Dante or Petrarch. Marriage figured in their works, when it
figured at all, as a goal to be pursued or as a simple fact, not as a sustained partnership of intimate companions. A significant exception in
Shakespeare was the marriage of the Macbeths, but that would hardly
serve as a model for an Edenic couple. Milton believed deeply that at
the center of marriage was intimate conversation between husband and
wife, but to imagine and depict such intimacy was largely uncharted
territory, not for him alone but for all of the literary culture in which
he had steeped himself.

If in his voluminous reading he had come across the twelfth-
century French play Le Jeu d'Adam, Milton would have encountered
Adam and Eve as amusing rustics. (Their dialogue is in the manner
of "Who was that snake you was talking to, missus?") Or if he had
ventured into still more popular French literature, he might have
found Adam and Eve depicted in the coarse comic tales known as the

fabliaux. God created Eve—goes a typical one called "The Cunt That Was Made by a Spade"—from a hard bone in Adam's side in order to show husbands that they should beat their wives regularly, preferably three or four times a day. The first woman was an attractive-enough creature, but God had carelessly left her incomplete by omitting her genitals. Assigned to finish the job, the Devil looked over all the available tools—"hammers, adzes,/chisel, mattocks, sharpened axes, cutting tools with double blades,/pruning hooks" and the like—and settled on a spade, for he knew that "with the sharp edge of the spade/a great, deep crevice could be made/in scarcely any time at all." After he made the gash, by pushing in the spade right up to the handle, the Devil finished up by farting on the woman's tongue. That is why, the tale concludes, all women have to chatter constantly.

Such wild, violently misogynistic materials were abundant in the literary archive that Milton inherited—they lurk under the surface at many times and in many cultures—but he wanted no part of them. He could easily see that they were a vulgar betrayal of the Bible's vision of the human pair. Yet what was left for him? What would perfect innocence actually resemble? How could he show convincingly what the first—the ideal—marriage was? What did the first humans look like? Did they eat like animals or did they prepare and serve meals? How did they spend their days? What did they talk about? Did they have sex? Did they dream at night, and, if so, did they ever, in their state of perfect happiness, have nightmares? Were they occasionally bored or annoyed or anxious in Paradise? Did they sometimes disagree with each other? And how did a relationship that promised perfect happiness go so catastrophically wrong?

For a start, Milton conjured up things he had seen when he still had the use of his eyes. He remembered landscapes he had loved, particularly in Tuscany, and these he merged with descriptions that he culled from the innumerable books he had himself read or that his assistants read to him. The garden that God—"the sovereign Planter"—made for the first humans was not, Milton was certain, one of those formal constructions then in vogue, with clipped hedges artfully arranged in elaborate geometrical patterns. It tended, if anything, to be overgrown, a richly verdant, well-watered plot of land situated at the top of a steep wilderness and encircled with immensely high trees. It must have been full of flowers, chosen not only for the exquisite variety of their colors but also for their rich fragrance. (Milton remembered sailors' reports of delicious odors wafted to their ships by prevailing winds from the coast of Arabia.) And though it was enclosed, it offered enchanting prospects of the kind the blind Milton could still see in his mind's eye, long vistas out over forests and rivers and distant plains. Paradise, as he imagined it, was something like a magnificent country estate: "A happy rural seat of various view" (4:248).

As for the lord and lady of this estate, Milton drew on paintings and prints of Adam and Eve that he must have stared at intensely both during his travels in Italy and again when he returned home. The images that stayed with him were not figures bent over in abjection and sadness. They were rather the naked pair, splendid in their dignity, vitality, and independence, of High Renaissance art. The first man and woman, he wrote, were "Godlike erect, with native honor clad" (4:289). Adam had a large forehead; his hair, parted at the front, hung clustering down, but not beneath his broad shoulders. Eve's golden hair was much longer; in wanton ringlets it reached all the way to her slender waist. Neither of them concealed "those mysterious parts" that humans now hide in guilty shame, for they yet knew neither guilt nor shame.

Milton did not want to depict Adam and Eve through a kind of mystical haze or delicately hidden from view by strategically placed fig leaves. He wanted to see them—and to have his readers see them—in all the vigor of robust youth. There was nothing ethereal about them. Deeply in love, Milton thought, they must have walked hand in hand through their delicious garden, stopping often to chat and kiss and indulge in "youthful dalliance" (4:338). When hungry, they sat down on a soft bank by a stream and ate the fruit that grew abundantly around them. "The savory pulp they chew," as the poem pictures the scene, "and in the rind/Still as they thirsted scoop the brimming stream" (4:335–36).

Milton was in part going out of his way to make a theological point. Adam and Eve were not allegorical emblems; they were flesh-and-blood people, better than we are, to be sure, but not different in kind and not philosophical abstractions. Even the angels, he proposed, should be understood in human terms, for our material nature does not cut us off from higher forms of life. Thus when the poem depicts a friendly visit to Eden by the angel Raphael, sent by God to warn Adam and Eve about Satan, it imagines the heavenly guest sitting down with the humans for a meal and eating not "in a mist, the common gloss/Of theologians, but with keen dispatch/Of real hunger" (5:435–37). Spiritual beings are made of matter, just as humans are. Milton went still further. He insisted that, if angels actually ate real food, then they must also, like humans, have digested it and eliminated whatever "redounded." But, he added, with a sidelong glance at his own lifelong digestive problems, at least angels did not suffer from any gastric discomfort: "what redounds, transpires/Through Spirits with ease."

But it was not only bodily existence that Milton had to represent vividly in order to ground in reality the literal truth of the first humans. That was the easy part, thanks to the Renaissance art that helped to shape his vision. It was their inner lives and the substance of their relationship that posed the far greater challenge. The most difficult question was how to make Adam and Eve's marriage come alive. If Shakespeare could not help him here, still less could Augustine or Luther or Calvin. Milton's years of public service, writing angry polemics and educational treatises and diplomatic correspondence, were of no use. He found the way forward in his most private experiences, in his passionate friendship with Charles Diodati, in the fantasies he cherished during the long years he struggled to preserve his chastity, and above all in the feelings aroused in him around the time of his first marriage and disastrous honeymoon. Only by tapping into these recesses, courageously and relentlessly, did he begin to discover what he needed. As a poet, he aspired to make his creation real—that was, he knew, not only Augustine's theological imperative but also the secret of the greatest literature. And he succeeded. In *Paradise Lost,* Adam and Eve took on a more intense life—the life both of fully realized individuals and of a married couple—than they had ever possessed in the thousands of years since they were first conceived.

In his conversation with the angel Raphael, Milton's Adam recalls the moment when God brought all of the animals before him, two by two. Adam duly gave the animals names—the poem discreetly avoids indicating how long the parade must have taken—but he found himself unaccountably missing something, though he was not sure exactly what it was. He turned to the divine figure standing next to him and asked, "In solitude/What happiness"? God smiled and asked what he meant by solitude: had the human not just been introduced to every species in the entire world? Some of these species, God added, are capable of reason, and Adam could find pastime with them. Adam persisted. All of the animals, even the best of them, were far below him. The fellowship he sought must be mutual; any attempt at conversation would otherwise soon prove tedious. He needed a mate, an equal. "Among unequals," he asked God, "what society/Can sort, what harmony or true delight?" (8:383–84).

The divine response was a strange one. What do you think of *me?* God asked Adam; I am alone for all eternity and without equal. All creatures I converse with are infinitely—literally infinitely—below me, not to mention the fact that they have all been made by me. "Seem I to thee sufficiently possessed/Of happiness, or not?" (8:404–5). This is an uncomfortable question to be asked by anyone, let alone by God, and it is not surprising that the human's answer was diplomatic to the point of incomprehensibility. But in the midst of his extravagant compliments and evasions, Adam did manage to observe that, while he would not venture to speak for God, he could attest to his own desire to have a conversation with another human and not with one of the lower animals. Moreover, he added that God, being perfect, has no need to propagate, but that he, the human, knew that he was somehow deficient.

Why the first man had this feeling of deficiency is not entirely clear. Genesis did not provide any guidance, so that Milton had to reach back to his own experience, to whatever it was that drove him in that fateful July of 1642 to end his solitary existence and take a wife. Adam must have been painfully aware, Milton thought, of what he called his "single imperfection," that is, the imperfection of being single.

At this point in the conversation God said something else that Adam must have found disquieting. He told Adam that he had only been testing him, to see if he would be willing to settle for any of the beasts brought before him. There is nothing in the Bible about a test. "It is not good that the man should be alone," God in Genesis says; "I will make him an help meet for him." The words clearly bothered Milton, as they had bothered many generations of commentators. Could it be that God only now noticed something that He had left out? How could an omnipotent God have made a mistake? Was it possible, as Rabbi Eleazar had suggested in the Talmud, that Adam actually tried sex with all of the animals before the creation of the woman? Milton, who had learned Hebrew, had pored over the rabbinical commentaries, but he found this idea too extreme. Better to imagine, he thought, that God, wanting to observe the human's powers of discrimination, had the animals brought before Adam to see if he would settle for one or another of them as a conversational partner. By holding out for a human interlocutor, Adam had passed the test, God declared, adding that he already knew before Adam spoke that it was not good for a human to be alone.

It was just as well that the test was over at this point, Adam tells Raphael, for the strain of conversing with God was so great that the human—"dazed and spent" (8:455)—was ready to collapse. Collapse he did, but then, as if in a trance, he was able to see himself lying on the ground and to watch while God stooped down, opened his left side and removed a rib, with "life-blood streaming fresh." The rabbis similarly considered the possibility that Adam could have witnessed the fashioning of the woman from his own bone, but they imagined that if he did so he would have been so disgusted by what he saw that God would have had to destroy the creature and start again. Milton, who may have had this midrashic comment in mind, insisted that for Adam the sight was only thrilling. Her looks, Adam recalls, "infused/ Sweetness into my heart, unfelt before" (8:475).

Others before Milton had at least implied the arousal of such feelings in Adam. In Hebrew, as he knew, the Genesis verses suggest them in a poem that repeats again and again the feminine pronoun *zo't*: "This one," "this one," "this one."

> This one at last, bone of my bones
>> and flesh of my flesh,
> This one shall be called Woman,
>> for from man was this one taken. (2:23, Alter trans.)

In Hieronymus Bosch's famously strange painting known as *The Garden of Earthly Delights,* Adam stares up at the newly created, nubile Eve with a look of rapt wonder. To convey such wonder, Milton could draw upon the great flowering of love poetry in the English Renaissance—"Who ever loved that loved not at first sight?" asked Christopher Marlowe—and he seems to have drawn as well upon his own first experience of love's sweetness. The Adam of *Paradise Lost*, the man who emerged in the poet's nightly dreams, articulates his feelings with extraordinary intensity and eloquence.

Awakening from his vision, Adam found that in comparison with Eve everything else in the world—and he was, after all, in Paradise—suddenly looked shabby. When he went off to seek her, he was certain that if he could not find her he would forever deplore her loss. God invisibly drew her to him, and though she initially turned away, she came to accept his suit and allowed herself to be led blushing to the "nuptial bower." There Adam experienced for the first time what he calls "the sum of earthly bliss."

Milton knew perfectly well that Catholic intellectuals had long speculated that in Paradise sexual intercourse was designed only to produce offspring and thus to be undertaken with a kind of cool detachment. He had read Augustine's claim that the act, performed without arousal or excitement, would have been entirely unremarkable and public. *Paradise Lost* imagines a kind of eyewitness testimony that this whole theological tradition was a lie. "Whatever hypocrites austerely talk/Of purity and place and innocence" (4:744–45), Milton insisted, Adam and Eve in Paradise had spectacularly good sex, and they had it in private. Their bower was enclosed, and it was theirs alone: no other creature, "Beast, bird, insect, or worm" (4:704), dared enter. Eve decked the nuptial bed with flowers and sweet-smelling herbs, and there they enjoyed exclusive possession of each other's body—the only form of private property, the poem remarks, in a world where everything else was held in common.

But how could boundless love and passionate mutual possession be compatible with hierarchical order—the man on top—that Milton thought was essential to marriage? Milton knew what such an order would have to feel and sound like. Adam tells Eve that the garden is getting overgrown and that they should wake up early the next morning to prune the branches. Eve responds in the compliant, adoring fashion that the newlywed Milton must have expected from the woman he married:

> what thou bidst
> Unargu'd I obey; so God ordains,
> God is thy Law, thou mine: to know no more
> Is woman's happiest knowledge and her praise. (4:635–38)

The perfect wife in all things submits cheerfully to her husband's will.

Eve has not, as the French fabliau proposed, been tamed or beaten into this submissive posture. In Milton's view, and that of many of his contemporaries, in Paradise the woman's submission would have come naturally. "Should the wife have been subject to the man in that state of innocence?" asked the seventeenth-century Puritan Alexander Ross. "Yes," he replied, answering his own question, "but this subjection of the wife should not have been unwilling, bitter, troublesome, as it fell out afterward by sin." In God's design Adam and Eve were both magnificent specimens of humanity, but they were by no means equal. "For contemplation he and valor formed,/For softness she and sweet attractive grace," Milton wrote, adding in a line that has become notorious for its complacent, self-congratulatory sexism, "He for God only, she for God in him" (4:297–99).

The surprise is not that Milton subscribed to this widely shared picture, but that he recognized in it a fundamental and unresolvable problem. That problem was not, as he conceived it, the unwillingness of the woman to submit; his is not a story about Lilith. Rather, there is something disruptive in the very experience of bliss, disruptive for men at least as much as for women.

Adam tries to explain the problem to Raphael. I understand, he tells the angel, that she is the inferior one. I know that, though we have both been made in the image of God, I resemble God more exactly than she does. I grasp that I am meant to be and to remain on top. But when

I approach her loveliness, he confesses, the official account no longer seems true. "So absolute she seems/And in herself complete" (8:547–48) that, if anything, it is she who seems the superior human being.

The angel's response—he contracts his brow and tells Adam to have more self-esteem—is not helpful. (Such responses never are.) How could an angel understand what a human feels who is deeply in love? Raphael warns Adam not to overvalue mere sexual pleasure, a pleasure, he says scornfully, that is vouchsafed to cattle and every other beast. Adam replies with dignity that it is not only what happens in bed, though he regards that with far greater reverence than Raphael's remark suggests, that accounts for the feelings he has tried to describe. Rather, he says, it is "those graceful acts,/Those thousand decencies" that bespeak a perfect union—"in us both one soul"—that so delight him in Eve. His love, the intimate physical and spiritual communion with his wife, cancels out the sense of superiority to which he knows that as a male he is meant to cling. Instead, he feels an overwhelming bond: "in us both one soul" (8:604).

There is in Adam's words an implicit refusal of the official line or at least a polite but firm suggestion that the angel and his heavenly cohort have a very imperfect grasp of human experience. Indeed, Milton's first human allows himself to wonder, given the angel's obtuseness, just what angelic sexual experience is like. "Love not the Heavenly spirits," he asks Raphael, "and how their love/Express they, by looks only?" Raphael does something extraordinary, at least for an angel: he blushes. "Let it suffice thee," he reassures Adam, "that thou know'st/ Us happy, and without love no happiness" (8:620–21). Like a parent who does not know when he has said enough, he goes on to try to be explicit and technical—something about angels having no membranes or "exclusive bars." Then, catching himself up and remarking how late in the afternoon it is, he flies back to heaven.

In his conversation with the angel, and even in his earlier conversation with God, Adam manifests a kind of stubborn human independence that would be completely shocking if one did not remember the Milton who was expelled from Cambridge by his enraged tutor, or who refused the easy career path in the church that had been laid out before him, or who rose up against the king and his bishops, or who was determined to work out his own personal theology. The Adam who took living form in Milton's imagination was precisely not someone who would simply accept the doctrine that had been handed down from on high. But in this case—the superiority in principle of the male over the female—Milton himself did not doubt that the conventional doctrine was true. The trouble was that this truth could not be reconciled with what it actually felt like to love someone. "Among unequals," Adam had asked God, "what harmony or true delight?" (8:583–84).

Eve is the answer to Adam's longing. But, though she is fashioned from the very stuff of which he is made and is in this sense his equal, she is not entirely the same. At the moment that she awoke into consciousness, she did not gaze up at the sky, as Adam did, in search of a creator. Instead, she made her way to a nearby lake and peered at her reflection in the clear, smooth water. It was only when a mysterious voice drew her away and when Adam gently seized her by the hand that she reluctantly abandoned the pleasing image of herself.

It is possible, of course, to interpret this moment of narcissism as a defect in Eve; centuries of misogynistic sermonizing made some such point. But Milton did not necessarily draw this conclusion. Instead, he imagined that the woman seemed less haunted than the man by a sense of innate imperfection, less needy. And it is out of this perception of difference that the poem generates its understanding of the disaster.

We have no idea what actually happened in those weeks in the summer of 1642—more than a quarter of a century earlier—when Milton came back to London with his young bride, when they briefly lived together, and when she left him. It is very unlikely that the experience was the direct model for the Adam and Eve who emerged in the poet's imagination. But perhaps Milton had at least come to recognize that there was a painful tension between conventional expectations and actual feelings. In *Paradise Lost*, the tension is transmuted into something rich and strange. The hierarchy—"He for God only, she for God in him"—begins to crumble under the weight of the husband's overwhelming recognition of his wife's beauty, kindness, and, above all, autonomy.

Eve's autonomy comes to the test on the morning after the angel's visitation, when the pair awakens to begin the day's tasks in the garden. The tasks are meant to be pleasant, the poem insists, but the work is real, not merely symbolic, and Eve echoes Adam's observation that it is getting out of hand. What they accomplish in the day—"Lop overgrown, or prune, or prop, or bind" (9:210)—is undone by the night's growth. Until "more hands/Aid us," she says, they are only falling further behind. She proposes an experiment, a new idea that she has come up with to address the problem that they have both recognized: "Let us divide our labors," she suggests, so that they lose less time in idle conversation.

Adam initially gives a "mild answer." Her proposal for the division of labor, he tells his wife, is praiseworthy—"for nothing lovelier can be found/In woman than to study household good"—but it is misguided, for this, after all, is Paradise, and work is not meant to be drudgery. For a brief moment he shifts ground: if perhaps what Eve is really saying is that she has been finding their conversation tiresome, he would be willing to let her go off briefly by herself, "For solitude sometimes is best society" (9:249). And then, not waiting for an answer and not leaving well enough alone, he makes the mistake of telling her that, with Satan possibly lurking about, she should not in any case leave his side.

Replying with "sweet austere composure," Eve gives voice to hurt feelings. That you should doubt my firmness, she tells Adam, "I expected not to hear." Poor "domestic Adam," as Milton calls him, tries to appease her. He only meant to suggest, he says, that they should face together any threat from Satan. But the damage is not so easily undone. Eve still speaks with "accent sweet," but this time she asks bluntly: "If this be our condition," she begins, "how are we happy"? We must have been created with sufficient moral strength—her word is "integrity"—to enable us to resist temptation, whether in company or alone. Let us not imagine, she says, that the Creator made us so "imperfect" as to require us constantly to cling to each other for defense: "Frail is our happiness, if this be so,/And Eden were no Eden, thus exposed" (9:340–41).

We know, of course, that all of this is heading for disaster, but it is difficult to refute Eve's argument, since we also know that Satan's threat is not a temporary one. Were they never going to part, even for a few hours? And, after all, her confidence in her own integrity mirrors Adam's admiring sense that she seems "in herself complete." Unhappy and exasperated, Adam bursts out, "O woman." As if called upon to defend the whole order of things, he declares that there is "Nothing imperfect or deficient" in anything God created. His defensiveness seems a bit strange, since this is precisely Eve's point, until we recall that he had earlier expressed to God his own feeling that by himself he was both imperfect and deficient. But now, in acknowledging that Eve cannot in principle lack the firmness she would need to resist temptation, Adam has backed himself into a corner. "God left free the will," he says, and in saying so, he has to permit Eve to leave his side. "Go," he says, "for thy stay, not free, absents thee more." "With thy permission then" (9:378), replies Eve, withdrawing her hand from his and going off on her own.

Anyone who has had an argument with a spouse—which is to say anyone who has ever lived with someone intimately for a significant length of time—will recognize how brilliantly Milton captures a peculiar seesaw of love, anger, hurt feelings, attempts at appeasement, insincere compliments, passive aggression, frustration, submission, independence, and longing. And the genius of this invention is all the more remarkable, given the fact that Milton needs to persuade the reader that this squabbling husband and wife are in Eden and still unfallen. This is what a domestic quarrel in Paradise sounds like.

The elaborate backstory—the war in heaven and Satan's malicious enmity toward the humans that God had created—helped to make sense of the mysterious role in Genesis of the serpent. But Milton could not accept the notion that the first humans were simply tricked by Satan into disobeying, the victims of a celestial plot. Adam and Eve must be intelligent, well-informed, forewarned. They must be free, and they must be innocent. But if they are both free and innocent, then there must be something disturbing in innocence and threatening in freedom.

What is disturbing in innocence is the impossibility of understanding evil, no matter how many warnings you receive, no matter how much you try to imagine it. What is threatening in freedom is glimpsed in the pain of Adam's acknowledgment, as he lets Eve go: "thy stay, not free, absents thee more." There are some things that you cannot compel, true intimacy being foremost among them. And Eve's loving, perhaps lightly ironic attempt to assume the mantle of submission— "With thy permission then . . ."—does not hide her persistent refusal or inability to give up her freedom. She might be persuaded, but she cannot and will not be compelled.

Freedom threatens innocence. But Milton clearly thought that innocence without freedom was worthless, a state of perpetual childishness or bondage. Everything in his life—in his politics, his religious faith, his educational theory, his views of marriage and divorce— focused on consent, freely given or freely withheld. This is why, even in the bitterness of the divorce tracts, Milton never claimed that his wife had no right to leave him. He could not have brought himself to insist that she stay against her will.

This sphere of personal freedom, the core of Milton's sense of any life worth living, is why, notwithstanding Adam's anxiety and frustration, it makes perfect sense for Eve to go off by herself for a few hours and why it is appropriate for her to be alone when she faces the fateful temptation. Freedom at its core is not a collective possession; it belongs to each individual.

Eve, in Milton's vision, could not have impulsively or thoughtlessly succumbed to temptation. There had to have been long exchanges between her and the serpent, and then, though she was quite hungry, she could only have made her fateful decision to eat the forbidden fruit after thinking through the implications of the serpent's arguments. Knowledge of good and evil, she reasoned to herself, must in itself be a good, "For good unknown, sure is not had" (9:756). Is it possible that the prohibition to eat the fruit "Forbids us good, forbids us to be wise?" That makes no sense: "Such prohibitions bind not." As for the death that is threatened to anyone who disobeys, "what profits then/Our inward freedom?" The prohibition, she concluded then, must be a divine test of the kind that readers of *Paradise Lost* have already witnessed when God proposed that Adam find a partner among the animals he has just named. To pass the test—to be worthy of the freedom that God has conferred upon humans—Eve determined to reach out, pluck, and eat the forbidden fruit. She chose to fall.

In the wake of her fateful act, Eve, in Milton's account, immediately found that she faced another choice. Should she tell Adam what she had done and urge him to join her in the newly acquired knowledge, or hold onto the advantage that, as she imagined it, eating the fruit had conferred upon her? If she were to decide, as she put it, to "keep the odds of knowledge in my power," she would make up for the inferiority attributed to the female sex, the inferiority which the angel Raphael had sternly urged Adam to keep in mind.

Like Adam, Eve believed that the truest love must be between equals. She could, she told herself, use her extra knowledge,

the more to draw his Love,
And render me more equal, and perhaps,
A thing not undesirable, sometime
Superior: for inferior who is free? (9:822–25)

Milton almost certainly understood that last question as a sign of something seriously amiss in Eve, a corruption that had already begun to occur in the wake of her transgression. And yet the humans who emerged in his imagination had achieved enough independent reality to insist on the force of their claims. Eve had reason to believe that Adam did not want to love an inferior, and even that an occasional reversal of hierarchical order, with the woman on top, would be "not undesirable."

In the end, Eve decided to share with Adam—she could not bear the thought that she might after all die and that Adam would then wed "another Eve." And Adam? Adam, in Milton's conception, was not deceived. He understood at once that Eve had made a catastrophic mistake, but he immediately decided to share her fate. "How can I live without thee?" He refused to accept the official superiority that had been conferred upon him; she was for him the "last and best/Of all God's works." And he refused to accept what he intuited would be the official solution: to have God "create another Eve." Even, as Adam put it to himself, could he afford another rib, the loss of the woman he loved would never leave him.

Adam's decision to eat the fruit completed the disaster of Original Sin. It was followed, in Milton's vision, by mutual intoxication and intense sexual pleasure that then gave way to the bitterness of shame. The marital intimacy, so subtly drawn in its complexity before the Fall, disintegrated into recrimination and misery. Adam's long lament—why did I do what I did? how can I bear the weight of my guilt? what is to become of me?—culminated in rage when Eve tried to approach him. He vehemently repelled her: "Out of my sight, thou serpent" (9:867).

In Adam's mind Eve had become indistinguishable from the hated agent of their ruin, and the sight of her—as Milton wrote in the divorce tracts—brought him only a sense of "trouble and pain of loss, in some degree like that which reprobates feel." Bitterly unhappy, the first man would, Milton was sure, have descended into a loathing not of Eve alone but of all womankind. "Why did God," Adam asked himself, create "This novelty on Earth, this fair defect/Of nature" (10:891–92)? Why should he or any man find himself married to an "adversary, his hate or shame?"

But if at this point Milton tapped into his own most toxic feelings in the wake of the breakdown of his marriage, he also remembered the moment in which he let those feelings go. He recalled the occasion in his friends' house in London when the woman who had, as he believed, deeply wronged him knelt at his feet and begged his pardon. Eve, not repulsed by Adam's misogynistic reproaches,

> with tears that ceased not flowing,
> And tresses all disordered, at his feet
> Fell humble, and embracing them, besought
> His peace. (10:910–13)

And Adam's "heart relented."

Had Milton's own heart actually relented in 1645, when he took up the weeping Mary and resumed the marriage? Was it from this moment and the years that followed that he derived the feeling of profound love that he attributed to Adam? The fact that they then had four children in quick succession—until the fourth childbirth took Mary's life in 1652—does not really give us an answer. *Paradise Lost* suggests at least that Milton passionately longed to imagine a full reconciliation between the estranged husband and his wife. After all, in his decision not to ask God for another Eve, Adam had deliberately refused the Edenic equivalent of divorce. In the wake of the Fall, Eve proposed that she should plead to bear alone the full consequences of God's wrath, but Adam rejected this idea, as he likewise rejected her proposal that they jointly commit suicide and her idea that they abstain from sex in order to remain childless. Slowly, as a married couple, they would have to put together their broken lives.

They began to do so by acting in unison, kneeling down together to confess their faults to God and implore his mercy. They still hoped, Milton makes clear, that they might be able to avert the divine punishment: "Undoubtedly," Adam reassured himself and his wife, God "will relent and turn/From his displeasure" (10:1093–94). And, he thought, if it remained their fate to return in the end to dust, at least they could expect "To pass commodiously this life, sustained/By him with many comforts." After all, they have been living in the most beautiful garden imaginable. Rising from his knees, Adam declared that he was confident that their joint prayers had been heard: "the bitterness of death/Is past," he told Eve, "and we shall live" (11:157–58).

Of course, as its title already suggests, *Paradise Lost* does not have so happy an ending. The bitterness of death is not past. Adam was closer to the truth when, in his most despairing mood, he intuited that God had chosen to inflict upon them "a slow-paced evil,/A long day's dying to augment our pain" (10:963–64). Expulsion from Paradise is decreed in order to make sure that the humans do not have the opportunity to reach out to the Tree of Life "and eat/And live forever" (11:94–95). Though Milton was simply quoting directly from Genesis at this point, he seems to have been uneasy with this archaic verse. He has God add a qualifier—"dream at least to live/Forever"—but the qualifier seems to undermine the motive for the expulsion.

Could God actually have feared that if the humans were left in the Garden, they might have eaten from a magical tree that would make them immortal? Milton uncharacteristically failed to wrestle the theological problem to its knees. He focused instead on the intense human anxiety caused by the divine decree. Adam stands stunned with sorrow; he could not speak. Eve weeps at the prospect of saying farewell forever to the flowers she had planted and the nuptial bower she had adorned. The archangel Michael, sent by God to announce and enforce the decree, simply tells the woman that she should not be "over-fond" of what was not hers in the first place. The disconnect between this angelic perspective and the perspective of humans being evicted from their home by an implacable landlord shapes the conclusion of Milton's poem.

For by the close of *Paradise Lost,* Adam and Eve had become so real in Milton's imagination that they began to crack open the whole theological apparatus that brought them into being. They had, as Augustine had fervently wished, altogether lost the shimmering air of allegorical figures. They possessed an insistent, undeniable, literal human presence. This was the kind of presence that Shakespeare had conferred upon Falstaff, Hamlet, and Cleopatra, a presence that signals the triumph of literature. But the triumph of literature came at a theological cost. Next to Adam and Eve, all of the other characters—Michael, Raphael, Satan, even God and his Son—seem somehow reduced in significance. Of course, Milton continued to insist upon their inconceivable vastness, power, and importance, compared to puny humanity, and he persisted in the belief that he was justifying the ways of God to men. But he could not control his deepest loyalty, and he was the greater artist for this apparent failure.

On God's orders, while Eve is made to fall into a deep sleep, the archangel Michael leads Adam to the top of a mountain and gives him a vision of human life as it is to become over time. The vision, dismaying in almost all of its details, includes a tour of a hospital, so that he could witness the full range of convulsions, epilepsies, kidney stones, ulcers, madness, and the like to which humans would be subject. It is all Adam's fault, Michael takes pains to underscore, "From man's effeminate slackness it begins" (11:634). We are back to the stern warning to hold on to his dominant place that Raphael had tried to give Adam before the Fall.

It is in the spirit of this warning that Michael concludes the long, painful tour of history: "He ended, and they both descend the hill" (12:606). But it is precisely here, in the descent from the grand angelic overview to the uncertain ground of ordinary human life, that Milton's own shift in loyalty makes itself most clearly felt. Adam does not seek to linger in the presence of the angel; on the contrary, he hastens to get away from the celestial visitor and return to his spouse: "Adam to the bower where Eve/Lay sleeping ran before." And Eve, who is already awake, speaks words that make it clear that she too is now focused entirely on her partner:

> With thee to go,
> Is to stay here; without thee here to stay,
> Is to go hence unwilling; thou to me
> Art all things under Heav'n, all places thou. (12:615–18)

The theological scheme, of course, is still in place. Milton believes both in the justice of the horrible punishments that will be visited on all humankind as a result of man's first disobedience and in the salvation that will be brought to the faithful by Christ. But what most arrests the poet's attention is not this grand vision of fall and redemption but rather the quiet intimacy of the married couple. Though he has run ahead in order to have time alone with her, Adam, as Milton imagines him, cannot reply to Eve's loving words, "for now too nigh/Th'Archangel stood." The things that a man and a woman say to each other at such a moment are not public utterances intended for an angelic audience. The cherubim, advancing with their flaming swords, take their stations and begin to change the temperate climate of Paradise into something that resembles the torrid heat of Libya. Michael seizes Adam and Eve in either hand, hurries them down through the gate onto the plain below, and then disappears.

What follows at the poem's end are among the most beautiful lines that Milton ever wrote. The lines continue to express faith in divine providence but still more in freedom, the freedom that Milton believed God had conferred on the first couple, the freedom that still belonged to all humans. At its close *Paradise Lost* liberates Adam and Eve from the story that gave them birth and watches them advance together toward an uncertain future:

> Some natural tears they dropped, but wiped them soon;
> The world was all before them, where to choose
> Their place of rest, and providence their guide:
> They hand in hand with wand'ring steps and slow,
> Through Eden took their solitary way. (12:646–49)

More than a thousand years after Augustine, Adam and Eve have finally become real.

12

Men Before Adam

Isaac La Peyrère must have been one of those children who give Sunday school teachers severe headaches. He asked too many questions, and the questions he asked were vexing ones. The pious Calvinists of Bordeaux, where La Peyrère was born in 1596 to a wealthy Protestant family, would have easily recognized the type: intellectually alert and full of spiritual zeal, but also annoyingly curious, argumentative, venturesome, and independent. He had the makings of a fervent believer, but at the same time he scrutinized as if from an odd distance the most cherished and familiar articles of the faith.

At that particular time and place it would have been reasonable to deduce that at least some of the boy's qualities might be traced back to Marrano roots—that is, to a concealed Judaism that his family, of Portuguese origin, had brought with them after the expulsion of the Jews from the Iberian Peninsula. The great essayist Michel de Montaigne, who had been mayor of Bordeaux in the 1580s, had on his mother's side a similar background, which may have contributed to his comparable independence of mind. The wars of religion—murderous conflicts between French Roman Catholics and Protestants that raged all through the second half of the sixteenth century—had, in any case, undermined for most thinking people, Catholic and Protestant alike, the settled assumptions of both society and creed.

The young La Peyrère displayed an intense interest in the Hebrew Bible and above all in the book of Genesis. And his restless curiosity was piqued by a peculiar detail early in the sacred book: in the wake of murdering his brother, Cain is driven forth and comes to dwell in the land of Nod, east of Eden. There, the Bible relates without further explanation, Cain "knew his wife, and she conceived . . . and he builded a city" (Gen. 4:17). Where, the schoolboy wondered out loud, did the woman Cain married come from? The traditional answer, scandalously enough, was that she was one of his sisters, though no daughters of Adam and Eve had been mentioned up to this point in Genesis.

There the Sunday school discussion was meant to end. But little Isaac's curiosity would not be quieted. A fugitive and a vagabond, Cain told God that he feared that "every one that findeth me shall slay me" (Gen. 4:14), but who could this "every one" possibly be, if the world was still unpopulated? And what was the woman Cain married doing in the land of Nod? And how could the fugitive have built a city there, without any other people around to inhabit it? Might all of these clues suggest, the boy asked himself, that there were already humans in the world before the creation of Adam and Eve, humans who lived outside the walls of the Garden of Eden and with whom Adam and Eve and their offspring interacted? It is not clear that the young La Peyrère dared to express this surmise openly. Even an irrepressibly curious schoolboy knew that such a question could get him into serious trouble.

There matters might have come to rest, as they probably had many times before for generations of overly inquisitive schoolchildren, had it not been for several peculiar twists and turns both in La Peyrère's life and in the culture into which he was born. Trained as a lawyer, he came to the attention of the powerful Prince of Condé, who brought him to Paris as his secretary. That position provided a measure of protection, enabling him to pursue his penchant for restless, potentially heretical inquiry wherever it happened to lead him. And he had access as well to a circle of daring philosophers, theologians, and scientists. Members of this circle were unusually alert to discoveries and encounters that had been taking place for more than a century but whose disturbing implications were still dangerous to speak about too openly.

The implications already began to emerge on October 12, 1492, when Columbus and his men made landfall in the Caribbean and witnessed huge crowds of natives. "All of them go around," the admiral recorded in his diary entry, "as naked as their mothers bore them; and the women also." Body paint yes, but no clothing. For the armed European adventurers this nakedness was good news, for it meant that the inhabitants were vulnerable. But at the same time it posed a theological problem: how was it possible for a whole, immense population to be exempt from the first and most basic consequence of the Fall, namely, shame? "And the eyes of them both were opened, and they knew that they were naked; and they sewed fig leaves together, and made themselves aprons" (Gen. 3:7).

Shame was not supposed to be a cultural acquisition; it was the inescapable, defining human condition in the wake of sin. Yet here were huge numbers of people parading around naked: Why did they not recognize their condition? And why did they not avail themselves of the means that God himself had given humans to cover their nakedness: "Unto Adam also and to his wife did the Lord God make coats of skins, and clothed them"?

It was possible to argue that the natives had lost all shame and forgotten the gift of clothing. Apes, it was widely thought, had once been like us, but had degenerated into their bestial state. So too, some argued, the New World natives were creatures who had fallen below the level of the human. In 1550 certain Spanish intellectuals presented such an argument at a formal debate in Valladolid. They proposed that, despite certain resemblances, the newly encountered creatures were not actually human and that what sounded like speech were only animal noises. The testimony of eyewitnesses who had communicated with them and could attest that the natives were indeed human was deemed insufficient. The position that they were beasts who lacked the use of reason was ultimately defeated not by empirical observation but by religious doctrine: the natives, the winning argument claimed, had souls that were ripe for conversion to Christianity. But, if the inhabitants of these islands were not beasts, that is, if they were persons who had descended, like everyone else, from Adam and Eve, what then to make of their nakedness?

The answer was hinted at by Columbus. On his third voyage and shaken in his belief that he had reached the Indies, the admiral began to entertain a new possibility. The world is not perfectly round, he wrote, but has instead the shape of a pear or ball on which there is "something like a woman's nipple." The new lands that he has discovered, with their perfect beauty and abundance, must be located on or very near that nipple, whose very center was the site of the Earthly Paradise. Columbus did not believe that he would be able to enter the garden itself, at least not in this mortal life. But it made sense that in their nakedness the people he saw, living so close to Eden, resembled its first inhabitants. Shame after the Fall evidently intensified with distance. It set in more deeply the further one moved from the original site of bliss.

Proximity to Paradise would explain the rushing currents of fresh water that the Spanish seamen observed with wonder in Trinidad's Gulf of Paria. After all, in Genesis it was written that four great rivers arose in the Garden of Eden. In 1498 the only alternative explanation Columbus could think of seemed even wilder: "And I say," he added, "that if it be not from the earthly paradise that this river comes, it originates from a vast land, lying to the south, of which hitherto no knowledge has been obtained." That thought—the idea of an unknown continent—was so difficult to fathom that he retreated to the safer ground of Eden: "But I am much more convinced in my own mind that there where I have said is the earthly paradise."

When, in the wake of further exploration, it became clear that there really was a vast land lying to the south—namely, the whole of South America—the idea that the site of Paradise was located nearby did not simply vanish. In the sixteenth and early seventeenth centuries, the Spanish chroniclers López de Gómara and Antonio de Herrera seriously entertained the possibility, as did the great naturalist Father José de Acosta in his *Historia natural y moral de las Indias*. In the mid-seventeenth century, Antonio de León Pinelo—like La Peyrère the son of Portuguese Marranos—proved to his own satisfaction at least that the Río de la Plata, the Amazon, the Orinoco, and the Magdalena were the four great rivers that surged up from the Earthly Paradise.

And, after the shock of the first encounter, what about the nakedness of the New World natives? Most European colonists, bent on ruthlessly exploiting the peoples they overpowered, conveniently interpreted it as a sign of their primitive state and left it at that. If the Great Debate in Valladolid concluded that the natives were human, it also concluded that they were what Aristotle had called "natural slaves," people whose debased condition made it legitimate and even merciful for them to be enslaved.

But at least one major figure, the great Dominican Bartolomé de las Casas, vehemently disagreed. Las Casas, who had originally come to the New World as a colonist, had been deeply shaken by the atrocities that he had witnessed against its inhabitants and that he denounced in a celebrated indictment, *A Brief Account of the Destruction of the Indies* (1542). He shared Columbus's conviction that the Americas were the likeliest site of the lost Garden of Eden. As for the natives, they were not only the same as all other humans, Christian and non-Christian alike, they were actually, as befitted their paradisal lands, morally superior. "God made all the peoples of this area, many and varied as they are," Las Casas wrote, "as open and as innocent as can be imagined.

The simplest people in the world—unassuming, long-suffering, unas-
sertive, and submissive—they are without malice or guile, and are
utterly faithful and obedient." They were not quite in Paradise—for
they lacked the Catholic faith—but, as their nakedness suggested, they
were very close.

"It was upon these gentle lambs," Las Casas lamented, "that from
the very first day they clapped eyes on them the Spanish fell like rav-
ening wolves upon the fold." The numbers of the dead staggered the
imagination: "At a conservative estimate, the despotic and diabolical
behavior of the Christians has, over the last forty years, led to the
unjust and totally unwarranted deaths of more than twelve million
souls, women and children among them, and there are grounds for
believing my own estimate of more than fifteen million to be nearer
the mark." (Modern demographic studies have concluded that Las
Casas's figures—long thought to be a polemical exaggeration—are
likely to be close to the truth.) If these tragic victims resembled the
Edenic innocence of Adam and Eve, what did that make the Spanish?
Las Casas did not hesitate to draw the conclusion: "The reader may ask
himself . . . whether these poor people would not fare far better if they
were entrusted to the devils in Hell than they do at the hands of the
devils of the New World who masquerade as Christians."

Las Casas's book became a European bestseller, and not only among
those whose main desire was to demonize the Spanish *conquistadores* or
the Catholic Church. His searing indictment lies behind Montaigne's
subversive questions, questions that extended to all European Christians: Why do we think that our ways are better than their ways? Who
are the genuinely civilized people and who the barbarians? Such questions had an unnerving relation to the basic story of primal innocence,
fall, and redemption through Christ. And it was not solely the viciousness of the colonists that proved so unsettling; it was the sheer number
of people in a hitherto unknown part of the globe, a part of which
there was no hint in the Bible. How could they possibly have gotten

there? Why should anyone think that there is a single, one-size-fits-all account of the entire world?

The size of the population that the European adventurers encountered in the Americas and the range of flora and fauna were difficult to reconcile with biblical chronology. The recent "discovery of the vast continent of America," wrote a distinguished mid-seventeenth-century English jurist, Matthew Hale, "which appears to be as populous with men, and as well stored with cattle [i.e., animals] almost as any part of Europe, Asia, or Africa, hath occasioned some difficulty and dispute touching the traduction of all mankind from the two common parents . . . namely *Adam* and *Eve.*"

The problem, as Hale notes, was "traduction": how was so much life carried across the ocean sea from one world to another? The Jesuit José de Acosta speculated—correctly, as we now know—that there must once have been a land bridge that linked Asia and the Americas. He had no physical evidence for its existence, but he needed to posit one in order to save the testimony of the Bible: "The reason which forces me to say that the first men of these Indies came from Europe or Asia is so as not to contradict the Holy Scripture which clearly teaches that all men descended from Adam, and thus we can give no other origin to man in the Indies."

To La Peyrère the idea of a land bridge seemed a desperate attempt—a Hail Mary, as it were—to save a bankrupt idea. No vanished bridge, he thought, could possibly account for the vast numbers of humans that, according to the orthodox account, would have had to descend almost immediately from the seven survivors on Noah's Ark and to spread with unimaginable rapidity throughout the globe. Even the sheer diversity of human cultures—Lapland nomads and Chinese courtiers, the fashionable ladies of Paris and the naked natives of the New World—posed what seemed to him a serious challenge to the accepted understanding of Adam and Eve as the progenitors of all the humans in the world.

La Peyrère was not alone in the doubts that seized him. In exactly the period when Milton set about to make Adam and Eve more intensely and fully real than they had ever been before, the credibility of the opening chapters of Genesis was being undermined on multiple fronts. Perhaps Milton was driven to write *Paradise Lost* in part by his very awareness of the challenges that were unsettling his contemporary La Peyrère. Though they reacted in different ways, they were registering the same seismic tremors: the vast expansion of the known world, the apparent absence of universal shame in many of its peoples, the viciousness of religious wars, the unnerving claims of Copernicus and Galileo.

These were not the only tremors that began to cause cracks in the Bible's origin story. Throughout Europe, humanists and artists had sparked a renewed interest in classical antiquity. The recovery of crucial texts from the ancient world gave new life to pagan theories of human origin that had been forgotten or ignored for centuries. No one rushed, as a result, to challenge the absolute authority of Genesis, but it was unsettling to become aware of alternatives.

One of the most powerful of these alternatives originated in the late fourth century BCE with the Greek philosopher Epicurus. Though his works were almost entirely lost, the long, brilliant poem written around 50 BCE by his Roman disciple Lucretius was found, copied, and returned to circulation by the Renaissance book hunter Poggio Bracciolini. Lucretius wrote that our species, along with all the others, emerged as a result of random atomic mutations over a limitless expanse of time. He argued that the universe was eternal and that nature ceaselessly experimented with the creation of new species. Most of these species perished—nature was indifferent to failure and waste—but a certain number of them, including our own, managed to survive, find food, and propagate.

Humans, Lucretius proposed, must have evolved only gradually and fitfully from savagery to civilization. The earliest humans were raw-boned, ignorant primitives scrambling to survive in a brutal environment. They had no sense of social order or the common good; by instinct each tried to seize what he could for himself. And the relations between man and woman had more to do with rape and barter than with anything like tender feelings: "The woman either yielded from mutual desire, or was mastered by the man's impetuous might and inordinate lust, or sold her favors for acorns or arbute berries or choice pears."

The recovery by Renaissance scholars of the knowledge of Greek and the translation of Greek classics into Latin made available many other pagan origin stories. The archaic Greek poet Hesiod offered a vision of a golden age, along with the myth of Pandora, so oddly reminiscent of Eve. The storyteller Aesop invoked a golden time in which the animals (along with stones, pine needles, and the sea) all spoke, as well as humans. Aristotle's student Dicaearchus of Messana wrote of primitive humans who lived like gods, were strict vegetarians, eschewed wars or feuds, and were by nature the best versions of ourselves. The Greek rhetorician Maximus Tyrius depicted Prometheus first creating man, a creature "in mind approaching very near to the gods, in body slender, erect, and symmetrical, mild of aspect, apt for handicraft, firm of step."

Vernacular translations, along with the printing press, made such accounts widely available, so that many people began to understand that Genesis was not alone or uncontested. Thus, for example, it was now relatively easy to come across the story, in Plato, of an earlier age in which humans were generated from the earth, without sexual reproduction. In that time long ago, the philosopher wrote, the climate was mild, and humans, dwelling naked and in the open air, had all that they needed: "The earth gave them fruits in abundance, which grew on trees and shrubs unbidden, and were not planted by the hand of man." There were no forms of government, no private ownership, no separate families competing with one another for scarce resources.

This and similar pagan stories could always be treated as distorted versions of the true origin story, the one that Moses had written, but the cumulative effect was still disturbing. It was not only the prestige of the classical authors that made it difficult simply to dismiss their accounts out of hand; the problem lay also in the chronology that they frequently invoked. A careful numbering of the generations recorded in the Hebrew Bible seemed to reveal that the world was some 6,000 years old. But Plato's dialogue *Critias,* with its description of the lost kingdom of Atlantis, speaks of founding events some 9,000 years ago. And the Greek historian Herodotus reports that he had extensive discussions with Egyptian priests who claimed to possess records that went back well more than 11,340 years. The Babylonian priest Berossus, from whom the West learned most of what it knew about ancient Babylon, calculated that there were some 432,000 years from the first king, the Chaldean Aloros, to the Great Flood. If that figure seemed utterly impossible (which it is), there remained a queasy sense that the biblical chronology was far too short.

Very few Catholics or Protestants in the Renaissance were eager to abandon the Bible's chronology, and it was, in any case, dangerous to admit to any serious doubts. In London in the 1590s a government spy reported that the playwright Christopher Marlowe went around saying that "the Indians and many authors of antiquity have assuredly written above 16,000 years ago, whereas Adam is proved to have lived within 6,000 years." In almost the same moment the renegade Italian monk Giordano Bruno asked how it was possible that so many people could continue to believe in the biblical chronology despite the fact that there is "a new part of the world, where are found memorials of ten thousand years and more." Marlowe and Bruno were compulsive risk-takers. One was mortally wounded with a knife stuck into his eye by an agent of Queen Elizabeth's secret police; the other was burned at the stake in Rome's Campo dei Fiori.

Still, rumors continued to circulate. La Peyrère heard that in Mexico the Aztec priests had written records far antedating Genesis but that the Spanish church authorities ordered them destroyed or buried. (Buried in the mid-sixteenth century, the Aztec Calendar Stone, now in the National Anthropology Museum in Mexico City, was not rediscovered until 1790.) It was obviously prudent to keep one's distance from such occasions for doubt, but for La Peyrère they served as confirmations of the theory that he had secretly harbored ever since he was a boy.

In the mid-1640s, La Peyrère spent several years in Sweden and Denmark, where he formed a close friendship with a celebrated physician and scholar named (quaintly enough, to English ears) Ole Worm. Worm was a passionate and inveterate collector of "curiosities." The wild array of objects he assembled in his home-based museum, known as the Wormianum, ranged from fossil bones to narwhal tusks, from an Eskimo kayak to an ancient Roman clasp, from a stuffed crocodile to an American tobacco pipe. It may have been the simple presence of these objects, or their shared interest in the sheer diversity of things, that inspired La Peyrère to tell his friend about the great idea that had been germinating in him since childhood.

Adam and Eve certainly existed, La Peyrère asserted, but they could not have been by any means the first humans on earth. There must have been innumerable others before them and all around them, peoples with diverse languages and cultures and histories. Long before the Fall, these peoples had struggled to survive, experienced their share of wars, plagues, and fevers, suffered the pangs of childbirth, and shared the fate of all mortals—not, that is, because of the eating of the forbidden fruit, but because such is the natural existence of humans.

La Peyrère told Ole Worm that he had written all of his theories up in a manuscript called the "Pre-Adamites" and that he had already shown a draft to a few others in the hope that they would be convinced. Their initial responses, he acknowledged, had not been encouraging. One of his readers, the distinguished Dutch philosopher Hugo Grotius, had become particularly upset. The American natives seemed to pose a problem for religious orthodoxy, Grotius conceded, but the problem was resolved if they were the descendants of the Viking expeditions of Eric the Red and Leif Erikson. La Peyrère's alternative suggestion should not be allowed to circulate: "If such things be believed, I see a great danger imminent to religion."

But surrounded by the precious objects he had collected, Ole Worm did not agree. Perhaps he was attracted by La Peyrère's claim that only the pre-Adamite theory could explain the existence of the American Indians and the Greenland Eskimos whose artifacts were so prominently featured in his museum. Undaunted by the warning signs, he helped La Peyrère in his research, introduced him to important friends, and encouraged him to make his views known to a wider world.

The result, in 1655, was the publication in Amsterdam of a book in Latin, the *Prae-Adamitae*, followed a year later in London by an English translation, *Men Before Adam*. The prince for whom he had originally worked had died, but the son and heir, the new Prince of Condé, kept La Peyrère on and must have made him feel secure, for his book holds nothing back. He recognized the risks: "As he who goes upon ice," he writes, "goes warily where he crack it . . . so I dreaded first, least this doubtful dispute might either cut my soles, or throw me headlong into some deep heresy." But now, after years of study and research, he walked on boldly, convinced that he was treading on safe ground.

Adam, La Peyrère explained, was not the father of all humankind; he was only the father of the Jews whom God had mysteriously chosen to receive the law and to be, though Jesus Christ, the agents of redemption. This particular genealogy is the reason that the time frame of Genesis seems so out of sync with "all profane records whether ancient or new, to wit, those of the Chaldeans, Egyptians, Scythians, and Chinensians [sic]," not to mention "those of Mexico, not long ago discovered by Columbus." The problems disappear, if you recognize that the world was already full of people before the creation of Adam.

But what about the consequences—work, pain in childbirth, death—that in Genesis follow from the transgression of Adam and Eve in the Garden? Did the earlier inhabitants live without these miseries? Not at all. "The natural death of men," La Peyrère wrote, "arises from the nature of man, which is mortal." So too women have always had natural pains in childbirth, just as serpents have always crawled in the dust. The curses pronounced by God in Genesis were spiritual punishments, added onto the ordinary, natural condition of existence. Wars, plagues, and fevers did not spring up as the result of eating the forbidden fruit; they were and are part of the "imperfection" of nature.

If so few readers of the Bible have understood these simple truths, it is, La Peyrère wrote with astonishing candor, because the Bible is such an imperfect document. The few things that we need for our salvation are made clear. But as for the rest, much of it is written "with so great carelessness and obscurity that sometimes nothing can be more obscure." How could Moses have been so careless? The answer is that the Bible, as we have it, is not Moses's own copy, handed down directly by him; after all, we read in it of his death. In the course of innumerable transcriptions, errors inevitably were introduced. It is no wonder that so many things are "confused and out of order": the Scriptures are "a heap of copy confusedly taken."

These confusions have led to innumerable absurdities in interpretation. Adam could not, as most commentaries claim, have been created as an adult. He must have been fashioned as an infant and have passed through the slow growth of childhood before God brought him to Paradise. How else could he have acquired the basic competencies that human beings only achieve in their early years? Then in Paradise the naming of the animals must have taken far longer than most people imagine. It could not possibly have been the work of a half-day,

for thither must the Elephant come from the furthest parts of *India* and Africk, who are of a heavy and a slow pace. What shall I speak of so many several species of creatures and fowls, unknown to our Hemisphere, who must swim so much Sea, pass over so much Land, to come from *America*, and there receive their names?

In such passages it sounds like La Peyrère is making fun of the Adam and Eve story, but the opposite is the case. We tend to think of belief as a kind of ON/OFF switch—either you accept or you do not accept a particular story as the truth. But there are many intervening stages between blind faith and outright rejection. Like Milton, La Peyrère was an heir to Augustine's insistence that the Bible's account of the first humans be taken literally. Yet from childhood he had been bothered by cracks that appear as soon as one tries to treat the myth as a description of reality. Determined, whatever the risks, to patch the cracks, he thought he could do so by reducing the Genesis narrative to a single strand—the origin of the Jews—in the much larger history of humanity.

That left room for a vaster world, with a more complex demographic history. Noah's Flood, for example, was a local rather than universal event; it "was not upon the whole earth, but only upon the Land of the Jews." Since God's intention was to destroy only the Jews, the revised understanding would allow for the global diffusion of peoples whose very existence early Christians like Lactantius and even the great Augustine doubted. "I would *Augustine* and *Lactantius* were now alive, who scoffed at the *Antipodes*," La Peyrère wrote,

> Truly they would pity themselves, if they should hear or see those things which are discovered in the East and West Indies in this clear-sighted age, as also a great many other countries full of men; to whom it is certain none of *Adam*'s posterity ever arrived.

Long before Adam and Eve were created, the pre-Adamites had been fruitful and multiplied and filled the earth.

For La Peyrère this correct understanding was not so much a demotion of the Genesis story as it was a promotion of the significance of the Jews. *Men Before Adam* was dedicated "To all the Synagogues of the Jews, dispersed over the face of the EARTH." His dedicatory epistle ends, "Bear up, and keep your selves for better things." The better things, he believed, would include salvation through Jesus, whom they had been chosen by the mysterious will of God to bring forth, just as they had been chosen to bring forth the Law.

That chosenness had nothing to do with any special virtue: "If you look upon the matter whereof the Jews were created, you will find nothing that shall make them appear worthy of the Election; For they were made up of the same flesh and blood as the gentiles, and were tempered with the same clay of which other men were framed." But their history as the chosen people is uniquely important, and for La Peyrère it is not fatally tarnished by their role in the Crucifixion. After all, if Jesus had not been crucified, he would not have been the savior of all mankind. The Jews in the first century did kill Jesus, he wrote, but Jews have already been amply punished over many generations for participation in this act. Persecution of the Jews now, he wrote, was almost the same crime as the deicide committed in the first century.

La Peyrère fearlessly proceeded to work out the implications of this argument, in terms that would have seemed to his contemporaries almost as shocking as his theory of the pre-Adamites. The world would soon witness, he wrote, the coming of a Jewish messiah. This coming will complete the history of the Jews—that small, finite fraction of the world's vast population—and in doing so it will also bring redemption to all humankind. There will be no distinction between pre-Adamites and descendants of Adam, no separating of the saved from the damned; no weeping souls driven to an eternity of torments in hell while other souls ascend to bliss. Everyone will be saved.

To accomplish the coming of the Messiah, La Peyrère wrote,

Jews and Christians should unite. Even though Christians may find Jews repulsive, anti-Jewish discrimination should be immediately stopped. Recognizing what ingrates they have been to the people who brought forth Jesus, Christians should begin to treat Jews decently. Working together, they will bring about the return of the Jews to the Holy Land from which they had been exiled, and in doing so they will fulfill the great design prophesied in the Bible. With the conversion of the Jews and their return to Israel, history will come to an end.

It is difficult to imagine a set of propositions more likely than these to provoke nearly universal outrage. The publication of *Men Before Adam* aroused vehement condemnation from Catholics, Protestants, and Jews alike. La Peyrère had stepped across boundaries very few others were willing to approach, let alone to cross. As the attacks mounted and his book was burned, he grew increasingly alarmed. His patron the Prince of Condé was in Catholic Brussels. There La Peyrère traveled to seek protection, but this move proved to be a disastrous mistake.

In February 1656 thirty armed men stormed into his room in Brussels and hauled him off to prison, charged with being "un hérétique détestable." At first, during long interrogations, he stubbornly upheld his view, but it became clear that neither the prince nor anyone else was going to intervene on his behalf. The situation was extremely perilous, but perhaps at this point La Peyrère's very notoriety as the author of the *Prae-Adamitae* helped him. If he recanted his errors, apologized to the pope, and became a Catholic, his captors informed him, he would be spared. By June, La Peyrère had accepted these terms and was taken to Rome, where he was personally brought before Pope Alexander VII. It is said that the pope smiled, saying, "Let us embrace this man who is before Adam." The General of the Jesuits, who was also present at the audience, remarked that he and the pope had had a good laugh when they read the *Prae-Adamitae*.

There is no record of La Peyrère's response to this merriment, but we do know that he set to work composing his recantation. He had been led astray, he wrote, by his Calvinist upbringing, which had erroneously taught him that he should interpret Scripture according to reason and his own conscience. That path brought him to the pre-Adamite theory, but now he understood: he had to follow neither the dictates of reason nor the promptings of conscience, but only the authority of the pope. He therefore renounced his claims about men before Adam, his account of the Flood as a local event, his denial of Moses's authorship of the entire Old Testament, and all the rest of his mistaken interpretations. His theory, he said, was like the Copernican hypothesis. If the pope said that it was wrong, then it must be wrong.

La Peyrère's recantation was accepted and printed. Two doctors of theology from the Sorbonne appended letters of approval. The pope, highly gratified, offered the repentant heretic a benefice and the opportunity to remain in Rome, but after a polite interval La Peyrère requested permission to return to Paris. There he resumed his service to the Prince of Condé. Though discreetly insinuating that he had not altogether abandoned his messianic dreams for a return of the Jews to the Holy Land, he managed to remain out of further trouble. He lived a long, quiet life in the shadow of his brush with an auto-da-fé. His wife and children, about whom we know next to nothing, probably predeceased him, and he spent his final years in a monastery.

What did it all amount to, this strange intellectual adventure? The Messiah failed to come, the Jews did not return to Zion, and the daring idea of the pre-Adamites, attacked from all sides, faded into oblivion. It was one of those dead-ends down which searchers for the truth venture, when conventional explanations and received assumptions begin to crumble. Not that the biblical origin story was crumbling yet. The problem was that it had become too real—the triumph of that long process that culminated in *Paradise Lost*. This reality—the palpable presence of Adam and Eve as sentient bodies in a particular geographical setting at the onset of historical time—forced a thoughtful obsessive like La Peyrère to try to fit them into the actual world as it had come to be known.

It is possible that La Peyrère did something more than hit a wall. He may have contributed in his odd way to persistent questioning that ultimately led to a more critical, anthropological, and historical approach to Genesis. He was both one of the precursors of Zionism and an impassioned voice for tolerance and for the redemption of all peoples. But his great idea turned out to be hopelessly wrong, and by a peculiar irony its most significant afterlife was as a justification for racism and slavery. In the late eighteenth and nineteenth centuries, La Peyrère's *Men Before Adam,* long sunk into oblivion, was revived by those who wanted to claim that the peoples of color whom they had enslaved were not in fact descendants of Adam and Eve. That La Peyrère himself did not rank on a scale of superiority the diverse populations of the globe, whether pre- or post-Adam, did not matter. His notion of multiple human origins—polygenesis, as opposed to monogenesis—gave the racists just what they needed.

As it happens, scientific studies of mitochondrial DNA overwhelmingly favor the notion of the shared African origin of all modern humans. Migration out of Africa was recent, by geological standards—that is, somewhere between 125,000 and 60,000 years ago—and it made use of such features as the land bridge that La Peyrère ridiculed. There is another mistake that proved crucial in the refutation of La Peyrère: as Malthus showed, populations multiply geometrically. There is therefore no mathematical reason why the human population should not have increased so rapidly—though the geographical distribution may have taken longer than the Bible allowed.

But the strange fate of La Peyrère's idea is a useful reminder of the leveling power that is always latent in the Adam and Eve story. Just as the medieval priest John Ball tapped into this power to challenge aristocratic fantasies of innate superiority—"When Adam delved and Eve span, who was then the gentleman?"—so too the slave-owners sensed that a single common ancestor pair at the origin of all humanity could give them trouble. They did not all depend on polygenesis—many Jews and Christians who believed fervently in universal descent from Adam and Eve were perfectly prepared to enslave their fellow descendants—but they knew that abolitionists would use our shared humanity as one of their most powerful moral arguments.

13

Falling Away

The threat of being burned at the stake—always an effective inducement to concentrate the mind—could force public recantations of skeptical propositions and unwelcome doubts. But it was not so simple. For "detestable heresies" like La Peyrère's were not the consequence of skepticism; they were the result of thinking of Adam and Eve as real. That is, they reflected the same forces that led Renaissance explorers to chart the location of their garden, Renaissance chroniclers to calculate the precise number of generations since their expulsion, Renaissance painters to give them bodily reality, and Milton, the consummate Renaissance poet, to confer upon them a complex marital relationship. The collective success of all of these efforts by believers—the triumphant fulfillment of the old Augustinian dream of a literal interpretation— had an unintended and devastating consequence: the story began to die.

Of course, the figures of Adam and Eve within the story were always understood to be mortal, the result of their transgression. But their coming into full life, through the power of Renaissance science, art, and literature, caused the whole structure in which they were embedded to become mortal. It did so because the gap between

convincingly real people and conspicuously unreal circumstances—
mysterious garden, magical trees, talking snake, God taking a walk in
the cool of the evening breeze—became increasingly untenable. So
too a vivid and humanly compelling Adam and Eve brought into ever
sharper and more uncomfortable focus the ethical problems that had
long haunted the story: the inexplicable move from perfect innocence
to wickedness, a divine prohibition that forbade the very knowledge
needed to observe the same prohibition, terrible universal punishments
for what appeared to be a modest local transgression. The problems
kept accumulating, and earnest good-faith attempts to solve them, such
as La Peyrère's, only opened up new problems.

The mortality of a narrative—one that has, as an article of faith,
been taken as true—is not the same as a human's. The aging process is not comparable; there are no telltale signs of impending collapse; no heirs crowd in by the bedside weeping or hoping for a legacy.
Above all, there is no moment in which the living myth decisively
stops breathing and a licensed physician hurries into the room to cer-
tify that indeed it has all come to an end. What happens instead is
simply that a significant number of people cease to believe that the
story convincingly depicts reality. Others may continue fervently to
believe after the decline has begun, but the ground has begun to shift,
and the process is usually irreversible. Even those who think that the
story is untrue may hold on to it for some time, whether because it is
awkward or dangerous not to do so, or because the alternative is not
clear, or because it still seems to convey something important about
life. But its key elements have begun to shimmer like a mirage. They
have ceased to be solid truths in the real world and have begun to drift
toward make-believe. The narrative becomes a just-so story, a fanciful
attempt to account for the way things are. If it is powerful enough, it
becomes a work of art.

The drift toward make-believe did not have to end in disillusion-
ment. After all, as we have seen, in the early history of the church

there were those who had argued strenuously that the story of Adam and Eve in the Garden was a tale that concealed a deep truth about human life but that it was not a description of history as it actually occurred. "Who could be found so silly?" the pious Origen asked in the third century CE, "as to believe that God, after the manner of a farmer, planted trees in a Paradise eastward in Eden?" But this position had been soundly defeated. "If there was no Paradise but in an allegory," the fourth-century bishop Epiphanius replied, then no trees; "if no trees, then no eating of the fruit; if no eating, then no Adam; if no Adam, then are there no men but all are allegories, and the truth itself is become a fable." Faced by this perceived threat, the defenders of Augustinian orthodoxy closed ranks. It was possible to read the Genesis account allegorically, medieval churchmen taught, just as it was possible to read it as a moral lesson for the present and a prophecy for the future, but only if it was also at the same time taken literally. For a millennium the strict accuracy of the biblical narrative remained dogma, underwritten by the incontrovertible words of Holy Scripture and by the authority of the church.

In the wake of this massive dogmatic investment, it was extremely difficult to make an about-face and return to the notion of allegory. It was all the more difficult to do so at the very time that the combined imaginative resources of Renaissance Europe were actually giving the story the life-likeness it so long had sought. The problem, as La Peyrère demonstrated, is that the life-likeness invited, even demanded, dangerous questions. The theologians themselves insisted on posing them, and the faithful followed suit. But hovering in the wings was skepticism, and skepticism was only a half-step from disbelief. In the 1630s, anxious authorities noted that some parishioners in Essex, northeast of London, were wryly asking where Adam and Eve obtained the thread to sew their fig leaves together.

This provincial irony was only a small foretaste of what was to come. Thirty years after Milton first published *Paradise Lost*, a French philosopher, Pierre Bayle, published what he called *A Historical and Critical Dictionary*. The title sounds anodyne enough, but the author, a Protestant at a time of fierce persecution in France, knew that he was venturing into dangerous territory. As the pressure for strict conformity mounted, he had fled to Holland, where he could more freely pursue his thoughts. They led him first and foremost to call for toleration; a Christian church that tried to achieve uniformity of faith by means of the rack and the stake, he wrote, was violating the very essence of Jesus's gospel. It was time, Bayle thought, to hold virtually everything up to careful scrutiny and to determine what it was proper to embrace or to discard.

The *Dictionary*, which first appeared in 1697 in Amsterdam, is a wild hodge-podge; essays on theological and philosophical concepts jostle for place with biographical sketches, textual inquiries, and strange stories, all festooned with fantastically detailed, often wryly ironic footnotes. Bayle's publisher and Bayle himself must have been astonished when it became a bestseller. Over the years, in successive editions, the work eventually grew to some 6 million words in length. There can be very few readers who actually waded through it all. But it was possible to plunge in almost anywhere and find startling things.

In each entry in the *Dictionary*, Bayle attempted to state clearly the basic, known facts about a given topic and then in the footnotes to consider any dubious claims or unresolved questions. As befitted their importance, the entries for Adam and Eve took many pages, but they consisted mostly of footnotes, for there was very little, in the welter of biographical details, that withstood Bayle's skeptical glance. By no means an outright unbeliever, he carefully rehearsed what he took to be the undeniable core truths. Yes, Adam was the first human, created by God from clay on the sixth day of creation. Yes, Eve was the wife of Adam, formed from one of his ribs. Adam gave names to the animals. He and his spouse were blessed by God, commanded to be fruitful and multiply, and warned not to eat from the Tree of the Knowledge

254 THE RISE AND FALL OF ADAM AND EVE

of Good and Evil. Both of them violated the prohibition—first Eve and then, on her instigation, Adam. For their disobedience, they were punished and driven from the Garden.

Thus much it was necessary to believe, Bayle averred, since the word of God positively affirmed it. But apart from these and a few other scriptural "facts," the rest, he thought, was open to doubt. The *Dictionary* then consigned to the rubbish heap legends that had slowly accreted over a thousand years and more. Adam was presumably "a fine person and well-made," Bayle wrote, but why should anyone credit the story that he was a giant or a hermaphrodite, or that he was born circumcised, or that he named all of the plants as well as the animals, or that he was in his spare time a great philosopher who wrote a book on creation? Did God originally give the first man a tail, as some commentators affirmed, and then, having changed His mind, did he cut it off and use it to form the woman? Was Eve truly so beautiful that Satan fell in love with her and seduced her? In the Garden did she break off a branch of the Tree of the Knowledge of Good and Evil, fashion it into a big stick, and beat her husband with it until he ate the fruit? Or was she herself, as others affirmed, the fatal tree whose fruit was prohibited?

Adam and Eve, Bayle thought, evidently did not have sex until after the expulsion, for it was only then that the Bible says that Adam "knew" his wife. But what about the rest of the innumerable speculations that had arisen about their lives? Did the first humans really have to consummate their marriage quickly in order to teach the animals, otherwise clueless, how to reproduce? Did Eve sleep with the serpent and give birth to demons? Was she pregnant every year, always with at least a son and a daughter, and sometimes with an even great number of children? How, despite these pregnancies, did she reach the ripe old age of 940, ten years older than her husband? Is it true that she instituted a religious order of young women who were always to remain virgins and to preserve unextinguished the fire that fell from heaven upon Abel's sacrifice?

Most of these time-honored claims have the musty odor, Bayle remarked, either of old books of romance or of "monkish" fantasy. There was nothing particularly new in dismissing any one of them, but the more details the *Dictionary* piled up, the less credible the entire story became. The imaginary name of one of the daughters of Adam and Eve might have slipped by, but a list of names culled from different sources and assembled in a footnote—Calmana, Azrum, Delbora, Awina, Azura, Sava, and so forth—served as a quietly ironic reminder that the Bible neglected to supply a single one. Bayle's mockery was rarely open—even in tolerant Amsterdam, he had vehement enemies, and besides, he seems to have been sincerely attempting to hold on to his core faith. But it was difficult for him to contain his irony within safe bounds.

Not everyone was amused. The Calvinist theologian Pierre Jurieu, who had earlier helped to bring Bayle to the safety of Holland, was outraged by the *Dictionary,* and he was not alone. He might have tolerated ironic reflections on the extravagant legends that had accumulated around Adam and Eve, but these reflections were in turn linked to disturbing questions about the origin of human sinfulness and about the justice of God's punishments. The responses in the *Dictionary* to these questions seemed to Bayle's enemies to undermine the Bible's creation account and thus to undermine faith in God.

If the world as it was first created had truly been pure and pristine, how was it possible, Bayle asked in several long philosophical essays, for evil ever to have entered into it? The traditional answers offered by orthodox theologians, the *Dictionary* stated flatly, were either pathetic or monstrous. Under the very thin cover of imagining what a heretic would say to these theologians, the full unnerving conceptual difficulties of the Adam and Eve story tumbled out.

How could an all-powerful god who was truly good, Bayle's imagined heretic asks, have exposed his beloved creatures to so much misery? Shouldn't a genuinely kind deity have taken pleasure in making humans happy and in preserving their happiness? Surely, the all-knowing Creator knew in advance that his creatures would fall and, in doing so, would bring down pestilence, war, famine, and unspeakable pain on all of their progeny. Was he not then like a ruler who supplies a man in a crowd with a very sharp knife, though he knows full well that the knife will be used in a crime that will lead to the death of thousands? Wouldn't preventing the catastrophe have been preferable?

Other orthodox arguments fare no better. To the idea that God chose to give his beloved creature free will, Bayle observed that we expect any good parent to save his child from wounding himself, not to look on with indifference or to withhold help when danger threatens, let alone to punish him violently after the disaster has occurred. You do not need to be a philosopher to grasp this, and you do not have to limit the comparison to parents and children. A simple peasant understands that there is much greater goodness in stopping a stranger from falling into a ditch than in letting him fall in and taking him out later.

These questions, as Bayle well knew, had long troubled readers of the Genesis story. Over the centuries many answers had been proposed, but they never succeeded in settling the matter, and the usual attempts to shut discussion down by dogmatic pronouncements, pious fervor, collective rituals, and—when necessary—torture did not bring about the desired silence. By the seventeenth century the questions had become more insistent than ever before, precisely because the Renaissance had made Adam and Eve seem more vividly alive than ever before. Bayle quoted a Latin couplet in which an angel sees Dürer's Adam and Eve and exclaims, "You are more beautiful than you were when I chased you out of the garden of Eden."

There was danger in conjuring up lives so powerfully. For Bayle, as for Milton, the compelling vividness of the first humans called attention to the cracks that had always existed in their narrative. This is certainly not the outcome Milton wanted, and it is probably not what Bayle wanted either. But what did Bayle want? Milton was confident, in spite of everything, that he could justify God's ways to man, but Bayle had no comparable confidence, and he saw the rage that his writing aroused. As a consequence of the questions he was asking, he had brought persecution down on his family; he had been driven into exile; he had turned his erstwhile friends and supporters into bitter enemies; he had suffered what we would now call a nervous breakdown. Though he had every reason to try to do so, he could not silence his doubts. And where—after the mighty wrestling with the problem of evil in the Garden of Eden—did he finally end up? Buried in a footnote to a footnote, deep in the 6 million words, is what he called his best answer. "The best Answer that can be naturally returned to the Question, *Why did God permit that Man should sin?* is this, *I don't know.*"

"I don't know": at this distance, it is difficult to grasp the depth charge hidden in the simple phrase and the courage required to write it. Though Bayle's world was in many ways tantalizingly close to our own—Copernicus had decentered the earth, Bacon had already laid the groundwork for the scientific revolution, Galileo and Newton had transformed the understanding of the heavens—the Adam and Eve story remained dangerous to handle in anything but a spirit of piety. In a religious context, shored up by professions of faith, it was safe to confess uncertainty; in a skeptical, secular context, it was far more risky. The little word "naturally" in the phrase "The best Answer that can be naturally returned to the Question" served as a minimal defense; it acknowledged the possibility of a different answer, a supernatural one. But Bayle was a philosopher, not a theologian, and, despite the dangers, everything in his being rebelled against abandoning his reason and taking shelter in dogma. Many wanted to silence him, but he continued to write and in the end achieved at least one small victory for toleration: though he was stripped of his professorship and reduced to poverty, when death came for him—in Rotterdam in 1706, in his fifty-ninth year—he was not in prison but at home in his bed.

At a dinner party one night in 1752 at the royal palace in Potsdam, the king of Prussia, Frederick the Great, and his guests entertained the idea of taking up Bayle's project and penning a dictionary of their own. They agreed to begin at once. The next morning only one of them arrived at breakfast with a sample entry, but that was the philosopher Voltaire. What he brought to the table served as the germ for the *Philosophical Dictionary* that he worked on for more than a decade. He was a risk-taker who made no secret of his contempt for religious orthodoxy. But even fifty years after Bayle, as a Europe-wide celebrity, with a handsome annual stipend of 20,000 francs and under the personal patronage of the Prussian king, Voltaire dressed himself in protective clothing when he approached the Garden of Eden.

In the first edition of the *Philosophical Dictionary,* published anonymously in 1764, Voltaire's entry on Adam exclaimed in a tone of wide-eyed innocence on how interesting it was that the names of the father and mother of the human race were unknown to anyone in the ancient world except for the Jews. What a delightful mystery! "It was God's pleasure that the origin of the great family of the world should be concealed from all but the smallest and most unfortunate part of that family."

Voltaire invited his readers to imagine a poor Jew telling Caesar or Cicero that they were all descended from one father, named Adam. The Roman Senate would have asked for evidence—they wanted to see the great monuments, the statues, the inscriptions on ancient buildings—but, of course, there was nothing to show. The senators would have laughed and had the Jew whipped: "so much," Voltaire wrote in his best deadpan manner, "are men attached to their prejudices!" Or again, he suggested, imagine a Christian paying a condolence visit to a queen of China, Japan, or India who has just lost her infant son and announcing that the prince royal is now in the clutches of five hundred devils who will torment him for all eternity. The grief-stricken queen would ask why devils should roast her poor child forever, and the Christian would have to explain that it is because the child's "great-grandfather formerly ate of the fruit of knowledge, in a garden."

Voltaire's tone recalls the irony pioneered by Bayle, but it is an irony that has been sharpened into a cruel weapon. Why do some infants die at the mother's breast? Why do others suffer months and even years of torments before they die an appalling death? Why does smallpox sweep away so many lives? Why in every age of the world "have human bladders been liable to turn into stone quarries?" Why pestilence, war, famine, and torture? It is all explained by the story of Adam and Eve. After all, Voltaire pointed out, one of the great champions of the Inquisition, the Spaniard Luis de Páramo, traced that splendid tribunal back to the Garden. God, calling the wrongdoer before Him with the words "Adam, where art thou?" was the first Inquisitor.

For Voltaire, who ended letters to his intimate friends with the injunction to "crush the infamous thing"—*Écrasez l'infâme*—the Adam and Eve story lay at the center of what most needed to be crushed. The story was not merely a ridiculous lie; it was the justification for some of the most hateful aspects of human actions and beliefs. The biblical prohibition—"Eat not of the fruit of the tree of knowledge of good and evil"—is very strange: "It is not easy to conceive that there ever existed a tree which could teach good and evil, as there are trees that bear pears and apricots." But that is not the main problem: "Why is God unwilling that man should know good and evil? Would not his free access to this knowledge, on the contrary, appear—if we may venture to use such language—more worthy of God, and far more necessary to man?" Wouldn't it have been preferable for God to command humans to eat more and more of the fruit? Why should religion enshrine a story that celebrates ignorance?

It is only ignorance, or rather the deliberate imprisoning of the human capacity to reason, that upholds belief in a benign God. Powerful institutions have a stake in fostering this belief, and their agents will stop at nothing to impose it on everyone. They will see to it that anyone who calls their fables into doubt or questions their vicious doctrines is violently punished. But the story of the omnipotent Creator and the magical garden makes no sense. Look around, Voltaire wrote,

> The globe on which we live is one vast field of destruction and carnage. Either the Supreme Being was able to make of it an eternal mode of enjoyment for all beings possessed of sensation, or He was not.

If the Creator was able to make the world a happy place and yet refused to do so, then you would have to conclude that that the god in the story of Adam and Eve was evil. But Voltaire was not urging a return to the old Manichaean heresy. Instead, he wanted his readers to conclude that God was simply limited in what he could do.

Voltaire knew that it was unsafe to voice such heterodox views in print, and, like Bayle, he donned a fig leaf of submission: "I address myself here solely to philosophers, and not to divines. We know that faith is the clue to guide us through the labyrinth." But he wanted to make perfectly clear that the submission was spurious: "We know full well," he added in a mock declaration of faith, "that the fall of Adam and Eve, original sin, the vast power communicated to devils, the predilection entertained by the Supreme Being for the Jewish people, and the ceremony of baptism substituted for that of circumcision, are answers that clear up every difficulty."

Bayle's questioning in 1695 had hardened by 1764 into outright mockery. Pressure from the church might compel a formal public acquiescence to its absurd fables, but only someone who had not actually thought about the story of Adam and Eve—only a fool or fanatic—could actually believe that it was literally true. As for the insane religious doctrines that had been extracted from the story, they reflected the infamous institution that they served. St. Augustine was the first, Voltaire wrote, who developed the strange notion of Original Sin, "a notion worthy of the warm and romantic brain of an African debauchee and penitent, Manichaean and Christian, tolerant and persecuting—who passed his life in perpetual self-contradiction." Ridiculous as the Hebrews were, they at least would have recognized how absurd and reckless it was to treat their origin fable as a depiction of real people in a real world. "The first chapters of Genesis—at whatever period they were composed—were regarded by all the learned Jews as an allegory," Voltaire wrote, "and even as a fable not a little dangerous."

By the late eighteenth century, allegory had experienced a resurgence. In the wake of the Enlightenment, there were too many contradictions in the origin story, too many violations of plausibility, too many awkward ethical questions to make it any longer comfortable to insist on a literal interpretation. Or rather what seemed at last like the real presence of Adam and Eve, in the art of the Renaissance and in Milton's great epic, had turned on the story itself and begun to tear it apart. To many believers, even within the church, the strongest way to shore up the story of Adam and Eve was to beat a hasty retreat from the literal. Others dug in and insisted more fiercely than ever on its unvarnished, undistorted truth.

As WAS SO OFTEN THE CASE, all possible positions were pushed to their logical extremes in the newly formed United States of America. Voltaire's *Philosophical Dictionary* was beloved by Thomas Jefferson, who purchased a bust of its author and placed it in Monticello. (Jefferson was also a great admirer of Bayle and included his *Dictionary* in the list of the one hundred books that would form the basis for the Library of Congress.) At the same time, hard-edged Calvinists, heirs to the Puritan founders, continued to preach fire-and-brimstone sermons about infant damnation and the universal taint of Original Sin.

The literal truth of the Genesis story was taken in a different direction by the founder of Mormonism, Joseph Smith, who in 1838 led his followers to a site seventy miles north of present-day Kansas City, Missouri, where he established a settlement he called Adam-ondi-Ahman. It was in that very place, Smith declared, that Adam had once lived. The idea did not die out when Smith was killed and his followers were driven further west. In the mid-twentieth century Mormon prophet Ezra Taft Benson, who served as the Secretary of Agriculture during Eisenhower's presidency, reiterated the original revelation. "This was the place," Benson wrote, "where the Garden of Eden was; it was here that Adam met with a body of high priests at Adam-ondi-Ahman shortly before his death and gave them his final blessing, and the place to which he will return to meet with the leaders of his people."

Even outside organized religious communities, it was clear to many Americans that there was a peculiarly intense and meaningful relation between their land and the Garden of Eden. The longing was not only to find the ancient traces of Adam's footsteps but also to encounter the first human here and now, at home in a world that had remained unspoiled and pure. "Adam in the garden," Ralph Waldo Emerson imagined himself in 1839, jotting in his journal ideas for a new series of lectures; "I am to new name all the beasts in the field & all the gods in the Sky. I am to invite men drenched in time to recover themselves & come out of time, & taste their native immortal air." So too, in his cabin by the small lake west of Boston, Henry David Thoreau dreamed of coming out of time and finding the way back to the primordial state. "Perhaps on that spring morning when Adam and Eve were driven out of Eden," he wrote in 1854, "Walden Pond was already in existence, and even then breaking up in a gentle spring rain accompanied with mist and a southerly wind, and covered with myriads of ducks and geese, which had not heard of the fall, when still such pure lakes sufficed them."

In his 1860 edition of *Leaves of Grass*, Walt Whitman took the literal identification with Adam, already glimpsed in Emerson and Thoreau, to a new level:

> As Adam, early in the morning,
> Walking forth from the bower refresh'd with sleep,
> Behold me where I pass, hear my voice, approach,
> Touch me, touch the palm of your hand to my body as I pass,
> Be not afraid of my body.

"Be not afraid of my body": the words well up at once from the Garden before the Fall and from the streets of a crowded city. But what accounts for the unembarrassed self-display and the strange demand for intimacy? What manner of man is asking us to touch him with the palm of our hands? It is as if sin, pollution, shame—the miserable consequences of the primal disobedience—have vanished, and with them the crucial distinction between an original state of innocence and an abject state of fallenness. Vanished too is the primordial couple; though he is evidently not alone, this is an Adam without an Eve.

The first man here is almost eerily alive. Accompanied by a startlingly vivid engraving of the poet—dressed in work clothes, his hat at a jaunty angle, his expression bold and direct—*Leaves of Grass* from the beginning made readers feel that Walt Whitman was physically present in his poem. But if Whitman seemed to embody Adam, bringing him back to a life almost palpable in its reality, the biblical story that gave birth to Adam in the first place, with its chronicle of crime and punishment, had, in Whitman's vision, completely faded away. Small wonder that Whitman was denounced, his poem called obscene. Nonetheless, *Leaves of Grass* quickly found ardent champions, who heard in it a voice that was at once eccentric and representative. By its final edition in 1891, Whitman was widely celebrated both for his radical originality and for his truthful depiction of what the literary critic R. W. B. Lewis has called the American Adam.

At almost the same moment that Whitman brought his great poem to completion, his contemporary Mark Twain wrote "Extracts from Adam's Diary," one of a succession of short pieces, some published and others left unpublished, that seem to reflect a virtually lifelong preoccupation with the Genesis story. More than twenty years earlier, in *Innocents Abroad,* a burlesque account of travels in the Middle East, he had become famous as a humorist for his mock-lament at the legendary tomb of Adam in Jerusalem's Church of the Holy Sepulcher:

> How touching it was, here in a land of strangers, far away from home, and friends, and all who cared for me, thus to discover the grave of a blood relation. True, a distant one, but still a relation. The unerring instinct of nature thrilled in recognition. The fountain of my filial affection was stirred to its profoundest depths, and I gave way to tumultuous emotion. I leaned on a pillar and burst into tears.

Now in "Adam's Diary" in 1892, Twain continued to mock credulous belief in the literal existence of the first human by projecting himself into him and playfully imagining what it would have been like to live at the dawn of time.

"This new creature with the long hair is a good deal in the way," the first diary entry reads,

> It is always hanging around and following me about. I don't like this; I am not used to company. I wish it would stay with the other animals. . . . Cloudy today, wind in the east; think we shall have rain. . . . WE? Where did I get that word—the new creature uses it.

That is Monday's entry; Tuesday's continues Adam's litany of complaints:

> I get no chance to name anything myself. The new creature names everything that comes along, before I can get in a protest. And

16. Dürer's depiction of the final moment of innocence, captured as if by a camera with a very fast shutter speed, became almost immediately famous. Albrecht Dürer, *Adam and Eve,* 1504.

17. In this preparatory study, Dürer plays with the idea that Adam himself plucks the fatal fruit. Sheet of studies for the hand and arm of Adam and for rocks and bushes for the engraving of *Adam and Eve,* 1504.

18. Dürer's fascination with the nakedness of Adam and Eve extends here to his own body. Albrecht Dürer, *Self-Portrait in the Nude,* 1505.

19. Eve is a sly seductress, while Adam is a rotting corpse. Hans Baldung Grien, *Eve, the Serpent, and Death, c.* 1510–1515.

20. Bosch shows Adam rapt in contemplation of Eve, while creatures in Eden eat each other. Hieronymus Bosch, *The Garden of Earthly Delights* (detail), 1504.

21. While a beautiful woman—perhaps Eve—looks on,
the spark of life seems to be passing from God's finger to Adam's.
Michelangelo, *The Creation of Adam,* 1508–1512.

22. Adam is already enervated by the fall. Jan Gossart, *Adam and Eve, c.* 1520.

23. A baffled Adam accepts the half-eaten apple from Eve. Lucas Cranach the Elder, *Adam and Eve*, 1526.

24. Is Adam attempting to restrain or to support Eve as she reaches for the forbidden fruit offered by a cherubic serpent? Titian, *Adam and Eve, c.* 1550.

© *Museo Nacional del Prado.*

25. The Virgin Mary and her son together crush the snake. Caravaggio, *Madonna dei Palafrenieri* (detail), 1605–1606.

26. With unnerving frankness, Rembrandt depicts the aging, all-too-human bodies of Adam and Eve. Rembrandt van Rijn, *Adam and Eve,* 1638.

27. Lelli's hyper-realistic figures of Adam and Eve were made from wax applied to human bones. Ercole Lelli, *Anatomical waxes of Adam and Eve,* eighteenth century.

28. The fruit Eve seems to be offering Adam is her breast. Max Beckmann, *Adam and Eve,* 1917.

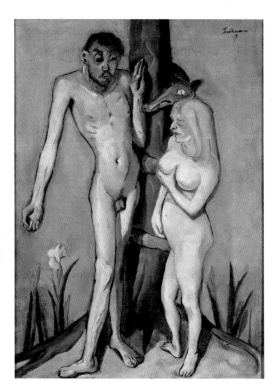

29. Based on surviving footprints, this imaginary scene of Lucy and her mate seems to invoke Adam and Eve exiled from Paradise. *"Lucy" (australopithecus afarensis) and her mate,* reconstruction by John Holmes under the direction of Ian Tattersall.

always that same pretext is offered—it LOOKS like the thing. There is a dodo, for instance. Says the moment one looks at it one sees at a glance that it "looks like a dodo." It will have to keep that name, no doubt. It wearies me to fret about it, and it does no good, anyway. Dodo! It looks no more like a dodo than I do.

Bayle's anxiety and Voltaire's outrage have morphed here into a comedy routine. Questions that haunted and on occasion tormented centuries of philosophers and theologians—how did the solitary figure in Paradise become a "we"? to what extent did Adam and Eve share their tasks? what did it mean to "name" the animals? what for theology is the status of extinct species?—have become wry jokes.

The jokes come at the expense of the naïve, innocent Adam and Eve but equally at the expense of a Bible story that had served for so many generations as the infallibly accurate account of the origin of the world. By the end of the nineteenth century Twain can count on his readers joining him in finding the account absurd: "She engages herself in many foolish things," Adam complains about Eve,

> among others, trying to study out why the animals called lions and tigers live on grass and flowers, when, as she says, the sort of teeth they wear would indicate that they were intended to eat each other. This is foolish, because to do that would be to kill each other, and that would introduce what, as I understand it, is called "death"; and death, as I have been told, has not yet entered the Garden.

Twain does not belabor the point. His interest in "Adam's Diary" and in the companion piece, "Eve's Diary," that he wrote to accompany it was less to ridicule the Bible than to explore with considerable tenderness and delicacy the comedy of sexual relations.

The light touch did not altogether forestall controversy. The book version of "Eve's Diary" that appeared in 1906 was accompanied by illustrations of the first pair that, though positively modest from our perspective, struck at least the librarians of one library, in Worcester, Massachusetts, as obscene. By and large, however, the pieces addressed a readership that no longer bristled at a humorous treatment of the Genesis story.

Twain, who knew the limits of his audience well, did not publish in his lifetime everything that he wrote on a subject that continued to preoccupy him. Among the pieces published only posthumously—and even then over the initial objections of one of Twain's daughters—are a series of further attempts to enter into the consciousness of Adam and Eve, as if they were recognizable human beings who found themselves trying to make their way through an entirely new and utterly unfamiliar world. In these, tenderness gave way to the irony and anger that seethed in Bayle and Voltaire. In one, Twain's Eve recalls asking her husband about a tree with a peculiar name, and being given an entirely unsatisfactory answer, since Adam has no idea what either "good" or "evil" means. "We had not heard them before, and they meant nothing to us."

The same perplexity besets them, of course, when they try to understand the new word "death." How could they possibly grasp it? They do not need, in this reimagining, the intervention of a serpent to induce them to eat the forbidden fruit. They only need perfect innocence and an earnest, well-intentioned curiosity:

> We sat silent a while turning the puzzle over in our minds; then all at once I saw how to find out, and was surprised that we had not thought of it in the beginning, it was so simple. I sprang up and said—
>
> "How stupid we are! Let us eat of it; we shall die, and then we shall know what it is, and not have any more bother about it."

Their act is deferred in Twain's retelling by the chance appearance of an interesting creature that they have not seen before and that they name "pterodactyl," but their dark destiny is already glimpsed.

Like the dodo in "Eve's Diary," the dinosaur sends up the whole account, but this time Twain does not deflect his sarcasm. There is, he makes clear, something inexcusably cruel in the story. In another of his unpublished pieces, a further version of "Eve's Diary," written after the expulsion from Eden, the indictment is made explicit:

> We could not know it was wrong to disobey the command, for the words were strange to us and we did not understand them. We did not know right from wrong—how should we know? . . . We knew no more than this littlest child of mine knows now with its four years—oh, not so much, I think. Would I say to it, "If thou touchest this bread I will overwhelm thee with unimaginable disaster, even to the dissolution of thy corporeal elements," and when it took the bread and smiled up in my face, thinking no harm, as not understanding these strange words, would I take advantage of its innocence to strike it down with the mother-hand it trusted?

The questions, in almost the same terms, had been posed two hundred years earlier by Pierre Bayle. And the doubt and anger they expressed had deeper roots still, extending all the way back two thousand years to the first surviving traces of the Adam and Eve story in the Nag Hammadi codices. For centuries after Augustine's doctrinal triumph, the moral paradoxes of the Genesis story seemed only to awaken more desire to reaffirm its truth and to fathom its underlying meaning. But by the time of Mark Twain, the tide of literal belief had decisively turned. The institutions that had once mobilized to suppress challenges were fatally weakened: the public library in Worcester, Massachusetts, was a far cry from the Inquisition. If Twain had published his more radical pieces during his lifetime, he might have lost some of his readers, but he would not have lost his life or even his livelihood.

This decisive change may be traced to the work that had been done, for more than two centuries, by Bayle and Voltaire and by the whole Enlightenment project that they bravely advanced. But it may be traced as well to the scientific discoveries represented by the creature that, in Twain's fantasy, appeared just in time to delay the Fall: the pterodactyl. Dinosaurs helped to destroy the Garden of Eden.

14

Darwin's Doubts

Darwinism is not incompatible with belief in God, but it is certainly incompatible with belief in Adam and Eve. Nothing in *The Descent of Man*, published in 1871, allowed for even the remotest possibility that our species originated in the form of two exemplary, fresh-minted humans at home in a paradisal garden. Darwin had already made public his evolutionary theory in his 1859 *The Origin of Species*. Written for nonspecialists, the book had had an enormous impact, but it had deliberately left humans out of the enormous range of species it discussed. It was possible for contemporary readers to take in the persuasiveness of the scientific argument for natural selection but to hold on to the notion that somehow humans were exempt from the biological processes that governed the struggle for life among all other creatures.

After 1871, there was no longer any doubt that Darwin himself shared the conclusions that his followers had already been drawing from the enormous mass of data that he had patiently collected and from the brilliant overarching theory that made sense of this data. There was no exemption for humans.

Paradise was not lost; it had never existed. Humans did not have their origins in the peaceable kingdom. They were never blessed with perfect health and abundance, a life without competition, suffering, and death. No doubt there were fat times, when food was plentiful, but those times would never last indefinitely, and our most distant forebears always had to share the bounty with other creatures whose needs were as exigent as theirs. Danger was rarely far off, and if they managed to hold the major predators at bay, they still had to reckon with army ants and intestinal parasites, toothaches, broken arms, and cancer. If circumstances were just right, human life could be extraordinarily sweet, but nothing in the whole vast landscape that Darwin surveyed suggested that there had ever been a magical time or place where all our needs were happily met.

As a species, humans were neither unique nor created once-for-all. Except in our dreams or fantasies, we could not possibly have emerged as fully formed adults, ready to speak, take care of ourselves, and reproduce. The particular kind of primate that we have become evolved over a vast span of time from extinct types of humans who shared many of our physical features: upright posture; walking on two feet; hands distinct from feet in form and function; small upper and lower canines; a chin. Exactly how and when this happened is still very much an open question.

Modern humans have particular qualities that mark us out as distinct—above all, language, moral consciousness, and the capacity to reason. But Darwin insisted that even these qualities were different in degree, not in kind, from those possessed by other animals to which our species is related. We exist in continuity not only with hominids— the primates, including chimpanzees, gorillas, and orangutans, whom we obviously closely resemble—but also with many other species. Recognizing this continuity did not, he thought, necessarily require specialized knowledge of the behavior of exotic animals; it could be grasped by looking attentively at birds and at dogs.

It is not surprising that Darwin, who tempered his scientific daring with a canny sense of what his contemporaries could bear, held off disclosing the full implications of what he had discovered. He had at home, in the person of his pious wife, an articulate and urgent witness to how upsetting his theories were. In the introduction to *The Descent of Man*, he wrote that for years he had collected notes on human origins, "without any intention of publishing on the subject, but rather with the determination not to publish, as I thought that I should thus only add to the prejudices against my views." Readers of *The Origin of Species* could always draw their own conclusions, but he had not intended to articulate them in print.

Even when he overcame his reservations and made his work public, Darwin was careful to make no mention at all of the Bible story—the story of the creation, the Garden of Eden, and the Fall of Man—whose claim to literal truth he knew that he was decisively destroying. The names of Adam and Eve do not appear anywhere in the work. But his theory of evolution grappled with the very questions that motivated the Genesis account of human origins: Where did humans come from? Why must we labor with such pain to survive and to reproduce? What is the shaping role of desire—the desire for particular individuals or features of individuals that Darwin termed "sexual selection"—in the long-term development of the species? Why do we suffer and die? Above all, Darwin and his successors attempted to account for the human inheritance of ancient drives, compulsions, and desires. Even when those drives are manifestly dangerous, even when they impel us toward actions that are violent, pathological, and self-destructive, they prove extremely difficult to surmount. It is as if our ancestors had passed along to us, through some hidden mechanism, a suite of experiences, accommodations, and choices that they had made in the remotest time and that remain active within us, despite the fact that our circumstances have radically changed.

As the heirs to this very problematical inheritance, we may become aware of at least some of the most harmful impulses and distance ourselves from them. But we cannot by any means always do so; in the course of a lifetime, we are almost certainly going to succumb, probably on many occasions. And what we succumb to is not, for the most part, *learned* behavior; it is what we have inherited from birth, before our distinct personalities in our distinct cultural settings have been formed and before we have acquired the capacity to reason. Those personalities and settings interact with this inheritance, and our reason can struggle against its most destructive urgings, but it can never be simply erased. We bear responsibility for our actions—we are not automata—but at the same time our freedom is severely constrained and compromised.

The interpreters of Genesis, particularly after Augustine, understood this whole legacy as punishment, consequent on the original sin of the first humans and our loss of Eden. But for Darwin there was no Eden. What we receive from our archaic forebears are not divine chastisements, but rather the living traces of successful accommodations our species made to the world over tens of thousands of years. Hence our sexual division of labor, our craving for sugar and animal fat, our mastery of fire, and our capacity for extreme violence take their place alongside our subtle social skills, our toolmaking, our expressive powers in language and imagery, all of which contributed to survival in a harsh, dangerous environment.

If for the Bible the ceaseless exhausting work that humans have to do in order to find enough to eat—ranging from rooting in the ground for tubers to the agricultural revolution that enabled us to cultivate, plant, and harvest our food—is the consequence of transgression, for Darwin it is a necessary achievement. If for the author of Genesis the pain human females experience in childbirth is one of the curses laid upon sinful Eve, for evolutionary biology it is a successful biological trade-off. That is, it is the price we pay for the combination of the maximum size of the pelvis in a creature that is bipedal and the minimal size of the skull in a newborn that allows our species to possess exceptionally large brains. Being able to stand upright on two legs enabled our species to see over the savanna grasses, to cover substantial distances in search of food, and to free our arms to throw projectiles. Possessing a large brain enabled us to develop a range of skills essential to survive and prosper, despite our relative lack of strength, sharp teeth, thick skin, and so forth. For Darwin these human traits are not penalties in consequence of transgression, but rather the essential, life-bearing gifts of random mutation and of skills acquired over vast tracts of time.

The number of generations that this evolutionary process required corresponded not to the relatively paltry succession of "begats" recorded in the Bible but rather to the scale found in an ancient pagan theory of human origins that Darwin certainly knew but that he was careful not to mention in *The Descent of Man*. That theory, which had deeply influenced his grandfather, Erasmus Darwin, held that humans must have originated not all at once in a purpose-built garden but in a primitive struggle for survival.

Genesis envisioned the early existence of the dominant species as orderly as well as easy. Even the prohibited fruit was, in its way, reassuring, for it signaled that the world had laws and a lawgiver. By contrast, Darwin's massive data and his overarching theory confirmed the pagan intuition that our earliest ancestors had no divine guidance, no assurance that their species would endure, no God-given laws, and no innate sense of order, morality, and justice. Social life as we know it, a life governed by a dense web of rules, agreements, and mutual understandings, was not a given but a gradual achievement.

In *On the Nature of Things*, Lucretius admired the ways that the earliest humans accommodated themselves to the harshness of the natural world and, in doing so, began to change their own nature. We would not have lasted long as a species, he wrote, had we not learned to modify our crudest instincts, to develop protective technologies, and to form social bonds. Fashioning clothing from skins, building huts, and mastering fire weakened our ancestors physically—

"It was then that human beings first began to lose their toughness: the use of fire rendered their shivering bodies less able to endure the cold beneath the pavilion of the sky"—and at the same time enabled them to begin to live together, to foster the young, and to protect the weaker members of the group. It was in this formative stage of social life that we developed one of our crucial species characteristics, the ability to speak.

This ability had nothing to do with the power of any one figure to create language and impose it on the world. As if he had read or at least heard a version of the Hebrew myth, Lucretius wrote flatly that "the hypothesis that in those early times someone assigned names to things, and that people learned their first words from him, is preposterous." Impressive as it is, our linguistic ability is continuous with the signification through variable sounds that we can observe in innumerable animals around us. A stallion's neighing in desire is distinct from its whinnying in fear; there are birds that change their raucous notes with the weather; fierce watchdogs snarl in menace, but "when they begin to lick their pups tenderly with their tongue, or when they cuff them with their paws and, snapping at them with checked teeth, pretend gently to swallow them, the whining they make as they fondle them is a very different sound from the howls they give when left alone to guard the house."

Lucretius's observations from the natural world strikingly anticipated what Darwin brought in such massive detail to support his overarching theory of natural selection: random mutations, a ceaseless struggle for existence, innumerable extinctions, the shared life of animals, slow cognitive growth, a history without purpose extending over an unimaginable expanse of time. Thanks to the indefatigable research of Darwin and his allies, these ideas no longer seemed like archaic philosophical speculations; they had begun to take on the status of scientific truth. And with them Adam and Eve, once so real as to be almost tangible, receded into the filmiest of daydreams.

It was chalk, curiously enough, that played a critical role in this history. For what made Darwin's theory of human origins seem entirely plausible—after centuries in which Lucretius was ridiculed for advancing strikingly similar ideas—were scientific advances in geology that brought a new sense of the immense age of the earth and with it a timescale that allowed for evolution's innumerable experiments. For English geologists like Charles Lyell, the celebrated White Cliffs of Dover served as Exhibit A: the familiar soft white porous rock, they showed, was formed by sedimentation that took tens of millions of years. A careful examination of the shape of this landscape, of the chalk, flint, and marl with which it is composed, of the fossils that may be found in it, leads to an inescapable and very unsettling conclusion: these are the consequence of geological events—sedimentations, displacements, upheavings, fractures—most of which occurred in what Lyell termed the Eocene Epoch, lasting from 56 to 33.9 million years ago.

There was, Lyell argued in the 1830s, no sign of progress in the long, long history of the earth, no indication of providential design, no record of a universal flood that destroyed all living things save those that had found refuge on the ark. The same processes that had been at work in the most distant past were at work now. And the overall rate of geological change was always the same.

A pious Christian, Lyell struggled to hold on to his faith in the light of what he had come to understand. But it was immensely difficult to do so. There was certainly no question of maintaining any longer a literal belief in the six days of creation and the Garden of Eden. It had been difficult enough to hold on to the biblical story in the wake of the scientific discoveries that began to unsettle the world from the sixteenth century onward. Copernicus had displaced the earth from the center of the universe; the telescope disclosed the existence of untold multitudes of worlds; medical anatomies unveiled the inner workings of the body; the microscope revealed the hidden recesses of matter. Each of these had required major efforts to reconcile with traditional tenets.

But geology was a nightmare for the faithful. Fossils, such as sea-shells found far from the sea and bones that belonged to no known animal, had long been a conundrum, but they had been explained away by arguing that they were nature's "sports," or that they had been deposited on mountaintops and in deserts by Noah's Flood, or by citing the biblical references to giants roaming the earth in its earliest days, or even by speculating on the enormous size of the first humans. Denis Henrion, a French mathematician born at the end of the sixteenth century, used fossil bones to estimate Adam's height at 123 feet 9 inches, Eve's at 118 feet 9 inches. But the deep time disclosed by eighteenth- and nineteenth-century geology made these explanations seem absurd.

In 1857 the distinguished English naturalist Philip Gosse—inventor, among other things, of the first seawater aquarium—published a book entitled *Omphalos,* the Greek word for navel. A fundamentalist lay preacher and Bible teacher, Gosse had been deeply unnerved by Lyell's *Principles of Geology,* which made the biblical time scheme seem childish. It was always possible to interpret that time scheme in symbolic ways by positing that each of the "days" in Genesis represented a much vaster temporal horizon. But Gosse understood the perils of this path toward allegory. He was committed, as to this day fundamentalism remains committed, to the literal interpretation of scriptures that had first been championed by Augustine.

The subtitle to Gosse's book was *An Attempt to Untie the Geological Knot*, that is, to acknowledge the force of the geological record and at the same time to hold on to his faith. His solution was simple and, or so he thought, ingenious. All living things, he observed, have built into them the signs of their development and history. This is true of the rings of a tree, the deposits of calcium carbonate that make up a seashell, the overlapping scales on a fish. These signs are detectable even in the youngest, most newly hatched of these creatures, and they are certainly detectable in humans as well.

Gosse then turned to "the newly-created form of our first progenitor, the primal Head of the Human Race." To conjure him up properly and to distinguish him from all the beasts that perish, he quoted—as if he were citing an eyewitness—John Milton:

> Of far nobler shape, erect and tall,
> Godlike erect, with native honor clad,
> In naked majesty, as lord of all.

Gosse let his eyes slowly survey this first human, and, describing in loving detail what he saw, he compiled what he called a physiologist's report.

The human was evidently a fine specimen whose features—"the perfected dentition, the beard, the deepened voice, the prominent larynx," and the like—all pointed to a man between twenty-five and thirty years old. But though we must conclude from the infallible words of the Bible that God created Adam at precisely this age, and not as an infant, Gosse noticed something strange: "What means this curious depression in the centre of the abdomen, and the corrugated knob which occupies the cavity?" This is, he answered exuberantly, "the NAVEL."

Adam *must* have had a navel; he would not otherwise have looked right, let alone perfect. All great painters—Van Eyck, Michelangelo, Raphael, and the like—depict him with one. But the navel, of course, is a sign of a past, a link to the mother, that Adam did not have. This means that God created Adam with a perfectly formed, scientifically convincing trace of a history that never existed. And now, Gosse declared, like a lawyer who knew that he had proved his case, we can at last understand those fossils, those vast sedimentary deposits, those marks of ancient cataclysms, those agonizingly slow glacial transformations, that geologists study. The geologists' findings are in their way perfectly correct; what they fail to understand is simply that the evidence was planted by God on the first day of creation.

Poor Gosse. His book was received with ridicule and contempt that dogged him for the rest of his long life. His contemporaries were emphatically not prepared to believe that God, as the Victorian writer Charles Kingsley put it, had "written on the rocks one enormous and superfluous lie for all mankind." The navel would not, as Gosse had hoped, serve as life support for a dying Adam and Eve.

Only two years after the debacle of *Omphalos,* Charles Darwin triumphantly published his *Origin of Species.* Darwin was fifty, but the book had long been in gestation, at least since the time that he had returned at the age of twenty-six from almost five fateful years circumnavigating the globe as a naturalist aboard the HMS *Beagle,* under the command of captain Robert FitzRoy. Darwin had taken a number of favorite books with him for his long sea voyage, foremost among them *Paradise Lost.* But the book that had the most far-reaching influence upon him was Lyell's *Principles of Geology,* which FitzRoy presented to him before they set sail. First on the Cape Verde islands and then on the coast and in the interior of South America, Darwin repeatedly saw confirmation of many of Lyell's key theories and began passionately to collect supporting evidence in the form of fossils and rock samples.

It was not only the immense age of the earth that struck Darwin, along with the fact that geological change could therefore happen at an almost unimaginably slow pace; it was also the realization that living species were not immune from this same slow process of change. It was difficult to track the transformations; the evidence was elusive, fragmentary, and enigmatic. "Following out Lyell's metaphor," Darwin wrote, "I look at the natural geological record, as a history of the world imperfectly kept, and written in a changing dialect." Of this vast history only the last volume has survived, and of this volume "only here and there a short chapter has been preserved; and of each page, only here and there a few lines." Nevertheless, enough of the record had survived to make it impossible to believe that "in the beginning" all the species on earth were created by God once and for all.

The crisis came to a head even before Darwin set foot on the Galápagos Islands and encountered the evidence that would lead to the theory of natural selection. The *Beagle* was carrying back to Tierra del Fuego three hostages who had been seized on a previous expedition, more than a year before, and brought to England. The hostages— called by the crew Jemmy Button, Fuegia Basket, and York Minster— had been nominally Christianized. Dressed in English clothes, they had become familiar companions during the months at sea. The young naturalist must have looked up at them repeatedly when he wanted to rest his eyes from the pages of *The Principles of Geology*. He chatted with them—Jemmy Button, short, fat, and merry, was the universal favorite—and learned something about their reception in England, where they were treated as celebrities and received by King William IV and his wife Queen Adelaide. They were living proof of the malleability of even the most primitive humans.

Hence perhaps the intensity of the young Darwin's shock when he witnessed the Yaghan people to whom the kidnapped converts, in their gloves and well-polished shoes, were being returned. Years later he still recalled with a shudder the effect that the sight had on him:

> The astonishment which I felt on first seeing a party of Fuegians on a wild and broken shore will never be forgotten by me, for the reflection at once rushed into my mind—such were our ancestors. These men were absolutely naked and bedaubed with paint, their long hair was tangled, their mouths frothed with excitement, and their expression was wild, startled, and distrustful. They possessed hardly any arts, and like wild animals lived on what they could catch; they had no government, and were merciless to every one not of their own small tribe.

"Such were our ancestors."

After three years in English captivity, Jemmy Button at first seemed diffident, disoriented, and ashamed of his own countrymen. But as the weeks passed, while the English explored, mapped, and collected samples, he was evidently absorbed again into the world from which he had been torn. Before the *Beagle* sailed on, Darwin encountered him for the last time and was amazed at what he saw. "We had left him plump, fat, clean, and well-dressed," he wrote; now he was "a thin, haggard savage, with long disordered hair, and naked, except a bit of blanket round his waist." Pained by this spectacle, Captain Fitzroy brought him aboard the *Beagle* and offered him the chance to return to England. Jemmy refused. In the evening, Darwin and the others saw what they took to be the reason for this otherwise inexplicable refusal: "his young and nice-looking wife."

For many years Darwin did not allow himself to articulate in public the full implications of this encounter. *The Descent of Man* was not published until four decades after he witnessed the Fuegians. But they at once haunted him and fortified his willingness to pursue the implications of the theory of evolution to its logical conclusion. That conclusion—that we were descended from ape-like ancestors—was widely viewed as a shameful insult to human dignity. For millennia humans had told themselves that they were the heirs to a perfect man and woman who had been made by God and had once lived harmoni- ously in the Earthly Paradise. Of course, the Fall had introduced sin and death into the world, but we could dream of an eventual recovery of our lost perfection and take pride in our glorious lineage. What Darwin saw for himself in Patagonia made him less inclined to cling to this pride of origin and less ashamed to recognize the actual line of descent. "He who has seen a savage in his native land," he wrote, "will not feel much shame, if forced to acknowledge that the blood of some more humble creature flows in his veins."

Darwin's critics called him the "Monkey Man" and excoriated him for besmirching our ancestry. But Darwin held his ground:

For my own part I would as soon be descended from that heroic little monkey, who braved his dreaded enemy in order to save the life of his keeper, or from that old baboon, who descending from the mountains, carried away in triumph his young comrade from a crowd of astonished dogs—as from a savage who delights to torture his enemies, offers up bloody sacrifices, practices infanticide without remorse, treats his wives like slaves, knows no decency, and is haunted by the grossest superstitions.

The legacy of this response—a bold insistence on humanity's primate inheritance braided together with a deep-seated Victorian belief in a cultural hierarchy among human populations—has haunted evolutionary biologists ever since.

THE FALL OF ADAM AND EVE—at least among virtually the entire scientific community—signaled a shift toward a different conception of human origins. The conception called into question an entire structure of thought, a structure based upon the collective project of conferring on the figures in Genesis the vividness of real people. But the persistence of the belief in Adam and Eve's literal existence suggests something more than the atavistic clinging to a discredited fiction. The story of Adam and Eve was the precipitate of a very long, complex creative endeavor and has been teased out, in all of its implications, for thousands of years by people who have found it thought-provoking, compelling, and morally instructive. In doing so they were guided by specialized labors of great creative artists and thinkers who invested themselves deeply in the imaginary figures. The account of Lucy and our other hominid forebears is recent, murky, and in effect primitive. That this account of human origins happens to be true, according to our best scientific lights, does not in itself make it good to think with.

On the contrary, its difficulty, its uncertainties, its resistance to narrative coherence, makes it one of the great challenges of our age.

The difficulty, apparent from the beginning, has led to repeated attempts to impose a satisfying plot of one kind or another on Darwinism. Some followers imagined natural selection as a triumphal progress toward higher and higher forms of life, culminating of course in our own species. The predestined dominion granted by God to the humans in Genesis was simply granted now by evolution. Others used Herbert Spencer's famous characterization of natural selection as "the survival of the fittest" to serve as a brief for free-market competition in a capitalist economy. Still others, led by Darwin's cousin Francis Galton, saw in the theory a justification for eugenics, the attempt to perfect the human race by ridding it of "undesirables." That sinister enterprise, drawing upon the German biologist Ernst Haeckel's views on race and evolution, had its demonic expression with the Nazis.

Each of these and related variations on Darwinian themes has been exposed as a betrayal of Darwin and a fatal distortion of the massive scientific evidence that has accumulated in the wake of his generative insights. There is no progress in evolution, no march toward perfection. The concept of evolutionary "fitness," from which the phrase "survival of the fittest" was derived, need have nothing to do with competition, let alone with particular economic systems or with warfare. And genetics has undone rather than underscored the whole notion of "race" as an evolutionary principle.

But the attempt to find a narrative in evolution, however much that narrative distorts the evidence, is in large part a consequence of the unsettling absence of a plot, an aesthetic shape, in Darwin's overarching vision. In his old age, he himself brooded on what had happened to him. "Up to the age of thirty, or beyond it," he recalled in the brief autobiography he wrote for his children, poetry of many kinds, such as the works of Milton, Gray, Byron, Wordsworth, Coleridge, and Shelley, gave me great pleasure, and even as a schoolboy I took intense delight in Shakespeare, especially in the historical plays.

These authors, familiar from his childhood, were among his principal companions during the round-the-world voyage on the *Beagle*. Milton in particular was with him, an intimate presence, when Darwin said farewell to Jemmy Button and Fuegia Basket, or dug in the limestone cliffs of South America for fossils, or measured the beaks of the Galápagos finches.

Yet though his imagination may have been shaped by *Paradise Lost* and *Henry IV*—and, for that matter, by the paintings and music that he loved—the stupendous theory he began slowly to formulate as the *Beagle* made its way across the Pacific ultimately changed everything in his mental universe. "Now for many years," he reflected, "I cannot endure to read a line of poetry: I have tried lately to read Shakespeare, and found it so intolerably dull that it nauseated me."

Darwin was not proud of this nausea and did not commend it to his children. "The loss of these tastes," he told them, "is a loss of happiness, and may possibly be injurious to the intellect, and more probably to the moral character." But he was honest enough to acknowledge it, and he struggled to understand how it had come about. It had, he believed, something to do with his particular enterprise as a scientist, the work with which he had been absorbed for decades, ceaselessly amassing evidence and assessing its significance: "My mind," he wrote, "seems to have become a kind of machine for grinding general laws out of large collections of facts, but why this should have caused the atrophy of that part of the brain alone, on which the higher tastes depend, I cannot conceive."

I have no solution to what baffled Darwin himself, but the problem

284 THE RISE AND FALL OF ADAM AND EVE

returns us to the continuing life of the story of Adam and Eve. For many people today, including me, that story is a myth. The long, tangled history from archaic speculation to dogma, from dogma to literal truth, from literal to real, from real to mortal, from mortal to fraudulent, has ended in fiction. The Enlightenment has done its work, and our understanding of human origins has been freed from the grip of a once-potent delusion. The naked man and woman in the garden with the strange trees and the talking snake have returned to the sphere of the imagination from which they originally emerged. But that return does not destroy their fascination or render them worthless. Our existence would in fact be diminished without them. They remain a powerful, even indispensable, way to think about innocence, temptation, and moral choice, about cleaving to a beloved partner, about work and sex and death. They are unforgettable embodiments at once of human responsibility and of human vulnerability. They convey with exceptional vividness the possibility of deliberately choosing in the pursuit of knowledge to disobey the highest authority or, alternatively, the possibility of being seduced into making a foolish choice whose catastrophic consequences will be felt for all time. They hold open the dream of a return somehow, someday, to a bliss that has been lost. They have the life—the peculiar, intense, magical reality—of literature.

Epilogue

In the Forest of Eden

On an uncomfortably hot and humid February morning, three of us—
the evolutionary biologist Melissa Emery Thompson, the field assistant
John Sunday, and I—had already walked for almost an hour in search
of the chimpanzees that lived somewhere in this part of Uganda's enormous Kibale National Park. Researchers from the scientific field station where I was staying, the Kibale Chimpanzee Project, had seen
them nest near here last night, John assured me, and we would almost
certainly find them. The local chimpanzees, called the Kanyawara
group, after the nearest village, would not run away from us, as apes
in the wild ordinarily would. A team of scientists, led by the evolutionary biologist Richard Wrangham, has been observing them inten-
sively for almost thirty years. In the first weeks, Wrangham told me,
he did not see them at all; it was months before he began tentatively to
name them; and four years passed before they were comfortable on the
ground with the scientists nearby. But over time these apes very slowly
became accustomed to the presence of humans.

I looked up for nests they might have made on the top branches,
but I could detect no signs of them. The density and the enormous

height of the trees made it difficult for me to make out anything, and the sweat dripping down into my eyes did not improve matters. In any case, chimpanzees have no fixed abode. Whether to be in the neighborhood of new food, to evade the stealthy approach of predators, or to keep their distance from competing chimpanzee groups with whom they are perpetually at war, they nest every night in a different place. That makes finding them a daily challenge.

We went further into the forest, pushing past vines, thorny brambles, and the long, trailing air roots of the strangler figs—those strange epiphytes that drop from above and surround the host trees, eventually killing them and turning them into supports for their own exuberant growth. We stepped carefully over a platoon of army ants on the move. A tiny frog, the exact color of the leaf on which it sat, hopped away. Tree bark that seemed to shimmer in the half-light revealed itself on closer inspection to be covered with hundreds of caterpillars. Astonishingly beautiful butterflies flitted through the air, as if someone had flung handfuls of old French banknotes from the sky. But no chimpanzees.

My back began to ache, and I was losing heart, when John abruptly stopped. He had heard something. He looked up and pointed. "Do you see anything?" he asked. At first I saw "nothing at all," as Hamlet's mother says when she fails to see the ghost, "yet all that is I see." But then high in the trees I began to perceive two black silhouettes, then two more on an adjacent tree. For animals so large, the apes were relaxing on what appeared to me to be alarmingly slender branches, but they seemed eerily confident in their perches, and I thought for a moment of trapeze artists in the circus who are immune to ordinary fear. One of them leapt casually from one branch to another, and I caught a glimpse of a pink rump.

Continuing to stare, I could just barely make out the fruit that the chimpanzees were methodically picking from the trees. They were in no hurry. One of them moved slightly, and I saw that what had first appeared to be a tuft of hair on its back was in fact a baby clinging to its fur. Nothing more happened; there was no history, no event, no adventure, unless the lazy chewing of fruit is deemed an adventure. This then, I thought, is what Paradise must have been: no permanent address, no weary labor, no planting or cultivating, and, at that dizzying height, no predators and no fear. I had glimpsed a part of the ancient dream: "Of every tree of the garden thou mayest freely eat."

I had come to Uganda in pursuit of that dream, or rather in search of any traces of the Bible story that might be found in what, after Darwin, is now thought to be the actual origins of our species. Moreover, as far as possible, I wanted to make vividly real for myself our modern, scientific origin story. To be sure, we did not descend directly from chimpanzees. Since our lineages diverged millions of years ago from what evolutionary biologists call the Last Common Ancestor, they are not our progenitors but rather our near cousins. Yet they are, many scientists believe, much closer to the Last Common Ancestor in their physical form and the form of their social existence than we are. This is in part because they continue to live in the same forest environment—tragically shrinking every day, through the devastating force of deforestation and human population pressure—in which our distant progenitors lived.

We hominins, by contrast, left the forest to forage on the savannas. In a stupendous evolutionary gamble, we gave up the magical power to live at the vertiginous heights. There were many experiments over millions of years, alternative human species that arose and then became extinct. At the glacial pace set by natural selection, we slowly lost the immense muscle strength and the knuckle-walking and the large canines. Instead, we developed the ability to walk and run upright on our two feet, and we pushed the size of our brains to the limit, the limit, that is, of the female pelvis. Over a vast expanse of time, we mastered fire, increased our ability to cooperate with one another, and, almost incredibly, invented language. This astonishing set of changes was our triumph, of course, but it was also a fall from the leisurely treetop life that I witnessed. Down on the ground, sur-rounded by fearsome predators, we gradually made our way, through our superior cleverness, to species dominance, transforming ourselves from prey into the greatest predators of them all.

Now, largely thanks to us, the chimpanzees are an endangered species. There are currently some 150,000 left in the wild, and unless drastic measures are taken, they are likely to shrink further, until they survive only in zoos or in the grim operating rooms of medical research facilities. But for the moment, in a few places, it is still possible to see them living lives that conjure up our own existence before we became the wise hominins—*Homo sapiens*—that we are.

The scientists in the Kibale Chimpanzee Project name each of the animals and recognize them almost instantly, the way we might rec-ognize Uncle Al and Cousin Beatie. They assess their personalities, chart their health, and track their fates. "That is Eslom," Melissa said, pointing to one of the shadowy forms above our heads, "and the one with the pink rump is Bubbles, carrying her child Basuta." The apes began to swing themselves down from the heights. In the intensely hierarchical chimpanzee society, Eslom, in his early twenties, was the current alpha male, the undisputed leader of the group of some fifty adult males and females and their offspring.

Eslom, the field assistant explained to me, was a great success story. His mother was an outsider, from the neighboring chimpanzee com-munity to the north. For the most part, chimpanzees are patrilocal; the mates stay put, and females generally take the risk, as Eslom's mother did, of migrating to a new group. (Without some such arrangement the small groups would in time suffer the genetic consequences of excessive inbreeding.) Her gamble had succeeded: she had survived the beatings and abuse with which new arrivals to a chimpanzee community are often greeted, usually at the hands of other females. Perhaps when she arrived, she was in heat, a condition highly visible in this species from the pink swelling of the skin around her genitals. The swelling would, researchers speculate, have functioned as a passport, giving the alluring stranger a measure of protection from one or more of the males.

Over the years, she bore three children, one of them being Eslom. But then she died, as did two of her offspring, leaving the sole survivor a young, unprotected, very low-ranking orphan. But Eslom proved to be adept in all the ways that matter. Agile and alert, he was one of the community's best hunters, snatching and killing the red colobus monkeys that chimpanzees love to eat as a delicacy. He quickly fathomed the complexities of the social system, grasping with whom to ally himself and when it was time to shift alliances. And, as he grew and matured, he became a master of what are called "displays": swaying back and forth, he would stand upright with his shoulders hunched and hair bristling out, so that he looked still more massive and intimidating. With his powerful arms, he would tear off tree branches or throw rocks. Then with blinding speed he would rush toward a rival, forcing him out of the way or slapping him. Through such tactics, endlessly repeated, he gradually rose in rank.

When the reigning alpha male died, there was a power vacuum. One by one, over an extended time, the higher-ranking males were compelled to acknowledge Eslom's authority. Finally, only one rival, Lanjo, was left to challenge him. The scientists know, from analyzing the urine and feces samples that they collect, that Eslom and Lanjo had the same father, Johnny. But Johnny was dead, and in any case chimpanzee males have no way of knowing who their fathers are. The rivals had no idea then that they were half-brothers on their father's side, and it would not have mattered if they did.

With the support of his mother, his maternal siblings, and other allies, Lanjo seemed the stronger candidate for supremacy. But when Eslom managed to sink his large fangs into Lanjo's neck, driving him screaming up a tree, the struggle for dominance was finally over. All the chimpanzees in the group, males and females alike, performed rituals of submission—known as pant-grunts—to him, while he pant-grunted to no one. Anyone who failed to submit risked slaps or full-scale beatings from the angry alpha or from his erstwhile rival, now the beta male.

Yet when the chimpanzees dropped to the ground, I saw before me not a display of power, but rather of mutual comfort. It was a vision of collective Edenic tranquility, as if the first humans had already managed to reproduce and multiply before they were expelled from the Garden. They lounged there, some eight or ten adult males and females with their children, and began to form pairs, carefully combing through their partner's fur for insects, dirt, and wounds, looking into each other's ears, gently scratching and stroking. The chimpanzees of Kibale and a few other places, to the great fascination of the scientists, have developed a special grooming technique: one chimpanzee raises a long arm into the air and another chimpanzee mimics the gesture, clasping hands or touching wrists together, while with the other hand they groom one another. The technique is distinctive enough, where it has been transmitted from one generation to the next, that some scientists have claimed that it is evidence that chimpanzees possess what we call culture.

This group of cultured chimpanzees stayed at it for a very long time, long enough for me to begin to know each of them by name. Outamba, in her late thirties, was the most fecund of the mothers; with six children as well as a grandson, she was once again pregnant. Several of her offspring were there and took turns grooming her. Stella, the eighteen-month-old daughter of another female in the group, was clearly hyperactive. She could not stay still for a minute, either to rest or be groomed, but constantly climbed over her mother and everyone else, slipping down their sides as if they were slides, throwing leaves in the air, breaking off small branches and swinging them recklessly around. I thought for sure that she would be slapped, but the adults were all amazingly tolerant of her zaniness. The adult male Bud nursed wounds he had received from an enemy group that he had encountered. He was lucky to have somehow escaped; had he not, they might have ripped off his testicles and beaten him to death. Big Brown, a huge male considerably larger than Eslom, sat quietly apart, chewing on the pith inside a shoot. Old for a chimpanzee in the wild—he was in his fifties—he had dropped to a low rank and had to pant-grunt to almost every other adult male. Years ago he had been the alpha, but his reign, characterized by his frequent beatings of the females, had come to an end. Eslom too on occasion beat the females—such is the manner of chimpanzee males—but, whenever he had caught and killed a monkey, he always shared the meat first with them, and in doing so he had patiently generated loyalty.

Eslom was less relaxed than the others in the group. He was preoccupied with the female Bubbles, whose rump, already visible high in the trees, revealed itself on the ground to be spectacularly swollen. In her mid-fifties, Bubbles was quite a bit older than the twenty-two-year-old Eslom, but she was in heat. Chimpanzee females continue to ovulate through most of their lifetime, and chimpanzee males are particularly aroused by older females who have demonstrated the ability to bear children. The alpha male, wanting her exclusively for himself, was engaged in what is called mate-guarding. Whenever another male came too close to her, Eslom's hair would ominously stand on end, and the ambitious suitor would beat a hasty retreat. Chimpanzee copulation is less about pleasure—it takes on average six seconds—than about reproduction: in principle the alpha's goal is to father all of the offspring.

Bubbles, for her part, would probably have been happy to mate with many of her suitors, for while it is in the interest of the alpha to monopolize her, females generally seek to have intercourse with as many of the senior males as possible. (Females, Melissa told me, go out of their way to copulate with the males who have been most aggressive toward them.) Promiscuity, scientists speculate, is a survival strategy, not for the females but for their offspring. For since chimpanzee mothers typically nurse their young for years and only go back into heat when they are weaned, the more powerful males may on occasion practice infanticide, in order to hasten a return to sexual availability. If the female has copulated with many males, the speculation goes, each will think that the newborn might well be his and will be less prone to violence.

But today at least, while I observed them, Eslom chased off all potential suitors. He was determined to cling to and merge with his desired partner. "This one," the alpha male insisted, with all the strength of his muscular body; "this one." Bubbles looked around and complied. She turned and presented her swollen rump for Eslom to inspect and admire. He looked, sniffed, and was content.

Observing this scene not as a legitimate natural scientist but merely as a writer fascinated by the biblical story of the primal pair, I felt an odd twinge of shame at my voyeuristic role. And this shame, of course, is part of the story: "The eyes of them both were opened, and they knew that they were naked; and they sewed fig leaves together, and made themselves aprons." The chimpanzees have no interest in leaves except on occasion to chew on them. They do not know that they are naked, and they feel absolutely no shame. Though they live in the shadowy depths of a remote forest, their lives are remarkably open to view. The scientists who tirelessly track them and watch their every movement and analyze their urine and fecal samples are able to describe each of them with a degree of intimacy that far exceeds what I could muster for even my closest friends, my children, or my parents.

Though there is some evidence that they can deceive one another, chimpanzees generally hold nothing back. They scratch, fart, shit, and do everything else in full view. When they are tickled, they grin; when they are angry, they bear their fangs and roar; when they are excited or threatened, they jump up and down and scream. When the female is ovulating, she shows it vividly for all to see. When the male is aroused, he spreads his legs and displays his erection. They copulate openly, with everyone looking on and often with their children climbing over them. This is what it means to be shameless, or rather to exist in a world where shame does not exist.

According to Genesis, before they had eaten the forbidden fruit, the first humans existed precisely in such a world. Of course, the Genesis story did not depict that existence in any detail, let alone in terms that made it resemble the lives of our chimpanzee cousins. All the text says is that "they were both naked, the man and his wife, and were not ashamed." Most Christian commentators speculated that their copulation would have been brief—perhaps no more than the apes' six seconds—and intended exclusively for reproduction. St. Augustine added that it would have certainly taken place openly in the presence of others, including offspring. But despite their mania for filling in the blank spaces in the biblical narrative, the theologians never fully imagined what it would be like to live lives that resemble ours minus any touch of shame.

Before they violated the divine interdict, there was another crucial feature of life for the first humans: they had not eaten of the Tree of the Knowledge of Good and Evil. The biblical contrast is not between a life governed by a moral code and a wild, lawless life. No, the contrast in Genesis is between a life lived *with* knowledge of good and evil— presumably, an awareness of the symbolic categories themselves and of the difference between them—and a life lived *without* such knowledge. The Bible clearly expects that its readers possess an understanding of what good and evil are, for we are all heirs to the humans who ate from the tree. But what it was like to be Adam and Eve before they ate from the tree—that is, what it was like to be humans without the knowledge of good and evil—is much less clear. Of course, we could say that any animal would serve as a model: a cat or a lobster will do. But Adam and Eve in the Garden were not any animal; they were our progenitors. Being perfectly innocent, as we are not, they could not have been identical to us, but they were still like us.

As virtually everyone has recognized from ancient times to the present, apes are not identical to us, but they are very much like us. The resemblance is startling. Yet they do not possess the knowledge of good and evil. This does not mean that they live in the state of nature that the seventeenth-century philosopher Thomas Hobbes famously characterized as "solitary, nasty, brutish, and short." The lives of chimpanzees are neither solitary nor short, and nasty is in the eye of the beholder. They are complex social beings; they solve problems; they use tools; they have distinct and varied personalities; they often survive to what, by the standards of most animals, is a ripe old age. But, as far as we can tell, their primal ancestors never ate from the fatal tree. Though they signal to one another, for example when danger is near, they do not possess symbolic concepts like good and evil. Chimpanzees are neither moral nor immoral; they are amoral.

A primatologist wrote a celebrated book in the early 1980s that likened chimpanzee behavior—their shifting alliances, betrayals, bribes, and punishments—to Machiavellian politics. But in *The Prince* Machiavelli assumed that politicians fully understood what was good and what was evil; the survivors among them simply understood when it was necessary to violate their moral code. "Thus it is well to seem merciful, faithful, humane, sincere, religious, and also to be so; but you must have the mind so disposed that when it is needed to be otherwise you may be able to change to the opposite qualities" (*The Prince*, chap. 18). Chimpanzees seem to function politically without the need for a conceptual understanding of either fidelity or betrayal, domination or submission.

For centuries, theologians—all men, of course—brooded uneasily about God's curse on Eve: "thy desire shall be to thy husband, and he shall rule over thee." Did not the husband, they asked, also rule over the wife in Paradise before the Fall? Yes, most of them reassured themselves: the man would always have ruled over the woman, for that was the natural order of things. But before eating from the Tree of the

Knowledge of Good and Evil, the woman did not understand that she was being dominated; after her transgression, she did understand, and she bitterly resented it. Chimpanzee sexual relations then are something like the theologian's dream of life before the Fall. The females are dominated, but they lack any concept of domination.

Chimpanzee females scream when they are hit, but there is no evidence that they dream it should or could somehow be otherwise. So too young males form raiding parties to murder chimpanzees from neighboring groups, but they lack the concept of murder. If one of her children dies, a mother may carry it about for a while, as if she were in mourning, but chimpanzees do not have an abstract notion of death, just as they cherish and nurture without having the words for love and mothering. This does not mean that all their actions are purely instinctual. The young are highly observant, learning how to behave by watching the adults, and they may even rehearse their roles. Researchers note that juvenile males break off sticks and practice hitting adult females with them, while juvenile females with sticks are more likely to carry them as if they were babies. None of this behavior is conceptual or self-conscious, for chimpanzees have no language in which to formulate ideas, but it would be absurd to regard them as automata.

We should be forever grateful to them. They enable us to see for ourselves what the Genesis origin story might have actually looked like, had it been real. Closely resembling us, they show us what it is to live without the knowledge of good and evil, just as they live without shame and without understanding that they are destined to die. They are still in Paradise.

Of course, very few humans in their right mind think that the life apes live in the forest is the life humans would actually want for themselves in Paradise. But that is because we construct our idea of Paradise from notions that we derive from our knowledge of good and evil. We are already fallen; they are not.

Medieval thinkers, reflecting on the striking resemblance of apes to humans, came to the opposite conclusion: they believed that simians too must have fallen, but even lower in the scale of being than we have. In Paradise, Adam and Eve were incomparably beautiful and huge in size. Now because of the legacy of sin, we have lost much of the beauty as well as the bulk of the first humans. The loss has been progressive: the earliest patriarchs and matriarchs retained some of the splendor of the first humans, but it is now almost entirely gone. "The fairest women compared with Sarah are as apes compared with a human being," an ancient commentator sadly remarked, and compared with Eve, Sarah too resembled an ape. Apes, of course, are the gold standard of human ugliness.

One legend held that at some point after the expulsion from the Garden, God visited Eve and asked her how many children she had. The truth is that she had a great many, but because she was afraid that the number of her offspring would indicate that she took too much pleasure in sex, she lied and only showed the Lord a few of them. God was not deceived: to punish her, He turned the children she had concealed into apes. Accordingly, apes were widely used in the Middle Ages as symbols not merely of ugliness but of carnal desire; they displayed in an exaggerated form the vice that contributed to our own fall. When in medieval paintings Adam and Eve stand by the Tree of the Knowledge of Good and Evil, an ape often lurks somewhere nearby.

It was only in the nineteenth century that the view decisively changed. The pivotal moment came at Oxford in 1860 when Darwin's friend and champion Thomas Henry Huxley engaged in a famous debate with Bishop Samuel Wilberforce. The bishop capped his sardonic refutation of evolutionary theory by turning to his opponent and wryly asking, "Is it on your grandfather's or grandmother's side that you claim descent from the apes?" Huxley slowly rose and said that while he would not be ashamed to have a monkey for an ancestor, he would be ashamed to be connected to a man who used great gifts to obscure the truth. Huxley's voice did not carry through the large room, but everyone understood his words to mean "I would rather be descended from an ape than a bishop." A woman in the audience fainted.

It was Darwin's position that ultimately prevailed in the modern scientific account of human origins. No one any longer believes that apes are degenerate versions of humans, metamorphosed as punishment for lust or idleness. The fossil evidence gathered now for many decades and still emerging in spectacular finds provides overwhelming evidence that our remote ancestors were ape-like creatures who somehow contrived to walk on two feet. How any of them survived, let alone flourished, is still not clear. As scientists have shown beyond a reasonable doubt, they were not the happy product of a once-and-for-all creation, destined from the beginning to be masters of the universe. They were a work-in-progress, over an unimaginably long time. A biologist writes that one key period of evolutionary ferment, long before the emergence of modern humans, was between 2.5 and 2 million years ago. He is attempting to narrow down the crucial time period, and so in a way he does. But he is talking about 500,000 years. All of recorded human history, as far back as we can get, is only about 5,000 years.

Over the course of this immense time span, our species evolved from diminutive, small-brained bipeds eating fruit, digging for tubers, and catching the occasional lizard to what we are now: animals, as Friedrich Nietzsche put it, who can make promises. In a provocative book published in 1887, the German philosopher argued that the crucial mechanism for the transformation of amoral ape-like creatures into moral human beings was pain—repeated, remorseless infliction of pain. Punishment was the means by which the healthy, exuberant, violent energies of the dominant males—Nietzsche called them "the blond beasts"—were gradually tamed. In the process, everything that those who had once ruled the earth regarded as good—the ruthless satisfaction of appetite, the swaggering insolence, the reckless blend of rapine and largesse, the unrestrained will to be the alpha male—was rebranded as evil. The mass of women and male weaklings who had once been glee-fully dominated by the blond beasts managed to proclaim their values of self-sacrifice, discipline, and pious fear as good. The transformation—Nietzsche termed it a "transvaluation of values"—was in effect a success-ful slave revolt. It must have been led, he thought, by an extremely clever priestly caste seething with resentment. He identified this caste with the Jews and declared that their culminating invention, in celebrating dis-eased suffering over amoral health, was Jesus, the new Adam.

This sinister philosophical parable points to questions whose answers lie still in the sphere of wild speculation: given the fact that chimpanzees (*Pan troglodytes*) and modern humans (*Homo sapiens*) share 96 percent of the same genes, how did it actually happen? What trig-gered the fantastically complex suite of features—long legs, hands with short fingers, feet unable to grasp things, prolonged childhood depen-dency, large brain size, cooperative social existence, capacity for sym-bolic thought, and many more—that characterize humans? How did we acquire language, religious beliefs, origin stories? Where did our moral conscience come from? And what do we still share with chim-panzees as an inheritance from the Last Common Ancestor?

Scientific interest has been drawn in recent years to bonobos, found in the wild in only a single area of Central Africa. At some point in the relatively recent past, as measured by evolutionary time, a group of chimpanzees became isolated south of the Congo River and formed their own world. Over time, while they retained many behav-ioral characteristics of common chimpanzees, their social life began to change. Researchers observe that males continue to be competitive with one another, but their aggression now rarely turns against the females, who enjoy greatly increased rank and status. Forming intense bonds with one another, by acting together the females are able to dominate most of the males. Sexual activity is greatly heightened. The females show signs of being in heat even when they are not fertile, so

that copulation is no longer exclusively linked to reproduction. Bonobos engage in fellatio; there is frequent male–male and female–female
sexuality; and, perhaps most remarkably, encounters with neighboring groups lead not to violence but to intercourse. Behavior then that
seemed constitutive of being a chimpanzee proved amenable, with isolation, the right environment, and enough time, to radical change.

Something of the same kind may account for the way in which our
species bafflingly combines characteristics found in both chimpanzees
and bonobos and has interlaced these together with entirely new features. While managing to retain a penchant for intense competition for
rank, group hunting, xenophobic violence, and a strong male impulse
to dominate females, we have at the same time developed pervasive
nonreproductive sexuality, friendship, cooperation, and the potential
for egalitarianism and the peaceful embracing of other groups. To all
of these we have added the fathomless complexities of toolmaking, art-
making, language, and the capacity to reason. Our grasp of the way this
came about is still at an early stage, and it is safe to say that in the years
to come there will be both steady advances and spectacular surprises.

But what the current scientific understanding still lacks—and may
never achieve or even want—is the focus on moral choice that lies at
the heart of the Adam and Eve story. The first humans in the biblical
account were free to observe or to violate the divine prohibition: "And
when the woman saw that the tree was good for food, and that it was
pleasant to the eyes, and a tree to be desired to make one wise, she took
of the fruit thereof, and did eat, and gave also unto her husband with
her; and he did eat." It is this transgression—a deliberate action, not an
impersonal, mechanistic process of random genetic mutation and natural selection—that determined the shape of our lives. The Adam and
Eve story insists that our fate, at least at the beginning of time, was our
own responsibility. Millions of people in the world, including many
who grasp the underlying assumptions of modern science, continue to
cling to the peculiar satisfaction that the ancient story provides. I do.

·   ·   ·

WHEN I ARRIVED at the scientific research station in western Uganda, I was not allowed to go out immediately to observe the chimpanzees. Since they are vulnerable to human diseases, there was a quarantine period to determine that I was not infectious. With time on my hands, I went to Anglican services on Sunday morning in nearby Fort Portal. Uganda is an overwhelmingly Christian country, roughly divided between Roman Catholics and Anglicans, with a small but growing number of Pentecostals. In my application to visit the Kibale Chimpanzee Project, I had initially written that I was eager to observe the modern scientific origin story that has replaced the ancient biblical one, but if it was couched in these terms, friends who had worked there told me, the application would almost certainly be rejected. Ugandan authorities do not regard chimpanzee research as the alternative to their religious faith.

In church—which happened to be called St. Stephen's—the sermon delivered by the priest, the Reverend Happy Sam Araali, centered on the creation story. (He must have been tipped off that I was coming.) We can dig wells, he said, but only God can create lakes and seas. That is a sign of how powerful God is, and it should make us respect him, since He can do things that are so much bigger and more difficult than anything we can do. So too with the creation of man. We can draw figures on a wall and confer upon them a certain vividness, Reverend Happy told the congregation, but only God could create the first humans and make them live by breathing the breath of life into their nostrils.

On the ride back to the field station, I asked the field assistant who had accompanied me whether he believed that the story of Adam and Eve was the literal truth. Yes, he did, he assured me; he was a good Christian. Then what did he make of the notion that we were closely related to chimpanzees? He laughed—"A very difficult problem," he said—and then we both fell silent. The next day, when we were out in the forest observing the Edenic scene of grooming and Eslom's mate-guarding, we did not pursue the subject.

The alpha male's cleaving to Bubbles set the stage for a scene I witnessed on the following morning that conjured up Genesis for me still more intensely. We were at breakfast at the camp when Melissa noticed a shadow near the entrance to the compound. At first she thought it was an elephant, but she realized quickly that it was a chimpanzee, and with the skill shared by all the scientists and field assistants, she immediately identified him as the beta male, Lanjo. We hurried down to see why he had come so uncharacteristically close to the human settlement.

He was sitting in a small patch of grass and leaves looking increasingly impatient. From time to time he slapped the ground noisily with his feet or hands. (I realized with a start where we get the otherwise inexplicable impulse to stamp our feet in frustration.) Then after ruffling the leaves, dragging a stick across the ground, and making a low noise, he reached out and gave a vine a violent shake. At last, the source of his impatience appeared: from out of the thick bush came a very uneasy female, nineteen-year-old Leona, looking over her shoulder and carrying her young child Lily. What had happened, the field assistant explained, was that Lanjo must have taken advantage of Eslom's mate-guarding preoccupation to lure away Leona, who was also showing signs of being in heat, though not as vividly as Bubbles. They had slipped off and embarked on what the scientists call a consort, a kind of honeymoon away from the group and the jealous gaze of the dominant male. They would be beaten if they were caught; hence perhaps Leona's anxiety and Lanjo's cunning decision to come near the human settlement, where the group rarely ventures.

Alone at last, Lanjo and Leona shared a moment of chimpanzee tenderness: they gently touched rumps. With Lily clinging to her back, Leona bent over and allowed Lanjo to examine her vulva with his finger which he then held to his nose and sniffed. But it was not just for the six-second copulation that they were together. Through violating the will of the supreme ruler and risking punishment, they had become a couple. They looked around the clearing and glanced quickly at us. Then, set on continuing their consort, they plunged together into the dense thicket where, set on continuing our spying, we struggled to follow. The world was all before them.

Appendix 1

A Sampling of Interpretations

Over the centuries there have been innumerable interpretations of the story of Adam and Eve. Many of the most influential interpretations figure in this book. But it is impossible to convey the full richness, variety, cunning, and on occasion wildness of the vast archive that has accumulated and that continues to grow. What follows are a few attempts to conjure up, in modern idiom, some fragmentary pieces of this archive. The language for the most part is my own, but I have stitched each of them together from one or more original sources listed in the notes.

WHEN EVE VIOLATED THE PROHIBITION and ate the forbidden fruit, Adam was not with her—some say that they had made love and that the man was taking a nap; others that he had gone off to conduct a survey of the Garden. The first sign he had that something was wrong was the fact that Eve had covered her genitals and her buttocks with fig leaves. At first Adam could not even understand what she had done— he thought that the leaves had stuck to her by accident. But then when he looked more closely, he realized that she had made small holes and threaded the leaves together with vegetable fibers.

[Abba Halfon b. Koriah. Genesis Rabbah (fourth and fifth centuries CE), 19:3; *The Book of Jubilees* 9c. 100–150 BCE[?]), 3:22]

THE FIRST HUMANS WERE perfectly beautiful and very wise, but
they lacked one of the five senses on which fallen humanity most
depends: sight. In their original state Adam and Eve were completely
blind. They had no need to see, since they were in a world designed to
meet their every need. If they wanted something to eat or drink, it was
always there within their grasp. And when God brought the animals
to Adam for him to name, Adam simply reached out and touched each
of them, knowing from the touch what name to assign. Perhaps their
happy blindness—happy, of course, because they did not know that
they could not see—helps to explain their transgression, since it must
have been difficult for them to distinguish the forbidden fruit from
all others, particularly since the Enemy was bent on deceiving them.
Their condition helps to explain their complete absence of shame, for it
was only after their Fall that God removed the coating that had blinded
their eyes. As soon as they could see, in the wake of their disobedience, they hastened to cover themselves: "And the eyes of the two were
opened, and they knew they were naked, and they sewed fig leaves and
made themselves loincloths."

[Clement of Alexandria (c. 150–c. 215)]

THE NEWLY CREATED HUMANS were physically mature—God
gave them the form and attributes of twenty-year-olds—and in many
ways they were impressively accomplished. But they were also newborns, only beginning to accommodate themselves to the world. It
was for this reason that God commanded them not to eat of the Tree
of the Knowledge of Good and Evil. The fruit of that tree was not in
itself poisonous. On the contrary, for a mature human it was the best
of all possible nourishment, and God fully intended Adam and Eve
to eat from it in due time. But as with all the foods we eat, some are

appropriate to infant stomachs and some are not. Paradise was unusual in having only a single fruit that was decidedly not appropriate, and God told the newborn humans that they could eat the fruit of every other tree. But Eve and Adam, deceived by the serpent into an act of rash impatience, tried to consume the fruit of the forbidden tree before they were ready for it. It was like an infant trying to gobble down a steak, and it is no surprise at all that the consequence to them was fatal.

[Theophilus of Antioch (fl. second century)]

EVE WAS HOLDING A BRANCH on which there was a ripe, red fruit, unmistakably the fruit of the forbidden tree. She said to Adam, "Take and eat." He had some difficulty hearing her, as if her voice were coming from some distant place, or as if the voice and the language it spoke were not quite hers. He felt confused and baffled and, above all, drowsy. He remembered, of course, that God had told him not to eat of the fruit of that particular tree, but he could not quite recall why. He realized that, since he did not know the meaning of the word "die," he had not really understood at the time what God was talking about. He could almost grasp the notion of a commandment—since the commandment to be fruitful and multiply had corresponded to his desire for Eve—but the notion of not doing something made no sense to him. He reached out languidly, took the fruit, and ate.

[Cappadocian Fathers (fourth century CE)]

WHILE EVE WAS OFF CONVERSING with the serpent, Adam had been staring intensely at the refulgent light of the heavens. Contemplating the glory of God—boundless, incomprehensible, and utterly overwhelming—was what filled his days and his nights. Everything was absorbed in this rapt contemplation, even his hours of sleep, his moments of calm sexual coupling with his wife, his simple breathing in and out, in and out. God was everywhere and everything. When Eve offered him the forbidden fruit, the fruit that God himself had warned them not to eat, Adam immediately took it and ate. Why? "I am exhausted," he said to himself. "I want to return now to the clay from which I was made. I want to die."

[Gregory of Nyssa (c. 332–395)]

HAVING FAILED TO FIND a suitable companion for the human among the creatures made out of clay, the Lord God decided to build one out of bone. He thought the human would find the whole process fascinating, so He let him watch as He deftly opened his side, removed a suitable bone with which to begin, and closed the wound He had made. He then set to work on the project, not modeling the new figure out of clay, as He had done with the first human and all the other animals, but rather constructing it as an architect might do: a vast network of veins, arteries, and nerves; a fabulously complex arrangement of internal organs able to interact with the environment, convert food to energy, regulate the creature's metabolism, and excrete waste; a brain whose involuted material could perform calculations with dazzling speed; a tongue, larynx, and vocal cords suitable for speaking and singing; and finally a graceful exterior, quite similar to that of the first human but sufficiently varied to excite interest and designed to facilitate sexual reproduction. God looked at what He had done and saw that it was very good. But then He noticed that the human for whom He had done all this had a look of disgust on his face. Adam found the interior of the new creature, the tangle of blood and soft tissue and pulsing organs, nauseating. The idea of living with this creature, let alone mating with it, was unendurable. God had to destroy what He had made and to start again.

[R. Jose. Genesis Rabbah (fourth and fifth centuries CE) 17:7]

WHEN THEY HAD EATEN of the forbidden fruit, Adam and Eve realized that, while they were doomed to die, the animals over which they
held sway were, as things stood, going to live forever. They knew they
had very little time, and so they began to rush everywhere, with the
forbidden fruits in their hands, feeding each of the animals so that all
would be mortal. Could they have explained why they were in such
a hurry to doom all living creatures? Perhaps they were mindful of
God's earlier command and feared that, by failing to hold sway over
the animals, they would be violating yet another divine edict. Perhaps
they did not want anyone else, even simple brutes, to enjoy what they
were condemned to lose. In any case, they succeeded in finding and
feeding all of the cattle and beasts and birds—an astounding feat—with
the exception of a single bird. That bird, the phoenix, still lives forever.

[R. Simlai(?) Genesis Rabbah 19:5 (fourth and fifth centuries CE)]

AND THE HUMAN SAID, "The woman whom you gave by me,
she gave me from the tree, and I ate." And the Lord God said to the
woman, "What is this you have done?" And the woman said, "The
serpent beguiled me and I ate." And Lord God called the serpent to
Him, and the serpent uneasily stepped forward. And the Lord God
took a sharp knife and cut off the serpent's feet and legs. This is why
from that day forward serpents crawl on their bellies.

[George Syncellus (fl. eighth century)]

THE IMMEDIATE EFFECT of his disobedience was to introduce into
Adam for the first time the sensation of gloom. At the very moment
that he ate the fruit, all his joy vanished and melancholy coagulated in
his blood, just as radiance disappears when a candle is blown out, leaving the wick, glowing and smoking, to stink. And there was a further

striking effect: Adam had once known the songs of the angels, and his own voice was sublimely tuneful. After his sin, however, there crept into his marrow an ugly wind that is now in every man. This wind in the marrow turned his blissful voice into the sounds of loud jeering and hooting. After bouts of great shaking laughter, tears would come to his eyes, in the same way that the foam of semen is expelled in the ardor of carnal pleasure.

[Hildegard of Bingen (1098–1179)]

BEFORE THE FALL, Eve did not menstruate. It was only after sinning that all women became animals whose menstrual fluxes must be counted among the world's monstrosities. For seeds touched with them will not germinate, trees will lose their fruit, iron will rust, bronze will grow black.

[Alexander Neckam (1157–1217)]

ADAM SAW PERFECTLY CLEARLY that his wife had been deceived and that the serpent had lured her into a trap from which she could not now escape. She will have to die, he thought, and God will offer to create a new companion for me, either from another one of my ribs or from some other source. But I do not want a new companion. I want this one and only this one. There is but a single way in which I can remain with her, and that is by conjoining my fate to hers. We will live—and when the time comes, we will rot—together.

[Duns Scotus (1266–1308)]

AND GOD BLESSED HIM, and God said to him, "Be fruitful and multiply and fill the earth and conquer it." And the human said to God, "How am I supposed to be fruitful and multiply? I am a single creature, made in your image. All the other creatures, the fish of the sea and the fowl of the heavens and the cattle and the wild beasts and all the crawling things that crawl upon the earth, are in pairs, male and female distinct and separate from one another. I see them mate with each other, and through that act they are fruitful. But I am one, both male and female. How can I fulfill your command?" And God took a knife and split the human in half, as an apple is split, making two where there was once one. And God drew flesh over the wounds he had made and left on the belly of each half the mark called a navel as a sign of what he had done. And God said "Now you will be able to multiply and to conquer the earth." After the cut was made, the two parts of the human, each desiring his other half, came together, and throwing their arms about one another, entwined in mutual embraces. The man and the woman were fruitful and multiplied and conquered the earth. But they always felt the wound of their original division and the impossibility, even in their mutual embraces, of healing the wound completely.

[Judah Abravanel (c. 1464–c. 1523)]

GOD WAS EVERYWHERE AND EVERYTHING. All the more baffling then that when Eve offered him the forbidden fruit, Adam immediately took it and ate. Why? He could scarcely have put it into words, but if compelled, he might have said: An eternity in this condition is unendurable. I hate the contemplation of the One who made me. I hate the overwhelming debt of gratitude. I hate God.

[Martin Luther (1483–1546)]

GOD NOT ONLY KNEW that Adam and Eve would violate his prohibition; He also actively and deliberately impelled them to do so. And if Adam had hesitated before he ate the fatal fruit, if he had dared to question the impulse that God Himself had planted in him, God would have rebuked him with these words: "O man, who art thou that repliest against God? Shall the thing formed say to him that formed it, Why hast thou made me thus? Hath not the potter power over the clay of the same lump to make one vessel unto honor, and another unto dishonor?"

[John Calvin (1509–1564)]

THE FIRST MAN was made out of clay, but it was not ordinary clay. His body was more pure and transparent than the finest crystal. It was lit from within with streams of light that illuminated his internal vessels, vessels containing liquids of all kinds and colors. This iridescent creature was larger in stature than humans are now. His dark hair was short and curly; a dark mustache adorned his upper lip. He did not have a penis. Where his genitals would have been, there was something with the shape of a face from which emerged delicious odors. In his belly there was a vessel that bred small eggs and another vessel that contained liquid capable of impregnating these eggs. When the man became enflamed with the love of God, desire that there might be other creatures to share in this adoration would overwhelm him, so that the liquid would boil over and, spreading itself over one of the eggs, would cause it in time to hatch into another perfect man. So at least it was meant to be, when God told the human to be fruitful and multiply. But it happened this way only once: the man that was hatched was the Messiah who turned himself into a fetus and awaited the time to enter Mary's womb. All other humans were born in a different way, when Adam and Eve were expelled from Paradise. Driven from the sacred precinct, their bodies coarsened and became like ours. They lost their crystalline transparency, their inward light dimmed and then went out; and their inner vessels became the internal organs whose sight only repels us. And in the place of the beautiful faces that once emitted such marvelous perfumes, there were now the ugly genitals that all humans cover in shame.

[Antoinette Bourignon (1616–1680)]

HUYNH SANH THONG, a MacArthur Fellow, has argued that snakes were ultimately responsible for the origin of language because mothers needed to warn their children about them. Snakes gave bipedal hominins, who were already equipped with a nonhuman primate communication system, the evolutionary nudge to begin pointing to communicate for the social good, a critical step toward the evolution of language and all that followed to make us who we are today.

[Lynne A. Isbell, 2009]

Appendix 2

A Sampling of Origin Stories

Almost every human culture that has been studied has one or more origin stories. What follows is a small selection of these stories.

Egypt

When I had come into being, being (itself) came into being, and all beings came into being after I came into being.

I planned in my own heart, and there came into being a multitude of forms of beings, the forms of children and the forms of their children. I was the one who copulated with my fist, I masturbated with my hand. Then I spewed with my own mouth.

They brought to me my Eye with them. After I had joined together my members, I wept over them. That is how men came into being from the tears which came forth from my Eye.

[Pritchard, *Ancient Near Eastern Texts*]

Greece

In those days God himself was their shepherd, and ruled over them, just as man, who is by comparison a divine being, still rules over the lower animals. Under him there were no forms of government or separate possession of women and children, for all men rose again from the earth, having no memory of the past. And although they had nothing of this sort, the earth gave them fruits in abundance, which grew on trees and shrubs unbidden, and where not planted by the hand of man. And they dwelt naked, and mostly in the open air, for the temperature of their seasons was mild, and they had no beds, but lay on soft couches of grass, which grew plentifully out of the earth.

[Plato, *Statesman*]

Greece

In the days of old, the gods distributed the earth among themselves and peopled their own districts. And when they had peopled them they tended us, their nurselings and possessions, as shepherds tend their flocks, excepting only that they did not use blows or bodily force, as shepherds do, but governed us like pilots from the stern of the vessel, which is an easy way of guiding animals, holding our souls by the rudder of persuasion according to their own pleasure.

[Plato, *Critias*]

Rome

An animal with higher intellect,
more noble, able—one to rule the rest:
such was the living thing the earth still lacked.
Then man was born. Either the Architect

of All, the author of the universe,
in order to beget a better world,
created man from seed divine—or else
Prometheus, son of Iapetus, made man
by mixing new-made earth with fresh rainwater
(for earth had only recently been set
apart from heaven, and the earth still kept
seeds of the sky—remains of their shared birth);
and when he fashioned man, his mold recalled
the masters of all things, the gods. And while
all other animals are bent, head down,
and fix their gaze upon the ground, to man
he gave a face that is held high; he had
man stand erect, his eyes upon the stars.
So was the earth, which until then had been
so rough and indistinct, transformed: it wore
a thing unknown before—the human form.

    [Ovid, *Metamorphoses* 1]

Rome

. . . from the bronze helmet, he [Jason] draws out snake's teeth
and scatters them on the plowed field as seed.
These teeth had first been steeped in potent venom;
earth softens them; they grow, take on new forms.
Just as a fetus gradually takes,
within its mother's womb, a human shape,
acquiring harmony in all its parts,
and only sees the light that all men share
when it is fully formed, so here, the likeness
of men, perfected in the pregnant earth,

sprang from the soil; and what is even more
miraculous, each man was armed and clashed
his weapons at his birth.

    [Ovid, *Metamorphoses* 7]

Rome

At long last, borne upon her dragons' wings,
Medea came to Corinth's sacred spring.
Here, when the world was born—so we are told
by ancient legends—mortal bodies sprang
from mushrooms risen in the wake of rain.

    [Ovid, *Metamorphoses* 7]

North America (Great Plains)

One day Old Man determined that he would make a woman and a
child; so he formed them both—the woman and the child, her son—
of clay. After he had moulded the clay in human shape, he said to the
clay, "You must be people," and then he covered it up and left it, and
went away. The next morning he went to the place and took the covering off, and saw that the clay shapes had changed a little. The second
morning there was still more change, and the third still more. The
fourth morning he went to the place, took the covering off, looked
at the images, and told them to rise and walk; and they did so. They
walked to the river with their Maker, and then he told them that his
name was *Na'pi*, old man.

    As they were standing by the river, the woman said to him, "How
is it? Will we always live, will there be no end to it?" He said: "I have
never thought of that. We will have to decide it. I will take this buf-
falo chip and throw it in the river. If it floats, when people die, in four
days they will become alive again; they will die for only four days.

But if it sinks, there will be an end to them." He threw the chip in the river, and it floated. The woman turned and picked up a stone, and said: "No, I will throw this stone in the river; if it floats, we will always live, if it sinks people must die, that they may always be sorry for each other." The woman threw the stone into the water, and it sank. "There," said the Old Man, "you have chosen. There will be an end to them."

[George Bird Grinnell, *Blackfoot Lodge Tales*]

Melanesia

The one who was first there drew two male figures on the ground, scratched open his own skin, and sprinkled the drawings with his blood. He plucked two large leaves and covered the figures, which became, after a while, two men. The names of the men were To Kabinana and To Karvuvu.

To Kabinana went off alone, climbed a coconut tree that had light yellow nuts, picked two that were still unripe, and threw them to the ground; they broke and became two handsome women. To Karvuvu admired the women and asked how his brother had come by them. "Climb a coconut tree," To Kabinana said, "pick two unripe nuts, and throw them to the ground." But To Karvuvu threw the nuts point downward, and the women who came from them had flat, ugly noses.

[P. J. Meier, *Mythen und Erzählungen der Küstenbewohner der Gazelle-Halbinsel (Neu-Pommern)*, in Joseph Campbell, *The Hero with a Thousand Faces*]

Siberia

When the demiurge Pajana fashioned the first human beings, he found that he was unable to produce a life-giving spirit for them. So he had to go up to heaven and procure souls from Kudai, the High God, leaving meanwhile a naked dog to guard the figures of his manufacture. The devil, Erlik, arrived while he was away. And Erlik said to the dog: "Thou has no hair. I will give thee golden hair if thou wilt give into my hands these soulless people." The proposal pleased the dog, and he gave the people he was guarding to the tempter. Erlik defiled them with his spittle, but took flight the moment he saw God approaching to give them life. God saw what had been done, and so he turned the human bodies inside out. That is why we have spittle and impurity in our intestines.

[W. Radloff, *Proben der Volksliteratur der türkischen Stämme Süd-Siberien,* in Joseph Campbell, *The Hero with a Thousand Faces*]

Zimbabwe

Maori (God) made the first man and called him Mwuetsi (moon). He put him on the bottom of a Dsivoa (lake) and gave him a ngona horn filled with ngona oil. Mwuetsi lived in Dsivoa.

Mwuetsi said to Maori: "I want to go on the earth." Maori said: "You will rue it." Mwuetsi said: "None the less, I want to go on the earth." Maori said: "Then go on the earth." Mwuetsi went out of Dsivoa and on to the earth.

The earth was cold and empty. There were no grasses, no bushes, no trees. There were no animals. Mwuetsi wept and said to Maori: "How shall I live here?" Maori said: "I warned you. You have started on the path at the end of which you shall die. I will, however, give you one of your kind." Maori gave Mwuetsi a maiden who was called Massassi, the morning star. Maori said: "Massassi shall be your wife for two years." Maori gave Massassi a fire maker.

[Leo Frobenius and Douglas C. Fox, *African Genesis*]

Togo

Unumbotte (god) made a human being. The Man was Unele (man). Then, Unumbotte next made Opel (antelope . . .). Then, Unumbotte made Ukow (snake . . .) named Snake. When these three were made there were no other trees but one, Bubauw (oil palm . . .). At that time, the earth had not yet been pounded (smooth). . . . Unumbotte said to the three: ". . . You must pound the ground where you are sitting." Unumbotte gave them seeds of all kinds, and said: "Plant these." Unumbotte went (away).

Unumbotte came back. He saw that people had not yet pounded the ground, but had planted the seeds. One of the seeds had sprouted and grown. It was a tree that had grown tall and was bearing fruit. The fruits were red. . . . Now, every seven days Unumbotte returned and plucked one of the red fruits.

One day Snake said: "We too would like to eat these fruits. Why must we be hungry?" Antelope said: "But we don't know this fruit." Then Man and his wife (. . . who had not been there at first . . .) took some of the fruit and ate it. Then, Unumbotte came down from Heaven. Unumbotte asked: "Who ate the fruit?" Man and Woman answered: "We ate it." Unumbotte asked: "Who told you that you should eat of it?" Man and Woman replied: "Snake told us." Unumbotte asked: "Why did you listen to Snake?" Man and Woman said: "We were hungry."

Unumbotte questioned Antelope: "Are you hungry too?" Antelope said: "Yes, I am hungry too; I'd like to eat grass." Since then Antelope has lived in the bush, eating grass.

Unumbotte then gave Idi (. . . sorghum) to Man, . . . yams and . . . millet. . . . And since then people have cultivated the land. But Snake was given by Unumbotte a medicine (Njojo) so that it would bite people.

[E. J. Michael Witzel, *The Origins of the World's Mythologies*]

Tierra del Fuego

Kenós was alone on the earth. "Someone Up There," Temaúkel, had appointed him to set everything down here in order. He was the son of the South and the Heavens. He wandered over the world, came back here and looked around, then went to a swampy place, dug out a lump of mud mixed with matted roots and grass tufts, shaped a male organ, and placed this on the ground. He dug another lump, squeezed the water out, shaped a female organ which he placed beside the first, then went his way. During the night, the two lumps of earth joined. From this arose something like a person: the first Ancestor. The two objects separated and, during the following night, joined again. Again someone arose who quickly grew. Night after night this occurred, with every night a new Ancestor. Thus their number steadily increased.

[Joseph Campbell, *Historical Atlas of World Mythology*]

Acknowledgments

Part of the pleasure of pursuing this topic has been the incentive it gave me to venture outside the disciplinary orbit in which I ordinarily circle. In the course of research and writing, I have incurred debts of gratitude to an unusually wide range of individuals and institutions. My greatest—and ongoing—institutional debt is to Harvard University, where I teach. I have benefited from wonderful colleagues and students in multiple disciplines, from the incomparable resources of its libraries and the tireless assistance of its staff, from the remarkable treasures housed in its art museums, and from the rich collections in the Semitic Museum, the Harvard Museum of Natural History, and the Peabody Museum of Archaeology and Ethnology. Familiarity is supposed to dull a sense of wonder, but over the years I have become ever more astonished by the very existence of great universities, and I have profited from the intellectual generosity that is a striking and often unrecognized characteristic of scholarly communities.

That generosity is spectacularly in evidence in two extraordinary research institutions to which I am also greatly indebted. The first is the Wissenschaftskolleg zu Berlin, where over many years I have forged enduring friendships, and from which I have derived a model for intense, ongoing conversations that bring the humanities together with the natural sciences. The second is the American Academy in Rome, with its visionary insistence that art-making and scholarship inhabit the same space of inquiry. With its inexhaustible ancient, medieval, and Renaissance resources, Rome is an ideal setting for work on Adam and Eve, and I have spent many happy hours in the city's innumerable churches, catacombs, museums, galleries, and libraries. I am particularly grateful to the staff of the libraries of the American Academy and the Vatican, with special thanks to Sebastian Hierl, the director of the Academy's library; to Umberto Utro, the Vatican's curator of Christian Antiquities; and to Angela Di Curzio at the Catacombe SS. Marcellino e Pietro.

I have had the opportunity to present pieces of this project, as it was unfolding, in several different places and to profit from the questions and comments of my audience. These include the Humanitas Lectures at the University of Oxford; the Mosse-Lecture at the Humboldt University, Berlin; the Cardin Lecture at Loyola University, Baltimore; a conference in honor of Thomas Laqueur at the University of California, Berkeley; the Wissenschaftskolleg and the Staatsbibliothek in Berlin; Northern Arizona University; and the Renaissance Society of America Annual Convention. All arrangements for these occasions were facilitated by my able assistant Aubrey Everett, to whom I am grateful for this and much other help, provided with unfailing cheerfulness, competence, and resourcefulness.

A significant part of the joy, as well as the daunting challenge, of this project is the number of distinct worlds in which Adam and Eve found a home over many centuries. As I am painfully aware of how much I have failed to understand in this long history, so too I am happily aware of how much help I have received in making sense of what parts of it I could grasp and in keeping the inquiry from breaking up into discrete pieces. My agent, Jill Kneerim, has, as usual, been there for me from the beginning of this project to its completion and has given me the gift of her unfailing professional and personal wisdom. This is the third book on which I have worked with my remarkable editor at Norton, Alane Mason. In each instance—and perhaps most of all in the writing of this book—I have been amazed by her special gifts. Those gifts include patience, a startling (and, on occasion, dismaying) intellectual acuity, an unflagging attention to detail, and an ability to elicit feats of rethinking, restructuring, and rewriting. These are rare qualities in anyone, and I can only hope that I can emulate them in my teaching, just as I have profited from them in my writing.

I am grateful to Shawon Kinew for invaluable assistance in tracking down and obtaining permissions for the images in this book. Among the many who have kindly assisted me, I want to acknowledge Salar Abdolmohamadian, Lilly Ajarova and the staff at the Ngamba Chimpanzee Sanctuary, Suzanne Akbari, Danny Baror, Shaul Bassi, Uta Benner, Homi Bhabha, Kathrina Biegger, Robert Blechman, Mary Anne Boelcskevy, Will Bordell, Daniel Boyarin, Horst Bredekamp, Georgiana Brinkley, Terence Capellini, David Carrasco, Maria Luisa Catoni, Christopher Celenza, Grazie Christie, Shaye Cohen, Rebecca Cook, Rocco Coronato, Lorraine Daston, Zachary Davis, Jeremy DeSilva, Maria Devlin, François Dupuigrenet Desroussilles, Ruth Ezra, Noah Feldman, Steven Frank, Raghavendra Gadagkar, Luca Giuliani, Anthony Grafton, Margareth Hagen, Jay Harris, Galit Hasan-Rokem, Stephen Hequembourg, Walter Herbert, David Heyd, Elliott Horowitz, Bernhard Jussen, Henry Ansgar Kelly, Karen King, Adam Kirsch, Jeffrey Knapp, Jennifer Knust, Meg Koerner, Ivana Kvetanova, Bernhard Lang, Thomas Laqueur, Jill Lepore, Anthony Long, Avi Lifschitz, Zarin Machanda, Peter Machinist, Hussain Majeed, Louis Menand, Eric Nelson, Morton Ng, Emily Otali and her staff at Kanyawara, Shekufeh Owlia, Elaine Pagels, Catalin Partenie, David Pilbeam, Lisbet Rausing, Meredith Ray, Robert Richards, Ingrid Rowland, Michal Ronnen Safdie, Moshe Safdie, Paul Schmid-Hempel, David Schorr, Charles Stang, Stephen Stearns, Alan Stone, Gordon Teskey, Michael

Tomasello, Normandy Vincent, Elizabeth Weckhurst, Adam Wilkins, Nora Wilkinson, Edward O. Wilson, and Richard Wrangham. To all of these, in addition to my thanks, I offer the usual indemnification: I alone am responsible for the mistakes, omissions, and inadequacies that will no doubt be discovered and duly noted.

The same blanket release from blame extends to those whose presence in these pages is even more marked and pervasive. I owe Robert Pinsky, Adam Phillips, and Rabbi Edward Schecter the deepest gratitude for years of patient listening, wise counsel, and unwavering friendship. With unstinting intellectual generosity, Meredith Reiches helped me find my way around the difficult, often confusing landscape of evolutionary biology and initiated me into the complex calculations of energy expenditure that governed her fieldwork on women in the Gambia. This work explores a world far away from the dreams of Eden, but it shed an illuminating light on those dreams. With Joseph Koerner, an art historian of singular brilliance, I have in recent years at Harvard cotaught both graduate and undergraduate courses on Adam and Eve. At various points in this book I acknowledge my voluminous debts to him, but I am conscious that they extend well beyond these gestures. It is the sweet peril of team-teaching and close friendship alike that the boundaries between one's own ideas and those of another become easily blurred.

To my three sons, Josh, Aaron, and Harry, I owe thanks for their patience in putting up with innumerable conversations about primates, for their thoughtfulness, humor, and insight, and for their unfailing love. The experience of love, as Milton understood so well, lies at the center of the story of Adam and Eve. It is all the more appropriate then that my deepest gratitude, in the writing of this book as in so much else, is to my wife, Ramie Targoff. She has brought me as close to the gates of Eden as I will ever get in my life.

Notes

Except where noted, citations from the Bible are to the King James Version, in *The English Bible: The Old Testament*, ed. Herbert Marks (New York: W. W. Norton, 2012), and *The English Bible: The New Testament and The Apocrypha*, ed. Gerald Hammond and Austin Busch (New York: W. W. Norton, 2012). The King James Version, one of the greatest literary accomplishments ever produced by a committee, is the translation that, since the early seventeenth century, has shaped the dominant reception of the Adam and Eve story in the English language. Readers (and I include myself) who lack a scholarly command of the Hebrew original can get at least some sense of key translation issues from *The New Oxford Annotated Bible* (New Revised Standard Version) 4th ed., ed. Michael D. Coogan (Oxford: Oxford University Press, 2010). I have found Robert Alter's translation—*The Five Books of Moses* (New York: W. W. Norton, 2004)—consistently illuminating. The Hebrew text is available online, along with many translations reflecting a wide range of denominations and interests. These may be readily compared for each verse.

  For full bibliographic details in the references that follow, please see the Selected Bibliography.

Chapter 1: Bare Bones

  6 **Poring over the words:** The rabbis recognized quite early that the story of the creation and first disobedience in Genesis could produce potentially dangerous speculations. According to the Mishnah—the first major redaction of the Jewish oral law—"the [subject of] forbidden relations may not be expounded in the presence of three, nor the work of creation in the presence of two, nor [the work of] the chariot in the presence of one, unless he is a sage and understands of his own knowledge" (Hagigah 2:1 [*Complete Babylonian Talmud*]). The Talmud applies the

last clause to all three prohibitions, meaning that these three particularly risky subjects—the laws regarding incest, the creation story in Genesis, and Ezekiel's vison of God's chariot—should only be taught to the wise. As for the precise age when one was presumed to be wise, there was considerable disagreement, ranging from twenty to twenty-five and even to forty.

6 **a particularly beautiful camel:** Muhammad ibn 'Abd Allah al-Kisa'i, *The Tales of the Prophets* (c. 1200 CE), in Kvam et al., *Eve and Adam*, p. 192. On Iblis, see *Qur'an, Surah 7:27,* in *Eve and Adam,* pp. 181–82. See Marion Holmes Katz, "Muhammad in Ritual," in *The Cambridge Companion to Muhammad,* ed. Jonathan E. Brockopp (New York: Cambridge University Press, 2010), pp. 139–57; Asma Barlas, "Women's Readings of the Qur'an," in *The Cambridge Companion to the Qur'an,* pp. 255–72.

10 **possess objects called holotypes:** At Harvard's Museum of Comparative Zoology, the great biologist E. O. Wilson opened a cabinet not long ago and showed me a few of the vast number of ant holotypes that he had collected, each one a distinct species affixed to a pin and labeled in almost microscopic writing.

11 **Bible commentaries traditionally posited:** Readers who wish to get a preliminary sense of this enormous field may profitably begin with James L. Kugel, *Traditions of the Bible*; Louis Ginzberg, *Legends of the Jews*; Bialik et al., *The Book of Legends: Sefer Ha-Aggadah*; Hermann Gunkel, *Genesis*; and Claus Westermann, *Genesis: A Commentary.*

11 **Alexander Ross:** Quoted in Philip C. Almond, *Adam and Eve in Seventeenth-Century Thought,* p. 49.

13 **"tangled bush":** Bernard A. Wood, "Welcome to the Family," in *Scientific American,* September 2014, p. 46.

14 **a cranium very much the size of ours:** Though we did not evolve from these creatures, it is estimated that for at least the "brief" period of five thousand years—the length of all known human history—we shared the world with them and on occasion interbred.

15 **rabbi Samuel ben Nahman:** In *Midrash Rabbah,* trans. H. Freedman, 8: 1. On the human's immense size, see R. Tanhuma in the name of R. Banayah, R. Berekiah in the name of R. Leazar, and R. Joshua b. R. Nehemiah and R. Judah b. R. Simon in the name of R. Leazar (8: 1); on the tail, see Judah B. Rabbi (14: 10). For further speculations, see Ginzberg, *Legends of the Jews,* 1: 47–100; and Bialik, *The Book of Legends: Sefer Ha-Aggadah,* p. 12ff.

Chapter 2: By the Waters of Babylon

23 **God instructed an angel:** Even here there is a telling confusion, since in one moment (Jubilees 1:26) the Angel of the Presence actually writes the book, while at others (2:1) Moses writes it from dictation.

23 **"And the Lord said to Abram":** Trans. Robert Alter, who points out in his note that Abram here "becomes an individual character, and begins the Patriarchal narratives" (p. 56).

24 **"By the waters of Babylon":** Psalm 137, in the King James translation (1611).
Cf. the Jewish Publication Society version (Tanakh Translation):

> By the rivers of Babylon
> there we sat,
> sat and wept,
> as we thought of Zion.
>
> (Berlin et al., *The Jewish Study Bible*, p. 1435.)

The psalms are extremely difficult to date, but the editors observe that the word
"there" (שָׁם) in the first verse of Psalm 137 implies that the Hebrews are now
somewhere else, presumably back in the land from which they had been exiled.

24 **the hanging gardens:** The actual "Hanging Gardens" were in all likelihood
located at Nineveh, and not in Babylon (where archaeologists have failed to find
any trace of them). Greek sources seem to have confused the two cities and their
respective empires. See Stephanie Dalley, "Nineveh, Babylon and the Hanging
Gardens," pp. 45–58.

27 **From this primordial intercourse:**

> When on high no name was given to heaven,
> Nor below was the netherworld called by name,
> Primeval Apsu was their progenitor,
> And matrix-Tiamat was she who bore them all,
> They were mingling their waters together.

From Distant Days: Myths, Tales, and Poetry of Ancient Mesopotamia, trans. Benjamin R. Foster, p. 11. For other translations and commentaries on this and related
Mesopotamian origin texts, see *Ancient Near Eastern Texts Relating to the Old Testament*, ed. James B. Pritchard; *The Harps That Once . . . : Sumerian Poetry in Translation*, trans. Thorkild Jacobsen; and *Myths from Mesopotamia: Creation, the Flood,
Gilgamesh, and Others*, trans. Stephanie Dalley.

28 **Life, with its energy and noise:** Thorkild Jacobsen suggests that the Babylonians were aware that they had founded their city and civilization on the foundations of their enemy the Sumerians and that this awareness is reflected in their
account of the killing of Apsu (Jacobsen, *The Treasures of Darkness*, p. 186). If this
interpretation is correct, it would suggest that, by rejecting the story of a primordial killing, the Hebrews, in their own origin story, were unwilling to acknowledge any such foundational debt.

29 **the divided female body:** Cf. Jacobsen: "The phenomena of winds and storms
Marduk reserved for himself. Below, he heaped a mountain over Ti-amat's head,
pierced her eyes to form the sources of the Euphrates and the Tigris (the Akkadians have but one word for 'eye' and 'source,' *inu*, and presumably considered them
in some way the same thing), and heaped similar mountains over her dugs, which
he pierced to make the rivers form the eastern mountains that flow into the Tigris.
Her tail he bent up into the sky to make the Milky Way, and her crotch he used to
support the sky" (*Treasures of Darkness*, p. 179).

29 **"I shall compact blood":** "I shall make stand a human being, let 'Man' be its
name. . . . They shall bear the god's burden that those may rest" (trans. Foster,

p. 38). To accomplish what he had conceived, Marduk needed blood. He asked who was principally responsible for Tiamat's rebellion and was told that it was "Qingu who made war,/Suborned Tiamat and drew up for battle." Accordingly, Qingu was bound and brought before Marduk's father, Ea:

> They imposed the punishment on him and shed his blood.
>
> From his blood he made mankind,
>
> He imposed the burden of the gods and exempted the gods. (39)

The material used to make mankind was thus drawn from a god executed for rebellion, though the text, at least as it has survived, does not speculate on whether this origin affected the result. The possibility that it might have done so, producing in humans an innate tendency to rebel, is the subject of a fascinating analysis in Paul Ricoeur, *The Symbolism of Evil*, p. 175ff.

29 **"the black-headed people"**: Savage-man, Pritchard explains, is probably a derivative of the ethnic name Lullu. "That the Lullu were linked by Akkadian sources with the remote and dim past may be gathered from the evidence . . . as well as from the fact that the flood ship lands on Mount Nisir, in Lullu country" (Pritchard, *Ancient Near Eastern Texts*, p. 68, n. 86).

29 **the supreme god Marduk**: Though Babylonians conferred upon their own city's god an absolute preeminence and gave that god a crucial role in the creation of man, there had been alternative accounts in Mesopotamia of the origins of things. In one of these accounts, humans were created not by a god but by a goddess, the wise Ninhursag. She is "the mother-womb,/The one who creates mankind" (Pritchard, *Ancient Near Eastern Texts*, p. 99), and in an incantation evidently used to facilitate childbirth, she is shown fashioning offspring to serve the gods: "Let him be formed out of clay, be animated with blood!" (ibid., p. 99). There was clearly an elaborate mythology constructed around this mother goddess—a mythology that included a place of perfect beauty called Dilmun and a wild succession of sexual couplings—but the cult of Marduk absorbed what it could and swept the rest away.

29 **the *Atrahasis***: Citations of this work are from Foster, *From Distant Days*. See the helpful introduction in Millard et al., *Atra-Hasis: The Babylon Story of the Flood*, pp. 1–30.

31 **imagined violence**: The fantasy of revenge serves as a symbolic warding off of a threatened assimilation, whether as entertainer or servant or suppliant, to the victor's culture. The enemies in this fantasy are simply "the children of Edom," that is, the descendants of Jacob's rival and brother, Esau. As such, they are restored to their place in the ancient mythic history that gives the Jews their sense of identity.

32 **Babylonians allowed the upper classes**: Cf. Marc Van De Mieroop, *A History of the Ancient Near East*, p. 284.

33 **enormous stone blocks**: What visitors see is in fact the magnified, grandiose form given it centuries later by Herod the Great. In 70 CE, some five hundred years after the initial rebuilding, those blocks were pried loose and flung down from the temple mount by the Roman soldiers who brought the city to its knees in yet another historical disaster.

33 **The prophets raged:** Ezekiel declared that the Lord brought him to the north gateway of the Temple, where women sat "weeping for Tammuz" (Ezek. 8:14–15). Jeremiah, who foresaw the destruction of Jerusalem by the Babylonians, passionately argued that the looming disaster was the consequence not of military or diplomatic incompetence but rather of the infidelity of God's people. In Jerusalem, he wrote, "the children gather wood, and the fathers kindle the fire, and the women knead their dough, to make cakes to the queen of heaven" (Jer. 7:18).

It is difficult at this distance to take in the horror and rage provoked by ceremonies that seem so appealingly familial and domestic. Who was "the queen of heaven" whose little cakes were deemed an intolerable affront? Though Jeremiah did not give her a name, the deity so honored was evidently the goddess associated with the planet Venus, whom the Babylonians called Ishtar or Inana, the Canaanites Astarte, and the Hebrews Asherah. Archaeologists have found ancient shrines to Asherah in the kingdoms of both Israel and Judah. The Hebrews may even have regarded her as Yahweh's consort.

The cult of God's domestic partner seems to have been suppressed by the Hebrew priests and prophets after Babylon's fall and their return to Jerusalem. The leading authorities in the community insisted that Yahweh lived alone in solitary, sexless splendor. There is evidence, however, that the goddess did not go quietly. Jeremiah described the response he received, when he reproached the men and women of Jerusalem for their idolatries:

> Then all the men which knew that their wives had burned incense unto other gods, and all the women that stood by, a great multitude . . . answered Jeremiah, saying, As for the word that thou hast spoken unto us in the name of the Lord, we will not hearken unto thee. (44:15–16)

The crowd refused to take the prophet's denunciation as the direct word of God. Why should they stop doing what had long suited them? As for the implication that the offerings were somehow all women's work, done behind the backs of the men, Jeremiah recorded the wives' indignant answer:

> And the women said, "When we burnt sacrifices to the queen of heaven and poured drink-offerings to her, our husbands knew full well that we were making crescent-cakes marked with her image and pouring drink-offerings unto her." (44:19; *New English Bible*, Oxford Study Edition)

35 **a new covenant:** William Rainey Harper, "The Jews in Babylon," in *The Biblical World*, pp. 104–11. To say that this whole topic is complex and contested would be a gross understatement. For a rapid overview, simply focused on the moment when the Adam and Eve story was possibly written, see Jean-Louis Ska, "Genesis 2–3: Some Fundamental Questions," in *Beyond Eden: The Biblical Story of Paradise (Genesis 2–3) and Its Reception History*, ed. Konrad Schmid and Christoph Riedweg, pp. 1–27.

35 **the People of the Book:** See Moshe Halbertal, *People of the Book*.

35 **multiple strands:** The recognition of multiple strands goes back at least to the early eighteenth century, when a German Protestant pastor, Bernhard Witter (1683–1715), published a thesis focused on the difference between the divine

names *Elohim* and *YHWH*. Given the extreme constraints on recognizing, let alone publicly acknowledging, the possibility of multiple strands, it took considerable intellectual fortitude to explore this subject. In addition to Witter, the key early figures were the Dutch philosopher Baruch Spinoza (1632–77) and the French priest Richard Simon (1638–1712). Hence the founding figures included a Protestant, a Jew, and a Catholic. To these brave voices, we should add Jean Astruc and his anonymously published 1753 work, *Conjectures sur les mémoires originaux dont il paroit que Moyse s'est servi pour composer le livre de la Génèse. Avec des remarques qui appuient ou qui éclaircissent ces conjectures.* For a popular overview of this complex subject, see Richard Elliott Friedman, *Who Wrote the Bible?*

37 **a committee of redactors:** The issues here are particularly complex and contentious. In *The Edited Bible: The Curious History of the "Editor" in Biblical Criticism*, John Van Seters vigorously questions the terms "editor" and "redactor" for the Bible, preferring to speak of "authors." Van Seters's arguments are reviewed and challenged by Jean-Louis Ska in "A Plea on Behalf of the Biblical Redactors," pp. 4–18. Ska observes persuasively that the compilers of the Bible—whether we call them redactors or "living channels of transmission" or "custodians of ancient sources"— had a deep respect for the texts they had received and a reluctance to rework those texts into a stylistically consistent, logically coherent whole. They opted instead for minimal changes and bridging passages linking together what we can now perceive as distinct traditions. To this extent, their work is quite different from the reworking of sources that we can follow in a text like *King Lear*. It is possible to discover the diverse sources that Shakespeare is stitching together and on occasion to catch contradictions in the resulting play, but he confers upon all of them his inimitable style and sensibility. The same is not true even of the first three chapters of Genesis, let alone of the Pentateuch in its entirety. Nonetheless, for many centuries—almost the entire history that my book surveys—the story of Adam and Eve (along with the whole of the Pentateuch) was taken as an inspired, holy text authored by Moses or transcribed by him from the words of an angel. This presumption of authorship led to the long and fateful reception history, one in which apparent textual contradictions and tensions were invitations not to redactional criticism but to sustained meditation, interpretation, and artistic representation.

Chapter 3: Clay Tablets

43 **discovery of a trilingual inscription:** The person who laid claim to the discovery, Sir Henry Creswicke Rawlinson, was one of those Victorian gentleman-adventurers who from this distance seem larger than life: supremely energetic, resilient, and egomaniacal, Rawlinson, as a young lieutenant with the British East India Company, helped to reorganize the shah's army, while displaying remarkable talents as a horseman, exploring the remoter regions of Kurdistan and Elam (now southwestern Iran), becoming fluent in Persian, and studying the traces of the past. In 1836 he learned of the intriguing inscription, part of an ancient monument to the Persian king Darius the Great located in Behistun, in the Zagros

Mountains between Babylon and Persia. The monument was visible from afar but virtually inaccessible, since it had been carved above a narrow ledge on a cliff some three hundred feet above the valley floor. Undaunted, Rawlinson scaled the cliff—along with a local boy who, as usual in these stories, received little money and less credit for risking his life—and obtained a copy of the inscription. In a gripping history, *The Buried Book: The Loss and Rediscovery of the Great Epic of Gilgamesh*, David Damrosch describes in detail how it happened. I am particularly indebted to this account. The inscription is transcribed in De Mieroop, *A History of the Ancient Near East*, p. 291.

45 **distant echoes:** The Hebrew God in the opening words still bears a plural name, Elohim, and he does not start from nothing. Apsu and Tiamat, to be sure, are nowhere to be found, but there is something called *tohu v' bohu*—chaotic, formless matter, as well as *tehom*, the deep or abyss. "When God began to create heaven and earth, and the earth then was welter and waste [*tohu v' bohu*] and darkness over the deep [*tehom*] and God's breath hovering over the waters, God said, 'Let there be light'" (Robert Alter, trans., *The Five Books of Moses*). For an account of some of the echoes, see Howard N. Wallace, *The Eden Narrative*; W. G. Lambert, "Old Testament Mythology in Its Ancient Near Eastern Context" [orig. pub. 1988], in Lambert, *Ancient Mesopotamian Religion and Mythology: Selected Essays*, pp. 215–28.

45 **any level of excitement:** See Damrosch, pp. 11–12. As he labored to put the pieces together, Smith made several significant mistakes—it is a wonder that he got so much of the assembling, transcribing, and deciphering right—but scholarly research over the ensuing century, along with a succession of further discoveries, generally confirmed that what he already perceived in the first seconds turned out to be correct. The clay tablets were in fragments only fully deciphered and sorted out in the 1960s.

47 **large-scale infant mortality:** Assyriologists have hypothesized that in a missing part of the *Atrahasis* the gods also agree to establish a natural end to the human life span. See W. G. Lambert, "The Theology of Death," in Lambert, *Ancient Mesopotamian Religion and Mythology: Selected Essays*; cited in Andrew George, *The Epic of Gilgamesh: A New Translation*, pp. xliv–xlv.

50 **arbitrariness and cruelty:** It is not as if the Genesis story is indifferent to moral values: Noah was saved because he "was a just man and perfect in his generations," while the rest of the earth "was filled with violence" (Gen. 6:9–10). And yet the same god who was deeply repelled by the spectacle of so much violence in the world he had brought forth—"It grieved him at his heart" (6:6)—decided indiscriminately to wipe out virtually all living things. Chapter 6:5–8 comes from the J source (most scholars posit), while starting with v. 9 through the end of the chapter is P. Evidently there are different theological conceptions visible here; in P, Elohim regrets nothing, even as in J, Yahweh regrets his creation. I owe this account to Professor Jay Harris, Harvard University.

50 **These questions had been there:** Particularly illuminating are two books by Elaine Pagels, *The Gnostic Gospels* and *Adam, Eve, and the Serpent*.

51 **he discovered Gilgamesh:** Unless otherwise noted, citations of *Gilgamesh* are to

the edition and translation by Benjamin J. Foster. The textual history of *Gilgamesh* is complex; there are multiple versions, none of them complete, from different periods and places. The key tool for differentiating these versions is Andrew George, *The Babylonian Gilgamesh Epic: Introduction, Critical Edition, and Cuneiform Texts*; see also George, *Gilgamesh: The Babylonian Epic Poem and Other Texts in Akkadian and Sumerian*. There is a modern translation in verse—not accurate as a scholarly rendering but beautiful and evocative—by David Ferry. I have also profited from the translations by Stephen Mitchell and by James B. Pritchard, *Ancient Near Eastern Texts,* and Stephanie Dalley, *Myths from Mesopotamia.*

51 **the first city:** This innovation—which has changed the course of all of our lives—was facilitated by a series of crucial technological developments, above all by the invention of the first system of writing. The cuneiform tablets recorded the complex computations, regulation of weights and measures, transactions, contracts, and laws that make possible and still characterize urban life, but they also registered an awareness of the symbolic significance of the new mode of existence. Uruk was an image of the cosmos, and its founding hero was more divine than human. Cf. Nicola Crüsemann et al., eds., *Uruk: 5000 Jahre Megacity.*

52 **pinches off a piece of clay:** In Pritchard, *Ancient Near Eastern Texts*, p. 74:

> Aruru washed her hands,
>
> Pinched off clay and cast it on the steppe.
>
> [or possibly, drew a design on it; or spat upon it].

53 **nature to culture:** Cf. from Bernard F. Batto, *Slaying the Dragon: Mythmaking in the Biblical Tradition*, p. 55:

Sumerian myth "Ewe and Wheat":

> Shakan (god of flocks) had not (yet) come out on dry land;
>
> Humankind of those distant days
>
> Knew not about dressing in cloth,
>
> Ate grass with their mouth like sheep,
>
> Drank water from the water-hole.

Similarly, another Sumermian text, Ur Excavation Texts 6.61.i.7'–10' (ibid.):

> Humankind of those distant days
>
> Since Shakan had not (yet) come out on dry land,
>
> Did not know how to dress in cloth;
>
> Humankind walked about naked.

56 **same-sex friendship:** Is Gilgamesh a "gay" epic? It is difficult to say. While there is no explicit abjuring of a sexual relationship between Gilgamesh and Enkidu, there is no representation of it either. What there is instead is precisely what Gilgamesh's wise mother says that there will be: a deep male bond that involves the sharing of danger and an absolute fidelity. Gilgamesh and Enkidu are the love of each other's life.

57 **to launch a new story:** We do not know whom the editors of Genesis chose to construct this new story. What we do know is that they chose brilliantly. If it seems plausible that the writer who wrote the first chapter reviewed a number of earlier accounts and used them to create his cosmology, it is still more plausible

that the writer of the second and third chapters was a cunning weaver of different strands. For several centuries now the verses have been carefully, even obsessively scanned in order to try to sort out just how many strands there might have been. The exact number remains uncertain, but the person who undertook the great task—the one biblical scholarship calls J, for Jahwist—almost certainly assembled a number of distinct ancient Hebrew oral legends and texts.

57 **one who dominates them:** So at least, before the rise of modern critical biblical scholarship, virtually all commentators to Genesis assumed, carrying over to the account of the clay human in chapter 2 the attributes of the human created in chapter 1.

59 **their proud tower:** In Hebrew the play on words is with *balal*, "to confound." Alter, in *Five Books of Moses*, observes that the story "is an extreme example of the stylistic predisposition of biblical narrative to exploit interechoing words and to work with a deliberately restricted vocabulary" (p. 59, n. 11:3).

59 **the garden, not the city, was the great good place:** For a detailed exegesis of the garden, with careful comparisons to other gardens in Near Eastern religions, see Terje Stordale, *Echoes of Eden*.

59 **digging irrigation ditches:** In Genesis 1 the world originates in a watery waste from which the earth emerges when God divides the waters and commands the waters under the heavens to be gathered together "in one place so that the dry land will appear" (1.9). In Genesis 2 the problem seems to be not an excess of water but the opposite, a condition of drought, along with the absence of anyone to work the land: "On the day the Lord God made earth and heavens, no shrub of the field being yet on the earth and no plant of the field yet sprouted, for the Lord God had not caused rain to fall on the earth, and there was no human to till the soil" (Alter, *Five Books of Moses*, 2:5–6).

60 **a piece of the man's own body:** One of the pleasures of fiction is that it can violate the rules of nature and realize a fantasy, here the fantasy that the original birth is not from the body of a woman but from the body of a man, along with the fantasy that the love object has been extracted from one's own body. The fashioning is represented as at once dream-like—it happens in the man's sleep—and surgical: his side is opened, a bone removed, the skin closed up again. Then the man greets the woman as a piece of himself returned to him, fusing with him emotionally. That fusion is described in ecstatic metaphorical terms, as if it were the original physical truth of the myth—bone of my bones, flesh of my flesh. Though we are not meant to imagine that the woman is actually, physically, returning to the man's body and once again becoming a single being, the whole force of the metaphor is the physical fantasy that underlies it.

61 **jubilant welcome:** "Jubilant welcome" is the felicitous phrase of Johann Gottfried Herder (1744–1803). Quoted in Claus Westermann, Genesis 1–11, p. 231.

61 *ishah . . . ish:* The play on "ishah" and "ish" (which are apparently not related etymologically) is a further confirmation of the "one flesh" experience, but it is at the same time an act of domination and subordination: that is, the man names the woman, just as he has named the other creatures. And, in rectification of the bio-

logical reality, he was not taken from the woman but rather the woman was taken from him. *Gilgamesh* also has domination and subordination, but it is established through physical contest, not through naming, and there is no "bone of my bones" feeling suffusing the relationship.

62 **bringing together of the man and the woman:** For the implications in the West of this formation of new families through "looser ties of descent," see Michael Mitterauer, *Why Europe: The Medieval Origins of Its Special Path*, trans. Gerald Chapple, pp. 58–98.

Chapter 4: The Life of Adam and Eve

64 **he rescued the rest and set it aside:** Circumstances, already strange enough, then took a stranger turn. A half year earlier Mohammed 'Ali's father, a night watchman, had been murdered, and, when they were alerted to the killer's whereabouts, the eldest son and his brothers exacted vengeance. Catching the culprit asleep and unprotected, they hacked off his limbs with their sharpened mattocks and then fished out and ate his heart. The authorities, alerted to the killing and anxious to stop the blood feud, began to question the villagers. Mohammed 'Ali and his brothers were briefly held and then released. Though many people presumably knew exactly what had happened, everyone remained silent.

With the police still nosing about the village and searching houses for evidence, Mohammed 'Ali was concerned that the old books, from which he still hoped to make some profit, would be found and confiscated. He entrusted one of them to a Christian priest. The priest's brother-in-law, a parochial schoolteacher, realized that the find might indeed be worth something. He proposed to contact people who could conceivably be interested.

For further details, see John Dart, *The Laughing Savior*; Jean Doresse, *The Discovery of the Nag Hammadi Texts*; Elaine Pagels, *The Gnostic Gospels*; James M. Robinson, *The Nag Hammadi Story*.

65 **all save one:** The single papyrus book that eluded the Egyptian authorities made it to the United States, where it was purchased, via a Dutch scholar, for the psychoanalyst Carl Jung's Institute in Switzerland. Slowly, scholarly work began on this codex, and slowly too the significance of the whole find began to be grasped.

66 **the most startling finds:** In one of the most remarkable of these texts, *The Secret Revelation of John,* the "first man" is a female figure known as Barbelo: "She became a womb for the All because she is prior to them all, the Mother-Father, the first Human, the holy Spirit, the triple male, the triple power, the triple named androgyne, and the eternal aeon among the invisible ones, and the first to come forth" (5:24–26, in Karen King, *The Secret Revelation of John*, p. 33).

67 **The Life of Adam and Eve:** Anderson et al., *A Synopsis of the Books of Adam and Eve*, enables the reader to compare the Greek, Latin, Armenian, Georgian, and Slavonic versions. See Michael E. Stone, *A History of the Literature of Adam and Eve*, and *Literature on Adam and Eve: Collected Essays*, ed. Gary A. Anderson et al. The tale of Adam and Eve's life after the expulsion had an immensely long, rich career

throughout the Middle Ages and beyond. See Brian Murdoch, *Adam's Grace*, and Murdoch, *The Medieval Popular Bible*. For a transcription and English translation of the Old French version, see Esther C. Quinn and Micheline Dufau, *The Penitence of Adam: A Study of the Andrius Ms.*

70 **Rabbi Samuel ben Nahman imagined:** In Freedman, *Midrash Rabbah*, 8:8.

71 **Rabbi Hanina suggested:** Ibid., 8:4.

71 **a grand narrative focused on the Prince of Darkness:** See Neil Forsyth, *The Old Enemy: Satan and the Combat Myth*; Elaine Pagels, *The Origin of Satan*; and Jeffrey Burton Russell, *The Devil: Perceptions of Evil from Antiquity to Primitive Christianity*.

73 **the visionary Sedrach:** The text, available in English translation at Christian Classics Ethereal Library (http://www.newadvent.org/fathers/1006.htm), is nominally Christian, but it seems to reflect questions that were asked at the time by Jews as well. See *Apocalypsis Sedrach*, ed. Otto Wahl, in *Pseudepigrapha Veteris Testamenti Graece,* 4 vols. (Leiden: Brill, 1977).

74 **Marcion drew the sharpest possible line:** Cf. Adolf von Harnack, *Marcion: The Gospel of the Alien God*.

74 **St. Paul had established:** Many scholars have reflected on why Paul made the crucial connection between Jesus and the story of Adam and Eve. The link obviously is bound up with Paul's origins in a Jewish world—with Paul, in Daniel Boyarin's phrase, as a "radical Jew." (Cf. Boyarin, *A Radical Jew: Paul and the Politics of Identity* [Berkeley: University of California Press, 1994]). But in its account of the origin of evil, traditional Jewish thought, as we have seen, did not typically dwell on the Adam and Eve story. Instead, it tended to turn to the story of the so-called "Watchers" in Genesis 6, that is, the "sons of God" who came down and took wives among the "daughters of men." From this union sprung up the giants to whom evil was attributed. The problem with this account is that the Flood supposedly killed off all of these mixed-blood giants, leaving the origin problem intact for the postdiluvian world. Beginning in the late second century BCE, with the Book of Jubilees, Jewish thought turned more often to Adam's transgression as an explanation. See John R. Levison, *Portraits of Adam and Early Judaism*. On the complex theological issues, see W. D. Davies, *Paul and Rabbinic Judaism*, esp. pp. 31–57.

74 **impossible to understand Christ:** And then he made the link still more explicit: "For as in Adam all dies, so also in Christ shall all be made alive" (1 Cor. 15:21–22). Again, in the Epistle to the Romans, Paul bound together the free gift brought by Jesus to something that happened at the beginning of time:

> Therefore as by the offence of one judgment came upon all men to condemnation; even so by the righteousness of one the free gift came upon all men unto justification of life. For as by one man's disobedience many were made sinners, so by the obedience of one shall many be made righteous. (Rom. 5:18–19)

Davies (*Paul and Rabbinic Judaism*, p. 44) argues that Paul introduced the doctrine of Christ as the Second Adam. Others, including C. F. Burney (*The Aramaic Origin of the Fourth Gospel* [Oxford: Clarendon Press, 1922]), believe that it was already at least implicit in the synoptic gospels. In any case, Paul set the ball in motion: after him most of the early Christian Fathers felt compelled to grapple with the opening chapters in Genesis.

74 **In the imagination of Christian theologians:** Victorinus, "On the Creation of the World," in Coxe, *The Ante-Nicene Fathers*, vol. 7, *Fathers of the Third and Fourth Centuries*, p. 341. In the Eastern Orthodox liturgy, attributed to St. Basil the Great, as in many other solemn ritual utterances throughout the Christian world, the overarching design was spelled out and ceaselessly reiterated:

> For, since through man sin came into the world and through sin death, it pleased Your only begotten Son . . . born under the law, to condemn sin in His flesh, so that those who died in Adam may be brought to life in Him, Your Christ.

74 **Typology insisted:** Reminding his congregants that Adam received the sentence "Cursed is the ground in thy labors; thorns and thistle shall it bring to thee," St. Cyril, a bishop of Jerusalem in the fourth century, concluded that it is "for this cause Jesus assumes the thorns, that He may cancel the sentence; for this cause also was He buried in the earth, that the earth which had been cursed might receive the blessing instead of a curse" (Edwin Hamilton Gifford, D.D., ed., "The Catechetical Lectures of S. Cyril, Archbishop of Jerusalem" in *Nicene and Post-Nicene Fathers of the Christian Church, Second Series*, vol. 7, p. 87). The thorns that sprang up from the ground after Adam's fall were genuinely sharp, but their full significance—their destiny, as it were—was only disclosed and at the same time annulled in the Crown of Thorns. On typology, see especially Erich Auerbach, "Figura," in *Scenes from the Drama of European Literature* (New York: Meridian, 1959), pp. 11–56, and Auerbach, "Typological Symbolism in Medieval Literature," in *Yale French Studies* 9 (1952), pp. 3–10.

75 *Against the Galileans:* In *Works of the Emperor Julian*, ed. Wilmer C. Wright (Cambridge: Harvard University Press, 1913–23), 1: 325–29.

76 **a single word: allegory:** See Philo of Alexandria, *On the Creation of the Cosmos According to Moses*, esp. 84–89. Though he may not have been able to read Hebrew—in his many works, he always quoted from the Septuagint—Philo professed the most extravagant admiration for Moses as the author of the Torah. Moses did not simply proclaim laws to be obeyed, Philo wrote, nor did he attempt like the pagan priests to befog the masses with trumped-up fictions and invented myths. Instead, he began the scriptures with an account of the creation of the world, implying that "the cosmos is in harmony with the law and the law with the cosmos" (p. 47).

76 **in six days the world was created:** There is no order without number, and "six is the first perfect number." It is equal to (the product of) its parts and is also formed by their sum, namely the three as its half and the two as its third and the unit as its sixth. It is also, so to speak, both male and female by nature, forming a harmonic union out of the product of each of them, for among existing things the odd is male and the female is even. The first of the odd numbers is the three, of

the even numbers it is the two, and the product of both is the six. So it was right that the cosmos, as the most perfect of the things that have come into existence, be built in accordance with the perfect number six (Philo, ibid., 49).

76 **and the actual garden:** "With the garden of delights he hints at the ruling part of the soul, which is filled with countless opinions just like plants, while with the tree of life he hints at the most important of the virtues, reverence for God, through which the soul is immortalized, and with the tree which makes known good and evil things at intermediate practical insight, through which things which are opposite by nature are discriminated" (Philo, ibid., 88).

77 **the course of Jewish exegesis:** This exegetical technique reached its high point in the great Sephardic philosopher Maimonides (1135–1204 CE). Maimonides, who remains today at the center of Orthodox Judaism, interpreted the verses in Genesis with profound learning and precision, but he had no commitment to reading them as the straightforward reporting of actual events. On the contrary, drawing on Greek philosophy as well as on the utterances of the Hebrew sages, he viewed Adam and Eve not as if they were characters in a novel but rather as the allegory of a single human in whom form and substance, intellect and passion, are conjoined.

To expound this idea, Maimonides cited one of those midrashic comments that might have seemed to a sophisticated reader the epitome of wrongheaded narrative elaboration. "The serpent had a rider," an ancient Sage had remarked, "the rider was as big as a camel, and it was the rider that enticed Eve: this rider was Samael." The passage, Maimonides acknowledges, is "most absurd in its literal sense; but as an allegory it contains wonderful wisdom, and fully agrees with real facts." Samael, he explains, was the name for Satan, and it makes perfect sense that Satan spoke not to the intellect, but to desire and imagination, that is, to the part of the human that in the allegory is called "Eve." Absurd in its literal sense but wonderfully wise as allegory. (Moses Maimonides, *The Guide of the Perplexed*, pp. 154–56.) On Maimonides' intellectual method and aims, see Moshe Halbertal, *Maimonides: Life and Thought.*

The allegorical interpretation of Adam and Eve was not a strategy of religious dissent or skepticism. On the contrary, it generated a wide spectrum of deeply pious thought. If it influenced the hyperintellectual, highly rational Maimonides, it also inspired the esoteric extravagances of the mystical kabbalists. In the foundational works of Jewish mysticism, the thirteenth-century *Zohar* and the sixteenth-century Lurianic Kabbalah, Adam in chapter 1 of Genesis was created in the likeness of Adam *Kadmon*, the primordial or heavenly Adam from whose head radiated streams of light. This purely spiritual higher Adam—associated in some strains of this tradition with the Messiah—is distinguished from a lower Adam, Adam *Ha-rishon*, who is the Adam we encounter in the scriptural narrative and who included within himself all future souls. The continuing vitality of the notion of the two Adams and of the allegorical method launched by Philo two thousand years ago can be seen in Joseph Soloveitchik's *Lonely Man of Faith,* published in the mid-1960s. For Soloveitchik, Adam in chapter 1 of Genesis is an allegory of "majestic man," dominating the universe through his knowledge and technology, while the Adam of chapter 2 is "covenantal man," saved from his existential loneliness by companionship and by his observance of the revealed law of God.

78 **"incredible and insipid":** The Jews "wove together some most incredible and insipid stories, viz., that a certain man was formed by the *hands* of God, and had breathed into him the breath of life, and that a woman was taken from his side, and that God issued certain commands, and that a serpent opposed these, and gained a victory over the commandments of God; thus relating certain old wives' fables, and most impiously representing God as weak at the very beginning (of things), and unable to convince even a single human being whom He Himself had formed" (Origen, *Contra Celsum* in *The Anti-Nicene Fathers*, 44:36).

79 **subtle philosophical problems:** Just as modern Jewish thought on Adam and Eve reflects the inheritance from Philo, so too among modern Christians there are many heirs to the allegorical method launched in the third century by Origen. The greatest philosopher of the European Enlightenment, Immanuel Kant, had no patience for theological obscurantism or scriptural literalism. Of all the ways of understanding the origin of moral evil and representing its spread through the members of our entire species, he wrote, "the most inappropriate is surely to imagine it as having come to us by way of inheritance from our first parents." We cannot possibly inherit our sinfulness; "every evil action must be so considered whenever we seek its rational origin, as if the human being had fallen into it directly from the state of innocence." The problem, Kant recognized, is that if we thus begin in a state of innocence, there is no way to explain how moral evil should have come into us. Faced with this dilemma, he turned back, in a way that Origen might have recognized and approved, to the story of the Garden and the snake: "Scripture," Kant wrote, "expresses this incomprehensibility in a historical narrative" (Immanuel Kant, *Religion Within the Boundaries of Mere Reason*, p. 65). The irrationality of the biblical account is a brilliant allegory for a philosophical problem that reason cannot solve. A succession of distinguished philosophers of the nineteenth and twentieth centuries, both Protestant and Catholic—Friedrich Schleirmacher, Søren Kierkegaard, Reinhold Niebuhr, Hans Urs von Balthasar—followed suit. But—unlike the case in modern Judaism—these modern instances of Christian allegorization are not the continuation of an unbroken line of thought. Instead, they constitute a revival in the wake of a very long eclipse.

Chapter 5: In the Bathhouse

81 **unchanged to the present:** It can be found more or less intact in the Rudas Baths in Budapest, the Al Pasha in Amman, the Suleymaniye Hamami in Istanbul, or, for that matter, on First Avenue in New York at the Russian and Turkish Baths.

82 **"saw the signs of active virility":** Augustine, *Confessions*, trans. R. S. Pine, 2:3, p. 45. The phrase "me ille pater in balneis vidit pubescentem et inquieta indutum adulescentia" leaves open the possibility that it was only his son's pubic hair that the father noticed, not an erection. I am inclined to think that the words *inquieta*

adulescentia imply something more than hair. Erection—and above all the involuntary experience of erection—turns out, in any case, to be crucial in Augustine's interpretation of the story of Adam and Eve and his understanding of the human condition after the Fall. All citations of the *Confessions* in English are to this translation. Citations of the Latin are to Augustine, *Confessions*, Loeb Classical Library.

84 **one brother:** The brother, Navigius, makes the briefest of appearance in the *Confessions*, in Ostia at the bedside of his dying mother. He expresses the thought that he wishes that his mother might die not in a strange land but in her own country, where she could be buried by the side of her husband. "See how he talks!" she exclaims, reproaching him for his worldly thoughts, and says that she does not care where her body is laid to rest. For Augustine's biography, I have relied principally on Peter Brown, *Augustine of Hippo*, and Robin Lane Fox, *Augustine: Conversions to Confessions*.

86 **grazes the skin:** "I did not seek the kind of sorrow which would wound me deeply, for I had no wish to endure the sufferings which I saw on stage; but I enjoyed fables and fictions, which could only graze the skin" (*Confessions*, 3.2. p. 57).

88 **indifferent to good and evil?:** Epicurus had argued that the universe as we know it emerged from the random and spontaneous collision of atoms and that the gods were indifferent to human behavior and deaf to human appeals.

91 **the Bible was accessible:** "Its plain language and simple style make it accessible to everyone, and yet it absorbs the attention of the learned" (*Confessions*, 6:5, p. 117).

94 **True, a grandson:** The child, Adeodatus, was baptized alongside his father and his father's friend, Alypius. Augustine marveled at his son's piety and intelligence, both entirely the gifts, he writes, of God, "for there was nothing of mine in that boy except my sin" (*Confessions*, 9:6, p. 190). Adeodatus died in his teens.

96 **"*Come and share*":** The final words are a quotation from Matthew 25:21. *Confessions*, 9:10, p. 198.

96 **"the most intense experience":** Rebecca West, *St. Augustine*, p. 91.

Chapter 6: Original Freedom, Original Sin

98 **he heard Ambrose proclaim:** Quoted in Augustine, "*De Gratia Christi, Et De Peccato Originali*," *Augustin: Anti-Pelagian Writings*, p. 214.

100 **a whole litany of sins:** See chapter 45 in *On the Holy Trinity* in *Nicene and Post-Nicene Fathers of the Christian Church, First Series*, vol. 3, *St. Augustin: On the Holy Trinity, Doctrinal Treatises, Moral Treatises*. Augustine began to write *On the Holy Trinity*, or *De trinitate*, around 400, three years after the *Confessions*.

101 **they, the humans, must bear the responsibility:** ". . . the reason for these evils must be either the injustice or impotence of God, or the punishment for the first and ancient sin. Since God is neither unjust nor impotent, there is only what you are forced unwillingly to confess: that the heavy yoke upon the children of Adam from the day of their coming out of their mother's womb until the day

of their burial within the mother of all would not have existed if the offense by way of origin had not come first to deserve it" (Augustine, *Saint Augustine Against Julian*, p. 240).

103 **the outrage that still lingered:** "Will any common sense observer agree that I was rightly punished as a boy for playing ball—just because this hindered me from learning more quickly those lessons by means of which, as a man, I could play at more shameful games?" (*Confessions*, 1:9:15).

105 **the innate stain of vice:** "Nothing that is good and evil, on account of which we are either praiseworthy or blameworthy, is born with us—it is rather done by us, for we are born with capacity for either" (cited in "St. Augustine on Original Sin" in *St. Caesarius of Arles Sermons*, p. 442). "Before the action of his own proper will, that only is in man which God made" (cited in Benjamin B. Warfield, "Introductory Essay on Augustin and the Pelagian Controversy" in *St. Augustin: Anti-Pelagian Writings*, p. 15). "As we are procreated without virtue, so also without vice."

105 **"The long custom of sins":** Cited in John M. Rist, *Augustine: Ancient Thought Baptized*. This Pelagian position was attacked from the beginning as hopelessly weak—how could "imitation" and "habit" explain the virtual universality of human sinfulness?—and continues to be an object of contempt or at least condescension. See, for example, Bonnie Kent, "Augustine's Ethics" in *The Cambridge Companion to Augustine*, p. 223, who remarks dismissively that "the works of Pelagius and his followers declare it absurd to suggest that Adam's sin damaged anyone but himself, except in the trivial sense that Adam set a bad example." In what sense is example, if properly understood, trivial? "Example" for Pelagius in effect means the whole glacial weight of human culture.

106 **To die is not a punishment:** This is early Pelagian doctrine; later Pelagians were willing to concede that death was introduced by Adam.

106 **accused of heresy:** James Wetzel, "Predestination, Pelagianism, and Foreknowledge," in *The Cambridge Companion to Augustine*: "It was his [Pelagius's] disciple, Caelestius, a Roman aristocrat, who first aroused the ire of the North African bishops. While in Carthage, Caelestius raised questions about the practice of infant baptism, suggesting it could be supported (as he in fact did support it) without having to appeal to an original sin that tainted every human birth. For the Africans, this was to question a hard-won dogma, and they denounced him in synod. Pelagius briefly escaped guilt by association when he was cleared of heresy at the synod of Diospolis, presided over by a council of bishops from Palestine in December 415. But in the years following his acquittal, the Africans, now led by Augustine, rallied their forces and eventually persuaded Pope Zosimus to condemn the heresy of Pelagius."

107 **torture infants:** Julian had argued, "There cannot be offense in infants, because there can be no offense without will, which they do not possess." (*Saint Augustine Against Julian*, p. 216). Augustine countered, "This assertion may be correctly made about a personal sin, but not about the contagion by way of origin of the first

sin. If there were no such sin, then infants, bound by no evil, would suffer nothing evil in body or in soul under the great power of the just God" (ibid., 116).

107 **all sinners, all damned:** "Whatever good is done by man, yet is not done for the purpose for which true wisdom commands it be done, may seem good from its function, but, because the end is not right, it is sin" (*Saint Augustine Against Julian*, 187). Augustine cited as proof the words of Paul's Epistle to the Hebrews—"Without faith it is impossible to please God" (ibid., 195) (Heb. 11:6). The outraged Julian argued that these words were being put to a use for which they were never intended.

108 **What the gloomy bishop of Hippo condemned:** "You divide, you define, you give a kind of clinical dissertation on the genus, the species, the mode, and the excess of concupiscence, asserting that 'Its genus is in the vital fire; its species is in the genital action; its mode is in the conjugal act; its excess is in the intemperance of fornication.' Yet, after all this supposedly subtle and truly prolix disputation, when I ask you briefly and openly why this vital fire plants the root of warfare in man, so that his flesh lust against his spirit, and it becomes necessary for his spirit to lust against his flesh—why he who wills to consent with the vital fire receives a mortal wound—I think the black ink in your book must turn red with blushing" (*Saint Augustine Against Julian*, 130). In the struggle against the Pelagians, Augustine had an advantage: though he had been married, Julian made clear that he was now chaste, as had been the ascetic Pelagius himself. What was the point of electing chastity, Augustine wryly asked, if there was nothing wrong with sex?

108 **"not performed without evil":** Concupiscence, he wrote, "acting now slackly, now with great violence, never ceases to urge marriage to the unlawful, even when the marriage makes good use of the evil of concupiscence in the propagation of offspring." (*Saint Augustine Against Julian*, 134.)

108 **pleasurable stirring:** Yes, that stirring is pleasurable; sexual intercourse as we know it—as Augustine knew it from long experience with his mistress and others—is "the greatest of all bodily pleasures." But that intensity of pleasure is precisely its dangerous allure. It would be better to beget children without this sweet poison. "What friend of wisdom and holy joys . . . would not prefer, if this were possible, to beget children without this lust?" (Augustine, *The City of God* in *Nicene and Post-Nicene Fathers, First Series*, vol. 2, *St. Augustin: The City of God, and Christian Doctrine*, pp. 275–76). See, likewise, "What lover of the spiritual good, who has married only for the sake of offspring, would not prefer if he could to propagate children without it or without its very great impulsion?" (*Saint Augustine Against Julian*, p. 228).

109 **Original Sin:** According to N. P. Williams, Augustine came up with the term in his treatise *"ad Simplicianum."* Cf. Williams, *The Ideas of the Fall and of Original Sin, a Historical and Critical Study*. In my sampling of the overwhelmingly vast literature on Original Sin, I found Williams's venerable book helpful, along with the still more venerable H. Wheeler Robinson, *The Christian Doctrine of Man* (Edinburgh: T. & T. Clark: 1913), and Frederick Robert Tennant, *The Sources of the Doctrines of the Fall and Original Sin* (Cambridge: Cambridge University Press, 1903).

109 **the vast body of rabbinical writing . . . the comparably vast Islamic tradition:** Of course, their vastness means that one can easily find exceptions. And, if pious Jews and Muslims did not embrace a full-blown concept of Original Sin, they did quite often dwell on the taint that Adam and Eve brought upon themselves and their descendants by their disobedience. "The waste that is excreted by us is a result of what we inherited because of the tree," a seventeenth-century Muslim traveler in France explained to a Christian interlocutor:

> It brought about uncleanness in the body, as a result of which man has to wash those unclean parts of the body. He washes his hands because our father Adam, peace be upon him, stretched out his hand to the fruit which God had prohibited; he washes his mouth because he ate of it, and his nose because he smelled the fruit, and his face because he turned toward it.

Ahmad bin Qasim, *Kitab Nasir al-Din ala al-Qawm al-Kafirin (The Book of the Protector of Religion against the Unbelievers)*, in *In the Land of the Christians: Arabic Travel Writing in the Seventeenth Century*, pp. 26–27.

109 **"of a virgin":** See chapter 18 in Augustine, *On the Holy Trinity* in *On the Holy Trinity, Doctrinal Treatises, Moral Treatises.* "Nor did that concupiscence of the flesh intervene, by which the rest of men, who derive original sin, are propagated and conceived; but holy virginity became pregnant, not by conjugal intercourse, but by faith—lust being utterly absent—so that that which was born from the root of the first man might derive only the origin of race, not also of guilt" (*On the Holy Trinity*).

110 **subtle allegory:** The words Augustine uses for his method of interpretation include not only *allegoria*, but also *figura, aenigma, imago, similitudo, mysterium, sacramentum, signum*, and *velum* [veil]. Cf. Augustine, *A Refutation of the Manachees* in *On Genesis: A Refutation of the Manachees, Unfinished Literal Commentary on Genesis, The Literal Meaning of Genesis*, p. 30. For "soulish," see Augustine, *On Genesis*, p. 78. In *A Refutation of the Manachees:* Eve was not in Paradise "in a local sense, but rather as regards her blissful feeling of Paradise" (Augustine, *On Genesis*, 2.41.20, p. 85). Cf. John M. Rist, *Augustine: Ancient Thought Baptized*, p. 98.

111 *in order that:* My italics. Augustine does not deny that there might be a literal truth to the words of Scripture, but that literal truth is not what most matters. "Even if the real, visible woman was made, historically speaking, from the body of the first man by the Lord God," he writes, "it was surely not without reason that she was made like that—it must have been to suggest some hidden truth." God "filled up the place of that rib with flesh, to suggest by this word the loving affection with which we should love our own souls." (*On Genesis, 2.12.1*, p. 83.) In some cases, the literal could come after the spiritual sense. Hence the blessing to "be fruitful and multiply" originated in a spiritual sense and then "was turned into a blessing of fertility in the flesh after sin." (*On Genesis, 1.19.30*, p. 58.) On Adam's labor as an anticipation of Christ's stretching out of his hand, see *On Genesis, 2.22.34*, p. 94.

111 **was a mistake:** Already by 393, only five years after the *Refutation of the Manichees,* Augustine was trying his hand, in a text he did not finish, at a more literal

interpretation, one that treated the opening chapters of Genesis as a depiction of historical characters and events. All the same, he did not entirely abandon allegorical reading. It left its mark particularly strongly in the closing books of *The Confessions*. Why did God in Genesis 1:28 bid the first humans "to increase and multiply and fill the earth"? After all, He did not give the same commandment to the fish and the birds and trees, presumably because he expected them to reproduce anyway, without a specific order to do so. God's commandment to the humans must therefore conceal a special meaning. "What mystery do these words contain?" Augustine asks God; "I see nothing to prevent me from interpreting the words of your Scripture in this figurative sense" (Augustine, *Confessions*, 13:24). The figurative sense in question reveals that the multiplying God has in mind for humans has nothing to do with sexual reproduction: "I take the reproduction of human kind to refer to the thoughts which our minds conceive, because reason is fertile and productive" (ibid., 13:24).

111 **Plunging into the project:** He had immense confidence in his ability, with God's help, to accomplish anything to which he set his mind. Consider the tone in this passage from *The City of God*: "Having disposed of the very difficult questions concerning the origin of our world and the beginning of the human race, the natural order requires that we now discuss the fall of the first man (we may say of the first men), and of the origin and propagation of human death" (*The City of God, in St. Augustin: The City of God, and Christian Doctrine*, p. 245).

112 **the most prolonged and sustained attention:** "To hardly any other of his works did Augustine devote such perseverance, such care and circumspection" (Augustine, *The Literal Meaning of Genesis* in *On Genesis*, p. 164). On the rejection of "riddling," see *The Literal Meaning of Genesis* in Augustine, *On Genesis*, p. 183.) [*Secundum proprietatem rerum gestarum, non secundum aenigmata futurarum*.] On the urging of his friends, see Letter 38 (Ep. CLIX), from 415 CE, to his fellow priest Evodius, in which he alludes to "the suspense of anticipation" among his friends to see the book (*St. Augustine Select Letters*, p. 277).

112 **"more questions were asked than answers found":** "Revisions [Retractiones]" in *On Genesis*, 2.24.1, p. 167. When he encountered problems like God's vocal cords, he took refuge in a principle he found himself forced to repeat: "If . . . in the words of God or of any person performing the prophetic office something is said which taken literally is simply absurd, then undoubtedly it should be understood as being said figuratively" (ibid., 11.1.2, pp. 429–30).

112 **lest he die:** If you ask how he could know what "death" meant, Augustine wrote, you should remind yourself that you know many things intuitively, without direct experience of them (cf. *On Genesis*, 8.16.34).

113 **the literal sense of the Bible's words:** We may be confident, Augustine wrote, that the apples on the fatal tree were the same kind as the apples Adam and Eve had already found to be harmless on other trees. We know that real snakes cannot speak, but the real snake in the real Garden of Eden did not have to speak: "It was the devil himself who spoke in the serpent, using it like an organ" (Augustine, *The Literal Meaning of Genesis* in Augustine, *On Genesis*, p. 449). Not all of the details

needed to construct a literal reading were necessarily specified in the Scriptures, but we can fill in the gaps by conjecture. And since it would not do to think that the devil had any independent power to compromise either God's power or the free will of the first humans, we should understand that his words would not have had any effect upon Eve if she had not already had a "love of her own independent authority and a certain proud over-confidence in herself." (*On Genesis*, 11.30.39, p. 451.)

113 **Far better had she clung:** *The City of God* in *St. Augustin: The City of God, and Christian Doctrine*, p. 271. Augustine writes that Adam too erred in presuming God's forgiveness. He was not deceived by the serpent or by his wife, but "he was deceived as to the judgment which would be passed on his apology." Presumably, he did not expect the death sentence for what he thought was a venial sin. In *Paradise Lost* Milton powerfully represents a distraught Adam making the same error.

114 **the sight aroused them:** Augustine, "A Letter Addressed to the Count Valerius, on Augustin's Forwarding to Him What He Calls his First Book 'On Marriage and Concupiscence'" in "Extract from Augustin's 'Refractions,' Book II, Chap. 53, on the Following Treatise, '*De Nuptiis et Concupiscenta*'" in *St. Augustin: Anti-Pelagian Writings*, p. 258.

114 **they had lost their freedom:** "Must not this bring the blush of shame over the freedom of the human will, that by its contempt of God, its own Commander, it has lost all proper command for itself over its own members?" (Augustine, *On Marriage and Concupiscence*, in *St. Augustin: Anti-Pelagian Writings*, p. 266). On the rise of shame, see Kyle Harper, *From Shame to Sin*. On the psychological and somatic experience of shame, see Michael Lewis, *Shame: The Exposed Self*.

115 **male sexual arousal:** *On Marriage and Concupiscence* , p. 266. On a few occasions he recognized that the woman's sexual experience might be different. He knew, for example, that for the man the release of seed is deeply pleasurable, but whether "such pleasure accompanies the commingling of the seminal elements of the two sexes in the womb," he wrote, "is a question which perhaps women may be able to determine from their inmost feelings; but it is improper for us to push an idle curiosity so far" (*On Marriage and Concupiscence*, p. 293).

115 **"acts against its will!":** *On Marriage and Concupiscence*, p. 266. In *City of God*, Augustine remarks on the weird unreliability of arousal: "This emotion not only fails to obey the legitimate desire to beget offspring, but also refuses to serve lascivious lust; and though it often opposes its whole combined energy to the soul that resists it, sometimes also it is divided against itself, and while it moves the soul, leaves the body unmoved" (*The City of God*, in *St. Augustin: The City of God, and Christian Doctrine*, p. 276).

115 **"Does it not engage the whole soul and body?":** "And does not this extremity of pleasure," Augustine continues, "result in a kind of submersion of the mind itself, even if it is approached with a good intention, that is, for the purpose of procreating children, since in its very operation it allows no one to think, I do not say of wisdom, but of anything at all" (*Saint Augustine Against Julian*, p. 228). On

the theological issues with which Augustine is grappling, see Peter Brown, *The Body and Society.*

116 **a crucially important difference:** Sexual reproduction was not the only difference. The Pelagians argued that death, being part of what it meant to be human, would inevitably have come to Adam and Eve as well. Augustine vehemently disagreed: the first humans had the possibility, by means of the Tree of Life, to be immortal. Adam would not have grown old if he had not sinned: he "was supplied with sustenance against decay from the fruit of the various trees, and from the tree of life with security against old age" (Augustine, *A Treatise on the Merits and Forgiveness of Sins, and on the Baptism of Infants,* in *St. Augustin: Anti-Pelagian Writings,* p.16). Had they not sinned, they would not have grown decrepit and would not have died. Though he was less certain of this, Augustine also doubted that the offspring of Adam and Eve, had they remained in Paradise, would have suffered the extreme helplessness all infants now experience. Natural scientists, in the ancient world as now, recognized that prolonged infancy was a hallmark of our species. Augustine believed it was punitive. The issue was not one of size: the constraints of the womb, he understood perfectly well, would have required that infants be very small. But if the first humans had not sinned, their offspring might at once have attained physical and mental competence. After all, he observed, many brute creatures, even when they are newborns, "run about, and recognize their mothers, and require no external help or care when they want to suck, but with remarkable ease discover their mothers' breasts themselves" (ibid., p. 43). A human being, by contrast, "at his birth is furnished neither with feet fit for walking, nor with hands able even to scratch; and unless their lips were actually applied to the breast by the mother, they would not know where to find it; and even when close to the nipple, they would, notwithstanding their desire for food, be more able to cry than to suck" (ibid., p. 43). This miserable state, he concluded, was almost certainly penal, the consequence of the Fall.

117 **"relaxed on his wife's bosom":** The description of sex in Paradise is worked out in detail in book 14 of *The City of God.*

117 **"his body's integrity":** There was obviously no physical equivalent in the male to the hymen, but just as Augustine imagined that the woman must have an equivalent to the stirrings of the erection, so too he imagined that the man must have a bodily integrity that is violated in sexual intercourse as we experience it.

118 **without a trace of involuntary arousal:** Would this public coupling in front of whoever wished to watch have been pleasurable? Augustine was not quite sure. It would, he was certain, have been without "carnal concupiscence," that is, without involuntary arousal. Cf. Augustine, *Marriage and Concupiscence,* in *St. Augustin: Anti-Pelagian Writings,* p. 288: "For why is the especial work of parents withdrawn and hidden even from the eyes of their children, except that it is impossible for them to be occupied in laudable procreation without shameful lust? Because of this it was that even they were ashamed who first covered their nakedness. These portions of their person were not suggestive of shame before, but deserved to be commended and praised as the work of God. They put on their covering when

they felt their shame, and they felt their shame when, after their own disobedience to their Maker, they felt their members disobedient to themselves."

Chapter 7: Eve's Murder

121 **the Qur'an depicted:** The Qur'an does not depict Eve eating the fruit before Adam, nor does it depict Adam laying the blame on Eve. Eve—in Arabic, Hawwa'—is not mentioned by name in the Qur'an; she is called Adam's "spouse" and is jointly guilty with her husband for the disobedience that led to their expulsion from Paradise. See Kvam et al. *Eve & Adam*, esp. pp. 179–202, 413–19, 464–76; Karel Steenbrink, "Created Anew: Muslim Interpretations of the Myth of Adam and Eve," in Bob Becking and Susan Hennecke, ed., *Out of Paradise: Eve and Adam and their Interpreters* (Sheffield, UK: Sheffield Phoenix Press, 2011); *Concise Encyclopedia of Islam*, entries on Hawwa' and Adam. Post Qur'anic legends in Islam reflect many of the rabbinic and Christian traditions.

As for the Jewish tradition, even when some Jews became interested in human culpability in the Genesis story, they tended to focus not on Eve but on Adam. Thus, for example, 4 Ezra 7.118:

O Adam, what have you done?

For though it was you who sinned,

the fall was not yours alone,

but ours also who are your descendants.

4 Ezra, also called 2 Esdras or the Apocalypse of Ezra, was a work composed to help its readers cope with the disaster of Jewish history in the wake of the destruction of the temple in 70 CE.

121 **"the morals of a bitch":** Citations of Hesiod are to Hesiod, *"Works and Days"* and *"Theognis."* There is a rich discussion of the afterlife of the story in Dora and Erwin Panofsky, *Pandora's Box:* "Curiously enough, the Fathers of the Church are more important for the transmission—and transformation—of the myth of Pandora than the secular writers: in an attempt to corroborate the doctrine of original sin by a classical parallel, yet to oppose Christian truth to pagan fable, they likened her to Eve" (11). See also, more recently, Stephen Scully, *Hesiod's "Theogony."*

123 **woman's incorrigible vanity:** Tertullian, *De Cultu Feminarum*, trans. Sydney Thelwall, 1.1.14. The expression of outrage at women's ornaments is altogether typical. See, for example, Tertullian's contemporary Clement of Alexandria: "For as the serpent deceived Eve, so also has ornament of gold maddened other women to vicious practices, using as a bait the form of the serpent, and by fashioning lampreys and serpents for decoration" (*Paedagogus,* in Clement of Alexandria, *The Anti-Nicene Fathers*, vol. 2, *Fathers of the Second Century: Hermas, Tatian, Athenagoras, Theophilus, and Clement of Alexandria,* 2.13).

123 **"in spite of the wrinkles of age":** "To Marcella," in Jerome, *St. Jerome: Select Letters*, p. 163. For marriage as "the forbidden tree," see p. 165.

124 **"Keep therefore as you were born":** "To Eustochium," in Jerome, *Select Letters,* p. 93. Perhaps to emphasize the harshness of marriage for women, Jerome

made a significant change in his translation of Genesis 3:16. Where the Hebrew reads, "And for your man shall be your longing [Heb. *teshukah*], and he shall rule over you" [Alter, *Five Books of Moses*], Jerome writes, "And you shall be under (the) power of the man, and he shall be lord over you" (*sub viri potestate eris et ipse dominabitur tui*). There is no linguistic basis for translating the Hebrew in the way that Jerome does, and modern Catholic versions correct it.

125 **First Epistle to Timothy:** 1 Timothy 2.11–14 (KJV). Cited by Jerome in his work against Jovinian. Much disputed now, the verses were taken at face value. Jerome has some difficulty with the following verse: "Notwithstanding she shall be saved in childbearing, if they continue in faith and charity and holiness with sobriety."

126 **"and the whole world was overthrown":** Guido de Baysio and Raymond de Peñaforte are both cited in Gary Macy, *The Hidden History of Women's Ordination*, p. 123.

128 *Eva* **became** *Ave*: On Eve and Mary, see Miri Rubin, *Mother of God*. esp. pp. 202–3, 311–12. A rich collection of images linking Eve and Mary is available in German in Ernst Guldan, *Eva und Maria*.

128 **in rapt wonder:** Illustration of Dante Alighieri, *Paradiso,* Yates Thompson MS 36, c. 1445. The artist may have been Giovanni di Paolo.

129 **between synagogue and church:** Breslau. Stadtbibliothek Cod. M 1006 (3v); in Guldan, plate 156.

129 **writhing snake:** Caravaggio made the painting for the altar of the Archconfraternity of the Papal Grooms. He did not invent the motif; it appeared in an earlier painting by the Lombard Ambrogio Figino. But Caravaggio gave it unnerving intensity and strangeness, so much so perhaps that the Grooms, after briefly exhibiting it, sold it to Cardinal Scipio Borghese.

129 **a defective or mutilated man:** Thomas Aquinas, *Summa Theologica,* 1a.q.92 a. 1 ad 1. See Harm Goris, "Is Woman Just a Mutilated Male? Adam and Eve in the Theology of Thomas Aquinas," in *Out of Paradise*.

130 **his frenzied attack:** St. Peter Damian, quoted in Gary Macy, *The Hidden History of Women's Ordination*, p. 113.

131 **"the air darkens":** Paucapalea, quoted in Macy, *The Hidden History of Women's Ordination* , p. 114. Such was the considered opinion of this twelfth-century canon lawyer who wrote a *Summa* on the work of his distinguished teacher Gratian. The account was advanced to support the argument that women should not be allowed to visit a church during menstruation or after childbirth. Other churchmen strongly disagreed.

132 **eager to justify what they had done:** *The Hammer of Witches: A Complete Translation of the Malleus Maleficarum,* trans. Christopher S. Mackay, p. 164.

133 **innate defectiveness of all women:** On the vigorous refutations of this misogynistic account and the exoneration of Eve, see Alcuin Blamires, *The Case for Women in Medieval Culture*, esp. pp. 96–125.

133 **had no such excuse:** *Dialogue on the Equal of Unequal Sin of Adam and Eve* (Verona, 1451), in Isotta Nogarola, *Complete Writings: Letterbook, Dialogue on Adam and Eve, Orations*, pp. 151–52.

134 **Christine de Pizan:** *The Book of the City of Ladies*, I.9.3.

135 **"the priceless bounty of free choice":** Arcangela Tarabotti, *Paternal Tyranny*, p. 51.

Chapter 8: Embodiments

139 **along the twisting paths of the catacombs:** For a rich account of the complex shifts from one burial option to another, see Thomas Laqueur, *The Work of the Dead*.

140 **wall paintings of the naked Adam and Eve:** I located no fewer than four representations of Adam and Eve in this site. I am grateful to my expert guide, the art historian Dr. Angela di Curzio, and to the Ispettore della Pontificia Commissione di Archeologia Sacra, Dr. Raffaella Giuliani, for granting me permission to visit parts of the catacombs not ordinarily open to the public.

142 **Other Christian sarcophagi:** Elizabeth Struthers Malbon, *The Iconography of the Sarcophagus of Junius Bassus*. There are approximately thirty-four Adam and Eve figures on surviving early Christian sarcophagi.

145 **Bernward's doors:** See William Tronzo, "The Hildesheim Doors," *Zeitschrift für Kunstgeschichte*: 347–66; Adam S. Cohen and Anne Derbes, "Bernward and Eve at Hildesheim": 19–38.

146 **The rule of shame:** For a sampling of images, see Sigrid Esche, *Adam und Eva: Sündenfall and Erlösung*. This is a very rough generalization to which exceptions, over such a long, iconographically complex period of time, may certainly be found. The famous early-sixth-century Vienna Genesis, for example, depicts a naked, upright Adam and Eve, but branches discreetly cover their genitals, and the figures are next depicted at the moment of expulsion, bent over in disgrace. See *Imaging the Early Medieval Bible,* ed. John Williams. For the new and surprising ways of representing nakedness exemplified here by Gislebertus's Eve, see Alastair Minnis, *From Eden to Eternity: Creations of Paradise in the Later Middle Ages.*

148 **that her body pivots:** For this observation, as for much else in my discussion of images, I am indebted to conversations with Joseph Koerner.

149 **modestly, if scantily, dressed:** Modesty aside, the covering made sense, since, as we read in Genesis, the first humans sewed fig leaves together in the wake of the fall, in response to their newfound experience of shame, and God, for his part, dressed them in skins before driving them out of paradise. So from a strictly textual point of view, the fig-leaved figures in the fresco were, if anything, underdressed. See James Clifton, "Gender and Shame in Masaccio's *Expulsion from the Garden of Eden,*" 637–55.

154 **a great Dürer scholar:** Erwin Panofsky, *The Life and Art of Albrecht Dürer.*

155 **"the whole beauty of the meanest living creature":** William Martin Conaway, *Literary Remains of Albrecht Dürer*, p. 244.

156 **nothing like it:** Joseph Koerner, *The Moment of Self-Portraiture in German Renaissance Art*, p. 239 and n. 43.

156 **he had to grasp himself:** Though Dürer took it further than anyone, the

underlying idea was a commonplace: Cf. the fifteenth-century Italian preacher Girolamo Savonarola: "Every painter paints, as the saying goes, actually himself" (cited in Koerner, *The Moment of Self-Portraiture,* p. 484, n. 2).

157 **it befitted him:** As he tried to articulate what it was that he and anyone comparably endowed with great skill should do, he invoked a situation that was strangely like Adam and Eve in the Garden: "For evil and good lie before men," Dürer wrote, "wherefore it behoveth a rational man to choose the good" (*Literary Remains of Albrecht Dürer,* p. 245).

159 **the way the hip rises:** The stance of the figures is known as *contrapposto,* described by the art historian Panofsky as follows: "the weight of the body (which is presented in full front view, with the head more or less turned to profile) rests on the 'standing leg' while the foot of the 'free leg,' touching the ground only with the toes, steps outward; the pelvis is balanced against the thorax in such a way that the hip of the standing leg is slightly raised whereas the corresponding shoulder is slightly lowered" (*The Life and Art of Albrecht Dürer,* p. 86).

159 **that served as the model:** This possibility has been observed (along with many other salient details) by Koerner: "the backlit folds of Dürer's own left flank and haunch as they play against the underside of his arm are akin to this area of Adam's body" (Koerner, *The Moment of Self-Portraiture,* p. 239).

160 **the exact proportions:** Cf. Koerner, *The Moment of Self-Portraiture,* p. 195. The proportions are most elaborately worked out in Albrecht Dürer, *Vier Bücher von menschlicher Proportion (1528): mit einem Katalog der Holzschnitte,* ed. Berthold Hinz (Berlin: Akademie Verlag, 2011). See also Christian Schoen, *Albrecht Dürer: Adam und Eva. Die Gemälde, ihre Geschichte und Rezeption bei Lucas Cranach d. Ä. und Hans Baldung Grien;* Anne-Marie Bonnet, *"Akt" bei Dürer.*

Chapter 9: Chastity and Its Discontents

164 **learned Anglican churchman:** Milton's less gifted younger brother Christopher was "designed" by his father, as one of the poet's early biographers put it, for the law. In *The Reason of Church Government,* Milton wrote that "by the intentions of my parents and friends, I was destin'd of a child" to the service of the church, "and in mine own resolutions, till comming to some maturity of yeers, and perceaving what tyranny had invaded the church, that he who would take Orders must subscribe slave . . . I thought it better to preferre a blameless silence before the sacred office of speaking, bought and begun with servitude and forswearing" (Milton, "The Reason of Church Government," in *Complete Prose Works of John Milton,* p. 108).

164 **ogling pretty girls:** Or so he claimed in a Latin poem written to his friend Charles Diodati: "Often here you can see groups of young girls pass by: stars breathing forth seductive flames. Ah, how many times I have been amazed at the miracles of a worthy figure which could reverse the old age of Jove!" ("Elegia Prima ad Carolum Diodatum," in *The Complete Poetry and Essential Prose of John Milton,* p. 174). All citations of Milton's poetry are to this edition. On the rustica-

tion, see Barbara Kiefer Lewalski, *The Life of John Milton: A Critical Biography*, pp. 21–22. When he returned to Christ's College, Milton took what was at the time the highly unusual step of finding a different tutor.

164 **"an inordinate and riotous youth":** Quoted by Milton in *An Apology for Smectymnuus*, 1642, in *Milton on Himself: Milton's Utterances Upon Himself and His Works*, p. 73.

165 **drinking and whoring:** A few encounters with his rapier tongue seem to have turned the tide. He became celebrated for his satirical orations (all in Latin, of course) and was even chosen by his fellow students to deliver the annual vacation address. The "Lady of Christ's" took the occasion to remark on "the new-found friendliness" (Milton, "The Reason of Church Government," in *Complete Prose Works of John Milton*) of his classmates—a surprising change from the "hostility and dislike" he had come to expect. "Why do I seem to them too little of a man?" he asked, reflecting on the nickname he had been given.

> It is, I suppose, because I have never brought myself to toss off great bumpers like a prize-fighter, or because my hand has never grown horny with driving the plough, or because I was never a farm hand at seven or laid myself down full length in the midday sun; or last perhaps because I never showed my virility in the way these brothellers do. (Ibid., p. 284)

It is characteristic of Milton that he carefully saved this and other of his undergraduate literary performances. More than forty years later he published them, still taking pleasure, it seems, in his riposte: "I wish they could leave playing the ass as readily as I the woman" (ibid., p. 284).

165 **It was to this intimate friend:** "Know that I cannot help loving people like you," he wrote to Diodati; "For though I do not know what else God may have decreed for me, this certainly is true: he has instilled into me, if into anyone, a vehement love of the beautiful" (*The Complete Poetry and Essential Prose*, p. 774).

165 **a great poet:** "By labour and intent study (which I take to be my portion in this life)," he reflected, "joyn'd with the strong propensity of nature, I might perhaps leave something so written to aftertimes, as they should not willingly let it die" (Milton, *The Reason of Church Government,* in *Complete Prose Works of John Milton*, vol. 1, p. 11).

167 **not the author's private statement:** The poet is not directly present, as he is in "Lycidas," where he worries that he too, like his drowned friend, will be cut off before his prime (*The Complete Poetry and Essential Prose*, pp. 100–110).

167 **concern with virginity focused on unmarried girls:** That is how it functions, for example, in Shakespeare's late plays, where there is an intense interest in the preservation of the virginity of the young heroines—Innogen, Marina, Perdita, and Miranda—and very little concern about the virginity of the young men who woo (and eventually marry) them.

167 **"both the image and glory of God":** Milton, *An Apology for Smectymnuus*, 1642, in *Milton on Himself: Milton's Utterances upon Himself and His Works,* p. 81; in Edward Le Comte, *Milton and Sex*, p. 18.

168 **resist the seduction:** Even as a young reader, Milton wrote, he taught himself to

distinguish firmly between the poetic skill on display in the works he most admired and the values that those works expressed. If there was anything that threatened to compromise chastity, he knew how to respond: "their art I still applauded, but the men I deplored" (*Milton on Himself: Milton's Utterances upon Himself and His Works*, p. 78). And the love poets he most admired—Dante and Petrarch—were never guilty of transgression. The problem, of course, is that the women they addressed, Beatrice and Laura, were both dead at the time they wrote their love poems. In poetry as in real life, desire for the living is an altogether different matter.

168 **"a prisoner"**: Milton, *Areopagitica*, in *The Complete Poetry and Essential Prose*, p. 950. Galileo had been confined since his condemnation in 1633.

169 **"the exact humanity and civility"**: See the account in Helen Derbyshire, *The Early Lives of Milton* (London: Constable & Co., 1932), pp. 56–57, cited in Lewalski, *The Life of John Milton: A Critical Biography*, p. 91.

169 **in a state of sexual innocence:** It is possible, of course, that Milton's sexual interests lay elsewhere. There was an unmistakable erotic intensity in his expressions of love for Charles Diodati, the young man to whose beauty he declared that he was drawn. In Florence he immediately struck up a friendship with a gifted nineteen-year-old scientist whose name—Carlo Dati—strikingly recalled that of his English friend. And in Italy the same air of arousal and availability certainly extended to homosexual as well as heterosexual liaisons. But Milton's anxiety about "the lewd and lavish act of sin" as a threat to spiritual and creative life would hardly have been suspended in the company of men.

169 **"was hated by the Italians"**: Quoted in Lewalski, *The Life of John Milton: A Critical Biography*, p. 99. "He both disputed freely about religion, and on any occasion whatever prated very bitterly against the Roman Pontiff." Heinsius, who had two illegitimate children with the daughter of a Lutheran minister, may have had personal reasons for resenting Milton's moral high-mindedness.

170 **"the lodging place"**: Milton, *Defensio Secunda*, in *Complete Prose Works of John Milton*, vol. 1, p. 609.

171 **mired in error:** Nominally Protestant, these ecclesiastical grandees, ardent supporters of the king, seemed to Milton virtually indistinguishable in theology as well as arrogance from the corrupt Roman Catholic prelates he had seen in Italy.

172 **Puritans:** The term, intended as a sneer, had, as Milton understood it, a core of truth, for these people were in fact determined to return England to the purity of scriptural Christianity and to a church worthy of that sacred origin.

172 **matters began to come to a head:** Parliament refused to grant the king the funds he demanded to support a war against the Scottish Presbyterians, who had rebelled against the bishops and the Anglican liturgy. Charles attempted to rule without Parliamentary consent, but his principal adviser, the Earl of Strafford, was tried for treason and executed. Loath to compromise, the king pursued his plans all the same, but the disciplined Scots, though greatly outnumbered, routed the poorly trained and underfunded English troops.

172 **"avarice, dotage, and diseases"**: *Animadversions upon the Remonstrants Defence, Against Smectymnuus*, in Milton, *Complete Prose Works of John Milton*, vol. 1, p. 655.

172 **"sanctified bitterness":** John Milton, *An Apology for Smectymnuus,* in *Complete Prose Works of John Milton*, vol. 1, p. 900.

173 **his purity:** "A certain niceness of Nature," as he put it in a characteristic piece of syntactically complex, sinuous prose, "an honest haughtiness, and self-esteem either of what I was, or what I might be (which let envy call pride), and lastly that Modesty, whereof though not in the Title-page, yet here I may be excus'd to make some beseeming profession; all these uniting the supply of their natural aid together, kept me still above those low descents of mind beneath which he must deject and plunge himself that can agree to saleable and unlawful prostitutions" (*Apology for Smectymnuus,* in *Complete Prose Works of John Milton,* vol 1, p. 890).

173 **he brought home with him a wife:** How this precipitous marriage came about is unclear. The principal source of information is Edward Phillips, Milton's nephew and one of those adolescents whom he was educating at home. Phillips was twelve at the time; more than fifty years later he recalled the surprising turn of events:

> About Whitsuntide it was, or a little after, that he took a Journey into the Countrey; no body about him certainly knowing the Reason, or that it was any more than a journey of Recreation. After a Month's stay, home he returns a married Man, who went out a bachelor. (Edward Phillips, "The Life of Milton," in *John Milton: Complete Poems and Major Prose,* ed. Merritt Y. Hughes, p. 1031)

Perhaps Milton himself was just as surprised.

174 **"must not be call'd a defilement":** *Apology for Smectymnuus,* in *John Milton: Complete Poems and Major Prose,* ed. Merritt Y. Hughes, p. 695. He had long brooded on the scene in the Book of Revelations when a voice sounded from heaven "as the voice of many waters, and as the voice of a great thunder," and the glorious sound was answered by "the voice of harpers harping with their harps: and they sung as it were a new song before the throne" (14:2–3). Milton, who longed to sing this song of the redeemed, read that they alone could sing it "which were not defiled with women, for they are virgins" (14:4). Would a married man then be excluded from this chorus? No, Milton declared, that was absolutely not the conclusion that any right-thinking Christian should draw.

174 **God Himself had instituted it:** Marriage, the Anglican marriage ceremony declared, is "an honourable estate, instituted of God in the time of man's innocency" (Brian Cummings, *The Book of Common Prayer,* p. 434).

175 **"on the same bolster":** John Aubrey, *Brief Lives,* p. 20.

176 **Mary stayed put at Forest Hill:** The Powells, Milton's nephew wrote, "began to repent them of having matched the eldest daughter of the family to a person so contrary to them in opinion, and thought it would be a blot in their escutcheon whenever that court should come to flourish again" (Edward Phillips, "The Life of Milton," in *John Milton: Complete Poems and Major Prose,* p. 1031).

177 **a London Underground station:** It is the tube station called Chiswick Park, and not the nearby one called Turnham Green, that is closest to the site of the battle.

177 **in his own way extraordinarily brave:** Abandoned by his wife after a few short weeks and snubbed by her family, Milton determined to pick up the pieces. Increasing the number of pupils he had undertaken to educate, he thought up and put in practice a new course of study, one that he hoped would serve as the basis for reforming England's educational system. His goal, characteristically, was not a modest one, and characteristically too in explaining it Milton reached all the way back to Adam and Eve. The ultimate purpose of an education, he wrote in a pamphlet describing his proposed curriculum, "is to repair the ruins of our first parents" (*Of Education,* in *Complete Prose Works of John Milton,* 2: 366).

177 **unbelievable courage or, alternatively, unbelievable self-absorption:** "I resolved at length," he wrote, reflecting on his own rash venture, "to put off into this wild and calumnious world. For God, it seems, intended to prove me, whether I durst alone take up a rightful cause against a world of disesteem, and found I durst" (Milton, *Judgment of Martin Bucer, Concerning Divorce,* in Milton, *The Divorce Tracts of John Milton,* p. 203).

178 **an annulment:** The grounds were that Catherine's earlier marriage to his deceased older brother Arthur rendered their union technically invalid according to canon law.

178 **the knot could not be untied:** A refusal or inability to consummate a marriage could be grounds for annulment, but as Milton never raised the issue, it was apparently not in question here. It is certainly possible that a husband who is unable to consummate his marriage or whose wife categorically refuses to sleep with him might choose not to broadcast that fact. But Milton's description in his divorce tracts of the unpleasantness of sexual intercourse in an unhappy marriage—"to grind in the mill of an undelighted and servile copulation" (*Doctrine and Discipline of Divorce,* in *The Divorce Tracts of John Milton,* p.118)—is more likely to suggest what actually occurred or rather what it felt like to him.

178 **cases of desertion:** After an absence of seven years, the abandoned husband or wife could petition to have the missing spouse ruled dead, but there were risks: one such spouse returned and claimed his place, though his wife had remarried.

178 **not just for him alone:** Milton had already given some thought to the question of divorce; it was implicit in the general Puritan interest in companionate marriage. But he had not worked out a serious argument in any sustained way.

179 **"the rubbish of canonical ignorance":** *Doctrine and Discipline of Divorce,* in *The Divorce Tracts of John Milton,* p. 95. Custom, Milton wrote, "puffs up unhealthily a certain big face of pretended learning" that intimidates credulous men and women. No one in his right mind should meekly submit to the "tyranny of stupid and malicious monks." The monks set up the whole repressive system, Milton wrote, because "having rashly vowed themselves to a single life, which they could not undergo," they "invented new fetters to throw on matrimony, that the world thereby waxing more dissolute, they also in a general looseness might sin with more favor" (*Judgment of Martin Bucer, Concerning Divorce,* in *The Divorce Tracts of John Milton,* p. 201). That is, unable to bear the yoke of celibacy, discontented cler-

ics knew that they would stand more of a chance of sexual adventures if the general married population was made miserable.

179 **Jesus reminds them:** Reasonably enough, the Pharisees then asked Jesus what he made of the Mosaic law (in Deut. 24:1 and elsewhere) that permits divorce. The Savior's response was apparently unequivocal and uncompromising: "I say unto you, Whosoever shall put away his wife, except it be for fornication, and shall marry another, committeth adultery" (Matt. 8–9).

179 **The New Testament was good news:** "Our Savior's doctrine is, that the end, and the fulfilling of every command is charity" (Milton, *Tetrachordon*, in *The Divorce Tracts of John Milton*, p. 291).

180 **"Loneliness is the first thing":** *Tetrachordon*, p. 254.

180 **He found the lesson unbearable:** Milton married—as almost everyone marries—in the hope and expectation of finding what he called "an intimate and speaking help, a ready and reviving associate." That was, he thought, the point of marriage for Adam before the Fall, and it is still more the point for all of us born after the Fall into an infinitely harsher, more painful world where we need all the help and intimacy we can get. To marry the wrong person is a disaster. He "who misses by chancing on a mute and spiritless mate," Milton wrote, glancing back on what had happened to him, "remains more alone than before" (*Doctrine and Discipline of Divorce*, in *The Divorce Tracts of John Milton*, pp. 113–14). Cf. *Tetrachordon* in ibid., pp. 256–57: Marriage, "if it bring a mind perpetually averse and disagreeable, betrays us to a worse condition than the most deserted loneliness."

181 **"when the minds are fitly disposed":** Two letters, both in Greek, survive from Diodati to Milton, and both dwell on conversation. "So much do I desire your company," Diodati writes in one of them, "that in my longing I dream of and all but prophecy fair weather and calm, and everything golden for tomorrow, so that we may enjoy our fill of philosophical and learned conversation." "I have no complaint with my present way of life with this one exception," he writes in the other surviving letter, "that I lack some noble soul skilled in conversation" (*The Complete Poetry and Essential Prose of John Milton*, p. 767).

182 **"to grind in the mill":** *Doctrine and Discipline of Divorce*, in *The Divorce Tracts of John Milton*, p.118.

182 **"two carcasses":** Ibid., p. 77. On the hate that Milton experienced in marriage, instead of conversation, see, p. 49; cf. p. 115.

183 **ridicule and outrage:** Some of the harshest attacks came from quarters where Milton might have expected to find allies, among the Presbyterians and Independent preachers who were themselves sworn enemies of the bishops. In a sermon, one such preacher, Herbert Palmer, warned members of Parliament that "a wicked book is abroad and uncensored, though deserving to be burnt." Another attacked Milton as the author of "a tractate of divorce in which the bonds are let loose to inordinate lust" (*The Divorce Tracts of John Milton*, pp. 52, 78). See Gordon Campbell and Thomas N. Corns, *John Milton: Life, Work, and Thought*, pp. 165–67. So much for his fantasy (*Doctrine and Discipline of Divorce*, p. 42) of being celebrated as one of the public benefactors of humankind.

183 **"blasphemy against Christ himself":** *An Answer to a Book, Intituled, The Doctrine and Discipline of Divorce*, in Milton, *The Divorce Tracts of John Milton,* p. 430.

183 **"except she can speak Hebrew":** Milton should have taken the time, his critics observed, to acquaint himself in advance with the woman he decided to marry. If he is now unhappy with her conversational abilities, he can go out and find a more suitable person to talk to, even another woman, "provided he meddles not with her body" (434). But he cannot dissolve his marriage and take another wife, for the social consequences of this behavior, writ large, would be disastrous: "Who sees not, how many thousands of lustful and libidinous men would be parting from their wives every week and marrying others: and upon this, who should keep the children of these divorces which sometimes they would leave in their wives' bellies?" (quoted in Gordon Campbell and Thomas N. Corns, *John Milton: Life, Work, and Thought*, p. 166). Think about those abandoned wives and infants, opponents of divorce warned, forced to turn to the parish for alms.

184 **"comfort in the married state":** *Tetrachordon*, in *The Divorce Tracks of John Milton,* p. 255.

184 **"brazen ass":** All terms of abuse in the *Colesterion.*

184 **a liberator who is spurned:** "I did but prompt the age to quit their clogs," he wrote in an unpublished sonnet. And, of course, it was not just "the age" in general that was weighted down, like an animal prevented from straying, by its clogs; it was Milton himself who could not recover his freedom. The owls and cuckoos, asses, apes, and dogs had trapped him.

185 **"a sort of rainbow":** Letter to Leonard Philaris, dated September 28, 1654, quoted in Lewalski, *The Life of John Milton: A Critical Biography*, p. 181.

185 **against censorship:** See *The Reason of Church Government* in *Complete Prose Works of John Milton*, vol.1, p. 784: "If to bring a numb and chill stupidity of soul, an unactive blindness of mind, upon the people by their leaden doctrine, or no doctrine at all . . . be to keep away schism, they [the clerical censors] keep schism away indeed. . . . With as good a plea might the dead-palsy boast to a man, 'tis I that free you from stitches and pains." "The censure of the church," Milton concluded, should "be quite divested and disintail'd of all jurisdiction whatsoever."

185 **"as kill a good book":** *Areopagitica*, in *The Complete Poetry and Essential Prose of John Milton*, p. 930.

185 **laws that he was convinced were unjust:** It was not only a matter of his public stance: Milton was determined not to bury his hopes for personal happiness. He made plans to move to a new, much larger house—where he would bring his father, now in his early eighties—and to take on new students. According to his nephew, he began to spend evenings in the company of a married woman of "great wit and ingenuity," Lady Margaret Lee, to whom he wrote a sonnet of praise. The point is not that Milton had an adulterous affair; given his moral high-mindedness, that seems highly unlikely. Rather, he seems to have set out to prove to himself that he could find with the right woman the "delectableness of converse" that his polemical enemies said could only be found in the company of another man. Moreover, his nephew wrote, Milton actually proposed marriage

at this time to "a very handsome and witty gentlewoman" who was, however, "averse" to his proposal. Small wonder that she was averse: Milton may have told himself (and her) that he was free simply to declare himself to be divorced, but the rest of the world would have regarded his remarriage as bigamy.

186 **the decisive battle of the Civil War:** Rage that must have been building up during the many months of attack and counterattack boiled over. Royalist troops who blundered into the hands of the victors were slaughtered. The captured wives and mistresses bought their freedom by parting with their money and jewels—the pillage was reckoned to equal £100,000 in gold—but more than a hundred poor whores and serving-women in the king's camp were hacked to death. (Cf. C. V. Wedgwood, *The King's War: 1641–1647*, pp. 427–28.)

187 **He took up his repentant bride:** His nephew, who was fifteen years old at the time, provides an account that he acknowledges is only conjecture: "He might probably at first make some show of aversion and rejection; but partly his own generous nature, more inclinable to Reconciliation than to perseverance in Anger and Revenge; and partly the strong intercession of Friends on both sides, soon brought him to an Act of Oblivion, and a firm League of Peace for the future" (Edward Phillips, in Hughes, *John Milton: Complete Poems and Major Prose*, p. 1032).

187 **her interfering mother:** Milton's early anonymous biographer reports that Mary later accused her mother of inciting her to her "forwardness" (William Riley Parker, *Milton: A Biography*, 2: 864).

188 **"till death us depart":** This is the phrase used in the 1559 Book of Common Prayer. It was revised in the 1662 Book of Common Prayer to "till death us do part." See Cummings, *The Book of Common Prayer: The Texts of 1549, 1559, and 1662.*

188 **"about 3 days after":** Parker, 2: 1009. Jotting down the precise date and time of a birth was conventional—probably a holdover, even in those who may not have believed in astrology, of the notations needed to make the correct divinations—but would not ordinary human ties have led a grieving husband to record the actual date when his wife passed away? One of Milton's most learned and admiring modern biographers wished to believe that Milton had, in the moment that Mary knelt down before him, realized that he still loved her (Parker, *Milton: A Biography*, 1: 299). It seems to me highly unlikely, but stranger things have happened. Perhaps in that case Milton's vagueness was not a sign of estrangement. Perhaps precision simply did not seem important either for the dead, whose earthly story was over, or for the living, who must now move on. Shortly after Mary's death followed the death of their fifteen-month-old son John, and in his Bible entry Milton was once again vague on the details: "And my son about six weeks after his mother" (Parker, 2: 1014).

Chapter 10: The Politics of Paradise

189 **his incendiary little rhyme:** ". . . servitude had been introduced by the unjust and evil oppression of men, against the will of God, who, if it had pleased Him

to create serfs, surely in the beginning of the world would have appointed who should be a serf and who a lord." Ball's reputed words were noted by his aristocratic enemy, Thomas Walsingham. Cf. Albert Friedman, "'When Adam Delved . . .': Contexts, of an Historic Proverb," in Benson, *The Learned and the Lewd*, pp. 213–30. Also Steven Justice, *Writing and Rebellion: England in 1381*. As it circulated more widely, Ball's reminder of the nature of the first humans was not always and necessarily a call to revolt; it could simply be a call to humility. Owst quotes the Dominican Bromyard:

> All are descended from the same first parents, and all come of the same mud. For, if God had fashioned nobles from gold, and the ignoble from mud, then the former would have cause for pride. . . . True glory does not depend upon the origin or beginning from which anything proceeds, but upon its own condition. (quoted in G. R. Owst, *Literature and Pulpit in Medieval England*, p. 292)

191 **"We must bring these histories home":** Robert Everard, *The Creation and Fall of Adam Reviewed*. I am grateful to Dr. Stephen Hequembourg for this and the reference to George Fox.

191 **the founder of the Quakers:** *The Journal of George Fox*.

191 **"A little Adam in a sphere/Of Joys":** Thomas Traherne, "Innocence," in Thomas Traherne, *Centuries, Poems, and Thanksgiving*, ed. H. M. Margoliouth, 2 vols. (Oxford: Clarendon Press, 1958), 2: 18. Cf. *Centuries* 3:1: "Adam in Paradice had not more sweet and Curious Apprehensions of the World, then I when I was a child" (1: 110).

193 **"being born free":** *Of Prelatical Episcopacy*, in *Complete Prose Works of John Milton*, 1: 625.

195 **Private property is the fatal fruit:** "The Apple that the first man eats, is not a single fruit called an Apple, or such like fruit; but it is the objects of the Creation" (Gerrard Winstanley, *New Law of Righteousness*, in *The Works of Gerrard Winstanley*).

195 **"And this is *Adam*":** Winstanley, *Fire in the Bush*, in *Works*, p. 220. For the wide range of visions of Adam in this period, see Julia Ipgrave, *Adam in Seventeenth Century Political Writing in England and New England*, and Joanna Picciotto, *Labors of Innocence in Early Modern England*.

195 **"the whole earth shall be a common treasury":** Winstanley, *New Law of Righteousness*, in *Works*, p. 184. This "communist" interpretation of Eden, with its roots in John Ball's radicalism, was vigorously disputed in seventeenth-century England by a conservative interpretation that saw in Adam the first patriarch, landowner, and ruler. See Robert Filmer, *"Patriarcha" and Other Political Works*, ed. Peter Laslett (New York: Garland, 1984): "This lordship which Adam by creation had over the whole world, and by right descending from him, the Patriarchs did enjoy, was as large and ample as the absolutest dominion of any monarch which hath been since the creation" (p. 58).

196 **"the floating vessel of our faith":** *The Reason of Church Government* in Milton, *Complete Poems and Major Prose*, ed. Hughes, p. 662.

199 **But these hideous deaths were not enough:** The object of greatest loathing,

Oliver Cromwell, had signed the death warrant and had served as the principal pillar of the Commonwealth that followed, but his death in 1658 put certain limits on the retribution the Royalists could take. Nonetheless, they did what they could: exhuming Cromwell's corpse from its grave in Westminster Abbey, where it had been moldering for more than two years, they dragged it face-down on a sled through the streets of London, along with the decaying corpses of John Bradshaw, who had served as president of the court that tried the king, and Henry Ireton, Cromwell's son-in-law and a general in the Parliamentary army. On the anniversary of the king's execution, the three dead men were hauled up onto a scaffold and hanged by the neck. At nightfall the remains—now dead twice over—were beheaded and thrown into an unmarked pit. Their heads were stuck on spikes in Westminster Hall, where the king had been tried, and remained there for years as a grisly warning.

199   **influential friends:** The principal friend is thought to be Milton's former assistant, the poet Andrew Marvell, who was serving in Parliament as the member from Hull. The poet and playwright William Davenant also claimed a hand in protecting Milton. Years before, when the Royalist Davenant was accused of treason and imprisoned in the Tower, Milton, then in power, intervened and helped save Davenant's life.

199   **"perpetual terror of being assassinated":** Reported by Jonathan Richardson, in Parker, *Milton: A Biography,* 1: 577.

Chapter 11: Becoming Real

208   **Satan leading a third of the angels:** Among the many accounts of the development of this backstory, see Neil Forsyth, *The Old Enemy: Satan and the Combat Myth* (Princeton: Princeton University Press, 1987), and, more recently, Dallas G. Denery II, *The Devil Wins.*

213   **whatever "redounded":** "Redounds" here refers to food that cannot be assimilated but must pass through the system and be excreted. Apart from his insistence on how sweet the Garden smelled, Milton did not directly speculate on this result, but Luther did: "non fuit foetor in excrementis," he wrote; that is, excrement in Eden did not stink (cited in Kurt Flasch, *Eva e Adamo: Metamorfosi di un mito,* p. 111, n. 27). Luther, who spoke of "my beloved Genesis," worked on commentaries and interpretations of it for much of his life. See Theo M. M. A. C. Bell, "Humanity Is a Microcosm: Adam and Eve in Luther's Lectures on Genesis (1535–45)," in *Out of Paradise: Eve and Adam and Their Interpreters,* ed. Bob Becking and Susanne Hennecke (Sheffield, UK: Sheffield Phoenix Press, 2011).

215   **Adam actually tried sex with all of the animals:** Yebamoth 63a. Part of the Mishnah (compiled in the first and second centuries ce), Yebamoth, a tractate of family law, takes off from a commentary on Deuteronomy 23:5 and 7–9.

216   **"This one":** Genesis 2:23, from *The Five Books of Moses,* trans. Robert Alter. The translation captures, better than the King James, the emphasis on "this one."

218   **"but this subjection of the wife":** Alexander Ross, *An Exposition on the Fourteen First Chapters of Genesis, by Way of Question and Answer,* p. 26.

220 **peered at her reflection:**

> As I bent down to look, just opposite,
> A shape within the wat'ry gleam appeared
> Bending to look on me, I started back,
> It started back, but pleased I soon returned,
> Pleased it returned as soon with answering looks
> Of sympathy and love. (4:460–65)

226 **Had Milton's own heart actually relented:** There is at least one sign—though still an ambiguous one—that Milton may have worked through the bitterness and reached a renewed and deeper emotional bond. Perhaps the most moving lyric he ever wrote was a sonnet about a dream in which he thought he saw his dead wife—"his late espousèd saint"—returned to him from the grave (John Milton, "Sonnet XXIII," in Milton, *Complete Poems and Major Prose,* p. 170):

> And such, as yet once more I trust to have
> Full sight of her in Heaven without restraint,
> Came vested all in white, pure as her mind:
> Her face was veiled, yet to my fancied sight,
> Love, sweetness, goodness in her person shined
> So clear, as in no face with more delight.
> But O as to embrace me she inclined,
> I waked, she fled, and day brought back my night.

It was long assumed that the "late espousèd saint" was the poet's second wife Katherine, but in the mid-twentieth century, Milton's great biographer, William Riley Parker, argued that the wife in question must have been Mary. Milton was already blind when he married Katherine, Parker noted, and he could therefore not have hoped "once more" to have full sight of her in heaven. It was Mary on whose face he had once looked with so much delight. This argument is a slender reed on which to construct a confident account of renewed love.

Chapter 12: Men Before Adam

232 **without any other people around:** In his Proeme to *A Theological System* (London, 1655), La Peyrère rehearses the "natural suspition" that the world did not begin with Adam. This suspicion springs from the more ancient accounts of other peoples. Also, he says, it sprung up in him already as a child, "when I heard or read the History of Genesis Where Cain goes forth, where he kills his brother when they were in the field; doing it warily, like a thief, least it should be discovered by any: Where he flies where he fears punishment for the death of his Brother: Lastly, where he marries a wife far from his Ancestors, and builds a City."

233 **circle of daring philosophers:** The group included such intellectual giants as Blaise Pascal, Marin Mersenne, Pierre Gassendi, Hugo Grotius, and Thomas Hobbes.

233 **in his diary entry:** *"Ellos andan todos desnudos como su madre los parió; y también las*

mugeres." *The "Diario" of Christopher Columbus's First Voyage to America, 1492–1493,* pp. 64–65.

233   **had degenerated into their bestial state:** Cf. H. W. Janson, *Apes and Ape Lore in the Middle Ages and the Renaissance* (London: Warburg Institute, 1952).

235   **"But I am much more convinced":** Cf. Stephen Greenblatt, *Marvelous Possessions,* pp. 78–79.

235   **the four great rivers that surged up:** Jean Delumeau, *History of Paradise,* pp. 156–57.

235   **Columbus's conviction:** "Not the Elysian Fields, like the pagans," he wrote, "but the earthy Paradise, as Catholic, was located there" (*no los Campos Elíseos, como los gentiles, sino, como católico, el paraíso terrenal*). Las Casas, *Historia de las Indias* II: 50, in Santa Arias, "Bartolomé de las Casas's Sacred Place of History," in Arias et al., *Mapping Colonial Spanish America,* p. 127.

236   **"without malice or guile":** Las Casas, *A Short Account of the Destruction of the Indies,* p. 9. "I have time and again met Spanish laymen who have been so struck by the natural goodness that shines through these people that they frequently can be heard to exclaim: 'These would be the most blessed people on earth if only they were given the chance to convert to Christianity'" (pp. 10–11).

236   **close to the truth:** Cf. Woodrow Borah and Sherburne F. Cook, *Essays in Population History.*

236   **Who are the genuinely civilized people and who the barbarians?:** "I think there is more barbarity in eating a man alive than in eating him dead," Montaigne writes in his essay "Of Cannibals," "and in tearing by tortures and the rack a body still full of feeling, in roasting a man bit by bit, in having him bitten and mangled by dogs and swine (as we have not only read but seen within fresh memory, not among ancient enemies, but among neighbors and fellow citizens, and what is worse, on the pretext of piety and religion), than in roasting and eating him after he is dead. (Montaigne, "Of Cannibals," in Montaigne, *The Complete Essays of Montaigne,* p. 155). The French Wars of Religion, to whose horrors Montaigne is referring, undermined for him and for many of his contemporaries any confident faith in the tenets of religious orthodoxy. It is telling that the close of his essay is an ironic joke about the natives' nakedness: "All this is not too bad—but what's the use? They don't wear breeches" (159).

237   **"hath occasioned some difficulty and dispute":** Matthew Hale, in Almond, *Adam and Eve in Seventeenth-Century Thought,* 49. See, similarly, La Peyrère, *Two Essays Sent in a Letter from Oxford to a Nobleman in London:* "The West-Indies, and the vast *Regions,* lately discovered towards the South, abound with such variety of Inhabitants, and New Animals, not known or ever seen in *Asia, Africa,* or *Europe,* that the *Origine* of them doth not appear so clear as some late *Writers* pretend . . . and their differences from all the rest of the *Globe,* in Manners, Languages, Habits, Religions, Diet, Arts, and Customs, as well as in their Quadrupeds, Birds, Serpents and Insects, render their Derivation very obscure, and their Origine uncertain, especially in the common way, and according to

the vulgar Opinions of Planting all the Earth from one little Spot." No surprise that this was published anonymously, even in 1695.

237 **the vast numbers of humans:** "The Bible indicates," he wrote, "that the survivors produced all of the Nations on earth in five generations. But could they really have produced the inhabitants of China, America, the Southland and Greenland, among others? Could this even account for the population of Europe?" (quoted in Richard Henry Popkin, *Isaac La Peyrère [1596–1676]: His Life, Work, and Influence*, p. 51).

239 **"acorns or arbute berries or choice pears":** Lucretius, *On the Nature of Things*, 5: 963–65.

239 **Maximus Tyrius:** In Arthur O. Lovejoy and George Boas, *Primitivism and Related Ideas in Antiquity*, p. 149.

239 **"not planted by the hand of man":** The Eleatic stranger in Plato's *Statesman*, in *Primitivism and Related Ideas in Antiquity*, pp. 121–22.

240 **Herodotus . . . Berossus:** Herodotus, *The Histories*, trans. Aubrey de Sélincourt, rev. John Marincola (London: Penguin, 1972), 2: 142. For Berossus, see Berossus, *The Babyloniaca of Berossus* (Malibu, CA: Undena Publications: 1978).

240 **a government spy:** Richard Baines, "Baines Note," in BL Harley MS.6848 ff.185–6 (http://www.rey.myzen.co.uk/baines1.htm).

240 **"memorials of ten thousand years and more":** *Spaccio della Bestia trionfante* (1584), in *Dialoghi italiani: Dialoghi metafisici e dialoghi morali*, 3rd ed., ed. Giovanni Aquilecchia, pp. 797–98; in Popkin, *Isaac La Peyrère*, p. 35.

242 **"a great danger imminent to religion":** Grotius, quoted in Popkin, *Isaac La Peyrère*, p. 6.

242 ***Men Before Adam:*** The English text is bound together with *A Theological System*.

243 **not Moses's own copy:** "I know not by what author it is found out, that the Pentateuch is Moses his own copy. It is so reported, but not believ'd by all. These Reasons make me believe, that those Five Books are not the Originals, but copied out by another, Because Moses is there read to have died. For how could Moses write after his death? They say, that Josuah added the death of Moses to Deuteronomie. But, who added the death of Josuah to that book which is so call'd?" (Popkin, *Isaac La Peyrère*, pp. 204–5). La Peyrère was not alone in noticing the problems with claiming a direct transmission from Moses. The authorship problem caused by the inclusion of Moses's death had long been noticed, and in the seventeenth century the French Protestant scholar Louis Cappel "had counted up eighteen hundred variants, amongst the various versions of the Hebrew Scriptures that had come down to his time" (ibid., p. 50).

244 **much larger history of humanity:** "There is great errour in reading the Scripture many times, when that is taken more more [sic] generally, which ought to be particularly understood: as that of Adam, whom Moses made first Father of the Jews, and whom we hyberbolically [sic] call the first Father of all men" (in Popkin, *Isaac La Peyrère*, p. 119).

245 **salvation through Jesus:** La Peyère struggled to work out the complex theology

that this argument entailed: The sin of Adam, he wrote, "was imputed backward unto those first men that were created before Adam" (in Popkin, *Isaac La Peyrère*, p. 46). Why? Not for their destruction but rather for their salvation. For it is only if they had sinned, on the similitude (as he puts it) of the transgression of Adam, that they could partake in the glory and salvation of Christ. "They had perished, had they not perished" (47). He argues also that no one, after Adam and Eve, could sin as they had sinned, since it was not possible to eat of the Tree of the Knowledge of Good and Evil. All subsequent sin was "according to the similitude of the transgression of Adam" (37).

246   **nearly universal outrage:** Already a century earlier the Greek-born Dominican friar Jacob Palaeologus had been beheaded in Rome for suggesting that all humans might not have descended from Adam and Eve and for proposing that Judaism, Christianity, and Islam all offer legitimate routes to salvation.

246   **the pope smiled:** Father Richard Simon heard this from La Peyrère. (In Popkin, pp. 14 and 181, n. 61.)

248   **no mathematical reason:** The problem indeed is not that there are too many people for the time allotted between Adam and Eve and the present, but rather that there are too few. See Dominic Klyve, "Darwin, Malthus, Süssmilch, and Euler: The Ultimate Origin of the Motivation for the Theory of Natural Selection."

Chapter 13: Falling Away

252   **"Who could be found so silly?":** Origen, quoted in Almond, *Adam and Eve in Seventeenth-Century Thought*, p. 66.

252   **"if no trees, then no eating of the fruit":** Epiphanius, quoted in Nicholas Gibbons, *Questions and Disputations Concerning the Holy Scripture.*

255   **Bayle's imagined heretic:** Pierre Bayle (1647–1706). *An Historical and Critical Dictionary. By Monsieur Bayle. Translated into English, with many additions and corrections, made by the author himself, that are not in the French editions*, 4: 2487).

256   **the knife will be used:** "I did not tell him to use the knife," Bayle imagines the ruler sputtering after the crime has been committed. "On the contrary, I specifically ordered him *not* to use it." But the defense is worthless: the ruler understood perfectly well that a man placed in those circumstances would do exactly what he did and bring about untold miseries. It was in the ruler's power to stop it, and yet he inexplicably chose not to do so.

256   **A simple peasant understands:** As for the supposed justice of the punishments inflicted on Adam and Eve and their offspring, Bayle wrote, surely it is far better "to hinder an Assassin from killing a Man, than to break him upon the Wheel after he has been permitted to commit the Murder" (2488). If the climactic Christian answer is that God wished to demonstrate His great goodness by ultimately redeeming sinful humankind, then the dilemma, Bayle insisted, is even greater. Such a deity would resemble a father who allowed his son to break his legs—

though he could easily have prevented it—in order to demonstrate to the whole city his skill in making a very nice cast. What kind of God is that?

257 *"I don't know"*: "La meilleure réponse qu'on puisse faire naturellement à la question, *Pourquoi Dieu a-t-il permis que l'homme péchât?* est de dire: *J'en sais rien"* (ibid., 504). In still another footnote he glossed the word "naturally." It meant, he explained, "without consulting revelation." It is impossible, I think, to determine whether there is any irony here.

262 **Adam-ondi-Ahman:** Ezra Taft Benson, *The Teachings of Ezra Taft Benson*, pp. 587–88.

262 **Emerson imagined himself:** Ralph Waldo Emerson, journal entry for October 18, 1839, in *The Journals and Miscellaneous Notebooks of Ralph Waldo Emerson*, p. 270.

262 **"Walden Pond was already in existence":** Henry D. Thoreau, *Walden* (Boston: Ticknor & Fields, 1864), chapter 9.

Chapter 14: Darwin's Doubts

269 **Darwinism is not incompatible with belief in God:** Darwinism has inspired rigorously nontheological accounts of the genesis of life, as in John Maynard Smith and Eörs Szathmáry, *The Origins of Life*. But such accounts have failed to dismantle faith. See, for example, Alvin Plantinga, *Where the Conflict Really Lies*, and Berry et al., *Theology After Darwin*.

270 **Exactly how and when:** Merlin Donald, *Origins of the Modern Mind*: "We are no more than about 5 million years from an ancestor we shared with the chimpanzee. The oldest species within genus Homo are now dated at less than 2 million years old; the oldest remains of fully modern humans are only 50,000 to 100,000 years old" (p. 22).

271 **"with the determination not to publish":** Charles Darwin, *The Descent of Man, and Selection in Relation to Sex* (1871), in *From So Simple a Beginning: The Four Great Books of Charles Darwin*, p. 777. On the impact of Darwin's thought on the biblical account of creation, see John C. Greene, *The Death of Adam: Evolution and Its Impact on Western Thought*.

273 **ancient pagan theory:** Lucretius, *On the Nature of Things*, 5:932.

275 **White Cliffs of Dover:** "In order to make the reader acquainted with the physical structure of the Valley of the Weald," wrote Charles Lyell in the 1830s, describing the rolling hills in southeast England, "we shall suppose him first to travel southwards from the London basin. On leaving the tertiary strata he will first ascend a gently-inclined plane, composed of the upper flinty portion of the chalk, and then find himself on the summit of a declivity. . . . The geologist cannot fail to recognize in this view the exact likeness of a sea-cliff, and if he turns and looks in an opposite direction, or eastward, towards Beachy Head, he will see the same line of height prolonged. Even those who are not accustomed to speculate on the former changes which the surface has undergone, may fancy the broad and level plain to resemble the flat sands which were laid dry by the receding tide, and the

different projecting masses of chalk to be the headlands of a coast which separated the different bays from each other" (Charles Lyell, *Principles of Geology, Being an Attempt to Explain the Former Changes of the Earth's Surface, by Reference to Causes Now in Operation*, 3 vols. [London: J. Murray, 1832], 3: 289–90).

276 **Fossils, such as seashells:** See Paolo Rossi, *The Dark Abyss of Time.*

276 **Denis Henrion:** Cited in Andrew Dickson White, *A History of the Warfare of Science with Theology in Christianity*, p. 182.

277 **"the primal Head of the Human Race":** Philip H. Gosse, *Omphalos: An Attempt to Untie the Geological Knot*, p. 274.

278 **only the last volume has survived:** *On the Origin of Species* (1859), in *From So Simple a Beginning: The Four Great Books of Charles Darwin*, p. 647.

Epilogue: In the Forest of Eden

287 **much closer to the Last Common Ancestor:** Among other arguments for the resemblance of chimpanzees to the LCA are their striking morphological similarities to gorillas, presumably because neither has greatly changed since the divergence from humans.

290 **some scientists have claimed:** The claim has been contested by Russell H. Tuttle in *Apes and Human Evolution*, p. 576.

292 **they jump up and down and scream:** Fiercely xenophobic, they cling to one another if they detect alien chimps nearby. Their hair standing on end from their distress and loathing, they vomit or have bouts of diarrhea. I did not see this for myself, but it is described in many scientific accounts, including Toshisada Nishida, *Chimpanzees of the Lakeshore*, p. 246.

294 **they are very much like us:** The ancient views must have been based principally upon observations of monkeys and baboons, though there may have been early glimpses of the higher primates. Samuel Purchas, the great seventeenth-century collector of travel narratives, published Andrew Battell's 1607 account of his captivity in Africa. Battell describes a "monster" called by the natives a "pongo": "This Pongo is in all proportion like a man but that he is more like a Giant in stature, then a man: for he is very tall, and hath a mans face, hollow eyed, with long haire upon his browes" ("The Strange Adventures of Andrew Battell of Leigh in Essex, Sent by the Portugals Prisoner to Angola," in Samuel Purchas, *Hakluytus Posthumus, or Purchas His Pilgrimes*, 6: 398). See Dale Peterson and Jane Goodall, *Visions of Caliban: On Chimpanzees and People.* Chimpanzees and gorillas were not identified as a species and described by scientists until the modern period.

294 **they are amoral:** Tuttle, *Apes and Human Evolution.* There is plenty of room for argument here on all sides: some researchers would claim that chimpanzees do indeed have something like a sense of good and evil; others would claim that, however much they pretend that they possess it, humans lack that very sense.

294 **Machiavellian politics:** Frans de Waal, *Chimpanzee Politics: Power and Sex Among Apes.* See Machiavelli, *The Prince*, chap. 18, in *The Prince and the Discourses*, trans. Christian Detmold (New York: Modern Library, 1950), p. 65.

295 **raiding parties to murder:** Richard Wrangham and Dale Peterson, *Demonic Males: Apes and the Origins of Human Violence.*

296 **Sarah too resembled an ape:** Louis Ginzberg, *Legends of the Jews*, 1: 167.

296 **an ape often lurks somewhere nearby:** Cf. H. W. Janson, *Apes and Ape Lore in the Middle Ages and the Renaissance.*

297 **"I would rather be descended from an ape":** These are unlikely to have been Huxley's actual words, and the woman may have fainted from the heat or the crowd. See J. R. Lucas, "Wilberforce and Huxley: A Legendary Encounter," for criticism of possible legendary exaggeration; but even if the actual words were not exactly as remembered, the story circulated as a symbolic turning point.

297 **period of evolutionary ferment:** Ian Tattersall, *Masters of the Planet*, p. 85.

298 **The sinister philosophical parable:** Friedrich Nietzsche, *The Genealogy of Morals.*

299 **characteristics found in both chimpanzees and bonobos:** See Richard Wrangham and David Pilbeam, "African Apes as Time Machines," in *All Apes Great and Small,* vol. 1: *African Apes.*

Selected Bibliography

A longer bibliography of works I have consulted in writing this book may be found on my website, stephengreenblatt.com.

Adam, a Religious Play of the Twelfth Century. Translated by Edward N. Stone. Seattle: University of Washington Press, 1928.

Adar, Zvi. *The Book of Genesis: An Introduction to the Biblical World.* Translated by Philip Cohen. Jerusalem: Magnes Press, 1990.

Allen, Don Cameron. *The Legend of Noah: Renaissance Rationalism in Art, Science, and Letters.* Urbana: University of Illinois Press, 1949.

Almond, Philip C. *Adam and Eve in Seventeenth-Century Thought.* Cambridge: University of Cambridge Press, 2008.

Alter, Robert. *The Art of Biblical Narrative.* Rev. & updated ed. New York: Basic Books, 2011.

———, trans. *The Book of Psalms: A Translation with Commentary.* 1st ed. New York: W. W. Norton, 2007.

———, trans. *Five Books of Moses.* New York: W. W. Norton, 2004.

———, and Frank Kermode, eds. *The Literary Guide to the Bible.* Cambridge: Harvard University Press, 1987.

Anderson, Gary A. *The Genesis of Perfection: Adam and Eve in Jewish and Christian Imagination.* Louisville, KY: Westminster John Knox Press, 2001.

———. *Sin: A History.* New Haven: Yale University Press, 2009.

———, and Michael E. Stone, eds. *A Synopsis of the Books of Adam and Eve.* 2nd rev. ed. Atlanta: Scholars Press, 1999.

Andrewes, Lancelot. "A Lecture on Genesis 2:18," *Apospasmata Sacra, or A Collection of Posthumous and Orphan Lectures.* London, 1657.

Arendt, Hannah. *Love and Saint Augustine*. Edited by Judith Chelius Stark and Joanna Vecchiarelli Scott. Chicago: University of Chicago Press, 1996.

Arias, Santa. "Bartolomé De Las Casas's Sacred Place of History." In *Mapping Colonial Spanish America: Places and Commonplaces of Identity, Culture, and Experience*. Edited by Santa Arias and Mariselle Melé. Lewisburg, PA: Bucknell University Press, 2002.

Aubrey, John. *Brief Lives*. London: Penguin Books, 2000.

Auerbach, Erich. *Time, History, and Literature: Selected Essays of Erich Auerbach*. Edited by James I. Porter and Jane O. Newman. Princeton: Princeton University Press, 2014.

Augustine. "*The City of God.*" *St. Augustin: The City of God, and Christian Doctrine*. Edited by Philip Schaff. Vol. 2. Grand Rapids: Wm. B. Eerdmans Publishing Co., 1956.

———. *Confessions*. Latin text with commentary by James J. O'Donnell. 3 vols. Oxford: Clarendon Press, 1992.

———. *Confessions*. (Latin) Loeb Classical Library, with English translation by William Watts (1631). 2 vols. Cambridge: Harvard University Press, 1912.

———. *Confessions*. Translated by Gary Wills. New York: Penguin, 2006.

———. *Confessions*. Translated by R. S. Pine-Coffin. Baltimore: Penguin, 1961.

———. *Concerning the City of God Against the Pagans*. Translated by Henry Bettenson. New York: Penguin, 1984.

———. "*De Gratia Christi, Et De Peccato Originali.*" In *St. Augustin: Anti-Pelagian Writings*. Edited by Philip Schaff. Vol. 5. Grand Rapids: Wm. B. Eerdmans Publishing Co., 1955.

———. *De Haeresibus*. Translated by Liguori G. Mueller. Washington, DC: Catholic University of America Press, 1956.

———. "Letter Addressed to the Count Valerius, on Augustin's Forwarding to Him What He Calls His First Book 'On Marriage and Concupiscence' in 'Extract from Augustin's Refractions,' Book II. Chap 53, on the Following Treatise, *De Nuptiis Et Concupiscenta.*" *St. Augustin: Anti-Pelagian Writings*. Edited by Philip Schaff. Vol. 5. Grand Rapids: Wm. B. Eerdmans Publishing Co., 1955.

———. *On Christian Doctrine*. Edited by D. W. Robertson. New York, 1958.

———. *On Genesis: A Refutation of the Manachees, Unfinished Literal Commentary on Genesis, the Literal Meaning of Genesis*. Translated by Edmund Hill. Hyde Park, NY: New City Press, 2012.

———. "On the Holy Trinity." In *St. Augustin: On the Holy Trinity, Doctrinal Treatises, Moral Treatises*. Edited by Philip Schaff. Vol. 3. Grand Rapids: Wm. B. Eerdmans Publishing Co., 1956.

———. "On Marriage and Concupiscence." In *St. Augustin: Anti-Pelagian Writings* Ed. Philip Schaff. Vol. 5. Grand Rapids: Wm. B. Eerdmans Publishing Co., 1955.

———. "On Original Sin." In *St. Caesarius of Arles Sermons, Volume 2 (81–86)*. Translated by Sister Mary Magdalene Mueller, O.S.F. Washington, DC: Catholic University of America Press, 1981.

———. *Saint Augustine Against Julian*. Translated by Matthew A. Schumacher. New York: Fathers of the Church, 1957.

————. *St. Augustine on the Psalms*. Edited by Dame Scholastica Hegbin and Dame Felicitas Corrigan. Vols. I and II. London: Longmans, Green & Co, 1960, 1961.

————. *St. Augustine Select Letters*. Translated by James Houston Baxter. New York: G. P. Putnam's Sons, 1930.

————. "A Treatise on the Merits and Forgiveness of Sins, and on the Baptism of Infants." In *St. Augustin: Anti-Pelagian Writings*. Edited by Philip Schaff. Vol. 5. Grand Rapids: Wm. B. Eerdmans Publishing Co., 1955.

Austin, William. *Haec homo: Wherein the Excellency of the Creation of Woman is Described, by Way of an Essay*. London: Richard Olton for Ralph Mabb . . . , 1637.

Avril, Henry, ed. *Biblia Pauperum, a Facsimile and Edition*. Ithaca: Cornell University Press, 1987.

Bailey, Derrick. *The Man-Woman Relation in Christian Thought*. London: Longmans, Green & Co., 1959.

Bal, Mieke. "Sexuality, Sin, and Sorrow: The Emergence of Female Character (A Reading of Genesis 1–3)." In *The Female Body in Western Culture: Contemporary Perspectives*. Edited by Susan Rubin Suleiman. Cambridge: Harvard University Press, 1986.

Barasch, Moshe. *Gestures of Despair in Medieval and Early Renaissance Art*. New York: New York University Press, 1976.

Barr, James. *The Garden of Eden and the Hope of Immortality: The Read-Tuckwell Lectures for 1990*. London: SCM Press, 1992.

Barr, Jane. "The Influence of St. Jerome on Medieval Attitudes to Women." In *After Eve: Women in the Theology of the Christian Tradition*. Edited by Janet Martin Soskice. New York: Marshall Pickering, 1990, pp. 89–102.

Batto, Bernard F. *Slaying the Dragon: Mythmaking in the Biblical Tradition*. Louisville, KY: Westminster John Knox Press, 1992.

Baudet, Henri. *Paradise on Earth: Some Thoughts on European Images of Non-European Man*. Translated by Elizabeth Wentholt. New Haven: Yale University Press, 1965.

Bayle, Pierre. *An Historical and Critical Dictionary. By Monsieur Bayle. Translated into English, with Many Additions and Corrections, Made by the Author Himself, That Are Not in the French Editions. . . . A-B*. London: MDCCX, 1710.

Bayless, Martha. *Sin and Filth in Medieval Culture*. New York: Routledge, 2011.

Beck, Jonathan. "Genesis, Sexual Antagonism, and the Defective Couple of the Twelfth-Century Jeu d'Adam." *Representations*, no. 29 (1990), pp.124–44.

BeDuhn, Jason. *Augustine's Manichaean Dilemma*. 2 vols. 1st ed. Philadelphia: University of Pennsylvania Press, 2013.

Beer, Gillian. *Darwin's Plots: Evolutionary Narrative in Darwin, George Eliot, and Nineteenth-Century Fiction*. 3rd ed. Cambridge: Cambridge University Press, 2009.

Bellah, Robert N. *Religion in Human Evolution: From the Paleolithic to the Axial Age*. Cambridge: Harvard University Press, 2011.

Benson, Ezra Taft. *The Teachings of Ezra Taft Benson*. Salt Lake City: Bookcraft, 1988.

Berlin, Adele, and Marc Zvi Brettler, eds. *The Jewish Study Bible*. New York: Oxford University Press, 2004.

Berry, R.J., and Michael S. Northcott, eds. *Theology After Darwin*. Milton Keynes: Paternoster, 2009.

Bertoli, Bruno. *Medieval Misogyny and the Invention of Western Romantic Love.* Chicago: University of Chicago Press, 1991.

Bettenson, Henry Scowcroft and Chris Maunder, eds. *Documents of the Christian Church.* 4th ed. Oxford: Oxford University Press, 2011.

Bevington, David, ed. *Medieval Drama.* Boston: Houghton Mifflin, 1975.

Biale, David. *Not in the Heavens: The Tradition of Jewish Secular Thought.* Princeton: Princeton University Press, 2011.

Bialik, Hayim Nahman, and Yehoshua Hana Ravnitzky, *The Book of Legends: Sefer Ha-Aggadah.* Translated by William G. Braude. New York: Schocken, 1992.

Blamires, Alcuin. *The Case for Women in Medieval Culture.* Oxford: Clarendon Press, 1997.

Bloom, Harold, and David Rosenberg. *The Book of J.* Translated by David Rosenberg. New York: Grove Weidenfeld, 1990.

Blum, Pamela Z. "The Cryptic Creation Cycle in Ms. Junius xi." *Gesta* 15, no. 1/2 (1976), pp. 211–26.

Boehm, Christopher. *Hierarchy in the Forest: The Evolution of Egalitarian Behavior.* Cambridge: Harvard University Press, 1999.

———. *Moral Origins: The Evolution of Virtue, Altruism, and Shame.* New York: Basic Books, 2012.

Boehme, Jacob. *Mysterium Magnum.* Translated by J. Sparrow. London, 1654.

Bonnet, Anne-Marie. *"Akt" Bei Dürer.* Cologne: Walther König, 2001.

Bottero, Jean. *Everyday Life in Ancient Mesopotamia.* Translated by Antonio Nevill. Edinburgh: Edinburgh University Press, 2001.

———. *Mesopotamia: Writing, Reasoning, and the Gods.* Translated by Marc Van De Mieroop and Zainab Bahrani. Chicago: University of Chicago Press, 1992.

———. *Religion in Ancient Mesopotamia.* Translated by Teresa Lavender Fagan. Chicago: University of Chicago Press, 2001.

Braude, William G., trans. *The Book of Legends: Sefer Ha-Aggadah.* New York: Schocken, 1992.

Brenner, Athalya. *The Intercourse of Knowledge: On Gendering Desire and Sexuality in the Hebrew Bible.* Bible Interpretation. Edited by R. Alan Culpepper and Rolf Rendtorff. Leiden: Brill, 1997.

Breymann, Arnold. *Adam und Eva in der Kunst des Christlichen Alterthums.* Wolfenbüttel: Otto Wollermann, 1893.

Brockopp, Jonathan E., ed. *The Cambridge Companion to Muhammad.* New York: Cambridge University Press, 2010.

Brodie, Thomas L. *Genesis as Dialogue: A Literary, Historical & Theological Commentary.* Oxford: Oxford University Press, 2001.

Brown, Peter. *Augustine of Hippo: A Biography.* New ed., with epilogue. Berkeley: University of California Press, 2000.

———. *The Body and Society: Men, Women, and Sexual Renunciation in Early Christianity.* New York: Columbia University Press, 2008.

———. *The Ransom of the Soul: Afterlife and Wealth in Early Western Christianity.* Cambridge: Harvard University Press, 2015.

―――. *Through the Eye of a Needle: Wealth, the Fall of Rome, and the Making of Christianity in the West, 350–550 A.D.* Princeton: Princeton University Press, 2012.

Browne, E. J. *Charles Darwin.* Princeton: Princeton University Press, 2002.

Browne, Thomas. *Pseudodoxia Epdimica: or Enquires into Many Received Tenants and Commonly Presumed Truths.* London: Edward Dod, 1646.

―――. *Religio Medici.* London: Crooke & Cooke, 1643.

Bruno, Giordano. *The Expulsion of the Triumphant Beast.* London: John Charlewood, 1584.

Bryce, Trevor. *Atlas of the Ancient Near East: From Prehistoric Times to the Roman Imperial Period.* New York: Routledge, 2016.

Burnet, Thomas. *The Sacred Theory of the Earth: Containing an Account of the Original of the Earth, and of All the General Changes Which It Hath Already Undergone, or Is to Undergo. . . .* London: J. Hooke . . . , 1726.

Cadden, Joan. *Meanings of Sex Difference in the Middle Ages: Medicine, Science, and Culture.* Cambridge: Cambridge University Press, 1993.

Cahill, Lisa Sowle. *Sex, Gender, and Christian Ethics.* Cambridge: Cambridge University Press, 1996.

Calvin, John. *Institutes and Commentary on Genesis.* Translated by Thomas Tymme. London: John Harison and George Bishop, 1578.

―――. *Institutes of the Christian Religion.* Translated by John Allen. Vol. 1. Philadelphia: Presbyterian Board of Christian Education, 1936, II: chap. 1.

Camille, Michael. *The Gothic Idol: Ideology and Image-Making in Medieval Art.* Cambridge: Cambridge University Press, 1989.

―――. "Visual Signs of the Sacred Page: Books in the 'Bible moralisée.'" *Word and Image* 5, no. 1 (1989), pp. 111–30.

Campbell, Joseph. *The Hero with a Thousand Faces.* New York: Meridian, 1956.

―――. *The Way of the Animal Powers. Part 2: Mythologies of the Great Hunt.* Edited by Robert Walter. Vol. 1. New York: Harper & Row, 1988.

Carver, Marmaduke. *A Discourse on the Terrestrial Paradise, Aiming at a More Probable Discovery of the True Situation of That Happy Place of our First Parents Habitation.* London: James Flesher . . . , 1666.

Cassuto, U. *A Commentary on the Book of Genesis. Part 1: From Adam and Noah.* Translated by Israel Abrahams. Jerusalem: Magnes Press, 1978.

Caxton, William. *The Golden Legend or Lives of the Saints as Englished by William Caxton.* London: J. M. Dent and Co., 1922.

Cecil, Thomas and Joseph Fletcher. *The Historie of the Perfect-Cursed-Blessed Man: Setting Forth Mans Excellency by His Generation, Miserie [by his] Degeneration, Felicitie [by his] Regeneration. By I.F. Master of Arts, Preacher of Gods Word, and Rector of Wilbie in Suff.* London: Nathanael Fozbrook . . . , 1629.

Chadwick, Henry. *Augustine of Hippo.* New York: Oxford University Press, 2009.

Charles, R. H., ed. *The Apocrypha and Pseudepigrapha of the Old Testament in English.* 2 vols. Oxford: Clarendon Press, 1913.

Charlesworth, James. H., ed. *The Old Testament Pseudepigrapha.* Garden City, NY: Doubleday, 1983 and 1985.

Charleton, Walter. *The Darkness of Atheism Dispelled by the Light of Nature.* London: William Lee . . . , 1652.

Christine de Pizan, *The Book of the City of Ladies* [1405]. Translated by Earl Jeffrey Richards. New York: Persea Books, 1982.

Clarkson, Lawrence. *The Lost Sheep Found: or, The Prodigal Returned to his Fathers House, After Many a Sad and Weary Journey Through Many Religious Countreys.* London, 1660.

Clement of Alexandria. "Paedagogus." In *Fathers of the Second Century: Hermas, Tatian, Athenagoras, Theophilus, and Clement of Alexandria.* Edited by A. Cleveland Coxe. Vol. 2. Grand Rapids: Wm. B. Eerdmans Publishing Co., 1995.

Cohen, Adam S., and Anne Derbes. "Bernward and Eve at Hildesheim," *Gesta* 40, no. 1 (2001), pp. 19–38.

———. *The Mosaics of San Marco in Venice.* 2 vols. Chicago: University of Chicago Press, 1984.

Cohen, Jeremy. *Be Fertile and Increase, Fill the Earth and Master It: The Ancient and Medieval Career of a Biblical Text.* Ithaca: Cornell University Press, 1989.

Coles, William. *Adam in Eden, or, Natures Paradise: The History of Plants, Fruits, Herbs and Flowers* . . . London: Nathaniel Brooke . . . , 1657.

Columbus, Christopher. *The "Diario" of Christopher Columbus' First Voyage to America, 1492–1493.* Translated by Oliver Dunn and James E. Kelley, Jr. Norman: University of Oklahoma Press, 1989.

Conaway, Sir William Martin. *Literary Remains of Albrecht Dürer.* Cambridge: Cambridge University Press, 1899.

Concise Encyclopedia of Islam. Edited by H. A. R. Gibb and J. H. Kramers. Boston: Brill, 2001.

Coogan, Michael D., ed. *The New Oxford Annotated Bible.* 4th ed. New York: Oxford University, 2010.

———, and Mark S. Smith. *Stories from Ancient Canaan,* 2nd ed. Louisville, KY: Westminster John Knox Press, 2012.

Cook, Sherburne F., and Woodrow Wilson Borah. *Essays in Population History: Mexico and the Caribbean.* Berkeley: University of California Press, 1971.

Corns, Thomas N., and Gordon Campbell. *John Milton: Life, Work, and Thought.* Oxford: Oxford University Press, 2008.

———, et al., eds. *The Complete Works of Gerrard Winstanley.* 2 vols. Oxford: Oxford University Press, 2009.

Crooke, Helkiah, Ambroise Paré, et al. *Mikrokosmographia: A Description of the Body of Man. Together with the Controversies Thereto Belonging* . . . London: Thomas and Richard Cotes . . . , 1631.

Crüsemann, Nicola, et al., eds. *Uruk: 5000 Jahre Megacity.* Petersberg: Michael Imhof Verlag, 2013.

Cummings, Brian, ed. *The Book of Common Prayer: The Texts of 1549, 1555, and 1662.* New York: Oxford University Press, 2001.

Cyril of Jerusalem. "The Catechetical Lectures of S. Cyril, Archbishop of Jerusalem." In *Cyril of Jerusalem, Gregory Nazianzen.* Edited by Edwin Gifford. Vol. 7. Grand Rapids: Wm. B. Eerdmans Publishing Co., 1955.

Dalley, Stephanie, trans. *Myths from Mesopotamia: Creation, the Flood, Gilgamesh, and Others*. New York: Oxford University Press, 1989.

Damrosch, David. *The Buried Book: The Loss and Rediscovery of the Great Epic of Gilgamesh*. New York: Henry Holt & Co., 2006.

Danielson, Dennis. *Milton's Good God: A Study in Literary Theodicy*. Cambridge: Cambridge University Press, 1982.

———. "Through the Lens of Typology: What Adam Should Have Done," *Milton Quarterly* 23 (1989), pp. 121–27.

Dart, John. *The Laughing Savior: The Discovery and Significance of the Nag Hammadi Gnostic Library*. New York: Harper & Row, 1976.

Darwin, Charles. *From So Simple a Beginning: The Four Great Books of Charles Darwin*. Edited by Edward O. Wilson. New York: W. W. Norton, 2006.

Davies, W. D. *Paul and Rabbinic Judaism: Some Rabbinic Elements in Pauline Theology*. 2nd ed. London: SPCK, 1955.

Dawkins, Richard. *The Selfish Gene*. 30th anniversary ed. Oxford: Oxford University Press, 2006.

De Foigny, Gabriel. *A New Discovery of Terra Incognita Australis, or, The Southern World, by James Sadeur, a French-man, Who Being Cast There by a Shipwrack, Lived 35 Years in That Country* . . . London: John Dunton, 1693.

Delumeau, Jean. *History of Paradise: The Garden of Eden in Myth and Tradition*. Translated by Matthew O'Connell. Urbana: University of Illinois Press, 2000.

Denery, Dallas G. *The Devil Wins: A History of Lying from the Garden of Eden to the Enlightenment*. Princeton: Princeton University Press, 2015.

Desmond, Adrian. *Huxley: The Devil's Disciple*. London: Michael Joseph, 1994.

———. *Huxley: Evolution's High Priest*. London: Michael Joseph, 1997.

Donald, Merlin. *Origins of the Modern Mind: Three Stages in the Evolution of Culture and Cognition*. Cambridge: Harvard University Press, 1991.

Doresse, Jean. *The Discovery of the Nag Hammadi Texts: A Firsthand Account of the Expedition That Shook the Foundations of Christianity*. Rochester, VT: Inner Traditions, orig. French, 1958; U.S. ed., 1986.

Doria, Gino. *Storia di una Capitale. Napoli dalle Origini al 1860*. 5. edizione riveduta. Milan and Naples: R. Ricciardi, 1968.

Doron, Pinchas. *The Mystery of Creation According to Rashi: A New Translation and Interpretation of Rashi on Genesis I–VI*. New York: Maznaim, 1982.

Dryden, John. *John Dryden (1631–1700): His Politics, His Plays, and His Poets*. Edited by Claude Rawson and Aaron Santesso. Newark: University of Delaware Press, 2003.

Du Bartas, Guillaume de Saluste. *The Divine Weeks and Works*. Edited by Susan Snyder. 2 vols. Oxford: Oxford University Press, 1979.

Dubin, Nathaniel, trans. *The Fabliaux: A New Verse Translation*. New York: W. W. Norton, 2013.

Duncan, Joseph. *Milton's Earthly Paradise: A Historical Study of Eden*. Minneapolis: University of Minnesota Press, 1972.

Ebreo, Leone. *Dialogues of Love*. Translated by Cosmos Damian Bacich and Rossella Pescatori. Toronto: University of Toronto Press, 2009.

Eco, Umberto. *The Search for the Perfect Language.* Translated by James Fentress. Edited by Jacques Le Goff. Oxford: Blackwell, 1995 (orig. 1993).

Edwards, Thomas. *Gangraena.* London: Printed for Ralph Smith . . . , 1646.

Eisenberg, Evan. *The Ecology of Eden.* New York: Knopf, 1998.

Ellingson, Terry Jay. *The Myth of the Noble Savage.* Berkeley: University of California Press, 2001.

Elm, Susanna, et al., eds. *Faithful Narratives: Historians, Religion, and the Challenge of Objectivity.* Ithaca: Cornell University Press, 2014.

Emerson, Ralph Waldo. *The Journals and Miscellaneous Notebooks of Ralph Waldo Emerson.* Vol. 7. Cambridge: Harvard University Press, 1969.

Empson, William. *Milton's God.* Norfolk, CT: New Directions, 1961.

Essick, Robert N. *William Blake and the Language of Adam.* Oxford: Clarendon Press, 1989.

Eppacher, Franz. "La Collegiata Di San Candido: Arte, Simbologia, Fede." Translated by Carlo Milesi. San Candido: Parocchia San Michele Arcangelo, 2011.

Esche, Sigrid. *Adam und Eva: Sündenfall und Erlösung.* Düsseldorf: Verlag L. Schwann, 1957.

Evelyn, John. *Acetaria.* London: Printed for B. Tooke . . . , 1699.

Everard, Robert. *The Creation and Fall of Adam Reviewed.* London, 1649.

Fallon, Stephen. "The Metaphysics of Milton's Divorce Tracts." In *Politics, Poetics, and Hermeneutics in Milton's Prose.* Edited by James Grantham Turner and David Loewenstein. Cambridge: Cambridge University Press, 1990.

Fermor, Sharon. *Piero Di Cosimo: Fiction, Invention, and Fantasìa.* London: Reaktion Books, 1993.

Ferry, David, trans. *Gilgamesh: A New Rendering in English Verse.* 1st ed. New York: Farrar, Straus & Giroux, 1992.

Filmer, Robert. *Patriarcha and Other Writings.* Edited by Johann P. Sommerville. Cambridge: Cambridge University Press, 1991.

Fish, Stanley. *How Milton Works.* Cambridge: Harvard University Press, 2001.

———. *Surprised by Sin: The Reader in Paradise Lost.* London: Macmillan, 1967.

Flasch, Kurt. *Eva e Adamo: Metamorfosi di un mito.* Bologna: Il Mulino, 2007. Orig. *Eva und Adam: Wandlungen eines Mythos.* München: C. H. Beck, 2004.

Flood, John. *Representations of Eve in Antiquity and the English Middle Ages.* New York: Routledge, 2011.

Fluck, Cäcilia, Gisela Helmecke, and Elisabeth R. O'Connell, eds. *Ein Gott: Abrahams Erbemn am Nil. Juden, Christen und Muslime in Ägypten von der Antike Bis Zum Mittelalter.* Petersberg: Michael Imhof Verlag, 2015.

Foster, Benjamin R., ed. *Before the Muses: An Anthology of Akkadian Literature.* 2 vols. Bethesda, MD: CDL Press, 1993.

———, ed. *From Distant Days: Myths, Tales, and Poetry of Ancient Mesopotamia.* Bethesda, MD: CDL Press, 1995.

———, trans. *Gilgamesh: A New Translation, Analogues, Criticism.* New York: W. W. Norton, 2001.

Fox, Everett, trans. *The Five Books of Moses: Genesis, Exodus, Leviticus, Numbers, Deuteronomy.* New York: Schocken, 1995.

Fox, George. *The Journal of George Fox.* London: n.p., 1649.

Franck, Sebastian. *The Forbidden Fruit: or, a Treatise of the Tree of Knowledge of Good or Evill.* Translated by John Everard. London, 1642.

Frankfort, Henri, et al. *The Intellectual Adventure of Ancient Man.* Chicago: University of Chicago Press, 1946.

Franxman, Thomas W. *Genesis and the "Jewish Antiquities" of Flavius Josephus.* Biblica Et Orientalia. Rome: Biblical Institute Press, 1979.

Freedman, H., trans. *Midrash Rabbah.* 2 vols. London: Soncino, 1983.

Friedman, Albert. "'When Adam Delved . . .': Contexts, of an Historic Proverb." In *The Learned and the Lewd: Studies in Chaucer and Medieval Literature.* Edited by Larry D. Benson. Cambridge: Harvard University Press, 1974.

Friedman, Matti. *The Aleppo Codex: In Pursuit of One of the World's Most Coveted, Sacred, and Mysterious Books.* Chapel Hill, NC: Algonquin Books, 2013.

Friedman, Richard Elliott. *Who Wrote the Bible?* New York: Summit Books, 1987.

Frobenius, Leo, and Douglas C. Fox. *African Genesis: Folk Tales and Myths of Africa.* Mineola, NY: Dover Publications, 1999.

Furstenberg, Yair. "The Rabbinic Ban on *Ma'aseh Bereshit*: Sources, Contexts and Concerns." In *Jewish and Christian Cosmogony.* Edited by Lance Jenott and Saris Kattan Gribetz (Tübigen: Mohr Siebeck, 2013).

Gell, Alfred. *Art and Agency: An Anthropological Theory.* Oxford: Clarendon Press, 1998.

Geller, Markham J., and Mineke Schipper, eds. *Imagining Creation.* Boston: Brill, 2008.

George, Andrew, ed. and trans. *The Babylonian Gilgamesh Epic: Introduction, Critical Edition, and Cuneiform Texts.* Oxford: Oxford University Press, 2003.

———, trans. *Gilgamesh: The Babylonian Epic Poem and Other Texts in Akkadian and Sumerian.* London: Allen Lane, 1999.

Ghiglieri, Michael Patrick. *The Chimpanzees of Kibale Forest: A Field Study of Ecology and Social Structure.* New York: Columbia University Press, 1984.

Gibbons, Nicholas. *Questions and Disputations Concerning the Holy Scripture.* London: Felix Kyngston, 1602.

Gibson, J. C. L. *Canaanite Myths and Legends.* New York: T&T Clark International, 1977.

Ginzberg, Louis. *Legends of the Jews.* Translated by William G. Braude. 2 vols. Philadelphia: Jewish Publication Society, 2003.

Giuliani, Raffaella. "The Catacombs of SS. Marcellino and Pietro." Translated by Raffaella Bucolo. Edited by Pontifica Commissione di Archaeologia Sacra. Vatican City: 2015.

Givens, Terryl L. *When Souls Had Wings: Pre-Mortal Existence in Western Thought.* New York: Oxford University Press, 2010.

Glanvill, Joseph. *The Vanity of Dogmatizing: The Three Versions.* Edited by Stephen Medcalf. Brighton, UK: Harvester Press, 1970.

———, and Henry More. *Saducismus Triumphatus: or, Full and Plain Evidence Concern-*

ing Witches and Apparitions . . . Translated by Anthony Horneck. London: J. Collins . . . , and S. Lowndes . . . , 1681.

Gliozzi, Giuliano. *Adamo e il nuovo mondo: La nascita dell'antropologia come ideologia coloniale, dalle genealogie bibliche alle teorie razziali (1500–1700).* Translated by Arlette Estève and Pascal Gabellone, Venice: La Nuova Italia, 1977.

Gmirkin, Russell. *Berossus and Genesis, Manetho and Exodus: Hellenistic Histories and the Date of the Pentateuch.* New York: T&T Clark International, 2006.

Godden, Malcolm and Michael Lapidge, eds. *The Cambridge Companion to Old English Literature.* Cambridge: Cambridge University Press, 2013.

Gollancz, Israel, ed. *The Caedmon Manuscript of Anglo-Saxon Biblical Poetry: Junius Xi in the Bodleian Library.* Oxford: British Academy, 1927.

Goodman, Godfrey. *The Fall of Man: or, the Corruption of Nature* . . . London: Felix Kyngston . . . , 1616.

Gordon, Cyrus H. *Ugaritic Literature: A Comprehensive Translation of the Poetic and Prose Texts.* Rome: Pontificium Institutum Biblicum, 1949.

———, and Gary Rendsburg. *The Bible and the Ancient Near East.* 4th ed. New York: W. W. Norton, 1997.

Goris, Harm. "Is Woman Just a Mutilated Male? Adam and Eve in the Theology of Thomas Aquinas." *Out of Paradise: Eve and Adam and Their Interpreters.* Edited by Susan Hennecke and Bob Becking. Sheffield: Sheffield Phoenix Press, 2011.

Gosse, Philip Henry. *Omphalos: An Attempt to Untie the Geological Knot.* London: John Van Voorst, 1857 (reprint 1998).

Gott, Samuel. *The Divine History of the Genesis of the World Explicated & Illustrated.* London: E.C. & A.C., 1670.

Gould, Stephen J., and Richard C. Lewontin. "The Spandrels of San Marco and the Panglossian Paradigm: A Critique of the Adaptationist Programme." *Proceedings of the Royal Society of London* 205 (1979): 581–98.

Grabar, André. *Christian Iconography, a Study of Its Origins* (The A. W. Mellon Lectures in the Fine Arts, 1961). Princeton: Princeton University Press, 1968.

Graves, Robert. *Wife to Mr. Milton: The Story of Marie Powell.* New York: Creative Age Press, 1944.

———, and Raphael Patai. *Hebrew Myths: The Book of Genesis.* New York: Greenwich House, 1963.

Green, Anthony, and Jeremy Black. *Gods, Demons, and Symbols of Ancient Mesopotamia.* London: British Museum Press, 1992.

Greenblatt, Stephen. *Marvelous Posessions: The Wonder of the New World.* Chicago: University of Chicago Press, 1991.

———. *The Swerve: How the World Became Modern.* New York: W. W. Norton, 2011.

Greene, John C. *The Death of Adam: Evolution and Its Impact on Western Thought.* Ames: Iowa State University Press, 1959.

Gribetz, Sarit Kattan, et al., eds. *Jewish and Christian Cosmogony in Late Antiquity.* Tübingen: Mohr Siebeck, 2013.

Grinnell, George Bird. *Blackfoot Lodge Tales: The Story of a Prairie People.* Williamstown, MA: Corner House, 1972 (orig. 1892).

Grotius, Hugo. *Adamus Exul*. Hagae Comitum, 1601.

Guillory, John. "From the Superfluous to the Supernumerary: Reading Gender into Paradise Lost." In *Soliciting Interpretation: Literary Theory and Seventeenth-Century English Poetry*. Edited by E. D. Harvey and Katharine E. Maus. Chicago: University of Chicago Press, 1990.

Guldan, Ernst. *Eva und Maria: Eine Antithese als Bildmotiv*. Graz–Cologne: Verlag Hermann Böhlaus Nachf., 1966.

Gunkel, Hermann. *Genesis*. Translated by Mark E. Biddle. Macon, GA: Mercer University Press, 1997.

Hailperin, Herman. *Rashi and the Christian Scholars*. Pittsburgh: University of Pittsburgh Press, 1963.

Hakewill, George. *An Apologie or Declaration of the Power and Providence of God in the Government of the World*. London, 1635.

Halbertal, Moshe. *Maimonides: Life and Thought*. Edited by Joel A. Linsider. Princeton: Princeton University Press, 2014.

———. *People of the Book: Canon, Meaning, and Authority*. Cambridge: Harvard University Press, 1997.

Hale, Sir Matthew. *The Primitive Origination of Mankind, Considered and Examined According to the Light of Nature*. London: William Godbid, 1677.

Halkett, John G. *Milton and the Idea of Matrimony: A Study of the Divorce Tracts and Paradise Lost*. New Haven: Yale University Press, 1970.

Haller, John S. "The Species Problem: Nineteenth-Century Concepts of Racial Inferiority in the Origin of Man Controversy." *American Anthropologist* 72.6 (1970): 1319–29.

Hammond, Gerald, and Austin Busch, eds.*The English Bible: The New Testament and the Apocrypha*. New York: W. W. Norton, 2012.

Harari, Yuval N. *Sapiens: A Brief History of Humankind*. Edited by John Purcell, Haim Watzman, and Neil Gower. 1st U.S. ed. New York: Harper, 2015.

Hardison, O. B. *Christian Rite and Christian Drama in the Middle Ages*. Baltimore: Johns Hopkins University Press, 1965.

Harnack, Adolf von. *Marcion: The Gospel of the Alien God*. Translated by John E. Steely and Lyle D. Bierma. Eugene, OR: Wipf & Stock, 1990 (orig. 1920).

Harper, Kyle. *From Shame to Sin: The Christian Transformation of Sexual Morality in Late Antiquity*. Cambridge: Harvard University Press, 2013.

Harper, William Rainey. *The Biblical World*. Chicago: University of Chicago Press, 1899.

Harris, Olvier J. T., and John Robb, eds. *The Body in History: Europe from the Palaeolithic to the Future*. Cambridge: Cambridge University Press, 2013.

Harrison, Robert Pogue. *Juvenescence: A Cultural History of Our Age*. Chicago: University of Chicago Press, 2014.

Heger, Paul. *Women in the Bible, Qumran, and Early Rabbinic Literature: Their Status and Roles*. Boston: Brill, 2014.

Heidel, Alexander. *The Babylonian Genesis: The Story of the Creation*. 2d ed. Chicago: University of Chicago Press, 1951.

———. *The Gilgamesh Epic and Old Testament Parallels*. Chicago: University of Chicago Press, 1946.

Hendel, Ronald S., ed. *Reading Genesis: Ten Methods.* Edited by Ronald S. Hendel, Cambridge: Cambridge University Press, 2010.

Hesiod. *"Works and Days" and "Theognis."* Translated by Dorothea Wender. Middlesex, UK: Penguin, 1973.

Heyd, David. "Divine Creation and Human Procreation: Reflections on Genesis in the Light of *Genesis.*" In *Contingent Future Persons: On the Ethics of Deciding Who Will Live, or Not, in the Future.* Edited by Nick Fotion and Jan C. Heller. Dordrecht: Kluwer Academic Publishers, 1997, pp. 57–70.

Hiltner, Ken, ed. *Renaissance Ecology: Imagining Eden in Milton's England.* Pittsburgh: Duquesne University Press, 2008.

Hobbes, Thomas. *Leviathan.* Edited by Richard Tuck. Cambridge: Cambridge University Press, 1996, chap. 4, pp. 24–25.

Hollingworth, Miles. *Saint Augustine of Hippo: An Intellectual Biography.* New York: Oxford University Press, 2013.

Holloway, Julia Bolton, Constance S. Wright, and Joan Bechtold, eds. *Equally in God's Image.* New York: Peter Lang Publishing, 1990.

Hooke, Robert. *Micrographia: or, Some physiological descriptions of minute bodies made by magnifying glasses . . .* London: Jo. Martyn and Ja. Allestry, 1665.

Hrdy, Sarah Blaffer. *Mothers and Others: The Evolutionary Origins of Mutual Understanding.* Cambridge, MA: The Belknap Press, 2009.

Huet, Pierre Daniel. *A Treatise of the Situation of the Terrestrial Paradise,* trans. Thomas Gale. London: James Knapton, 1694.

Hutchinson, Lucy. *Order and Disorder: or, The World Made and Undone . . .* London: Margaret White for Henry Mortlock, 1679.

Huxley, T. H. *Evidence as to Man's Place in Nature.* London: Williams & Norgate, 1863.

———. *Science and the Hebrew Tradition.* London: Macmillan, 1993.

In the Land of the Christians: Arabic Travel Writing in the Seventeenth Century. Edited and translated by Nabil Matar. New York: Routledge, 2003.

Innocent III. *On the Misery of the Human Condition: De miseria humanae conditionis.* Edited by Donald R. Howard, translated by Margaret M. Dietz. Indianapolis, IN: Bobbs-Merrill 1969.

Isbell, Lynne A. *The Fruit, the Tree, and the Serpent: Why We See So Well.* Cambridge: Harvard University Press, 2009.

Jacobsen, Thorkild, ed. *The Harps That Once . . . : Sumerian Poetry in Translation.* New Haven: Yale University Press, 1987.

———. *The Treasures of Darkness: A History of Mesopotamian Religion.* New Haven: Yale University Press, 1976.

Janson, H. W. *Apes and Ape Lore in the Middle Ages and the Renaissance.* London: Warburg Institute, 1952.

Jerome. *Saint Jerome's Hebrew Questions on Genesis.* Translated by C. T. R. Hayward. Oxford: Clarendon Press, 1995.

———. *Select Letters.* Translated by F. A. Wright. Cambridge: Harvard University Press, 1933.

Jonas, Hans. *The Gnostic Religion.* Boston: Beacon Press, 1972.

Jospe, Raphael. "Biblical Exegesis as a Philosophic Literary Genre: Abraham Ibn Exa and Moses Mendelssohn." *Jewish Philosophy and the Academy*. Edited by Raphael Jospe and Emil L. Fackenheim. Madison, NJ: Fairleigh Dickinson University Press, 1986.

Judovits, Mordechai. *Sages of the Talmud: The Lives, Sayings, and Stories of 400 Rabbinic Masters*. Jerusalem: Urim Publications, 2009.

Justice, Steven. *Writing and Rebellion: England in 1381*. Berkeley: University of California Press, 1994.

Jütte, Daniel. *The Strait Gate: Thresholds and Power in Western History*. New Haven: Yale University Press, 2015.

Kahn, Paul W. *Out of Eden: Adam and Eve and the Problem of Evil*. Princeton: Princeton University Press, 2007.

Kahn, Victoria. "Embodiment," in *Wayward Contracts: The Crisis of Political Obligation in England, 1640–1674*. Princeton: Princeton University Press, 2004, pp. 196–222.

Kant, Immanuel. *Religion Within the Boundaries of Mere Reason*. Translated by Allen Wood. Cambridge: Cambridge University Press, 1998.

Kapelrud, Arvid Schou. "The Mythological Features in Gen 1 and the Author's Inentions." *Vetus Testamentum* 24 (1974): 178–86.

Kass, Leon R. *The Beginning of Wisdom: Reading Genesis*. New York: Free Press, 2003.

Kauffman, Stuart A. *Reinventing the Sacred: A New View of Science, Reason, and Religion*. New York: Basic Books, 2008.

Kauffmann, C. M. *Biblical Imagery in Medieval England, 700–1550*. London: Harvey Miller, 2003.

Kee, Howard Clark, et al. *The Cambridge Companion to the Bible*. Cambridge: Cambridge University Press, 1997.

Kelly, Henry Ansgar. "Hic Homo Formatur: The Genesis Frontispieces of the Carolingian Bibles." *Art Bulletin* 53, no. 2 (1971), pp. 143–60.

———. "The Metamorphoses of the Eden Serpent during the Middle Ages and Renaissance." *Viator* 2, no. 1, (1971), pp. 301–27.

———. "Reading Ancient and Medieval Art." *Word and Image* 5, no. 1 (1989), p. 1.

Kent, Bonnie. "Augustine's Ethics." *The Cambridge Companion to Augustine*. Edited by Norman Kretzmann and Eleonore Stump. Cambridge: Cambridge University Press, 2001.

Kerenyi, C. *Prometheus: Archetypal Image of Human Existence*. Translated by Ralph Manheim. New York: Pantheon, 1963.

Kierkegaard, Søren. *Eighteen Upbuilding Discourses*. Edited by Howard V. Hong and Edna H. Hong. Princeton: Princeton University Press, 1990.

King, Karen L. *The Secret Revelation of John*. Cambridge: Harvard University Press, 2006.

Kirchner, Josef. *Die Darstellung des Ersten Menschenpaares in der Bildenden Kunst von der Ältesten Zeit bis auf Unsere Tage*. Stuttgart: F. Enke, 1903.

Kirkconnell, Watson. *The Celestial Cycle: The Theme of Paradise Lost in World Literature, with Translations of the Major Analogues*. Toronto: University of Toronto Press, 1952.

Kitcher, Philip. *Living with Darwin: Evolution, Design, and the Future of Faith*. Oxford: Oxford University Press, 2006.

Klyve, Dominic. "Darwin, Malthus, Süssmilch, and Euler: The Ultimate Origin of the Motivation for the Theory of Natural Selection." *Journal of the History of Biology* 47 (2014), pp. 189–212.

Koerner, Joseph Leo. *Bosch & Bruegel: From Enemy Painting to Everyday Life*. Princeton: Princeton University Press, 2016.

———. *The Moment of Self-Portraiture in German Renaissance Art*. Chicago: University of Chicago Press, 1997.

Konowitz, Ellen. "The Program of the Carrand Diptych." *Art Bulletin* 66.3 (1984): 484–88.

Kramer, Samuel Noah. *The Sumerians: Their History, Culture, and Character*. Chicago: University of Chicago Press, 1963.

Kreitzer, Larry. *Prometheus and Adam: Enduring Symbols of the Human Situation*. New York: Lanham, 1994.

Kristeva, Julia. *This Incredible Need to Believe*. New York: Columbia University Press, 2009.

Kugel, James L. *Traditions of the Bible: A Guide to the Bible as It Was at the Start of the Common Era*. 2nd ed. Cambridge: Harvard University Press, 1998.

Kuper, Adam. *The Reinvention of Primitive Society: Transformations of a Myth*. New York: Routledge, 1988.

Kvam, Kristen E., Linda S. Schearing, and Valerie H. Ziegler, eds. *Eve & Adam: Jewish, Christian, and Muslim Readings on Genesis and Gender*. Bloomington: Indiana University Press, 1999.

La Peyrère, Isaac. *Du Rappel Des Juifs, 1643*. Translated by Mathilde Anqueth-Aulette. Edited by Fausto Parente. Paris: Honoré Champion, 2012.

———. *Men Before Adam, or, A Discourse upon the Twelfth, Thirteenth, and Fourteenth Verses of the Fifth Chapter of the Epistle of the Apostle Paul to the Romans, by Which Are Prov'd that the First Men Were Created Before Adam*. London, 1656.

———. *A Theological System*. London, 1655.

———. *Two Essays Sent in a Letter from Oxford to a Nobleman in London: The First Concerning Some Errors About the Creation, General Flood, and the Peopling of The World: In Two Parts: The Second Concerning the Rise, Progress, and Destruction of Fables and Romances, with the State of Learning*. London: R. Baldwin, 1695.

Lambert, W. G. *Ancient Mesopotamian Religion and Mythology: Selected Essays*. Edited by A. R. George and Takayoshi Oshima. Tübingen: Mohr Siebeck, 2016.

Lane Fox, Robin. *Augustine: Conversions to Confessions*. New York: Basic Books, 2015.

Lanyer, Aemelia. *Salve Deus Rex Judaeorum*. London: Valentine Simmes for Richard Bonian, 1611.

Laqueur, Thomas. *The Work of the Dead: A Cultural History of Mortal Remains*. Princeton: Princeton University Press, 2015.

Las Casas, Bartolomé de. *A Short Account of the Destruction of the Indies*. Translated by Nigel Griffen. London: Penguin, 1992.

Le Comte, Edward. *Milton and Sex*. New York: Columbia University Press, 1978.

Leibniz, G. W. *Theodicy: Essays on the Goodness of Go , the Freedom of Man, and the Origin of Evil*. Translated by E. M Huggard. London: Routledge & Kegan Paul, 1951.

Leonard, John. *Naming in Paradise: Milton and the Language of Adam and Eve*. Oxford: Clarendon Press, 1990.

Lerner, Anne Lapidus. *Eternally Eve: Images of Eve in the Hebrew Bible, Midrash, and Modern Jewish Poetry*. Waltham, MA: Brandeis University Press, 2007.

Levao, Ronald. "'Among Equals What Society': *Paradise Lost* and the Forms of Intimacy," *Modern Language Quarterly* 61.1 (2000), pp. 77–107.

Levison, John R. *Portraits of Adam in Early Judaism: From Sirach to 2 Baruch*. Sheffield, UK: JSOT, 1988.

———. *Texts in Transition: The Greek Life of Adam and Eve*. Atlanta: Society of Biblical Literature, 2000.

Lewalski, Barbara Kiefer. *The Life of John Milton: A Critical Biography*. Oxford: Blackwell Publishers, 2000.

Lewis, Michael. *Shame: The Exposed Self*. New York: Free Press, 1992.

Lewis, R. W. B. *The American Adam: Innocence, Tragedy, and Tradition in the Nineteenth Century*. Chicago: University of Chicago Press, 1955.

Liere, Frans van. *An Introduction to the Medieval Bible*. Cambridge: Cambridge University Press, 2014.

Lin, Yii-Jan. *The Erotic Life of Manuscripts: New Testament Textual Criticism and the Biological Sciences*. Oxford: Oxford University Press, 2016.

Lombard, Peter. *The Sentences*. Edited by Giulio Silano. Toronto: Pontifical Institute of Mediaeval Studies, 2007.

Loredano, Giovanni Francesco. *The Life of Adam*. Translated by J. S. London: Printed for Humphrey Moseley . . . , 1659.

———. *The Life of Adam (1640)*. Edited by Roy C. Flannagan and John Arthos. Gainesville, FL: Scholars' Facsimiles & Reprints, 1967.

Lovejoy, Arthur O., and George Boas. *Primitivism and Related Ideas in Antiquity*. Baltimore: Johns Hopkins University Press, 1935.

Lowden, John. "Concerning the Cotton Genesis and Other Illustrated Manuscripts of Genesis." *Gesta* 31, no. 1 (1992), pp. 40–53.

Lowie, Robert Harry. *Primitive Society*. New York: Boni & Liveright, 1920.

Lucas, J. R. "Wilberforce and Huxley: A Legendary Encounter." *Historical Journal* 22.2 (1979): 313–30.

Lucretius. *On the Nature of Things*. Translated by Martin Ferguson. Indianapolis: Hackett, 2001.

Luther, Martin. *Commentary on Genesis*. Translated by J. Theodore Mueller. 2 vols. Grand Rapids: Zondervan, 1958.

Mackay, Christopher S., trans. *The Hammer of Witches: A Complete Translation of the Malleus Maleficarum*. Cambridge: Cambridge University Press, 2009.

Maclean, Ian. *The Renaissance Notion of Woman: A Study in the Fortunes of Scholasticism and Medical Science in European Intellectual Life*. Cambridge: Cambridge University Press, 1980.

Macy, Gary. *The Hidden History of Women's Ordination: Female Clergy in the Medieval West*. Oxford: Oxford University Press, 2007.

Maimonides, Moses. *The Guide of the Perplexed.* Edited by M. Friedländer. London: Trübner, 1885.

Maimonides, Moses. *The Guide of the Perplexed.* Edited by Shlomo Pines and Leo Strauss. Chicago: University of Chicago Press, 1963.

Malan, Solomon Caesar, ed. *The Book of Adam and Eve: Also Called the Conflict of Adam and Eve with Satan, a Book of the Early Eastern Church.* London: Williams & Norgate, 1882.

Malbon, Elizabeth Struthers. *The Iconography of the Sarcophagus of Junius Bassus.* Princeton: Princeton University Press, 1990.

Mâle, Emile. *The Gothic Image: Religious Art in France of the Thirteenth Century.* New York: Harper, 1958.

Malebranche, Nicolas. *Father Malebranche His Treatise Concerning the Search After Truth* . . . Translated by Thomas Taylor. London: Printed by W. Bowyer for Thomas Bennet . . . , 1700.

Margalit, Baruch. *The Ugaritic Poem of AQHT: Text, Translation, Commentary.* Berlin: De Gruyter, 1989.

Marks, Herbert, ed. *The English Bible: The Old Testament,* New York: W. W. Norton, 2012.

Marrow, James H. "Symbol and Meaning in Northern European Art of the Late Middle Ages and Early Renaissance." *Simiolus* 16, no. 2/3 (1986), 150–69.

Marsden, Richard, et al., eds. *The New Cambridge History of the Bible.* Cambridge: Cambridge University Press, 2012.

Martz, Louis. *The Paradise Within: Studies in Vaughan, Traherne, and Milton.* New Haven: Yale University Press, 1964.

Matt, Daniel C., trans. *The Zohar, Pritzker Edition.* Vol I. Stanford, CA: Stanford University Press, 2004.

McAuliffe, Jane Dammen, ed. *The Cambridge Companion to the Qur'ān.* Cambridge: Cambridge University Press, 2006.

McCalman, Iain. *Darwin's Armada: Four Voyages and the Battle for the Theory of Evolution.* New York: W. W. Norton, 2009.

McColley, Diane. *A Gust for Paradise: Milton's Eden and the Visual Arts.* Urbana: University of Illinois Press, 1993.

Meeks, Wayne A., and John T. Fitzgerald, eds. *The Writings of St. Paul: Annotated Texts, Reception and Criticism.* 2nd ed. New York: W. W. Norton, 2007.

Merchant, Carolyn. *Reinventing Eden: The Fate of Nature in Western Culture.* New York: Routledge, 2003.

Mettinger, T. N. D. *The Eden Narrative: A Literary and Religio-Historical Study of Genesis 2-3.* Winona Lake, IN: Eisenbrauns, 2007.

Meyers, Carol. *Discovering Eve: Ancient Israelite Women in Context.* New York: Oxford University Press, 1988.

Mieroop, Marc Van De. *A History of the Ancient Near East Ca. 3000–324 B.C.* Malden, MA: Blackwell Publishing, 2007.

Miles, Jack. *God: A Biography.* New York: Knopf, 1995.

Miles, Margaret Ruth. *Carnal Knowing: Female Nakedness and Religious Meaning in the Christian West.* Boston: Beacon Press, 1989.

Millard, A. R., and W. G. Lambert, eds. *Atra-Hasis: The Babylonian Story of the Flood*. Oxford: Clarendon Press, 1969.

Miller, Kenneth R. *Finding Darwin's God*. New York: HarperCollins, 2009.

Milton, John. *The Complete Poetry and Essential Prose of John Milton*. Edited by William Kerrigan, John Rumrich, and Stephen M. Fallon. New York: Modern Library, 2007.

———. *The Complete Prose Works of John Milton*. Edited by Don Marion Wolfe. New Haven: Yale University Press, 1953.

———. *The Divorce Tracts of John Milton: Texts and Contexts*. Edited by Sara J. van den Berg and W. Scott Howard. Pittsburgh: Duquesne University Press, 2010

———. *John Milton: Complete Poems and Major Prose*. Edited by Merritt Y. Hughes. New York: Odyssey Press, 1957.

———. *Milton on Himself: Milton's Utterances upon Himself and His Works*. Edited by J. S. Diekhoff. New York: Oxford University Press, 1939.

———. *Paradise Lost*. London: Printed, and are to be sold by Peter Parker . . . , 1668.

———. *Paradise Lost*. Edited by William Zunder. New York: St. Martin's Press, 1999.

———. *The Poems of John Milton*. Edited by John Carey and Alastair Fowler. Harlow, UK: Longman, 1968.

Minnis, Alastair. *From Eden to Eternity: Creations of Paradise in the Later Middle Ages*. The Middle Ages. Edited by Ruth Mazo Karras. Philadelphia: University of Pennsylvania Press, 2016.

Mitchell, Stephen, trans. *Genesis*. New York: HarperCollins, 1996.

———, trans. *Gilgamesh: A New English Version*. New York: Free Press, 2004.

Montaigne. *The Complete Essays of Montaigne*. Translated by Donald M. Frame. Stanford, CA: Stanford University Press, 1958.

Moore, James, and Adrian Desmond. *Darwin's Sacred Cause: Race, Slavery, and the Quest for Human Origins*. London: Allen Lane, 2009.

Morey, James H. "Peter Comestor, Biblical Paraphrase, and the Medieval Popular Bible." *Speculum* 68, no. 1 (1993), pp. 6–35.

Moser, Stephanie. *Ancestral Images: The Iconography of Human Origins*. Ithaca: Cornell University Press, 1998.

Murdoch, Brian. *Adam's Grace: Fall and Redemption in Medieval Literature*. Cambridge, UK: D. S. Brewer, 2000.

———. *The Medieval Popular Bible: Expansions of Genesis in the Middle Ages*. Cambridge, UK: D. S. Brewer, 2003.

Myers, Carol. *Discovering Eve: Ancient Israelite Women in Context*. Oxford: Oxford University Press, 1988.

Nagel, Alexander. *Medieval Modern: Art out of Time*. New York: Thames & Hudson, 2012.

Nemet-Nejat, Karen Rhea. *Daily Life in Ancient Mesopotamia*. Westport, CT: Greenwood Press, 1998.

Nietzsche, Friedrich. *The Genealogy of Morals*. Translated by Francis Golffing. Garden City, NY: Doubleday, 1956 (orig. 1887).

Nishida, Toshisada. *Chimpanzees of the Lakeshore: Natural History and Culture at Mahale.* Cambridge: Cambridge University Press, 2012.

Nogarola, Isotta. *Complete Writings: Letterbook, Dialogue on Adam and Eve, Orations.* Translated by Diana Robin and Margaret L. King. Edited by Margaret L. King and Albert Rabil, Jr. Chicago: University of Chicago Press, 2004.

Norton, David. *A History of the Bible as Literature. Volume 1, From Antiquity to 1700.* Cambridge: Cambridge University Press, 1993.

Numbers, Ronald. *The Creationists: From Scientific Creationism to Intelligent Design.* New York: Knopf, 1992.

Nyquist, Mary. "The Genesis of Gendered Subjectivity in the Divorce Tracts and *Paradise Lost.*" In Christopher Kendrick, ed., *Critical Essays on John Milton.* New York: G. K. Hall, 1995, pp. 165–93.

Olender, Maurice. *The Languages of Paradise: Race, Religion, and Philology in the Nineteenth Century.* Translated by Arthur Goldhammer. Cambridge: Harvard University Press, 1992.

Oppenheim, A. Leo. *Ancient Mesopotamia: Portrait of a Dead Civilization.* Chicago: University of Chicago Press, 1964.

Origen. "Contra Celsum." *Tertullian, Part Fourth; Minucius Felix; Commodian; Origen, Part First and Second.* Edited by A. Cleveland Coxe. Vol. 4. Grand Rapids: Wm. B. Eerdmans Publishing Co., 1974. The Anti-Nicene Fathers.

Ostovich, Helen, Elizabeth Sauer, and Melissa Smith, eds. *Reading Early Modern Women: An Anthology of Texts in Manuscript and Print, 1550–1700.* New York: Routledge, 2004.

Overton, Richard. *Man's Mortality.* Amsterdam: Printed by John Canne, 1644.

Owst, G. R. *Literature and Pulpit in Medieval England.* Oxford: Clarendon Press, 1961.

Pächt, Otto, and J. J. G. Alexander, eds. *Illuminated Manuscripts in the Bodleian Library, Oxford.* Oxford: Clarendon Press, 1966.

Pagels, Elaine. *The Gnostic Gospels.* 1st ed. New York: Random House, 1979.

Paleologus, Jacobus. *An omnes ab uno Adamo descenderit* (1570).

Panofsky, Dora, and Erwin Panofsky. *Pandora's Box: The Changing Aspects of a Mythical Symbol.* New York: Pantheon, 1956.

Panofsky, Erwin. *The Life and Art of Albrecht Dürer.* Princeton: Princeton University Press, 2005.

Pardes, Ilana. *Countertraditions in the Bible: A Feminist Approach.* Cambridge: Harvard University Press, 1992.

Parker, William Riley. *Milton: A Biography.* 2 vols. Oxford: Clarendon Press, 1996.

Patrides, C. A. *Milton and the Christian Tradition.* Oxford: Clarendon Press, 1966.

Patterson, Annabel. "No Meer Amatorious Novel?" In *Politics, Poetics, and Hermeneutics in Milton's Prose.* Edited by David Loewenstein and James Grantham Turner. Cambridge: Cambridge University Press, 1990, 85–102.

Peterson, Dale, and Jane Goodall. *Visions of Caliban: On Chimpanzees and People.* Athens: University of Georgia Press, 1993.

Pettus, Sir John. *Volatiles from the History of Adam and Eve: Containing Many Unquestioned Truths and Allowable Notions of Several Natures.* London: T. Bassett . . . , 1674.

Phillips, Adam. *Darwin's Worms.* London: Faber & Faber, 1999.

Phillips, Edward. "The Life of Milton." In *John Milton: Complete Poems and Major Prose.* Edited by Merritt Y. Hughes. New York: Odyssey Press, 1957.

Phillips, John. *Eve: The History of an Idea.* New York: HarperCollins, 1984.

Philo. *On the Creation.* Edited by F. H. Colson, Vol. 1. Cambridge: Harvard University Press, 1958.

———. *On the Creation of the Cosmos According to Moses.* Edited by David T. Runia. Boston: Brill, 2001.

Picciotto, Joanna. *Labors of Innocence in Early Modern England.* Cambridge: Harvard University Press, 2010.

Pilbeam, David, and Richard Wrangham. *All Apes Great and Small, Vol. 1: African Apes.* New York: Kluwer Academic Publishers, 2001.

Plantinga, Alvin. *Where the Conflict Really Lies.* New York: Oxford University Press, 2011.

Platt, Rutherford Hayes, ed. *The Lost Books of the Bible and the Forgotten Books of Eden.* Cleveland: World Publishing Co., 1950.

Pollmann, Karla, ed. *The Oxford Guide to the Historical Reception of Augustine.* Vols. 2 and 3. Oxford: Oxford University Press, 2013.

Pongratz-Leisten, Beate, and Peter Machinist, eds. *Reconsidering the Concept of Revolutionary Monotheism.* Winona Lake, IN.: Eisenbrauns, 2011.

Poole, Kristen. *Radical Religion from Shakespeare to Milton: Figures of Nonconformity in Early Modern England.* Cambridge: Cambridge University Press, 2000.

Poole, William. *Milton and the Idea of the Fall.* Cambridge: Cambridge University Press, 2005.

Popkin, Richard H. *Isaac La Peyrère: His Life, Work, and Influence.* Leiden: Brill, 1987.

Pordage, Samuel. *Mundorum Explicatio: or, The Explanation of an Hieroglyphical Figure: Wherein Are Couched the Mysteries of the External, Internal, and Eternal Worlds . . .* London: Printed by T.R. for Lodowick Lloyd . . . , 1661.

Price, David. *Albrecht Dürer's Renaissance: Humanism, Reformation, and the Art of Faith.* Ann Arbor: University of Michigan Press, 2003.

Pritchard, James B., ed. *Ancient Near Eastern Texts Relating to the Old Testament.* 3rd ed. Princeton: Princeton University Press, 1970.

Purchas, Samuel. *Hakluytus Posthumus, or Purchas His Pilgrimes.* Glasgow: James MacLehose, 1905 (orig. 1625).

Quenby, John, and John MacDonald Smith, eds. *Intelligent Faith: A Celebration of 150 Years of Darwinian Evolution.* Winchester, UK: O Books, 2009.

Quinn, Esther Casier, and Micheline Dufau, eds. *The Penitence of Adam: A Study of the Andrius Ms.* University, MS: Romance Monographs, 1980.

Ralegh, Walter. *History of the World.* London: Printed by William Stansby for Walter Burre, 1614.

Reeve, John, and Lodowick Muggleton. *A Transcendent Spiritual Treatise upon Several Heavenly Doctrines . . .* London: 1652.

Richardson, Sarah S. *Sex Itself: The Search for Male and Female in the Human Genome.* Chicago: University of Chicago Press, 2013.

Richter, Virginia. "The Best Story of the World: Theology, Geology, and Philip Henry Gosse's *Omphalos.*" In *The Making of the Humanities.* Edited by Rens Bod, Jaap

Maat, and Thijs Weststeijn. Vol. 3: *The Modern Humanities*. Amsterdam: Amsterdam University Press, 2010, pp. 65–77.

Ricoeur, Paul. *The Symbolism of Evil*. Edited by Emerson Buchanan. Boston: Beacon Press, 1969.

Rist, John M. *Augustine: Ancient Thought Baptized*. Cambridge: Cambridge University Press, 1994.

Robbins, Frank Egleston. *The Hexaemeral Literature: A Study of the Greek and Latin Commentaries on Genesis*. Chicago: University of Chicago Press, 1912.

Robinson, James M., ed. *The Nag Hammadi Library in English*. Translated by Members of the Copic Gnostic Library Project. New York: Harper & Row, 1977.

Robinson, John A. T. *The Body: A Study in Pauline Theology*. Philadelphia: Westminster Press, 1952.

Rogers, John. "Transported Touch: The Fruit of Marriage in *Paradise Lost*." In C. G. Martin, ed., *Milton and Gender*. Cambridge: Cambridge University Press, 2004, pp. 115–32.

Rosenblatt, Jason P. *Torah and Law in Paradise Lost*. Princeton: Princeton University Press, 1994.

Ross, Alexander. *An Exposition on the Fourteen First Chapters of Genesis, by Way of Question and Answer*. London, 1626.

Rossi, Paolo. *The Dark Abyss of Time: The History of Earth and the History of Nations from Hooke to Vico*. Translated by Lydia G. Cochrane. Chicago: University of Chicago Press, 1984 (orig. 1979).

Rubin, Miri. *Mother of God: A History of the Virgin Mary*. New Haven: Yale University Press, 2009.

Rudwick, Martin J. S. *Bursting the Limits of Time: The Reconstruction of Geohistory in the Age of Revolution*. Chicago: University of Chicago Press, 2005.

———. *Worlds Before Adam: The Reconstruction of Geohistory in the Age of Reform*. Chicago: University of Chicago Press, 2008.

Russell, Helen Diane. *Eva/Ave: Woman in Renaissance and Baroque Prints*. New York: Talman Company, 1990.

Russell, Jeffrey B. *The Devil: Perceptions of Evil from Antiquity to Primitive Christianity*. Ithaca: Cornell University Press, 1977.

———. *Lucifer, The Devil in the Middle Ages*. Ithaca: Cornell University Press, 1984.

———. *Satan: The Early Christian Tradition*. Ithaca: Cornell University Press, 1981.

Sabine, George H., ed. *The Works of Gerrard Winstanley, with an Appendix of Documents Relating to the Digger Movement*. Ithaca: Cornell University Press, 1941.

Salkeld, J. *A Treatise of Paradise. And the Principall Contents Thereof: Especially of the Greatnesse, Situation, Beautie, and Other Properties of That Place* . . . London: Edward Griffin for Nathaniel Butter, 1617.

Saurat, Denis. *Milton: Man and Thinker*. New York: Dial Press, 1925.

Scafi, Alessandro. *Mapping Paradise: A History of Heaven on Earth*. Chicago: University of Chicago Press, 2006.

Schiebinger, Londa. *Nature's Body: Gender in the Making of Modern Science*. New Brunswick: Rutgers University Press, 1993.

Schiller, Gertrude. *Iconography of Christian Art.* 2 vols. Translated by Janet Seligman. Greenwich, CT: New York Graphic Society, 1971.

Schnapp, Alain. "The Preadamites: An Abortive Attempt to Invent Pre-History in the Seventeenth Century?" In *History of Scholarship.* Edited by Christopher Ligota and Jean-Louis Quantin. Oxford: Oxford University Press, 2006, pp. 399–412.

Schneidau, Herbert N. *Sacred Discontent: The Bible and Western Tradition.* Berkeley: University of California Press, 1976.

Schoen, Christian. *Albrecht Dürer: Adam und Eva. Die Gemälde, ihre Geschichte und Rezeption bei Lucas Cranach d. Ä. und Hans Baldung Grien.* Berlin: Reimer, 2001.

Schoenfeldt, Michael. "'Commotion Strange': Passion in *Paradise Lost.*" In Gail Kern Paster, Katherine Rowe and Mary Floyd-Wilson, eds., *Reading the Early Modern Passions: Essays in the Cultural History of Emotion.* Philadelphia: University of Pennsylvania Press, 2004.

Scholem, Gershom, ed. *Zohar: The Book of Splendor: Basic Readings from the Kabbalah.* New York: Schocken, 1963.

Schroeder, Joy A., ed. *The Book of Genesis.* Grand Rapids: Wm. P. Erdmans Publishing Co., 2015.

Schwartz, Jeffrey, and Ian Tattersall. *Extinct Humans.* New York: Westview Press, 2000.

Schwartz, Stuart B. *All Can Be Saved: Religious Tolerance and Salvation in the Iberian Atlantic World.* New Haven: Yale University Press, 2008.

Schwartzbach, Bertram Eugene. *Voltaire's Old Testament Criticism.* Geneva: Librairie Droz, 1971.

Scroggs, Robin. *The Last Adam: A Study in Pauline Anthropology.* Oxford: Basil Blackwell, 1966.

Scully, Stephen. *Hesiod's "Theogony": From Near Eastern Creation Myths to "Paradise Lost."* Oxford: Oxford University Press, 2015.

Senault, J. F. *Man Become Guilty: or, The Corruption of Nature by Sinne, According to St. Augustines Sense.* Translated by Henry Carey, Earl of Monmouth. London: Printed for William Leake . . . , 1650.

Sennert, Daniel. *Hypomnemata Physica.* Frankfurt: Clement Schlechius, 1636.

Shakespeare, William. *The Norton Shakespeare.* Edited by Stephen Greenblatt et al. 3rd edition. New York: W. W. Norton, 2016.

Shapiro, Robert. *Origins: A Skeptic's Guide to the Creation of Life on Earth.* New York: Summit, 1986.

Shelton, Kathleen. "Roman Aristocrats, Christian Commission: The Carrand Diptych." *Jahrbuch für Antike und Christentum* 29 (1986): 166–80.

Silver, Larry, and Susan Smith. "Carnal Knowledge: The Late Engravings of Lucas van Leyden." *Nederlands Kunsthistorisch Jaarboek* 29, no. 1 (1978), pp. 239–98.

Silvestris, Bernardus. *Cosmographia.* Translated by Winthrop Wetherbee. New York: Columbia University Press, 1973.

Ska, Jean-Louis. "A Plea on Behalf of the Biblical Redactors." *Studia Theologica—Nordic Journal of Theology* 59.1 (2005): 4–18.

Skinner, John. *A Critical and Exegetical Commentary on Genesis.* 2nd ed. Edinburgh: T. & T. Clark, 1930.

Slotkin, James Sydney. *Readings in Early Anthropology*. Chicago: Aldine Publishing Co., 1965.

Smith, George. *Assyrian Discoveries; an Account of Explorations and Discoveries on the Site of Nineveh, During 1873 and 1874*. London: Chiswick Press, 1875.

———. "The Chaldean Account of the Deluge." *Transactions of the Society of Biblical Archaeology* 2 (1873).

Sober, Elliott. *Evidence and Evolution: The Logic of the Science*. Cambridge: Cambridge University Press, 2008.

Soloveitchik, Joseph Dov. *The Lonely Man of Faith*. Northvale, N.J.: Jason Aronson, 1997.

Stanton, Elizabeth Cady. *The Woman's Bible: A Classic Feminist Perspective*. Mineola, NY: Dover, 2002.

Steinberg, Justin. *Dante and the Limits of the Law*. Chicago: University of Chicago Press, 2013.

Steinberg, Leo. "Eve's Idle Hand." *Art Journal* 35, no. 2 (1975–1976), pp. 130–35.

Stordalen, Terje. *Echoes of Eden: Genesis 2-3 and Symbolism of the Eden Garden in Biblical Hebrew Literature*. Leuven: Peeters, 2000.

Stott, Rebecca. *Darwin's Ghosts: The Secret History of Evolution*. New York: Spiegel & Grau, 2012.

Sulloway, Frank. *Freud, Biologist of the Mind: Beyond the Psychoanalytic Legend*. New York: Basic Books, 1979.

Szathmáry, Eörs, and John Maynard Smith. *The Origins of Life: From the Birth of Life to the Origin of Language*. Oxford: Oxford University Press, 1999.

Tarabotti, Arcangela. *Paternal Tyranny* (1654). Translated by Letizia Panizza. Edited by Margaret L. King and Albert Rabil, Jr. Chicago: University of Chicago Press, 2004.

Tasso, Torquato. *Creation of the World*. Translated by Joseph Tusiani. Binghamton, NY: Medieval and Renaissance Texts and Studies, 1982.

Tattersall, Ian. *Becoming Human: Evolution and Human Uniqueness*. New York: Harcourt Brace & Co., 1998.

———. *Masters of the Planet: The Search for Our Human Origins*. New York: Palgrave Macmillan, 2012.

Taylor, Jeremy. *Deus Justificatus. Two Discourses of Original Sin Contained in Two Letters to Persons of Honour, Wherein the Question Is Rightly Stated* . . . London: Printed for Richard Royston, 1656.

Tertullian. *The Ante-Nicene Christian Library*. 24 vols. Edited by Alexander Roberts and James Donaldson. Edinburgh: Kessinger, 1868–1872.

———. *De Cultu Feminarum*. Translated by Sydney Thelwall. In *The Ante-Nicene Christian Library*. 24 vols. Edited by Alexander Roberts and James Donaldson. Vol. 4: *Fathers of the Third Century*. Edinburgh: Kessinger, 1868–1872.

Thompson, Bard, ed. *Liturgies of the Western Church*. 1st Fortress Press ed. Philadelphia, 1980.

Thoreau, Henry D. *Walden*. Boston: Ticknor & Fields, 1864.

Traherne, Thomas. *Centuries of Meditations*. London: The Editor, 1906.

———. "Innocence." *The Poetical Works*. Edited by Bertram Dobell. London: The Editor, 1906.

Trible, Phyllis. *God and the Rhetoric of Sexuality*. Minneapolis, MN: Fortress Press, 1978.

Tronzo, William. "The Hildesheim Doors: An Iconographic Source and Its Implications." *Zeitschrift für Kunstgeschichte* 46:4 (1983), pp. 357–66.

Turner, James G. *One Flesh: Paradisal Marriage and Sexual Relations in the Age of Milton*. Oxford: Clarendon Press, 1987.

Tuttle, Russell H. *Apes and Human Evolution*. Cambridge: Harvard University Press, 2014.

Twain, Mark. *The Bible According to Mark Twain: Writings on Heaven, Eden, and the Flood*. Edited by Howard G. Baetzhold and Joseph B. McCullough. Athens: University of Georgia Press, 1995.

Ulrich, Eugene. "The Old Testament Text and Its Transmission." In *From the Beginnings to 600*. Edited by Joachim Schaper and James Carleton Paget. Vol. 1. Cambridge: Cambridge University Press, 2013.

Upton, Bridget Gilfillan. "Feminist Theology as Biblical Hermeneutics." In *Cambridge Companion to Feminist Theology*. Edited by Susan Frank Parsons. Cambridge: Cambridge University Press, 2002.

Van Helmont, Franciscus Mercurius. *Some Premeditate and Considerate Thoughts, on the Early Chapters of the Book of Genesis*. London: S. Clark . . . , 1701.

Van Reybrouck, David. *From Primitives to Primates: A History of Ethnographic and Primatological Analogies in the Study of Prehistory*. Leiden: Sidestone Press, 2012.

Van Seters, John. *The Edited Bible: The Curious History of the "Editor" in Biblical Criticism*. Winona Lake, IN: Eisenbrauns, 2006.

Velleman, David J. "The Genesis of Shame," *Philosophy and Public Affairs* 30 (2001), pp. 27–52.

Vermès, Géza, ed. *The Complete Dead Sea Scrolls in English*. New York: Penguin, 2004.

Veyne, Paul. *When Our World Became Christian, 312–394*. Edited by Janet Lloyd. Malden, MA: Polity, 2010.

Victorinus. "On the Creation of the World." In *Fathers of the Third and Fourth Centuries* Edited by A. Cleveland Coxe. Vol. 7. Grand Rapids: Wm. B. Eerdmans Publishing Co., 1951.

Voltaire. *Philosophical Dictionary*. Edited by Peter Gay. New York: Basic Books, 1962.

Voss, Julia. *Darwins Jim Knopf*. Frankfurt am Main: S. Fischer, 2009.

Waal, Frans de. *Chimpanzee Politics: Power and Sex Among Apes*. Baltimore: Johns Hopkins University Press, 1982.

Wallace, Howard N. *The Eden Narrative*. Edited by Frank Moore Cross. Atlanta: Scholars Press, 1985.

Wallace, William. *The Logic of Hegel*. Oxford: Clarendon Press, 1892.

Waltzer, Michael. *In God's Shadow: Politics in the Hebrew Bible*. New Haven: Yale University Press, 2012.

Warburg, Aby. *The Renewal of Pagan Antiquity: Contributions to the Cultural History of the European Renaissance*. Edited by Kurt Walter Forster. Los Angeles: Getty Research Institute for the History of Art and the Humanities, 1999.

Warfield, Benjamin B. "Introductory Essay on Augustin and the Pelagian Controversy." In *St. Augustin: Anti-Pelagian Writings.* Edited by Philip Schaff. Vol. 5. Grand Rapids: W. B. Eerdmans Publishing Co., 1955.

Webster, Charles. *The Great Instauration: Science, Medicine, and Reform 1626–1660.* London: Duckworth, 1975.

Wedgwood, C. V. *The King's War: 1641–1647.* London: Collins, 1958.

Weiner, Joshua. *From the Book of Giants.* Chicago: University of Chicago Press, 2006.

Weitzmann, Kurt, and Herbert Kessler. *The Cotton Genesis: British Library, Codex Cotton Otho B VI.* Princeton: Princeton University Press, 1986.

Werckmeister, Otto-Karl. "The Lintel Fragment Representing Eve from Saint-Lazare, Autun." *Journal of the Warburg and Courtauld Institutes* 35 (1972), pp. 1–30.

West, Rebecca. *St. Augustine.* London: Peter Davies, 1933.

Westermann, Claus. *Genesis: A Commentary.* 3 vols. Minneapolis: Augsburg Publishing House, 1984–86.

Wetzel, James. "Predestination, Pelagianism, and Foreknowledge." In *The Cambridge Companion to Augustine.* Edited by Norman Kretzman and Eleonore Stump. Cambridge: Cambridge University Press, 2001.

White, Andrew Dickson. *A History of the Warfare of Science with Theology in Christianity.* 2 vols. New York: D. Appleton & Co., 1896.

Whitehead, Alfred North. *Science and the Modern World: Lowell Lectures, 1925.* New York: Macmillan, 1925.

Willet, Andrew. *Hexapla, That Is, A Six-Fold Commentarie vpon the Most Diuine Epistle of the Holy Apostle S. Pavl to the Romanes . . .* London: Printed for Leonard Greene, 1620.

Williams, Arnold. *The Common Expositor: An Account of the Commentaries on Genesis, 1527–1633.* Chapel Hill: University of North Carolina Press, 1948.

Williams, Bernard. "The Makropulos Case: Reflections on the Tedium of Immortality." In *Problems of the Self.* Cambridge: Cambridge University Press, 1973.

Williams, George H. *The Radical Reformation.* Philadelphia: Westminster Press, 1962.

Williams, John, ed. *Imaging the Early Medieval Bible.* University Park: Pennsylvania State University Press, 1999.

Williams, Norman Powell. *The Ideas of the Fall and of Original Sin.* London: Longmans, Green & Co., 1927.

Williams, Patricia A. *Doing Without Adam and Eve: Sociobiology and Original Sin.* Minneapolis, MN: Fortress Press, 2001.

Wills, Gary. *Saint Augustine.* New York: Viking, 1999.

Wilson, Edward O. *The Social Conquest of Earth.* New York: Liveright, 2012.

Witzel, E. J. Michael. *The Origins of the World's Mythologies.* Oxford: Oxford University Press, 2012.

Wrangham, Richard W. *Catching Fire: How Cooking Made Us Human.* New York: Basic Books, 2009.

———, and Dale Peterson. *Demonic Males: Apes and the Origins of Human Violence.* Boston: Mariner Books, 1996.

The York Cycle of Mystery Plays: A Complete Version. Edited by J. S. Purvis. London: S.P.C.K., 1957.

Zevit, Ziony. *What Really Happened in the Garden of Eden.* New Haven: Yale University Press, 2013.

Zornberg, Avivah Gottlieb. *The Murmuring Deep: Reflections on the Biblical Unconscious.* New York: Schocken, 2009.

Zuberbühler, Klaus. "Experimental Field Studies with Non-Human Primates." *Current Opinion in Neurobiology* 28 (2014): 150–56.

Illustration Credits

Frontispiece: Hans Baldung Grien, *The Fall of Humankind* (*Lapsus Humani Generis*), 1511, print, Rijksmuseum, Amsterdam.

Inserts

1. *Adam and Eve,* third century CE, fresco, Catacombe SS. Pietro and Marcellino, Rome, photo © Pontifical Commission for Sacred Archaeology, Vatican.
2. *Sarcophagus of Junius Bassus* (detail), c. 359 CE, marble, Museo Storico del Tesoro della Basilica di San Pietro, Vatican (Scala/Art Resource, NY).
3. *Adam in the Garden of Eden,* fifth century, ivory, Florence, Museo Nazionale del Bargello.
4. Bernward Doors, c. 1015, bronze, courtesy of the Dom-Museum Hildesheim.
5. *The Creation of Eve* (detail from the Bernward Doors), photo by Frank Tomio, courtesy of the Dom-Museum Hildesheim.
6. *The Judgment of Adam and Eve by God* (detail from the Bernward Doors), photo by Frank Tomio, courtesy of the Dom-Museum Hildesheim.
7. St. Albans Psalter, HS St. God. 1, p. 18, twelfth century, property of the Basilica of St. Godehard, Hildesheim © Dombibliothek Hildesheim.
8. Gislebertus, *The Temptation of Eve,* c. 1130, stone, Musée Rolin, Autun, © Ville d'Autun, Musée Rolin.
9. *Crucifix,* c. 1200, wood, Collegiata di San Candido, photo courtesy of the Parrocchia di San Michele Arcangelo in San Candido.
10. Vat. Lat. 5697 fol. 16r (detail of God creating Eve from Adam's rib), fifteenth century © 2017 Biblioteca Apostolica Vaticana.

28. Max Beckmann, *Adam and Eve,* 1917, oil on canvas, Nationalgalerie, Staatliche Museen zu Berlin, © bpk Bildagentur/Nationalgalerie, SMB/Jörg P. Anders/ Art Resource, NY.

29. *'Lucy' (australopithecus afarensis) and her mate,* reconstruction by John Holmes under the direction of Ian Tattersall, photo by J. Beckett and C. Chesek, © American Museum of Natural History.

Index

Page numbers beginning with 325 refer to endnotes.